Praise for *The Revolution Was Televised*

**One of *New York Times* book critic
Michiko Kakutani's Ten Favorite Books of 2012**

**One of *Hollywood Reporter*'s Twelve Best
Hollywood-Related Books of 2012**

"A spirited and insightful cultural history . . . A terrific book."

—Michiko Kakutani, *New York Times*

"Mr. Sepinwall is an astute critic but also a dogged reporter.
Part critical appraisals, part history lessons . . . it adds up to
something like an oral history of Mr. Sepinwall's small-screen
'revolution.'"

—Sonny Bunch, *Wall Street Journal*

"A smart and substantive walk through the past fifteen years
of television drama, making a lucid case for the auteurist
mentality among modern showrunners."

—Emily Nussbaum, *New Yorker*

"TV fans have a new must-read."

—*USA Today*

"[A] thoroughly detailed and immensely entertaining stroll
through the new Renaissance of American television. . . .
Addictive."

—*Hollywood Reporter*

"Sepinwall is a sharp and prolific critic. . . . In *Revolution*, though, he admirably often stands back and lets his subjects' words speak for themselves . . . with insights that will make you see anew just how a *Friday Night Lights* or *Buffy* season truly worked, while tossing off the kind of dead-on descriptions that make his blog a blast to read."

—*Time*

"The best book by a journalist on American television that I've read in at least 20 years . . . in all its ultrasmart hyperbole and eye- and brain-opening glory."

—*Buffalo News*

"While it is bracingly readable and full of Alan's passion about these shows, it is also a valuable reference work. . . . Solidly reported."

—*Akron Beacon Journal*

"I can't recommend this engaging history highly enough."

—Maureen Ryan, *Huffington Post*

"A must-read for anyone who has ever fallen hard for a TV show."

—Salon.com

THE
REVOLUTION
WAS
TELEVISED

How *The Sopranos, Mad Men, Breaking
Bad, Lost,* and Other Groundbreaking
Dramas Changed TV Forever

Alan Sepinwall

Touchstone

New York   London   Toronto   Sydney   New Delhi

TOUCHSTONE
An Imprint of Simon & Schuster, Inc.
1230 Avenue of the Americas
New York, NY 10020

This Touchstone trade paperback edition December 2015

TOUCHSTONE and colophon are registered trademarks
of Simon & Schuster, Inc.

For information about special discounts for bulk purchases,
please contact Simon & Schuster Special Sales at 1-866-506-1949
or business@simonandschuster.com.

The Simon & Schuster Speakers Bureau can bring authors
to your live event. For more information or to book an event, contact
the Simon & Schuster Speakers Bureau at 1-866-248-3049
or visit our website at www.simonspeakers.com.

Manufactured in the United States of America

1   3   5   7   9   10   8   6   4   2

ISBN 978-1-4767-3967-0
ISBN 978-1-4767-3968-7 (ebook)

This book is dedicated to two people I dearly wish were still here to read it:

Dr. Jerry Sepinwall, who always encouraged my love of reading and writing,

David Mills, who gave me my first peek behind the curtain

CONTENTS

PREVIOUSLY, IN *THE REVOLUTION WAS TELEVISED*...

Why an updated version?

The original edition of *The Revolution Was Televised* was always going to be incomplete, because only 10 of the 12 shows profiled had finished their runs at the time of publication. *Mad Men* and *Breaking Bad* were too important to the book's larger story to leave out, but I knew I wanted to revisit things after we had seen their final episodes, in the same way the other 10 chapters all had closure.

And while I was covering the end of both those shows for Hit-Fix.com, I witnessed smaller changes to the stories of some of the other series (like David Chase making several public comments about what may have happened in that final *Sopranos* scene, or *24* being revived as a miniseries four years after it was canceled), and some major expansion of the TV universe that was opened up by the shows in this book.

What's new in this version?

The *Mad Men* and *Breaking Bad* chapters have been significantly rewritten, not only to discuss how each show ended, but also to add context to earlier parts of the story. (Vince Gilligan, for instance, told me how *Breaking Bad* Season 1 would have ended if not for the writers strike, while I finally had a chance to talk to Matthew Weiner about the origins of *Mad Men*.) There have also been some tweaks to other chapters, and updates to the Where Are They Now? section. (Sections that remain essentially the same: *Oz, The Wire, Deadwood, The Shield, Buffy the Vampire Slayer, Battlestar Galactica,* and the original epilogue.)

In addition, I wrote a bonus epilogue to discuss all the changes that have swept the TV business in the three years since this book was originally published.

If you were to have added a 13th show, what would it have been?

At the time, *Six Feet Under* was the toughest omission. It was distinct from the other vintage HBO dramas in that its complex themes and characterization weren't hidden inside a familiar genre like *The Sopranos* or *The Wire*, but it didn't make the original cut because I didn't want the book to become too focused on HBO in the early '00s. Had I started writing a year or two later, I might have considered *Louie*, because the one-man band aspect of it renders it distinct from the 12 shows in the book, while still feeling like a part of that movement, as opposed to the Netflix shows or *Fargo*.

One of the misconceptions about *Revolution* when it was originally published was that it was a look at the best TV dramas ever made, which resulted in a lot of questions about the absence of *West Wing* and others. That was never the idea, though of course many of the shows featured would be inner circle Hall of Famers. Rather, the book was my attempt to tell the larger story of what happened in TV around the turn of the century that fundamentally altered the way TV dramas were both made and viewed. The

12 shows in question demonstrated different facets of that change: *Oz* and *The Sopranos* as the start of the HBO boom, *The Shield* as the first HBO-style show on basic cable, *24* and *Lost* as broadcast network shows grappling with intense serialization, *Buffy* as a look at an alternate path to cable innovation that was open briefly in the late '90s, *Friday Night Lights* as a network show that survived due to an unusual business arrangement, etc.

There are certainly great essays to be written about *West Wing*, *Justified*, *Game of Thrones*, and other wonderful shows that ran concurrently with one or more of these 12, but they weren't part of this specific story.

Was "Why isn't (insert your favorite show here) the most frequent question you got last time?"

Probably, though the biggest reaction was more outrage over how many of the creators talked about having improvised major long-term arcs of their shows. There's this school of thought that insists any kind of serialized drama must be mapped out largely in advance, or else its storylines are somehow invalid. But that's just not realistic for most ongoing TV productions, given the number of moving parts involved year after year. Even something like *The Wire*, often held up as the patron saint of this particular religion of predestined storytelling, had to zig and zag at times to suit the whims of both actors and HBO executives. And nearly everything that fans loved most about *Breaking Bad* was improvised as that show went along, whereas one of its more divisive plot twists—the plane crash in the Season 2 finale—was among the few elements where Vince Gilligan knew the end well in advance.

And after this book was first published, a different kind of serialized show demonstrated the folly of trying to plan too much ahead of time. Creators of the CBS sitcom *How I Met Your Mother* had, during their second season, filmed a scene involving narrator Ted's future children that they intended to save and use in the series finale, however many years later, in which it would be revealed that the eponymous Mother had recently died, and now the kids were encouraging Ted to get back together with his old girlfriend Robin. It was a clever plan, given how much the audience at the time loved Ted and Robin as a couple and wished the narration hadn't explicitly ruled her out as the Mother, but it backfired enormously: by the time they actually used it, many fans had both soured on the idea of a Ted/Robin pairing and fallen for the actual Mother after she was introduced in the final season. The creators stuck with their original plan, even though the show they were making had long since evolved to the point where it was a bad idea, and the response was uglier than even what the *Lost* guys dealt with.

In an ideal world, creators should have some idea of where their show will go in success, but a flexible imagination is ultimately more important than a detailed series bible written before the pilot's even shot.

Will there ever be a third edition?

If David Milch ever manages to get that *Deadwood* reunion movie made, or if I answer the phone one day and it's David Chase saying, "Okay, here is *exactly* what happened to Tony right after Meadow walked into Holsten's," then sure. But failing that, this particular story feels complete.

INTRODUCTION

*A**nd they pay you for this?"*

Once upon a time, any conversation I had with a stranger about my job as a television critic led to that question. Some were amused that this was the way I made my living. Others were disdainful, insisting that they didn't watch much television (or even own a TV). More often than not, the conversation would hit a dead end when I said that I didn't also write about movies.

But if my job didn't make sense to these strangers, it made perfect sense to me. I had stumbled onto the best gig in the world. I was being paid to watch television. I was, of course, also being paid to *write* about television, which not everyone could do, and there were times where it wasn't so much that I *got* to watch television for a living, but that I *had* to watch it (where have you gone, *Homeboys From Outer Space?*), but overall, it was a dream come true.

It was a dream I had fallen into by continually being in the right place at the right time for someone with my interests. I matriculated at the University of Pennsylvania with the first class of non-engineers to receive an email address and a Unix shell account, and I began using both to write obsessively about *NYPD Blue*, first on

Usenet, then on a website I set up on the campus server (where it still sits, a monument to cutting-edge web design circa 1994). Online reviews of anything were still a novelty when I graduated in '96, and that website helped me land a features internship at *The Star-Ledger* of northern New Jersey—my hometown newspaper—in a summer when the paper's longtime TV critic couldn't make it to the TV critics press tour in LA. My editors gambled on sending me in his place, I didn't embarrass myself, and they offered me a full-time job as the back-up TV writer. In college, I'd been told I would be extraordinarily fortunate to land a full-time job as an entertainment critic at a small paper within five years; I'd lucked into one at a big paper within five weeks.

Even better, it seemed like the best time in entertainment history to be a television critic. From where I sat, TV was in the middle of another golden age, filled with smart comedies and, more importantly, dramas like *NYPD Blue* and *Homicide* that I felt tapped into what I had seen for years as the limitless potential of TV storytelling. I loved movies, but I'd also seen in shows like *Hill Street Blues* and *St. Elsewhere* that the small screen had certain advantages over its bigger, more prestigious cousin. It could tell very long stories. It could allow characters to grow over extended periods of time. And by coming into my home rather than making me go to it, it could forge a more intimate bond with me. As I grew up, very few shows were willing or able to exploit those advantages to the fullest, but by the time I arrived at *The Star-Ledger*, more and more were figuring it out.

I was, I said to myself often, privileged to be covering a medium that had become as good as I had always dreamed it would be—that was, possibly, as good as it could ever possibly be.

I was wrong.

I thought I had seen the TV universe at its most vast and impressive. Instead, I was about to witness a big bang of sorts, one that would greatly expand the boundaries of this universe, and the way we viewed it.

I was about to see *The Sopranos.*

I was about to see *Oz. The Wire. Deadwood. The Shield. Lost. Buffy the Vampire Slayer. 24. Battlestar Galactica. Friday Night Lights. Mad Men. Breaking Bad.*

I was about to see television achieve its full potential, and step out from the shadow of the cinema.

I was about to see a revolution.

And the revolution began not just with the talented creators of these shows—television had, after all, been no stranger to creative geniuses, going back to Rod Serling and Paddy Chayefsky—but with dynamic shifts in the television business itself, and in the many ways people watched TV.

When I started at the *Ledger* in the summer of 1996, you had the broadcast networks, and then you had everyone else. (And within the network universe, Fox had only begun to be treated as anything but a novelty; the WB and UPN were runts fighting over table scraps.) HBO had a few original comedy series and its movies, but if you wanted scripted television, you mostly went to ABC, CBS, NBC, and occasionally Fox.

A few years before, Bruce Springsteen had put out a song called "57 Channels (And Nothin' On)," whose title became almost instantly dated on both ends. Soon, everyone's cable package was ballooning way past 57, and channels that had been satisfied airing nothing but reruns and old movies began putting on their own original programming—and the mass audience that had been the bread and butter of television began to fracture into a group of ever-smaller niches.

Commercially, this presented a huge problem for a business built on a big-tent philosophy, where you succeeded with the broadest, most palatable, least challenging work. Creatively, though, the fragmented audience was the best thing that could have happened to television. Certainly, some corners of the TV business leaned heavily on programming that was as broad and/or cheap as possible (the year after *The Sopranos*, *Survivor* set off the reality TV boom). But many smart executives realized that they could do very well making shows those smaller audiences would care passionately about. You can make money on a show watched by three million people, if they're the "right" three million people, paying close attention.

Many of these shows came from veteran producers still stinging from mistakes made in past projects. Often, these modern masterpieces were first written under the assumption that no one would ever see them. That combination of regret and abandon led to a wave of bold and exciting new dramas the likes of which TV had never seen before.

And as *The Sopranos* was followed by *The Wire*, *The Shield*, and all the rest, an interesting role reversal happened with the movie business, which was dealing with some audience uncertainty of its own. Where once there had been blockbusters, art films, and a large swath of movies in between—many of that last group geared to adults—the 21st century slowly saw the extinction of the middle-class movie. If a film couldn't either be made on the cheap or guarantee an opening weekend of $50 million or more, it was out.

As *Sopranos* creator David Chase—who once upon a time wanted nothing more than to get out of the TV business and write films—puts it, "Movies went from something really interesting to what we have now."

TV stepped in to fill that void. If you wanted thoughtful drama for adults, you didn't go to the multiplex; you went to your living room couch.

The rise of this movement came at the perfect technological time, as DVRs, On Demand, and especially DVD box sets and video streaming made it easy for people to catch up on that great-but-complicated new show they'd heard so much about. (DVDs allowed fans to turn their friends onto new discoveries the way rock fans used to pass around albums from their favorite up-and-coming new band.) And the spread of the internet into every corner of modern life made it easier to discuss and make sense of shows that might have seemed too challenging back in the day, whether you were trying to solve the mysteries of *Lost* or understand what Tony Soprano's dreams meant.

Once upon a time, people seemed impressed when they heard what I did (first at the *Ledger*, later at HitFix.com) only because it seemed like an easy gig. After a while, though, when I would tell them that I was a TV critic, they would get this glint in their eyes, leaning in to tell me how much they loved Omar on *The Wire*, or talk about how *Friday Night Lights* always made them cry. We'd been going home with television every night for years, but suddenly we had reason to respect it in the morning.

This book is the story of that transformation in both the medium and how we saw it, through the prism of the best and/or most important shows of the era. I'll talk about why these shows were great and the role they played in the larger story; I'll also let the creators, executives, and actors responsible for that greatness explain how these shows came to be.

"It was a unique time, and there was a new generation taking over in television," says *Deadwood* creator David Milch. "And television, in its own way, the best of it was as good as anything."

PROLOGUE

Let's be careful out there...
The shows that paved the way

There's already a school of thought—one that a book like this admittedly plays into—arguing that true quality television didn't exist before *The Sopranos*. But while the adventures of Tony Soprano and the many complicated characters who followed him elevated TV to another level of both quality and cultural respect, they didn't come out of thin air. The millennial wave of revolutionary dramas was built on the work put in by a group of other series, particularly the ones created from the early '80s onward(*). Here are some of the crucial building blocks for the revolution:

(*) And even there, I would accept the argument from older TV historians that I'm leaving out significant even-earlier work. David Chase learned his craft writing for The Rockford Files, *for instance, even if* The Sopranos *has only a passing resemblance to it, and there were many important dramas in the '50s and '60s. But from my point of view, there's a more tangible connection between, say,* Hill Street Blues *and* The Wire *than between* The Defenders *and* Breaking Bad.

All in the Family **(CBS, 1971–1979):** It wasn't a drama, but it was capable of amazing dramatic moments, like the episode where Edith barely escapes being raped on her 50th birthday. More importantly, though, *All in the Family* was the first show to succeed with a blunt approach to the sorts of taboo subjects and deeply flawed central characters that would come to typify the great dramas not only of the '80s and '90s, but of this century. Archie Bunker would be disgusted by Tony Soprano (though Tony would justify many of Archie's beliefs about Italian-Americans), but the public's embrace of a character like Archie, whom they should have hated, would one day lead to a show like *The Sopranos*.

Hill Street Blues **(NBC, 1981–1987):** One night in our college dorm, a friend of ours admitted she had never seen *Casablanca*, a hole in her cultural memory we aimed to fill in as quickly as possible. To our dismay, she spent most of the movie complaining about how predictable and clichéd it all was, and our arguments that it had *invented* most of those clichés fell on deaf ears.

That's the danger with coming to a classic late: if a work is good enough, the rest of the entertainment industry will strip-mine it until the original work somehow seems derivative of the others that blatantly copied it. And I imagine if you were to show an episode of *Hill Street Blues* to someone who came of age with *The Wire*, they'd react to it about as favorably as our friend did to *Casablanca*. But in 1981, Steven Bochco and Michael Kozoll—and, later, writers like David Milch and Jeffrey Lewis—took every assumption viewers had about primetime dramas in general and cop shows in particular and turned each one on its ear.

Previous TV dramas tended to tell simple, easily digestible stories that began and ended within the space of an hour, featuring clear good guys and bad guys, that played on your emotions but rarely taxed your brain or your moral compass. With *Hill Street Blues*, nothing was ever simple.

The series took place in a run-down police precinct where the cops were fighting a holding action against the ever-increasing amount of gang violence and other brutal crime, while the police commissioner and local politicians preferred to act like the entire neighborhood would be better off forgotten. Stories didn't begin and end neatly within the space of an hour, but would continue for weeks on end, sometimes over an entire season. Though there was a clear central character in Daniel J. Travanti's righteous precinct captain Frank Furillo, the narrative bounced around constantly among a huge, diverse cast. Scenes might begin by focusing on one character, then immediately shift their attention to a different character who passed him in the hallway, then flip around to yet a third set of characters before cutting away to the next location. Furillo was for the most part a virtuous hero, but the other characters existed along a wide moral spectrum, and even Frank had his moments of weakness. The show mixed bleak drama with a twisted sense of humor (undercover cop Mick Belker had a tendency to growl and bite suspects), and the violence, language, and sex scenes were all considered fairly graphic for TV of the period.

Much of *Hill Street* would seem incredibly tame today, yet it feels less dated than a 30-year-old drama should. It was such a huge step forward in terms of what TV drama could do with complex narratives of moral shades of grey that you can still find strands of its DNA in many dramas being made today—both the ones I'll be talking about in this book, and less edgy material like *Grey's Anatomy* and the *CSI* shows—so it still feels very much a part of the current era. Without *Hill Street Blues*, maybe another show makes the evolutionary leap that eventually brings us to Don Draper and Walter White. Or maybe we're still watching simplistic, easy-to-digest dramas, even on HBO.

St. Elsewhere (NBC, 1982–1988): This hospital drama was so close in its chaotic style and cynicism to *Hill Street Blues* that it could have been a spin-off. But where *St. Elsewhere* distinguished itself, and blazed a trail for many that followed, was with its willingness to experiment with its own structure and even level of reality. At various points, *St. Elsewhere* did a two-parter flashing back over 50 years of history at the hospital; an episode involving a patient who believed himself to be Mary Richards from *The Mary Tyler Moore Show* (who ran into both Betty White playing a new role and Jack Riley as his character from *The Bob Newhart Show*); an episode where the doctors went to Cheers to have a beer and be insulted by Carla; and another where Howie Mandel's character was shot and journeyed between Hell, Purgatory, and Heaven (where he met a God who looked an awful lot like Howie Mandel).

   St. Elsewhere not only proved that the formal chaos of *Hill Street Blues* could be transplanted to another setting and creative team, but that your characters, your stories, and your world didn't have to be confined to a familiar box. You could take your audience anywhere, if you did it well enough. *St. Elsewhere* also set the bar very high—or very low, depending on your point of view—for memorable, challenging series finales. The closing scene revealed that the entire series had been the fantasy of the autistic son of the show's main character, who spent his days staring at a snow globe containing the hospital's familiar exterior. Some fans were dazzled by it; others felt it was the show judging them harshly for having watched it all these years. (Tommy even places the globe on top of the TV set right before we fade out.) It neatly presaged many of the anger-inducing finales to come in the 21st century.

Cheers **(NBC, 1982–1993):** Stick with me on this one. The through line from Sam Malone to Al Swearengen might seem tenuous, other than that they both ran bars, but I believe Glen and Les Charles and their writing staff were responsible for a crucial step in the evolution of how people watched television. *Hill Street Blues* and *St. Elsewhere* were critical darlings, but modestly rated. *Cheers* was a flop itself at first, but eventually became one of the most popular sitcoms of all time—and it did it while hooking viewers on an ongoing narrative about the on-again, off-again, on-again relationship between Sam and Diane, and later Sam and Rebecca, Rebecca and Robin Colcord, etc. *Cheers* wasn't weaving some kind of elaborate tapestry where you would be lost if you hadn't seen the previous 13 episodes. But the sitcom as a genre had to that point—with rare exceptions (like the seasons of *I Love Lucy* where they traveled through Europe or stayed in Hollywood)—been a form where each episode was self-contained, designed to exist independently from the one before and the one after. *Cheers* was a show that was always aware of what had already happened to its characters, and that built both jokes and important character beats serially on that. The show's success paved the way for even more heavily serialized sitcoms like *Friends* and *Seinfeld* (and later many of the HBO comedies, *Arrested Development*, *The Office*, *Parks and Recreation*, etc.). It also helped condition viewers to the basic idea that their TV shows weren't disposable, that it was possible to see characters transform beyond just seeing sitcom kids get older with each season.

Miami Vice (**NBC, 1984–1989**): There are so many creation myths around *Miami Vice*—the most famous of them involving NBC president Brandon Tartikoff writing the phrase "MTV cops" on a napkin and handing it to writer Anthony Yerkovich and director Michael Mann—that it's become all but impossible to separate the facts from the legend. What's indisputable is that the show Yerkovich and Mann went on to make demonstrated that you could adopt a cinematic look (and yes, music-video-style editing) on the budget and schedule of a weekly TV drama.

Wiseguy (**CBS, 1987–1990**): Stephen J. Cannell built a long, lucrative career as a master of TV drama as comfort food. The shows he created were well-crafted (*The Rockford Files* is still the best private-eye show ever) but never taxing on the brain. You tuned in for an hour and got a complete story that was easy to follow, usually with some combination of a catchy theme song, good jokes, a car chase and/or a shootout. But just because Cannell didn't often do complex didn't mean he couldn't. In 1987, Cannell and Frank Lupo—who had previously teamed up on the proudly lowbrow *The A-Team*—created *Wiseguy*, a dark, moody intelligent drama starring Ken Wahl as Vinnie Terranova, a federal agent assigned to infiltrate different criminal organizations.

What distinguished *Wiseguy* from similar shows that came before it—and makes it feel 20 years ahead of its time—was the duration of these assignments. Vinnie didn't bust the bad guys at the end of each episode. It took him many episodes to close each case, with one story arc taking a dozen hours to complete and others clocking in at a half-dozen hours or more. Many other dramas had featured recurring villains—even something as simple as *Hawaii Five-0* would bring back arch-nemesis Wo Fat now and again—

but not even *Hill Street Blues* had devoted so many episodes in a row to a single storyline this way. The format allowed Cannell and Lupo to dig deep with the characterization, and to give unlikely guest stars—a young, unknown Kevin Spacey as an incestuous, heroin-addicted mobster or Jerry Lewis as a garment-industry executive—among the best dramatic roles of their careers.

The idea of villains lasting long enough for both the protagonist and the audience to really get to know them is one that translated well to the revolutionary cable dramas, whether it was *The Sopranos* (where Tony seemed to have a new nemesis each season), *Breaking Bad* (which employed *Wiseguy* alum Jonathan Banks, and cast Gus Fring very much in the mold of a *Wiseguy* villain) or even *Dexter* (which also brought in a new major antagonist each year), to name just three.

(In between, there was also Bochco's *Murder One*, a mid-'90s legal drama for ABC that devoted its first season to a single case, and its second to three long arcs. *Murder One* mainly demonstrated how difficult it was to pull something like that off, but *24* would be far more successful in the next decade.)

***thirtysomething* (ABC, 1987–1991):** This drama about a close-knit group of yuppie friends was criticized in some quarters for being whiny, plotless, and self-indulgent. Today, it would instead be lauded as introspective, narratively unconventional, and stylistically ambitious. *thirtysomething* was a show very much ahead of its time, working without a traditional TV "franchise" (doctor, lawyer, cop) to generate story, and assuming its characters' inner lives would be rich enough that its target audience would need nothing more. Its spiritual DNA can be found in *The Sopranos* (where Carmela was yet another wife questioning her choice of partner), *Six*

Feet Under (which also got by without a franchise to drive the plot) and *Mad Men* (and not just because thirtysomething hero Michael was also in advertising), and the show's creators Marshall Hersko-vitz and Ed Zwick would later (on their brilliant-but-canceled teen drama *My So-Called Life*) help mentor a young playwright named Jason Katims, who would go on to run *Friday Night Lights*.

***Twin Peaks* (ABC, 1990–1991):** As strange as *St. Elsewhere* and some other '80s shows had been, nothing quite prepared audiences for *Twin Peaks*, a baroque mix of murder mystery, soap opera, '50s movie melodrama, and the 100% pure weirdness that comes with any project from the show's co-creator, David Lynch. Lynch, com-ing off the cult classic film *Blue Velvet*, was given carte blanche by ABC to see if his style would translate to television, and boy did it—for a little while. The series took place in an overcast corner of the Pacific Northwest where everything was slightly askew, includ-ing a local resident who wandered around town carrying a small log in her arms—as the local sheriff (named Harry Truman, of course) explained simply, "We call her the Log Lady."

Into this peculiar setting, Lynch and co-creator Mark Frost—who, like many of the producers in this book, made a show they assumed no one would ever watch, and that wouldn't last long enough for them to deal with the consequences of their creative decisions—dropped the body of a dead teenage girl, wrapped in plastic, and then a handsome but eccentric FBI agent to investigate her murder, and eventually a dancing dwarf who spoke backwards, a one-armed man, a malevolent spirit named BOB, and even an alternate dimension filled with evil doppelgangers of all our heroes.

It was a bizarre show on nearly every level—and yet, for a short while, it was also a hit. For a few weeks in the spring of 1990, viewers went nuts over who killed Laura Palmer, what the Log Lady's deal was, why there was a fish in the percolator, and whether Audrey Horne had a saxophone player following her at all times. It helped that all the quirkiness was married to a sense of real forward momentum for the investigation and all the personal drama in the town. But when the show's success led to an unexpected second season, Lynch and Frost had no idea what to do other than to dial up the weirdness at the expense of the plot, and everyone lost interest long before we found out that BOB had murdered Laura while controlling the body of her father.

But the show was an obvious influence on *The X-Files*, on *Alias* and *Lost* and *Fringe* and many other millennial dramas, including something as relatively straightforward as AMC's *The Killing*. It showed that strangeness didn't have to be a barrier for entry; if you told your story well enough and put interesting enough characters inside that strangeness, you could do very well with an audience.

(The popularity of its successor shows, and the constant praise their creators reflected back on it, also led to a *Twin Peaks* revival—to be written by Lynch and Frost, with the promise of Lynch directing every episode—set to debut on Showtime within the next two years.)

***Homicide: Life on the Street* (NBC, 1993–1999):** If *Homicide* had done nothing but provide David Simon a transition from his newspaper job to TV writing, it would still likely merit mention here. But the Baltimore-based drama, like the New York–set one that would debut a few months later, was an important transitional step, in addition to being one of the best cop shows ever made. Run by Tom Fontana—the man behind the *St. Elsewhere* finale and many of that show's other lunatic moments—*Homicide* was a cop drama that was rarely afraid to sacrifice plot in favor of character, or to sacrifice action for good dialogue. If cases got closed—usually through the silver-tongued salesmanship of Andre Braugher's master interrogator Frank Pembleton—so be it. And if they didn't—as in the story of murdered girl Adena Watson, which played out for much of the first season and haunted the rest of the series—that was often even more interesting. *Homicide* was never a hit, but it lasted seven seasons, and expanded the level of artistry that was possible in such a traditional, largely standalone format.

NYPD Blue (ABC, 1993–2005): Steven Bochco and David Milch, together again, this time looking to push the outer edge of the envelope even farther than they did on *Hill Street Blues*. In the early '90s, Bochco looked at a TV landscape where more and more homes were getting cable, and where his shows had to compete with racy movies on HBO, and decided that the only way for the networks to stay relevant would be to introduce their own programming with mature content.

Enter *NYPD Blue*, a cop drama that, if not quite R-rated, was still more adult in its use of language and nudity than anything before it. The graphic content helped pave the way for *The Sopranos* and company, but so did cop Andy Sipowicz: a deeply flawed character who, in an earlier age, would have been the villain, but instead was portrayed with such shading, depth, and empathy that we began rooting for him despite ourselves.

The X-Files (FOX, 1993–2002): TV science fiction is always an iffy commercial proposition, because no matter how great a particular series may be, there's still a stigma attached to the genre that will keep some people from watching. The genius of Chris Carter's

X-Files was in the way it drew in an audience that would ordinarily run screaming from stories of aliens and monsters. *X-Files* was a sci-fi series, but because the two main characters were FBI agents in plain business suits—one of them a skeptic who thought all this stuff was ridiculous—it gave a mainstream audience an out: *I'm not watching some nerd-fest; this is just a cop show where weird things happen.* The series was able to borrow the bizarre atmosphere of *Twin Peaks* and make it more sustainable, and in the process paved the way for the likes of *Lost*, which also essentially tricked viewers into watching science fiction by introducing it in the guise of a mystery.

X-Files also pioneered the concept of "mythology," in which a show has a complex backstory and elaborate ongoing story arc, parceled out to viewers a little bit at a time. Of course, *X-Files* also became the first show to disappoint its viewers when it became clear that the mythology didn't make any sense. Writers on the show—alums include *Breaking Bad* creator Vince Gilligan and longtime *24* showrunner Howard Gordon—insist that, early on, Carter did have a plan, but the huge success of the series (including a feature film that debuted after the fifth TV season) forced him to elongate and tinker with the story until it eventually became gibberish. And as the mythology unraveled, it prepared the next generation of fanboys and -girls for the frustration they would feel when *Lost*, *Battlestar Galactica,* and other iconic sci-fi series didn't always pay things off in a satisfying manner.

***ER* (NBC, 1994–2009):** On a commercial level, *ER* was the end of the era that preceded the one I'll be discussing in this book: a mass-appeal scripted drama that at its George-Clooney second-season height was averaging 32 million viewers a week, and once did an episode that attracted 48 million. On an artistic level, it was an important link in the chain, because of what it did to increase both the pace of the TV drama and the amount of trust shows could place in their audience.

ER was a hospital drama by genre, but an action movie in style. Even compared to something like *Hill Street Blues* or, the year before, *NYPD Blue*, this sucker *moved*—from doctor to doctor, patient to patient, often throwing the audience right into the middle of a story without bothering to explain anything about what was happening or what all the medical lingo meant. If you go back and look at the dramas leading up to it, there was a lot of over-explaining of the minutiae of these professions—there's a retrospectively hilarious *Hill Street* episode where Furillo and the other cops are baffled to learn of a legal concept called "fruits of the poisonous tree"—but *ER* assumed that its viewers would be smart enough to keep up. The ratings proved them right, which gave license to other ambitious network dramas (*The West Wing* shared producer John Wells) to do the same, and helped inform what was about to happen on cable.

And though many accounts of the cable-driven revolution tend to begin with *Sex and the City* or *The Sopranos*, this story begins earlier, with a show whose title evoked the phrase "there's no place like home," that was unlike anything seen on television before.

CHAPTER 1

What we were don't matter...
Oz *blazes a trail*

The Rolling Stones don't have a name or a sound without Muddy Waters. "Clapton Is God" signs don't pop up around London if Slow Hand doesn't first listen to Robert Johnson. And *The Sopranos* doesn't get on television without *Oz*.

The Sopranos was the first commercial success of the revolution, but it wasn't the first revolutionary cable drama of the period. That honor belongs to *Oz*, the prison drama HBO and creator Tom Fontana made almost as a lark, that became the foundation for everything that followed.

HBO had been pairing its movie library with original programming since the 1970s. There were critically acclaimed comedies like *Tanner '88* and *The Larry Sanders Show*, anthologies like *The Hitchhiker* and *Tales from the Crypt*, and more, but "the original programming was an afterthought," says Chris Albrecht, who became president of HBO Original Programming in 1995 (and later ascended to CEO thanks to his work in this period). "Even *Sanders* was an afterthought." In the mid-'90s, though, Albrecht and his boss Jeff Bewkes decided to take a more serious approach to original scripted television.

Meanwhile, Fontana was in the midst of running *Homicide: Life on the Street*, an artful cop drama that his bosses at NBC kept pushing him to make less artful and more commercial. (With each passing season, the cast became more conventionally attractive, while the philosophical conversations made way for shootouts, helicopter chases, and evil drug dealers.)

Fontana grew up in Buffalo, and had been fascinated by the nearby Attica prison riots. He says that as he made a television show where, at least every other episode, the detectives would send someone to jail, "I thought, 'Boy, every TV cop show ends with someone being put away, and you never hear about them ever again. Could you do a series about that?'"

He tried pitching gentle variations on the idea—a juvenile detention center, a "Club Fed" for white-collar criminals—but found little interest at the big networks. "So then I had to wait for HBO to decide they were going to do scripted television," he says.

Albrecht was talking with studio executive Rob Kenneally—one of the few in the business Fontana had mentioned the prison idea to who *hadn't* dismissed it out of hand—about HBO's plans to do a scripted drama series, and mentioned in passing that the network had found surprising success with its documentaries about life in prison.

"Rob heard the word 'prison,'" recalls Fontana, "and virtually left the meeting, got on his phone, called me in New York and said, 'Get your ass out here. I've finally found someone who will do your stupid television show.' It's just one of those kismet moments. I wouldn't have known otherwise."

Fontana and his *Homicide* partner Barry Levinson pitched the prison show to Albrecht and HBO executive Anne Thomopoulos. Albrecht wasn't sure it could work, but told them, "I'll give you a million dollars: shoot as much as you can."

Levinson and Fontana were able to put together a 17-minute pilot presentation for *Oz* (the title is the nickname for the show's fictional Oswald State Penitentiary), telling the story of wiseguy Dino Ortolani, a violent inmate who winds up burned to death by a rival convict.

"Chris said to me, 'I don't care if the characters are likable as long as they're interesting,'" says Fontana. "And he asked me, 'What's the one thing you've always wanted to do in the pilot of a broadcast television show that you've never been allowed to do?' And I said, 'Kill the leading man.' And he said, 'I love that! Do that!'"

At the broadcast networks, there was layer upon layer of executives to go through to get a new show on the air. At HBO at that time, things were so informal that Albrecht invited Fontana and Levinson to screen the *Oz* prototype in his office.

"It was the first and only time in my career where I flew out with a tape or a disc and the executive said, 'Come on, let's watch it!'" says Fontana. "And I go, 'I'm going to watch it with the head of the network. He won't have any defenses. He won't be able to hide behind the research and the hoo-ha.' So we sat there, and I must have looked back and forth from the screen to him. I hope I wasn't just staring at him."

Albrecht was impressed. "It was the first thing we had seen for premium television that was a true dramatic series," he says. "And it was startling how much different it felt from everything else on television." He ordered *Oz* to series.

The Ortolani story would survive to the finished version of the pilot, while Fontana began sketching out the characters who would outlast Dino inside the walls of Oz. He conceived of two administrators to represent the schism between those who believe prisons exist for retribution, and those who think the goal is to rehabilitate: respectively, Warden Leo Glynn (Ernie Hudson), and Tim McManus (Terry Kinney), manager of an experimental prison unit called Emerald City. As a point-of-view character for the audience, Fontana created Tobias Beecher (Lee Tergesen), a middle-class white attorney—"Beecher was the HBO subscriber," he says—sent to Oz after killing a nine-year-old girl while driving drunk. The other inmates were more serious criminals, including white supremacist Vern Schillinger (J.K. Simmons), who turns Beecher into his slave, branding a swastika onto his rear end to prove his dominance; black gang leader Jefferson Keane (Leon); Ryan O'Reily (Dean Winters), an Iago-like schemer with a gift for getting others to do his dirty work; Kareem Said (Eamonn Walker), a Muslim radical threatening a riot from the moment he enters the place; and Miguel Alvarez (Kirk Acevedo), a young gangbanger whose father and grandfather are also doing time in Oz.

Some actors were ones Fontana had worked with before (Hudson did a memorable stint on *St. Elsewhere* as an injured fireman, while Tergesen and Edie Falco—cast as prison guard Diane Wittlesey—had played husband and wife in a couple of *Homicide* episodes). Others, he had always wanted to work with (Tony winners B.D. Wong and Rita Moreno played the priest and nun tasked with the inmates' spiritual health), and still others were unknowns with interesting auditions.

A hulking black actor named Adewale Akinnuoye-Agbaje wandered in to read for the role of one of Keane's buddies, and "it was terrible," Fontana says. But the man's presence and charisma were undeniable, so Fontana invited him to stay and talk, and discovered that he was actually English (and much more comfortable when not faking an American accent), with Nigerian ancestry. Fontana's wheels started spinning, and he invented Simon Adebisi, a malevolent force of nature in a comically small hat who took whatever (and whomever) he wanted within the prison's walls.

This was one of the most racially diverse casts ever assembled for a TV series. Even the progressive dramas of the '80s and '90s tended to have merely token minority representation; it was so unusual for *Homicide* to have a scene featuring a bunch of black cops conversing among themselves (and not about race) that it sadly merited special mention by TV critics.

"That was one of the things I laid out first when I was first pitching it," says Fontana. "The prison population could represent the population of America, but the percentages were not representative."

Because he knew the average prisoner was even less likely to open up about his innermost feelings than the average homicide detective, Fontana decided to have each episode narrated by wheelchair-bound inmate Augustus Hill, played by Harold Perrineau.

"It really came out of the Greeks," Fontana says, "and Greek tragedy, where you would have this chorus of somebody in the community who would step out and talk about themes and bigger ideas. My original concept was John Leguizamo, but he thought about it and decided he didn't want to do it. I wanted the person to be a minority, either Latino or black, because I felt like this idea that a person had to be from an environment in which they had much more depth of experience than just being in a prison."

In addition to being one of McManus's charges in Em City(*), Hill would address the audience directly multiple times in each episode, musing on problems universal to the prison experience, or to life outside the walls of Oz.

(*) Fontana killed off Hill at the end of the fifth season so Perrineau would be free to appear in The Matrix *sequels, but kept Hill as the narrator for the final season (where he was often joined by other dead characters), since Perrineau could come in and film those monologues in chunks.*

"Oz is where I live," Hill announces midway through the first episode. "Oz is where I will die, where most of us will die. What we were, don't matter. What we are, don't matter. What we become, don't matter... Does it?"

"The thing about the *Oz* experience that stuck with me the most is that, compared to how things are now, it was utterly, 'Let's see what happens,'" recalls Carolyn Strauss, an HBO executive who became Chris Albrecht's top lieutenant during this era. "'Let's cast this guy, let's do this, let's do that. Let's experiment with form.' Not only was there a narrator, but the narrator was going to be shot differently by every director. The main character was going to be killed at the end of the first episode. It was very much a 'let's see what happens' attitude rather than a 'we need to know exactly what happens every step of the way.' It was a black-box theater, rather than the main stage. I think that gave people a tremendous sense of freedom and experimentation, and just a great sense of, 'You know what? We can try it. It's not going to be the end of the world if something doesn't work.'"

Hill Street Blues had laid out the template for ensemble dramas, which bounced back and forth between different stories over the course of each hour. It was a template Fontana knew well from *St. Elsewhere* and *Homicide*, and one he decided to step away from here. *Oz* episodes told multiple stories, but they tended to be presented one at a time, all the way through: first O'Reily scheming, then Moreno's Sister Pete counseling Alvarez, then Schillinger oppressing Beecher, etc.

He chose to experiment "because it was HBO, and they said you could do anything you want. I had written so much in the broadcast form, and I thought, 'Why not make each episode like a little collection of short stories?' Some weeks, the Beecher story would be five minutes, and some weeks it would be 15 minutes. The freedom to be able to do it differently every week, and decide what order they were coming in, was very liberating from a storytelling point of view. You weren't bound by, 'Oh, I've got to get to this point by the commercial so that I can get them back from the commercial,' or 'I haven't serviced this character in the second act.' None of the old rules applied, and it was wonderful. 'Oh, you can just tell the story for the length of time it needs to be told in this episode.'"

"One of the great things about the guys who did the first couple of big drama and comedy series on HBO is almost all of them had a lot of schooling on network series," says Strauss. "They knew the rules of series television. They knew how to tell stories, knew the rules they needed to keep and knew the rules they could throw out. They had a lot of fun with that. There was a lot of esprit, in terms of going at it in a whole new way."

When Fontana had pitched even mild versions of *Oz* to the broadcast networks, he says he was told, "'Oh, they're all too nasty. Where are the heroes? Where are the victories?'" These questions simply didn't apply at HBO. There were no obvious heroes in *Oz*—even the idealistic McManus had myriad flaws—and the villains tended to win, usually in the most gruesome way possible. O'Reilly and Adebisi team up to take out the prison leader of the Italian mob by grinding broken glass into his food until he slowly bleeds to death internally; when the man's son comes looking for revenge, Adebisi rapes him. A rare victory of sorts comes when Beecher finally fights back against Schillinger, savagely beating him with weightlifting equipment in the prison gym, then tying him down and literally defecating onto his tormentor's face.

Fontana's bosses at NBC likely would have fired him on the spot if he had put such a scene into a *Homicide* script. Chris Albrecht had no major objections to any of the content.

"Chris is not only leaving me alone," says Fontana, "he's encouraging me to be incorrigible. He was literally saying to me, 'Go as far, take as big a risk as you possibly want.' He never dictated any specific thing, but every time we spoke of the show and he had read a script or seen a screening, he was absolutely encouraging about the risk-taking."

Fontana says the only time in the run of the series when an HBO executive strongly objected to the content involved a flashback to an inmate who had murdered an entire family, including two young children. Strauss didn't even have an issue with the crime itself, but on how long the scene dwelled on the killer pointing a gun at the kids.

"So I just sped up the amount of time it was pointed," Fontana says. "I figured one note every five years, I'd be an asshole not to change it."

If *Oz* had just been about the brutality, it would have been the best-cast exploitation film of all time. The violence was inherent to the setting, but Fontana had higher aims. He wanted viewers to confront the dehumanizing nature of the prison experience, but also use these criminals as proxies to talk about race, addiction, sexuality, religion, elder care and any other hot-button issue he had on his mind.

The setting, and the rapid turnover in the cast (Em City had a very high body count), allowed Fontana to keep bringing in interesting faces to play prisoners: rap star Method Man, former teen idol Luke Perry, NBA veteran Rick Fox, KISS drummer Peter Criss, even Gavin MacLeod from *The Love Boat*. The longer the show was on, the more obvious it became that it was a fun place for actors to try roles unlike anything in their careers to that point.

"It was thrilling" says Fontana. "And I have been very blessed in my career. Starting with *St. Elsewhere(*)* and then doing *Homicide*, I can't really say I had a shitty time doing those shows. I had a great, joyous time doing those shows. But this was like 'Eat all the chocolate you want, and you won't get fat.' It was extraordinary. It made me rethink all the rules I assumed were unchangeable. Suddenly, you could change it. From a writer's point of view, it was so liberating. I would get up every morning at five and just be chuckling that I was going to get to write this stuff again."

(*) In addition to breaking new ground for cable drama with Oz, *Fontana had blazed a trail with the* St. Elsewhere *finale that revealed the show as a fantasy of the main character's autistic son—a polarizing ending that presaged the divisive conclusions to* The Sopranos, Lost, Battlestar Galactica, *and others. Though Fontana hadn't meant to anger his fans with the* St. Elsewhere *ending, he was relieved by the reaction to these other conclusions: "I was like, 'Oh, thank God there's other people in the room with me now! It's so lonely in there being the guy who had somehow infuriated half of our audience.'"*

Before *Oz* debuted on July 12, 1997, Fontana says the running joke on the set was, "Oh, that's turning into a great scene, but who's going to watch it?" Everyone was having a great time making this strange show, but nobody knew if there would be an audience for it. But HBO marketed the show well, and in time they found that while it wasn't an enormous hit (certainly not compared to many of the shows that followed), it had—perhaps because of the diverse cast and storylines—a broad constituency.

"I didn't even know they were doing research until a year or two into the show," says Fontana, "and they told me, 'For the HBO subscriber, it's pretty much across the board: it's black, it's white, it's young, it's old, it's rich, it's poor. It's gay, it's straight. It appeals to a lot of different parts of our subscriber base.' But the biggest single group was black women, which I found fascinating."

Because HBO doesn't have advertising, ratings have never been the most important metric, and in that early period were barely considered at all.

"For that brief period of time, Chris didn't care about a big hit," says Fontana. "He wanted just to make noise. I remember an op-ed piece in a newspaper about *Oz*, and he was thrilled about that, because we weren't on the TV page. That's what he considered a success."

For six seasons, Fontana kept devising creative, twisted ways to kill people. Many were adapted from real-life prison murders, and nearly all of them involved the Sicilian concept of poetic justice: "The way people died on the show had to come out of character or had to relate to the crime involved," Fontana explains. "If somebody tells a lie about you to a cop, you cut their tongue out." He kept bringing in interesting new performers—near the end of production of the final season, J.K. Simmons told me, "You keep thinking, 'They've got to have used every actor in New York by now,' and then Joel Grey turns up"—and letting his characters experience rare triumphs and abundant tragedies.

The spine of the series turned out to be the vendetta between Beecher and Schillinger, and the way it was complicated when Schillinger's predatory friend Chris Keller (Chris Meloni) fell in love with Beecher, and vice versa. So long as Fontana had some new combination of what he dubbed "the unholy trio" of *Oz*, the series still had legs, and Albrecht was willing to keep it going.

"One of the reasons that I stopped was I wasn't sure what to do with them after that season," he says of the decision to conclude the show after six years. "I was worried that it was going to become like a repetition, or a joke."

With no future to worry about, the final season is especially bloody, including the violent deaths of Kareem Said and Leo Glynn. Schillinger and Beecher play the lead roles in a prison production of *Macbeth*, and Keller, looking to cause trouble, replaces Beecher's prop knife with a real one so he'll unwittingly stab Schillinger to death in the final act (after each man has recited several Shakespeare passages that evoke their own mutually destructive relationship). Beecher rejects Keller's attempt to reconcile; spurned one last time, Keller commits suicide in a way that makes it look like Beecher murdered him.

"When God was designing the universe," a frustrated Beecher asks Sister Pete, "why did He make something wonderful so fucking painful?"

"I think He thought we could handle it," she replies.

It turns out that before Keller died, he had sent a biological agent to the prison mailroom to murder several of Schillinger's Aryan cronies, which forces an evacuation of Oz. We conclude with images of the darkened, empty prison, hear snippets of dialogue from the past six years, then get one final monologue from the late Augustus Hill, who tells us, "The story is simple: a man lives in prison, and dies. How he dies, that's easy. The who and the why is the complex part—the human part, the only part worth knowing. Peace."

HBO had followed the debut of *Oz* with a slew of unconventional hits both dramatic (*The Sopranos, Six Feet Under*) and comedic (*Sex and the City, Curb Your Enthusiasm*). Fontana kicked the door open, and many others followed him through.

"I would say that *Oz* gave us some confidence and momentum," says Carolyn Strauss. "We really enjoyed the process of working on it—working with Tom and building a presence in New York. It also helped us as we tried to define our series presence as bringing HBO viewers continuing stories and characters that they could not find on ad-supported television: complex, well-told stories, featuring conflicted human characters that dealt with adult subject matter."

Fontana jokes that "We were the farm team" for the series that followed: *The Sopranos*(*) hired Edie Falco to play Carmela (Fontana let her go, not wanting to deprive her of a lead role so she could continue a fairly minor one on his series) and *The Wire* would use more than a dozen *Oz* actors in its cast.

(*) *Fontana's initial reaction to* The Sopranos *pilot was to call his casting director, Alexa Fogel, to say, "Please tell me that James Gandolfini hasn't been in my office and I said no to him." (He hadn't.)*

Fontana had suspected that if *Oz* worked, it would be the first of many shows in a far more adventurous vein than what had been allowed on network television—and, that if he failed, this new era could be over before it started.

"When I first sat down with Chris, and he said, 'I'm going to give you as much creative freedom as you want,' I thought, 'This is great.' But you also go, 'Man, if I fuck this up, the next guy who comes in here, Chris is gonna say, "Yeah yeah yeah, I gave Tom Fontana all the creative freedom, and he fucked me." So I felt this incredible burden of responsibility for my brother and sister writers. And I was so thrilled that the shows that came after were so completely different than *Oz*, and succeeded. They kept building on HBO's reputation."

Oz and *The Sopranos* both filmed in New York and New Jersey, and the casts of the two shows would attend each other's parties, go to boxing matches together at Madison Square Garden, and find other ways to feel like a tight-knit community. Fontana had mentored *The Wire* co-creator David Simon, and overlapped at the MTM studio with *Deadwood* creator David Milch when Fontana was doing *St. Elsewhere* and Milch was on *Hill Street Blues*. He doesn't resent the shows that followed him for being more popular and/or enduring, but he does get frustrated when stories about the period skip over his contribution to it.

"Every once in a while, I feel like I'm the short guy in the back of the picture who keeps jumping up, going, 'I'm here, too,'" he says. "But what are you going to do? So much of that stuff, if you let it affect you too much, I think it burns away at your creative soul. I think it's better to go, 'Okay, it is what it is.' I can't do anything to change it. I move on from that. I don't sit up at night cursing the darkness saying, 'When am I getting my fair share of pats on the back?' The reality is, I got to make a show that I really wanted to make. And that was a huge reward."

Fontana got his reward (as did *Oz* fans), and TV audiences got to enjoy the other shows that *Oz* made possible.

CHAPTER 2

All due respect... The Sopranos
changes everything

G uy walks into a psychiatrist's office.

He complains, "It's good to be in something from the ground floor. I came too late for that, I know. But lately, I'm getting the feeling that I came in at the end. That the best is over."

The punchline—not that Tony Soprano could ever understand it—was that the show that told his story represented not the end of something, but the thrilling ground floor.

Other shows had made the revolution possible, but *The Sopranos* is the one that made the world realize something special was happening on television. It rewrote the rules and made TV a better, happier place for thinking viewers, even as it was telling the story of a bunch of stubborn, ignorant, miserable excuses for human beings.

And all of it came from the mind of a man who wanted nothing more than to be out of the TV business at the time he wrote that first script.

"I was never that happy in television," *Sopranos* creator David Chase admits. He'd been writing TV dramas for a couple of decades—had worked on *The Rockford Files, Kolchak: The Night Stalker* (the short-lived '70s drama that helped inspire *The X-Files*), *Northern Exposure*, and *I'll Fly Away*, among other impressive resume lines, and had created a critically well-regarded but short-lived series called *Almost Grown*—and in the mid-'90s he signed a development deal with the Brillstein-Grey production company, for reasons he couldn't quite understand.

"They made this development deal with me, and people there said they believed I had this great TV series in me," he says. "I thought, 'Me? A great TV series? I'm not even crazy about doing TV. I want to break out and do movies.'"

Given the shows he had written for, what exactly was so burdensome about the business for him at that point?

"I was really lucky," he says, "in that I worked for and with some really talented people. And on my own. But I'd had, either by myself or with these other people, had to sit through these moronic meetings, in which every timid, weak, vapid idea was always preferred to anything revolutionary or new. That was one thing: I was never surprised watching hour-long TV. And I never saw anyone on there who behaved like real human beings."

The Sopranos would not be timid, weak or vapid. It would surprise everyone in the business—including Chase, who never expected the thing to get made, much less in an environment where it could both succeed and stay true to his vision.

Among the ideas he was fighting against was the notion that a TV series had to have a likable character at its center. Why, TV executives had been asking for 50 years, would viewers want to come back week after week to watch a jerk, a crook, or worse? There's a famous scene in Paddy Chayefsky's script for *Network* (a movie that predicted the reality/tabloid state of our pop culture with stunning accuracy, but didn't have the optimism to allow for the flip side demonstrated by shows like *The Sopranos*) where a bored development executive rattles off the descriptions of the shows under consideration for next season; every one of them has a main character described as "crusty but benign." That was "complex" TV characterization for decades: a hero could have the faintest hint of an edge, but only if we were reminded early and often that he was ultimately pure of heart. Even Sipowicz from *NYPD Blue*—introduced to viewers as a drunken, profane, sexist, out-of-control bigot—ultimately sobered up, had a pair of sincere romances, fathered two babies, became a mentor, and by the finale had cleaned up his act to the point where it wouldn't have been implausible if he'd been made a candidate for sainthood.

Tony Soprano, on the other hand? Tony was crusty, sure.

He was not, however, benign.

We meet him in the waiting room of Dr. Jennifer Melfi's psychiatric practice, agitated at the thought of what he's about to do. ("It's impossible for me to talk to a psychiatrist," he barks early in that first session.) He says he's in "waste management," but as he walks her through the day of the panic attack that brought him to her, we see how he actually makes his living, starting with a scene in which he gleefully runs down a deadbeat gambler with his nephew Christopher's car, followed by Tony realizing he can force the guy to participate in a hustle involving non-existent MRI scans.

Of course, Tony is also presented as a relatable (second cousin to "likable") husband and father, grappling with pressures at both home and work (here differentiated as lower- and upper-case family and Family), moving through a suburban landscape not unlike that occupied by much of the show's audience. He's in a feud with his Uncle Junior (a fellow *capo* in the North Jersey mob), has debts to collect and legs to break, but he also has to throw a birthday party for Anthony Junior, attend daughter Meadow's volleyball game, keep wife Carmela happy, and find a way to convince his mother Livia to move to a "retirement community." He lives in a familiar neighborhood (even if you'd never been to the North Jersey locations where the show filmed, you knew some version of it from your area), shops at familiar stores, and has familiar problems. He just also has a very unfamiliar second life as a wiseguy.

And that was the show's genius. Chase didn't set out to write a mob drama. He set out to write a show about his troubled relationship with his late mother—his wife Denise "always said I should write a show about my mother, because my mother was very funny—unintentionally so"—here embodied by the marvelously passive-aggressive Livia Soprano. He just wanted to find a way to make the stakes high enough that viewers would care. Would anyone want to watch a show about a precision optics salesman (or, as a friend of Chase's had suggested, a TV writer) being henpecked by his mother? But what if the henpecked son is a wiseguy capable of incredible acts of violence, and under constant threat of incarceration or death? Then all of it—the mundane suburban drudgery, the lower-case family conflicts that were so resonant with so many viewers—takes on a much greater weight, doesn't it?

Chase first had the idea for *The Sopranos* sometime in the 1980s, but envisioned it as a movie, which would have dealt with Uncle Junior and Livia conspiring to murder Tony for his imagined slights against them, and concluded with Tony smothering Livia with a pillow. (Basically, the first season of the series, with a slightly darker ending.)

But he never bothered to write a script, and had largely forgotten about it until someone at Brillstein-Grey began pressing him to try something *Godfather*-esque. They had a pitch meeting at Fox, which was still a relatively young network looking to make a splash.

"In the pitch meeting, they were delighted," Chase recalls. "I thought they really got it. And I sat down to write it, and every step of the way, having spent so long writing for television, I thought, 'Uh-oh. This isn't going to fly. Oh boy.'"

He often jokes that the only way Fox would have made a pilot at that point was if Tony were revealed to be an FBI agent using the Mafia job as a cover to catch terrorists. Fox passed, and other networks showed tepid interest at best. A year later, Fox tried to revive the project as a vehicle for actor Anthony LaPaglia, but the network and the actor couldn't close a deal.

This was around the time that HBO debuted *Oz*, and HBO's Chris Albrecht recalls that that show, while only a modest commercial success, sent a message to the creative community.

As he puts it, "I think the people who were most affected [by *Oz*] was that group who were then inspired to go, 'All right, wait a minute: this thing that I've been thinking about, that I'll never sell anywhere, maybe I can take it to them.' Or, 'I have an idea that I've never even thought about because I never thought there was a home for something like that.' It became a calling card for what was possible."

One of those people paying attention was Albrecht's old friend Brad Grey, co-founder of Brillstein-Grey, who set up a meeting between Albrecht and Chase. This was not like any of the previous network meetings Chase had been through. Albrecht had questions—about where the show would be filmed (Chase wanted to shoot it in the actual Jersey locations as much as possible), and whether Tony and Melfi would have sex (they wouldn't, and didn't)—but the only part of the pitch that seemed to give him any pause at all was the idea that Chase, who had never been behind the camera before, might direct the pilot.

Chase wanted to be a filmmaker, and viewed directing the pilot as the next big stop on that road. Albrecht wasn't sure he should trust such a task to a novice, and after they had decided to make the script(*), he called Chase in for the meeting, intending to tell him gently that someone else would have to direct. Instead, Chase won the first of many debates with his new boss.

(*) HBO's Carolyn Strauss recalls that the other contender for HBO's first post-Oz drama spot was a very different, but still excellent, script from My So-Called Life *creator Winnie Holzman about a female business executive. The new golden age of drama that* The Sopranos *triggered has largely involved shows built around middle-aged male anti-heroes—as the saying goes, imitation is the sincerest form of television, even if it's innovative television—and I do wonder what the revolution would have looked like if Oz had been followed by the Holzman show.*

"He came in the room," Albrecht recalls, "and he talked about how he saw the show, how he saw Jersey as a character, and I listened to him and thought, 'I will never find anyone who sees this the way this guy sees it.'"

It was a level of attention to detail that would become familiar to everyone who ever worked on the show. Chase seemingly remembered every place he had ever been to in North Jersey, and had an almost obsessive grasp of how each character fit into this world. Production designer Bob Shaw once told me about the location that was chosen for Melfi's house. Shaw hadn't noticed that a mirror in the foyer reflected a nearby hat collection; when Chase saw it, he chewed Shaw out, insisting, "Melfi does not have *a collection of hats!*"

"David committed his life to that show," says Albrecht. "This is a guy who didn't have a whole lot of fun doing other things."

He was, however, having fun making *The Sopranos* pilot.

"HBO at the time," Chase says, "we didn't know they were the HBO they were going to become. But I realized, however it had happened, I had been given a great opportunity to do something different. And I didn't think it would succeed. And I didn't care. I was so fed up with TV at that time, and so frustrated with my lack of success at getting into features that I didn't care. I just wanted to make the best TV pilot I possibly could. And so I had license in terms of language and action and story development and flow and pace, and I thought, 'Just go for it.'"

Because nobody knew what HBO was about to become, name actors weren't beating down their door for the chance to play Tony Soprano or his wife Carmela. Albrecht and Strauss briefly pondered reaching out to LaPaglia again, to see if he was still interested, but the decision ultimately came down to three men Chase liked: little-known character actors Michael Rispoli and James Gandolfini, and longtime Bruce Springsteen guitarist Steven Van Zandt.

Chase had long been fascinated by Van Zandt's stage presence at Springsteen shows, but he was out of the running quickly. (He would wind up in the comic-relief role of Tony's *consiglieri* Silvio Dante.)

As for the other two, Albrecht says, "Rispoli was great. He was funnier than Jimmy, just because of the normal rhythms that he had. And we talked about it, and David said, 'It's a very different show if you put Rispoli in it or Jimmy in it, but the show I envisioned is the show that's got Jimmy in it. It's a much darker show with Jimmy in it.' I think we sat with that for a moment. 'Dark' is not really a word you ever want to go for in television, but the other one was 'more real.' So we cast Jimmy."

Gandolfini "just inhabited the tone of the script," says Chase. "At one time, I had said that this thing could be like a live-action *Simpsons*. Once I saw him do it, I thought, 'No, that's not right. It can be absurdist, it can have a lot of stupid shit in it, but it should not be a live-action *Simpsons*."

Some of the supporting actors were more familiar from mob movies (Michael Imperioli, Lorraine Bracco, and Tony Sirico were among a large contingent of *Goodfellas* alums in the regular and recurring cast, while Dominic Chianese played Hyman Roth's right-hand man Johnny Ola in *The Godfather Part II*), and Nancy Marchand, who played Tony's mother Livia, had been Mrs. Pynchon on *Lou Grant*. But anyone who hadn't seen his brief but memorable appearance in *True Romance* had no idea who James Gandolfini was at that time. And only fans of *Oz* really knew Edie Falco, who was cast to play Carmela Soprano.

There was little concern inside HBO at the time that they were building this series around two non-stars—"It's not like now," says Strauss. "Now there's so much *tsuris* about stuff. Back then, it was, 'If it doesn't work, it doesn't work'"—and Chase found it to his advantage to have a pair of actors at the center that the audience had no expectations for.

He could make Tony Soprano do just about anything without fearing an audience member would object, "Oh, James Gandolfini wouldn't do that." And it helped that Gandolfini himself never tried to protect his image in the way he suspects most actors would have in the part. If anything, Gandolfini often took things further than Chase had planned, like a scene in the pilot where Tony discovers Christopher has discussed writing a mob-movie script for a cousin who works in Hollywood. The scene called for Tony to slap Christopher lightly across the face; instead, Gandolfini picked up the smaller Imperioli to make his displeasure clear.

"And I went, 'All right, I got it. This is big shit. This is serious,'" says Chase.

Filming the pilot went better than Chase could have hoped, but in the long period between when it was shot and when the series was picked up, his dream was that HBO would pass, after which he would scrounge together maybe $500,000 to film a second hour, turn it into a movie, and take it to Cannes. Instead, HBO ordered *The Sopranos* to series, premiered it on January 10, 1999, and Chase found himself making a television show without any of the constraints that had nearly driven him from the business.

Of that time making the first season, he says, "I felt like after floating on a raft in the middle of the Pacific for about 25 years, I had washed up on Paradise Island."

The lesson Gandolfini had taught Chase about Tony Soprano eventually led to the series' fifth episode, "College," which cemented the show's place in TV history—and its great leap forward from all that had come before. In an hour that brings the Family/ family conflicts into sharper focus, Tony takes Meadow on a tour of small liberal-arts schools in New England, a journey that's familiar to many parents and children. Along the way, he happens to spot Febby Petrulio, a wiseguy who turned rat years before and disappeared into the witness protection program. Tony tracks Febby down and, while Meadow's in the middle of an interview at one school, slips away to strangle him to death.

Though Tony has participated in violence earlier in the series, and given orders that led to others being hurt, this is the first time we see him actively kill a man. It isn't self-defense, nor putting down a vile threat to society, the only two circumstances under which TV protagonists had previously been allowed to kill. Febby disappeared into civilian life, ran a travel agency, and if he was still committing crimes, it was small-time stuff. He tried to take a shot at Tony earlier in the episode after realizing he was being followed, but Tony doesn't know that. This is revenge, pure and simple, taken in bloody close-up, and it left no possible confusion about what kind of man we were watching and what kind of show this was.

Chase says he felt the moment was essential to the series at this point:

"We were four episodes in, and we were telling a story about a Mafia guy, and he had killed nobody. I realized this was a Mafia show. Part of the reason people go to that was to see revenge extracted, justice done quickly."

Albrecht—who, again, had green-lit *Oz* and allowed Tom Fontana to let his inmate characters commit all manner of depraved acts for two years before *The Sopranos* debuted—was convinced this would be a crippling mistake for such a young show, and once again let Chase convince him he was wrong(*).

(*) *Strauss says of her former boss, "Chris's philosophy has always been, 'I'm going to give you my opinion, but I'm never going to make you do something.'" Albrecht says, "Early on in my career I would argue with some guys, and I would realize, 'Was my idea really better?'"*

"I said, 'David, you can't do this. He can't kill this guy. You haven't earned it yet. The audience is going to hate him. It's the fifth episode. Wait 'til the end of the season.' And David said to me, 'If Tony Soprano were to find this guy and doesn't kill him, he's full of shit, and therefore the show's full of shit.' And I said, 'Okay, that's a good point.'"

"College" featured the first of many murders we would see Tony Soprano commit. *The Sopranos* was a violent show from its first episode to its last (both of them featured auto vs. pedestrian incidents), and it was easy for many viewers to focus on that familiar, visceral part of the series. I once asked Chase whether any of the network executives he had pitched the show to pre-HBO had any qualms about the violence. He laughed and said that when he brought it to CBS, he was told they would have been fine with even more violence than he was suggesting; it was the psychiatry they wanted to get rid of.

But *The Sopranos* without the psychiatry wouldn't have been *The Sopranos*, it's that simple. It's not a coincidence that the series starts with Tony meeting Melfi, not with Tony and Christopher making collections, or ogling strippers at the Bada Bing, or gathering for a family dinner at Tony's house. This was a show dedicated to going deep inside the psyche of a millennial man, figuring out what made him tick, what his hopes and fears were, and ultimately what made him a craven, hypocritical sociopath. *The Sopranos* without Dr. Melfi is a *Goodfellas* knock-off done for television.

The show *with* psychiatry, on the other hand? That was something special.

Before the series debuted, it was compared endlessly to the then-upcoming Billy Crystal/Robert DeNiro film *Analyze This*. It's even a joke in a second-season episode; a new therapist nervously invokes the film in front of Tony, who spits the title back at him like a rotten hunk of *moozadell*. By that point, though, there was no need to be defensive, because it was clear just how seriously the show took these journeys into Tony's mind—and how it took advantage of the serialized drama format to gradually expand what we knew of this man and his troubles.

Tony is rarely 100% honest with Melfi. There are too many barriers between them, from cultural (she's a woman, he's a sexist pig) to legal (doctor-patient privilege doesn't extend to acts you haven't committed yet) to plain personal (Tony Soprano trusts no one). But Tony, especially in the series' earliest days, is able to open up to her in a way he can't or won't with Carmela, Christopher, or Big Pussy. Tony makes himself vulnerable in that office. He tells Melfi things about himself that he would never speak of outside those walls. Those sessions allow us to see how much he's lying to the rest of the world, and render him an incredibly rich character even before you factor in the enormous contributions from Gandolfini.

The psychiatry starts off as a practical thing: Tony is having panic attacks, and that's unacceptable in his line of work. But over the course of his relationship with Dr. Melfi, he admits to his shortcomings as a husband and father, confronts a childhood that he's convinced himself was no worse than any other—despite a violent wiseguy for a father and an emotional leech for a mother—and at times despairs about the state of the world at large. When Livia dies unexpectedly at the start of Season 3 (Nancy Marchand had been deeply ill for the show's first two years, but Chase had cast her despite the risk of losing his story's chief antagonist at any moment), Tony glibly asks Melfi, "So, we're probably done here, right? She's dead." But the work continues, at first because the panic attacks have to be treated (Melfi figures out the root cause— a childhood trauma where Tony saw his father chop off a butcher's finger—in the very next episode), and then because Tony simply enjoys coming there. (In one of the series' final episodes, he calls their sessions "an oasis in my week.")

Whatever his motivations, whether at the start or in later seasons, Tony keeps going, and those sessions with Melfi—along with other Soprano relatives (and Dr. Melfi herself) seeing their own therapists, Tony having increasingly strange and elaborate (and, among the fans, divisive) dreams, or Tony at times using other friends and relatives as surrogate shrinks—helped add enormous depth, pathos, and at times comedy to what could have easily been a conventional, straightforward mob drama. We saw relationships ebb and flow, and realizations come slowly with time. In the series premiere, Livia just seems like a stubborn old crank; by the end of the first season, it's become entirely believable that she would plot to have her own son murdered.

The psychiatry and the mob conflict were beautifully married in that first season, in which Tony and Uncle Junior battle for control of the North Jersey mob after acting boss Jackie Aprile (played by Rispoli in a consolation prize role) dies of stomach cancer. It's a family conflict and a Family one all wrapped together, as Junior's dislike of Tony is as much about his nephew not respecting his elders as it is about anything business-wise—"How many fucking hours did I spend playing catch with you?" he complains when Tony disrespects him—and Junior is egged on for much of the season by Livia, who resents the son who took her out of her house and put her in a home. So Tony goes to Melfi to lament his strained relationships with his mother and his uncle, yet ultimately it's the discovery of the therapy itself that becomes the wedge Livia uses to push Junior towards having Tony whacked.

It's a brilliantly structured season, one that nearly every significant cable drama that followed would try to emulate in some way. The climax becomes less about what will happen to the Family (Junior goes to jail for an unrelated crime, and Tony and his guys take out most of Junior's crew) than about what Tony will do to the mother he finally accepts has absolutely no love in her heart for him. Chase decided early on to scrap the original pillow-smothering ending; fate intervenes in the form of a stroke, and all a homicidal Tony can do is rant about how she's smiling while orderlies wheel her away. Tony's immediate family (plus a handful of wiseguys like Silvio and Paulie Walnuts) wind up at Vesuvio for dinner in a torrential rainstorm, where Tony tells his kids, "Someday soon, you're gonna have families of your own. And if you're lucky, you'll remember the little moments, like this, that were good."

It was a fine moment in a season full of them (as if to acknowledge that, the second-season premiere opens with Frank Sinatra's "It Was a Very Good Year"). It was also just the beginning for a series whose audience had already grown significantly from the start (nearly 2 million more people watched the finale than had watched the series premiere) and would only get bigger as it went on. (The peak came—ironically, and yet true to the success curve for most hit phenomena—with the show's weakest stretch, the fourth season, which averaged nearly 11 million viewers each Sunday night.)

The show's increasing popularity belies much of what we knew then, and know now, about what the audience is supposed to be for a challenging adult drama, yet almost by accident *The Sopranos* displayed an unlikely crossover appeal. It wasn't designed with this in mind, but the mix of therapy and mob violence made it a show with something for everyone: *Come for the whacking, stay for the dream analysis!* People who never would have watched a series built around therapy and family issues watched for the mob action, and vice versa. It was a show that could be incredibly crude and blunt in its humor (not since the glory days of Mel Brooks had fart humor had such a filmed showcase), and also one that could be just as sensitive and sophisticated (A.J. Soprano is driven into a suicidal funk from reading W.B. Yeats's "The Second Coming").

I ask Chase about that marriage of highbrow and lowbrow(*), and he admits, "To tell you the truth, I really don't know if that show is a comedy or a drama. I honestly don't."

(*) *Chase on fart jokes: "Farts are a part of life. You can quote me on that."*

At times, though, that versatility was both a blessing and a curse. Because there were so many different aspects and flavors of the show to latch onto, many of its viewers started to build their own mental picture of what *The Sopranos* was, and railed against the parts of the show—parts that had been there from the very beginning—that existed outside the borders of that picture. Covering television for *The Star-Ledger* (the newspaper that Tony picked up from the end of his driveway at the start of most seasons) while the show aired, I was in the capital of Soprano Country, and heard equally from all camps. During the third season—particularly during a three-episode stretch that saw Dr. Melfi get raped, Bobby Bacala Sr. cough himself into a fatal car crash after the show's bloodiest assassination to date, and *capo* Ralphie Cifaretto beat his stripper girlfriend to death in the Bing parking lot—all we heard were complaints that the show had grown too ugly and violent. The following season drew the opposite reaction, as another segment of the audience objected to the low body count. There was a section of the fan base that would cry foul any time an episode featured a dream sequence, even though discussion of Tony's unconscious mind had been a strong element from the start. (Season 1's penultimate installment, "Isabella," is considered one of the show's best episodes, but some people only seem to remember Tony fighting off a pair of assassins, and ignore the long sequence where he's hallucinating about the idealized Italian woman next door.)

That refusal to be all things to all people was another key part of what made *The Sopranos* so revolutionary. For 50 years, TV had operated under a big-tent philosophy: you tried to rope as many people into the tent as possible, and once they were in, you gave them the same thing they wanted over and over until they got bored. *The Sopranos* had a wide appeal, but people watched it for many different reasons, and Chase never seemed interested in pleasing them all simultaneously. He hated the idea of just giving viewers exactly what they wanted, and would at times deliberately steer away from conflicts that seemed obvious precisely because he knew it was expected.

Ask any *Sopranos* fan which stories they felt the show didn't offer a satisfying enough payoff for, and they will name one or all of the following: 1) Dr. Melfi is raped, and when her attacker goes free on a technicality, she briefly ponders siccing Tony on him before changing her mind at the last minute; 2) In the classic "Pine Barrens" episode, Christopher and Paulie are stranded overnight in New Jersey's most famous woods after chasing a Russian mobster, who seemingly vanishes into thin air; 3) Season 4 seems to be building to a confrontation between Tony and his bodyguard Furio over a mutual attraction between Furio and Carmela, but instead Furio runs back to Italy, never to be seen again. Chase has explained his individual reasoning for each of these—with the rapist, for instance, he felt Melfi's decision to not tell Tony what happened was the end of the story, despite the audience's desire to see the guy suffer some Old Testament justice—but why, collectively, did none of these characters and stories return?

"Because I felt it was more interesting that they didn't," Chase says. "I like mystery. I like allusion. A lot of times, I prefer that to knowing what happened.

"I came up in the late '60s/early '70s," he adds, "when European and Japanese film was very popular. They were much more oblique in their storytelling. You could go to a Fellini movie and say, 'Wow, I loved that! Now what was it about?' And I loved that feeling."

That could be maddening on occasion—most tropes become tropes because they work—but at the same time, *The Sopranos* was rarely clumsier than when it tried to directly address viewer concerns. Season 4's "Christopher," in which actor/writer Michael Imperioli spent an hour satirizing the Italian-American advocacy groups who had objected to *The Sopranos'* existence, is widely viewed as a series low point(*).

(*) I found it funnier than others did, but mainly because I was being deluged with calls, letters and emails from the people Imperioli was publicly debating.

The Sopranos challenged its audience, rather than coddling it. Tony was not only a bad guy, but an increasingly unapologetic one as the series aged. Where previous dramas had humanized edgy characters over time, *The Sopranos* did the opposite. Gandolfini kept putting on weight, and whether that was deliberate or just the spread of middle age, the show visually reveled in his expansion from the relatively sleek man of action shown in the opening title sequence into the great, heavy-breathing bear he became in later seasons. Aesthetics aside, for all the time Tony spent in therapy, he made little progress as a human being. Dr. Melfi eventually stopped the panic attacks, but emotionally, Tony only got worse. The therapy was no longer useful as anything but a break in Tony's day—or, worse, a chance for him to use Melfi as an unwitting tool, letting him plan strategy for how to deal with Ralphie, Paulie and the rest. Whatever lessons he seemed to be learning in each session were forgotten the moment he stepped back into the real world—or misused to gain him leverage with an enemy. He might lament to Melfi about how he and sister Janice were afflicted with the famous Soprano temper, but once he saw Janice successfully managing her anger, his jealousy kicked in, and he goaded her into an explosion at the dinner table(*). If there was such a thing as a relatable sociopath, Tony had become one by the end of the series.

(*) That scene is followed by one of my favorite music cues of a series that took enormous pleasure in its use of rock 'n' roll, as Tony walks proudly out of the house while The Kinks' "I'm Not Like Everybody Else" plays. I once asked Chase why he chose that song for that moment. He laughed and said, "This one's pretty self-explanatory."

Tony's lack of forward progress wasn't a case of a TV show refusing to change because it would disrupt a successful formula, but an expression of what seemed to be the show's deeply cynical take on humanity. Time and again throughout the series, characters were presented with the choice between what is right and what is easy, and with one notable exception—Melfi refusing to use Tony as her instrument of vengeance against the rapist—they inevitably took the easy choice. They might pretend to change, like Janice returning from Seattle as a blissful New Age type called Parvati, but pretending was all it was. Even genuine attempts at self-transformation were strangled in the crib by the world these people lived in. When Tony survives being shot by a senile, confused Uncle Junior in the Season 6 premiere, he declares that "Every day is a gift" and vows to be a better, more patient person. But the demands of his job, and his own deep-seated emotional issues, bring back the same ol' Tony in short order.

Melfi aside—and even she treats Tony longer than she probably should, simply because he adds excitement to her life—every character chooses the path of least resistance over sacrifice. In Season 3, Melfi refers a depressed and lonely Carmela to an older, blunter therapist, who tells her she has to get away from Tony and raise the kids without his "blood money." She ponders the idea briefly, but instead, she stays—after guilting Tony into giving a $50,000 donation to Meadow's university so she can feel better about herself (and get her name on the wall of a new student center). In the final season, A.J. becomes fixated on the conflict in the Middle East(*) and other problems that are far more important than the petty beefs his father deals with every day, but by the end of the series he's been distracted by a fancy job and a shiny new car. Meadow has many bouts of conscience throughout the series and talks of getting as far away from her family and their lifestyle as possible, but in the finale gets engaged to Patsy Parisi's son Patrick.

(*) The series spent much of its second half touching on geo-politics. 9/11 took place during the long hiatus between the third and fourth seasons, and the show returned with one cosmetic change (in the opening credits, the Twin Towers no longer appeared in Tony's rearview mirror as he drove away from Manhattan and back home to Essex County) to reflect the strange new world, and frequent in-story references to the world at large, as seen through the selfish, ignorant prism of the show's characters. In the fourth-season premiere, Bobby Bacala laments that his mother's health started going downhill after 9/11, and tells Tony, "You know, Quasimodo predicted all this." Carmela tries to use 9/11 to guilt Tony into setting up an insurance trust for her and the kids, yelling, "Let me tell you something—or you can watch the fucking news—everything comes to an end!" Christopher becomes concerned with a pair of Middle Eastern men hanging around the Bing, and Tony is later able to leverage information about them to keep the FBI off his back on another matter. To Tony and his associates, the War

on Terror became just one more inconvenience—or, in some cases, one more angle to play.

The show's suggestion that most people act primarily from self-interest transcended race, creed, and even age. The final season's "Kennedy and Heidi"—best known as the episode where Tony smothers Christopher to death after a car accident because he's concerned Chris *might, one day*, prove an inconvenience—gets its name from the pair of teenage girls in the car that runs Tony and Christopher off the road; the scene briefly cuts to Kennedy in the passenger seat suggesting that they should go back to help, and Heidi replies, "Kennedy, I'm on my learner's permit after dark."

Saying that wiseguys and their friends and relatives are hypocritical narcissists is easy, but on this show, *everyone* was selfish and full of it on one level or another. Like many of the millennial dramas that followed it, *The Sopranos* used a familiar genre to sneak in a discussion of the state of America as a whole—and the show suggested that Chase and company felt the state wasn't very strong. What Tony says to Melfi about feeling like he came in at the end applies not just to the North Jersey mob, but to everything. In the first episode of the series, Tony takes Meadow aside to show her a church her great-grandfather helped build, and laments that few men today have the skills and work ethic to help produce such a lasting, beautiful structure. The last episode of the series, meanwhile, is called "Made in America," and mostly dwells on Tony and Carmela bringing A.J. back to his materialistic roots. This, the show seemed to be saying, is what we make in America today: not anything or anyone of value, but lazy, spoiled, myopic parents and children.

Though Chase in general doesn't like to explain what the show was about(*), he does take issue with the notion that his message was "people don't change," or that people are in some way inherently bad or selfish.

(*) Of the post-Sopranos trend of show creators doing interviews where they explain the meaning of their shows in great detail, he says, "I see people talking about their shows, and I go, 'Why are you doing that? You made this really great show, it's got everybody talking. Why are you explaining it? Why didn't you just write the explanation first and send it out as a flier?' I don't know what the impulse is there. It's more pleasurable for me to be left with the mystery or the possibility when I watch other people's work, than when they go, 'This means this, and this means that, and the snake in the dream means his penis.'"

"I believe people have said that the whole theme of *The Sopranos* was that change is impossible," he says. "That was never the theme of *The Sopranos*. That was never what I meant to say or meant to imply. Of course change isn't impossible. It's very, very difficult. It's very rare. Even the thing about 'Every day is a gift,' there's a quote, in *Our Town*, where Emily asks the stage manager, 'Do any human beings ever realize life while they live it—every minute?' And the stage manager says, 'No. The saints and poets, maybe they do some.' And to live every day saying 'Each day is a gift, I get it,' it means that every day you're thinking about death."

Of his and/or the show's take on people in general, Chase suggests, "My view of it is people do their best. They just muddle through. They do their best and they try to do the right thing. And there's nothing guiding us, and we know it, and we feel it, and we feel that lack, and don't know what to do. I think the overall feeling of the show, the thing about life isn't that it's good or bad, but that it's sad. There's a lot of sadness in *The Sopranos*. People want to cry, and don't, or can't."

Whether you choose to look at *The Sopranos* as cynical or sad, the series itself was never depressing, and rarely dull. Viewers may have learned to stop waiting for Tony to evolve, but they didn't give up on the show when he stayed the same miserable bastard as always(*).

(*) Though some people have a difference of opinion on the admirable nature of the show's main characters. Edie Falco sometimes tells stories about meeting women who looked up to Carmela as some kind of role model, for instance. One year, at the after-party for the screening of the Season 4 premiere, I waited on line at the bar behind a woman who wanted to talk about the episode. She expressed dismay about a scene where Christopher shoots heroin between his toes, because, "He's such a good boy." I raised a skeptical eyebrow and pointed out that the episode ends with Christopher murdering a cop, all because of a fairly shaky story from Tony about how the cop killed Christopher's father years before. The woman shrugged and said the cop got what was coming to him. Based on other encounters I had with fans over the years, she was not an anomaly.

A lot of the credit for that goes to the cast Chase and his team assembled, and then kept on subtracting from and adding to as the series went along. As Tony's enemies and allies alike got killed off, the show would bring in new actors (Joe Pantoliano, Steve Buscemi, Frank Vincent) to cause new headaches for our man, but just as often, some player from deep down the series' roster of characters would be called on to deliver, and they almost always did. In the show's early days, Drea de Matteo's Adriana was little more than eye candy, and a symbol of the gravitational field even a low-level wiseguy like Christopher could generate. By the fifth season, when Adriana is trapped in an inescapable circumstance as a cooperating FBI witness, de Matteo's performance was so powerful and sympathetic that many viewers clung to the belief that Adriana didn't die, simply because Silvio shot her slightly off-camera.

In some ways, every season after the first was a kind of ever-expanding contingency plan. Chase hadn't mapped out some grand design for the series at the beginning, so he had to start over from scratch with the second season. Then Nancy Marchand died, necessitating an entirely different third season than the one he'd outlined—involving Tony's reluctant attempt to woo Livia back to his side, keeping her from testifying against him about some stolen airline tickets—and forced Chase to refocus the series as a whole, now that the source of so much of Tony's anguish was gone.

Chase imagines that Livia likely would have died over the course of the series, anyway. Though losing Marchand was an enormous blow, her absence forced him to think through some other maternal psychiatric tropes, which led to one of his favorite story arcs of the series, in which Tony falls for sexy car saleswoman Gloria Trillo, only realizing deep into the affair that she's a younger version of Livia.

Later, the writers realized they had inadvertently put Buscemi's Tony Blundetto into a position where he had to die at the end of Season 5, even though they'd expected him to be a major player for the rest of the series. And the sixth and final season was expanded and then split in two after it was already in production, which required a number of storylines to get more screen time than anyone had expected. (Case in point: gay *capo* Vito Spatafore flees to a quaint, tolerant New Hampshire hamlet for several episodes.)

But again, a grand plot design wasn't really what the show was about. Christopher spends much of the series pursuing his dream of being a screenwriter, and his adventures in that field allowed Chase and his writers to take shots at various bits of TV and movie hackery. In Season 1's "The Legend of Tennessee Moltisanti," Christopher reveals his film ambitions to Paulie, then admits that the screenwriting software he bought hasn't done as much of the work as he'd expected it to; he only has 19 pages out of what should be around 120. Worse, he isn't sure what the story of his own life is about.

"It says in these movie-writing books that every character has an arc, you understand?" he says. "Everybody starts out some-where, then they do something or something gets done to them that changes their life. That's called their arc. Where's *my* arc?"

Because people on the show either chose not to change or weren't allowed to by the world around them (those that tried usu-ally ended up slapped down or dead), *The Sopranos* couldn't prac-tice the kind of character growth and improvement that can fuel dramas in their later years. (*ER*, for instance, got plenty of mileage out of John Carter's evolution from callow med student to sea-soned veteran doctor.) And because Chase disliked pat resolutions (and, at times, any kind of resolution), the story arcs were rarely as clean as people expected them to be.

Those later seasons often excelled, then, at crafting memorable episodes that largely stood on their own, while still tying into the main characters' ongoing problems and conflicts. One of the more overused clichés of the TV industry (which began getting trac-tion around the time of this series) is the phrase "we're making a one-hour movie every week," but in the case of *The Sopranos* at its best, this was true. The Buscemi-directed "Pine Barrens" was a black-comic masterpiece, the greatest movie the Coen brothers never made. Season 6's "Mr. & Mrs. John Sacrimoni Request..." took place at a wedding for the daughter of incarcerated New York boss Johnny Sack, and allowed the show to pay its most overt tribute to *The Godfather* films, while still being about these specific characters and their world. "Soprano Home Movies," the opener of the back half of that final season, sends Tony, Carmela, Janice, and poor Bobby Bacala off to a lake house in upstate New York for some *Who's Afraid of Virginia Woolf?*–style family hell-raising.

That final season is fascinating; the characters can almost sense they're in the final season of a great TV show, and are worrying about their legacy. Tony gets shot, and spends two episodes floating through a kind of fantasy(*) where he's a man who made very different choices in life. Johnny Sack prepares to die of lung cancer, and asks how he'll be remembered. Christopher finally makes a movie (a micro-budget horror film inspired by his role in Adriana's murder), which invites Tony to say, "100 years from now, we're dead and gone, people'll be watching this fucking thing."

(*) In an interview at the start of that season, I commended Chase on the bold choice to do a two-part dream episode, given how divisive they had been in the past. "I, frankly, would not call those dreams," he said cryptically at the time, inspiring many theories (including my own) about Tony moving through Purgatory or some other section of the afterlife. Asked now what those episodes (in which Tony is mistaken for a salesman named Kevin Finnerty) represented, Chase says, "Alternate universes. Now, I have no proof. That's what I consider them, as an artist. Something spiritual was happening with Kevin Finnerty; it wasn't in 'The Test Dream.'" The sequence was inspired by Chase's longtime friend John Patterson, who directed many episodes of the series before dying of cancer in 2005. At one point in his cancer fight, Patterson found himself in a hospital, muttering the same words—"Who am I? Where am I going?"—that Chase would put into the mouths of both Tony in his hospital bed and Kevin Finnerty in the alternate reality. "The way my mind worked," Chase says, "I wondered

what he was seeing when he said that... The line between dreaming and reality, and death and sleep and all that—I'm into that whole thing." Whatever you want to call it, the fans who hated the things Chase would actually consider dream sequences weren't any fonder of Kevin Finnerty's adventures in Costa Mesa.

Yet the legacy of the series doesn't seem to be what it should be. Because the show's later seasons could be so rambling and/or random (and with ever-widening gaps between them); because so many of the shows that followed *The Sopranos* were able to build on its foundation while often telling tighter stories; and because the end was so polarizing, many serious TV fans I know now consider the show at best to be a distant third to its HBO contemporaries *The Wire* and *Deadwood*, and I've even encountered people who would rank it well below descendants like *Mad Men* or *Breaking Bad.*

And that's just silly, as great as all those shows are.

It's not just that none of those shows would have been possible without *The Sopranos*. It's that *The Sopranos*, on its own defiant (if at times frustrating) terms, was an incredible piece of work. Its heart was black and its despair was high, yet I defy you to not be moved while watching Carmela break down in the hospital hallway after Tony has been shot, or as Adriana rides with Silvio to what will obviously be her own murder, or as a tearful, addled Junior is unable to respond when Tony asks him, "Don't you love me?" That bifurcated final season gets dumped on in some corners for Vito's New Hampshire getaway, or Christopher's extended junkie misadventures, but it also featured a number of episodes—notably "The Second Coming," with A.J.'s failed suicide attempt, and "The Blue Comet," where Bobby dies, Silvio is irreparably wounded, and Dr. Melfi finally kicks Tony out of her life for good—that I would put with the best work not only of the series, but of TV drama as a whole.

Let's face it: what drives people nuts in retrospect is the finale—specifically, the last six minutes of the finale.

Until we get to Tony, Carmela, and A.J. eating onion rings at Holsten's ice cream parlor while Meadow struggles to parallel park and a guy in a Members Only jacket(*) goes to the bathroom, it's a finale very much in line with the way the previous seasons ended, with a mix of plot closure (Tony makes peace with New York and has his guys take out Phil Leotardo) and reflection (Tony takes pity on Junior as his uncle slips further into dementia, and Tony and Carmela bribe A.J. back into spoiled brat-hood). Had the show ended on Tony walking away from Junior, or even on a more conventionally shot and edited family dinner, that episode, that final season, and the series as a whole would be remembered very differently. Instead, it almost feels bigger than the show it dropped a curtain on. It's a scene that some love and others despise, while even within those groups there's a deep division over what actually happened when Journey's "Don't Stop Believing" cut off and the picture went to black.(**)

(*) *God, Members Only Guy. Rarely has a TV clothing choice stirred up more analysis, particularly involving a character who had no dialogue, no name, and was barely a half step up from every other background extra. "Members Only" was both the title of the Season 6 premiere and the out-of-fashion jacket worn by that episode's main character, doomed Soprano soldier Eugene Pontecorvo, who hanged himself when he found himself trapped between Tony, the FBI, and a family that desperately needed to get away from Jersey, but couldn't with him alive. Because the jacket was so distinctive, so evocative of Eugene (he was mocked for wearing it), and because the actor play-*

ing Members Only Guy vaguely resembled actor Robert Funaro, who played Eugene, viewers who were set on edge by the scene's editing took him for a man who intended Tony harm. He glances in Tony's general direction a couple of times, but without real interest, then just heads to the men's room.

(**) Chase originally wanted the black screen to run a long time, with no end credits at all, but the various Hollywood guilds wouldn't allow it.

Chase admits he didn't realize people would focus so heavily on that final scene at Holsten's, forgetting everything that had happened earlier in the episode—or, in some cases, the entire series.

"I think that ending so enraged some people that it affected their whole view of the show," he says. "Why it would, I don't know."

Though he always wanted the work to speak for itself, Chase bristles when I suggest that he must enjoy the fact that people are still debating the ending years later, and likely will for as long as anyone cares about the show.

"If I say I enjoy that fact," he says, "how that gets interpreted is, 'He's a sadist. He likes to fuck with people. He's a mean guy.' I like to entertain people. I like to give them what's entertaining, and if it has to be different and it has to rile them up, then it has to rile them up. So if I say I enjoy the fact that people are still analyzing the finale, it will come out as self-aggrandizing, sadistic, and [like] I was always playing head games.

"That show was very, very important to me," he continues. "Those characters were very important to me. I loved each and every one of those characters. I did not throw them away lightly or deal with them lightly. And it goes all the way from, 'Oh, it's so he could do the movie,' to 'He got tired, he couldn't figure it out,' to 'He just wanted to fuck with us.' None of that was the case."

I ask, then, why he chose to present the final scene in the way he did, and his mood shifts abruptly. Any frustration at how he's been depicted in the media, and by fans of the show he slaved over for seven seasons, vanishes. He is suddenly much quieter, much more uncertain.

"It just seemed right," he suggests. "You go on instinct. I don't know. As an artist, are you supposed to know every reason for every brush stroke? Do you have to know the reason behind every little tiny thing? It's not a science; it's an art. It comes from your emotions, from your unconscious, from your subconscious. I try not to argue with it too much. I mean, I do: I have a huge editor in my head who's always making me miserable. But sometimes, I try to let my unconscious act out. So why did I do it that way? I thought everyone would feel it. That even if they couldn't say what it meant, that they would feel it."

Based on the reaction to the finale that he's aware of, does he think people felt it?

"Yeah. I do."

That said, feeling and understanding are two different things, and he acknowledges that with everyone focusing so much on that abrupt cut to black, something was missed.

"There were filmic things that I was doing there," he says, "that I wanted to say about life, which people have not really... Only one person I read actually saw it. That's where the center of the episode was for me, and that's where the ending was. And people have not connected it."

A lot of the audience decided that the cut to black meant Tony had just died, presumably at the hands of Member's Only Guy. They spun elaborate defenses for that theory—including the 20,000-word online essay "*The Sopranos:* Definitive Explanation of

'THE END' "—some based on actual elements from the series, or the handful of words that Chase either uttered(*) or wrote in the months after the finale aired. Many of these were well-constructed arguments that discussed the unusual editing choices Chase made in what was otherwise a normal family dinner scene, or all the death imagery of the final season. (The finale, for instance, opens on Tony lying in bed, looking very much like a body in a coffin.) Some were based on faulty remembrances of the show itself, like the people who convinced themselves that, when Tony and Bobby Bacala spend a boat trip discussing what happens when you die, Bacala says that everything goes to black. (The actual quote is "You probably don't even hear it when it happens.") But all were resolute that this was the only possible—only valid—interpretation of what happened.

(*) A few of those words were to me, in that interview I conducted the morning after the finale aired. It was an interview Chase didn't particularly want to do, as he had decided before the finale aired that he wanted to let it stand for itself, and that he wasn't going to discuss it at all, ever. The problem was, he had already promised me a post-finale interview months earlier, and he was a man of his word. We got on the phone and spent a half hour talking around his lack of interest in, as he put it, "explaining, defending, reinterpreting, or adding to what is there." Still, what little he said provided lots of fodder for analysis, particularly his statement, "Anybody who wants to watch it, it's all there."

I tended to see things the other way. While it's not unreasonable to look at our last glimpse of Tony and decide that it's the very last moment of his life, I felt more comfortable residing in the Tony Lives camp. Even factoring in the unusual style with which Chase shot that scene, I felt that the idea of Tony's death flew too much in the face of everything the show had previously done in terms of narrative and theme.

Narratively, this was never a show that cheated, or tried to trick its audience. This was never a show told only from Tony's point of view. We knew most everything going on in his world: who was on his side, who was against him, who was honest and who was lying to him. If a character went to work for the FBI, for instance, we either saw it happen, or it was such a minor character (like *capo* Ray Curto, so obscure that most fans couldn't tell him apart from Patsy Parisi) that it didn't matter(*).

(*) The major exception to that rule was Big Pussy in Season 1, but that was back when Chase didn't realize he was making a show that would last. He didn't expect to do a second season, and when he did, he didn't expect Pussy to be a part of it, until he kept hearing from fans on the street, "Hey, what happened to Pussy?" On that one occasion, Chase did what the fans requested—and Pussy was revealed as a rat within an episode of his return.

At the moment Tony walks into Holsten's, there's no one we know of who has murder in his heart for the guy. He's made a deal with new New York boss Butchie; his own inner circle is mostly dead or medically irrelevant; even the one *capo* who promises to be trouble just sounds like a cooperating federal witness. For Members Only Guy (or someone else in Holsten's) to be acting on the orders of an enemy we've never met (or whom we haven't heard of in years, like the Russians) simply isn't the sort of thing the show ever did, and seems too abrupt a shift for the final moments.

Beyond the issue of *who* did it, the mere idea of Tony's dying in (or immediately after) the final seconds of the show simply didn't seem like the kind of thing Chase would do.

This is a man whose opinion on the idea of story arcs was probably well expressed by Big Pussy, who once told Christopher, "You know who had an arc? Noah." People kept expecting the series to function like a TV show with a traditional narrative structure, even as the evidence kept piling up, hour after hour, season after season, that this show didn't work like that. The amount of mental energy expended solely on theories about when and how the "Pine Barrens" Russian would emerge from the woods to rain hell down on Paulie and Christopher—even well after that season ended and it was clear he was never, ever coming back(*)—was so huge it could have solved Fermat's Last Theorem under other circumstances.

(*) Chase has never understood his audience's fascination with the missing Russian, Valery, feeling like it was a one-off story that needed no closure. "Who gives a shit about this Russian?" he recalls thinking. "We did that show! I don't know where he is! Now we've got to go and figure that out?!?!" Terence Winter, who wrote "Pine Barrens" and many of the series' other memorable outings, agreed with the fans on this one, much to Chase's frustration, and kept pushing his boss to add a coda to that story in the final season. They finally hit on an idea everyone would be happy with: Tony and Christopher pay a visit to the local Russian mob boss, where they find Valery sweeping the floor, not recognizing Christopher thanks to a traumatic brain injury suffered when Chris and Paulie were shooting at him. (It would be explained that a local Boy Scout troop found him with part of his skull missing, and saved his life.) At the last minute, Chase changed his mind, and he recalls a despondent Winter insisting, "God, you're making a huge mistake leaving that on the table!"

Again and again, the show zigged when we expected a zag. Every cooperating witness would die before they could provide anything of value to the FBI. Seasons would frequently build to what seemed like a huge crescendo, only to offer resolution out of left field. Before Richie Aprile can go to war with Tony, Janice murders him over a punch in the face. Melfi never tells Tony about her rapist. Furio runs back to Italy. And still people expected a familiar narrative(*).

(*) In the fifth-season premiere, we see Carmela take a gun out of a cabinet in the house that also holds a grenade. Every week for the rest of the season, I would get emails asking when and how I expected the grenade to come into play, with many of the emails invoking the familiar Chekhov quote about how a gun shown onstage in the first act has to go off by the third. Though Chase understands Chekhov's theory, he never took it as literally as that; the grenade was never seen again, let alone used.

At the start of the fourth season, Tony confesses to Dr. Melfi that there are really only two ways a guy like him can end up: "Dead, or in the can." Viewers took the comment as foreshadowing the only two ways the series itself could end, yet whenever I would bring the line up to Chase, he would wince. His view of the show was too iconoclastic to believe that there were only two possible fates for Tony, each of them a kind of punishment for his misdeeds. Tony had clearly become the villain of his own story by that point; his getting killed in the finale, regardless of who was doing it or why, felt like too predictable an ending, even if the way it was presented (with viewers left to infer the murder based on editing choices and conversations from previous episodes) was unconventional.

For the longest time, Chase refused to say much of anything about that scene. In 2008, he did a radio interview with actor Richard Belzer, pointing to the Tony/Bacala scene on the boat, and to a murder that happens right next to Silvio, as clues to the ending—which the Tony Dies camp understandably took as more evidence for their cause—but largely evaded discussing it at all.

In the summer of 2014, Vox published a story by a reporter

who claimed Chase had flat-out told her that Tony survived the diner scene—a quote Chase said was taken wildly out of context. He insisted in a statement, "The final scene of *The Sopranos* raises a spiritual question that has no right or wrong answer."

Perhaps fed up with the public fixation on that question—and attempts to definitively answer it—above everything else about the finale, and the series, Chase wrote a shot-by-shot analysis of the Holsten's sequence for a 2015 issue of *DGA Quarterly*. Near the end of it, he wrote, "Whether this is the end here, or not, it's going to come at some point for the rest of us. Hopefully we're not going to get shot by some rival gang mob or anything like that. I'm not saying that [happened]. But obviously he stood more of a chance of getting shot by a rival gang mob than you or I do because he put himself in that situation. All I know is the end is coming for all of us."

That answer—that Tony, like Schrödinger's cat, has the potential to either be dead or alive when we look inside the box, but will be dead eventually no matter what—is as explicit as I expect Chase to ever get about a show, and conclusion, that he so often preferred to leave open to interpretation. Ask me on Monday, Tuesday, Thursday, Wednesday, and I'd still probably tell you that I believe Tony's life goes on (and, as Journey's Steve Perry sang, on and on and on), and the only punishment he has to face is continuing to be the fat, miserable fuck that is Tony Soprano. His children won't be involved in organized crime themselves—Chase argues that Tony and Carmela's ability to prevent that is the show acknowledging that people and generations *can* change, to a degree—but they also aren't who and what he hoped they would be, and he sees in lonely, penniless, senile Uncle Junior that even a long life for the boss of New Jersey is no great reward.

But ask me Friday, Sunday, Saturday? Then I'm not so certain.

But the very fact that we're still having these debates—about both the quality and the content of that final scene—speaks to the boldness of *The Sopranos* and the mark it left on not only television, but all of popular culture. That Chase would present a scene so open to interpretation(*)—even if, as he insisted, "It's all there"(**)—as his closing statement isn't something anyone would have expected from a TV show prior to this one.

(*) One of the other songs we see on the jukebox list before Tony chooses "Don't Stop Believing" is another Journey hit, "Any Way You Want It." And for those who want to do even more analysis, Chase tells me that one of the other songs he considered in lieu of Journey was Al Green's "Love and Happiness," particularly for the verse that goes, "Something's going wrong, someone's on the phone, three o'clock in the morning."

(**) "It's all there" could have meant "All the little clues pointing to Tony's death are there if you look carefully for them," or he could have meant, "What you saw is what happened, and anything after that is up for you to imagine."

American TV viewers had seen great series finales prior to June 10, 2007, and terrible ones, wholly satisfying wrap-ups and cliffhangers that never got resolved due to cancellation, but we'd never seen... *this.* No one had challenged his audience not only up to the last frame of footage, but for many seconds beyond that. (The most common complaint I still hear about the finale is that it made some people think their cable had gone out.) Chase not only never worried about having a likable main character; he didn't need a likable series. He didn't care about giving his audience what they wanted, didn't need to give them the warm fuzzies in the finale. Instead, he took a kind of scene (Tony gathers the family for a meal at the end of the season) that had been familiar from throughout the show's run, turned it on its head through music and editing, and either went away by pulling the rug out from under his viewers one last time, or by killing his main character in a way that (barring some kind of deathbed confession or other abrupt change of heart) could fuel arguments from here to the end of Western civilization.

And at this point, Chase had amassed enough power and trust at HBO and among his staff that no one objected to the surprising ending.

"The first time I saw the first cut," says Chris Albrecht, "I was completely jarred. My stomach wrenched. I think, for everybody, it was over before they wanted it to be—in any scenario. It was over before they wanted it to be in that episode, and it was over before they wanted it to be because they had to fill in the blank. There was a blank screen, and they filled it in. You could fill it in in the next five minutes, in the next five years, in the next 50 years. So I was stunned."

Carolyn Strauss recalls that her initial reaction was, "'Hmm. Bold choice!' It's one of those things where I think there was such a build-up to what it was going to be that it was a really, really difficult fork in the road. Personally, I kinda liked it, but there were so many people who had their hair on fire about it."

(Strauss, for what it's worth, falls into the camp that the ending means "they just went on in their lives," and is pleased Chase has vowed to never explain it. "I love that. It's perfectly David. I would be disappointed if he did.")

When Chase told his writing staff what the plan was, he recalls, "They were all for it. But in the end, it was my call. I don't know what I was looking for from them. I don't know what I would have done if they had said, 'Are you crazy?' But after working together all that time, they knew it probably wasn't going to be a good use of time to argue with me if they didn't like it, because they knew in the end we didn't have [that kind of relationship] before that."

He invokes the name of Quinn Martin, a successful television producer who, in the '60s and '70s, made a lot of money with the kinds of formulaic dramas (*The Streets of San Francisco, Cannon, Barnaby Jones*) Chase was rebelling against when he made *The Sopranos*.

"This was an auteur's vision," he says, "and it belonged to the auteur to say. And that didn't really happen before. Quinn Martin may have been an auteur, but a lot of what the network said, he did."

Quinn Martin never had the creative freedom that David Chase had, and thanks to the commercial and artistic success of *The Sopranos*, television had finally entered its own age of the auteur.

CHAPTER 3

All the pieces matter… **The Wire**
as the Great American Novel for television

It happens virtually the same way every time: someone (be it a friend, Twitter follower, or in one case a cousin) will approach me and say, "I am ready to watch *The Wire*." And they all phrase it like that—like it's a religious obligation they are about to undertake, rather than viewing a modestly rated HBO drama: *I am ready to take my vow of poverty. I am ready to be bar mitzvahed. I am ready to watch* The Wire.

Few TV shows are discussed in that kind of reverent tone, or encourage their fans to proselytize on its behalf the way *Wire* believers try to convert the uninitiated. Then again, few TV shows have the breadth, depth, or power of *The Wire*, a show that—at least as much as *The Sopranos*, if not more—helped redefine how we looked at the TV drama.

When these novices tell me they're ready to experience *The Wire* for the first time, they ask me for suggestions on how to maximize the experience, having heard from friends that it's not quite like anything else they've watched before. And I tell each of them the same thing: "Carve out a block of time where you can watch at least the first two episodes, and preferably the first four, in a row. You will understand everything much more easily, you will be able to tell Stringer apart from Wee-Bey, and by the end of the fourth episode, you will know if this is a show for you or not."

Because the thing is, as an hour of television—at least, as I understood television back in the summer of 2002, when HBO sent me a pair of videocassettes containing those first four episodes for review—*The Wire* pilot isn't very good. It's confusing. It introduces far too many characters to reasonably keep track of, and only two—Dominic West as Baltimore cop Jimmy McNulty, and Larry Gilliard Jr. as mid-level drug dealer D'Angelo Barksdale—really distinguish themselves as important people with recognizable personalities. We're introduced to some conflicts: D'Angelo adjusts to a new position in his uncle Avon's organization after beating a murder rap, while McNulty agitates for a police task force to go after the whole Barksdale crew. But there isn't anything even vaguely resembling a stand-alone story. The hour hurls a whole bunch of people, problems, and slang at you, and then it doesn't so much end as simply stop. There were some interesting individual moments, but had both HBO and the show's co-creator David Simon not already earned the benefit of some doubt (HBO for *Oz* and *Sopranos* and *Six Feet Under*; Simon for his non-fiction books and earlier TV work on *Homicide,* and the HBO miniseries *The Corner*), I don't know how eagerly I'd have watched another hour.

And television in 2002 simply didn't work this way—even the ambitious HBO kind of television. The pilot episodes of *Oz* or *The Sopranos* might not have given an indication of the heights those shows would later achieve, but they at least gave you a clear sense of the major players, and they provided some stories that had a beginning, middle, and end within the confines of that hour.

(The *Sopranos* pilot, for instance, has Tony resolving the matter of Uncle Junior's desire to kill Little Pussy Malanga at Artie Bucco's restaurant.) For all of David Chase's disdain for the clichés of television, he had worked in the medium for so long that he couldn't help but work with certain storytelling devices the audience had come to expect, including a conflict that could be both introduced and solved by the end of the hour. (Most *Sopranos* episodes have at least one.)

But Simon and his partner Ed Burns didn't believe they were making a TV show. They were making a novel for television—one that, by the end of the series, had as good an argument as any printed book for the title of The Great American Novel.

Given their backgrounds, and how they came to work together, it's not a surprise that Simon and Burns wouldn't want to write a TV show as a TV show. Neither started out intending to write for television, and each stumbled into the medium almost by accident.

When the two met in the mid-'80s, Burns was a veteran homicide detective in Baltimore, Simon a young reporter at the *Baltimore Sun* looking to make a splash on the police beat. Burns had just closed a sprawling wiretap investigation into local drug kingpin Melvin Williams(*) as part of a joint DEA task force, and Simon made the case into the subject of his first big feature for the *Sun*. Though cops and reporters are often natural enemies, Simon and Burns frequently found themselves on the same wavelength— "Ed was kind of a free thinker in a lot of ways," says Simon—and Simon would often use Burns as a source.

(*) Williams would not only serve as one of the inspirations for the show's Avon Barksdale, but act on the series in the recurring role of a wise and humble church deacon.

Simon took a sabbatical from the newspaper to embed himself with the homicide unit for a year; out of that came the non-fiction book *Homicide: A Year on the Killing Streets*, which Tom Fontana and Barry Levinson would eventually turn into the NBC drama *Homicide: Life on the Street*. Burns barely figures into the book, as he was busy with yet another wiretap case, much to the frustration of several other detectives who had to pick up his slack in the rotation. Burns took his 20-year pension in 1992, intending to become a teacher, but when Simon's book editor suggested his follow-up book be about a corner in Baltimore, Simon's thoughts immediately turned to the idea of drug corners, and he recruited Burns as his partner. The two spent a year at the intersection of Fayette and Monroe Streets, chronicling the lives of the addicts, dealers, and other residents, in what became *The Corner: A Year in the Life of an Inner-City Neighborhood*.

Meanwhile, Fontana invited Simon to write a script for *Homicide*, and Simon in turn recruited former college classmate David Mills(*) to team with him on "Bop Gun," which guest-starred Robin Williams as a tourist trying to keep it together for his kids after the random murder of his wife. The second-season premiere, it remains one of the best hours that show produced. Simon stayed at the *Sun* for a few more years, but joined the *Homicide* writing staff full-time in 1996.

(*) Mills would go on to write for NYPD Blue—he and I became friends through our different associations with that show—and ER; created his own very different series about the drug war for NBC, the Godfather-esque Kingpin; and re-teamed with Simon at various points in his career on The Corner miniseries, The Wire, and Tremé. Mills died of a brain aneurysm during the production of the first season of Tremé.

"He came to me and said he was being downsized from the *Sun* paper and would I be interested in hiring him?" says Fontana. "I said, 'Absolutely. But you're like a guy who's been playing football who's now going to play basketball. You've got to trust Yosh [*Homicide* producer James Yoshimura] and me to help make the transition.' And he was wonderfully open and completely ego free. It turned out to be a lot of fun. He and Yoshimura became like blood brothers."

Simon was learning a lot from Fontana, Yoshimura, and the other TV veterans on the *Homicide* staff, but television never really felt like his medium. He had a standing job offer at the *Washington Post*, and was seriously considering it when Fontana showed him the original pilot presentation for *Oz*.

"I'm watching that initial pilot," Simon recalls, "and thinking, 'This is going on television? HBO's going to do stuff like this? I'll be goddamned.'"

He understood the appeal of *Homicide* to television executives—as he puts it, "It's cops and killers"—but watching *Oz* was the first time he realized someone might be interested in adapting *The Corner*. Fontana helped arrange a meeting with HBO, and Simon's head filled with ambitious thoughts of an ongoing series that might start on a drug corner before quickly expanding. In this vision, the project would cover the cops, politicians, and other figures associated with the War on Drugs, which Simon and Burns both believed to be a colossal waste of time and money as well as an attack on the underclass. He was ready, in other words, to pitch what became *The Wire*, only to discover that the meeting was with executives with HBO's miniseries division, who had loved *The Corner* and wanted a faithful adaptation of that.

HBO's Chris Albrecht recalls that the choice was between

The Corner and a project adapting Taylor Branch's books about
the civil rights movement. Ultimately, he decided, "Anybody
could do the Taylor Branch miniseries; only HBO could do *The
Corner.*"

Burns, still teaching middle school, had expressed an interest in
joining Simon to adapt *The Corner* for television, but HBO execs
were more interested in seeing Simon reunite with David Mills,
who was African-American. "They were scared of the material,"
says Simon, noting that HBO had done several acclaimed movies
and miniseries about black America, but that in this case, "They
were very conscious of the fact it was a white guy talking to them."

Instead, Simon told Burns to get started outlining a potential follow-up project, covering all the parts of the story that the
more intimate *Corner* couldn't—the macro versus the micro. They
would start off with a fictionalized version of a wiretap case Burns
had worked in a Baltimore high-rise project, involving a kingpin
named Warren Boardley and a stick-up artist named Donnie Andrews (who would be the inspiration for *The Wire*'s Omar Little,
in the same way McNulty was loosely based on Ed Burns himself).
That case would let them deal with all the questions of social policy, race, economics, and more that *The Corner* had no place for.

The Corner won three major Emmys (writing, directing, and
outstanding miniseries) and was even the subject of a front-page
story in the *New York Times*. Simon had proved his value to HBO.
HBO's Carolyn Strauss bought the initial *Wire* script, then asked
Simon and Burns to write scripts for two additional episodes before she would agree to shoot a pilot. Like everyone watching the
finished product, she didn't know entirely what to make of it at
first, though she was intrigued.

"It was dense," Strauss recalls. "It was heavy going, but it was always interesting. It may not have been exactly scrutable yet, but you knew it was going to get there."

Though Simon had learned how to write episodic television while on staff at *Homicide*, it never felt natural to him.

"My rhythms are prose rhythms to an extent," he says. "In the beginning, the one thing prose could do that TV couldn't do was tell a sophisticated, complicated story. Television couldn't do that because they needed the episodes to stand alone."

Simon and Burns were about to prove that you could make very satisfying television even if the individual episodes weren't neatly self-contained.

"I remember the first couple of episodes of *The Wire*," says Strauss, "but especially that pilot, thinking, 'Where are we? What are we doing? Can we get a shot of the door that says what it is on it?' It takes about four episodes of that series to really orient yourself. It challenges you. It doesn't play anyone for a fool. But it's so worthwhile to stay with it."

In later years, Albrecht would take his sweet time deciding to order more seasons, but the renewal for the second season came quickly, after he saw the final cut of the fifth episode. Albrecht called up Simon with the good news, and said that the show took a while to get going, but was getting better with every episode.

"And what I thought was, 'All the episodes were good,'" Simon recalls. "What I thought he was saying without saying it is the story's going up the hill, which is what stories are supposed to do. If you're not more invested with every chapter, then the writer has failed. And if you get to the end of the story and all the components of the story—the characters and the plotlines—weren't there for a reason, then the writer has failed. I remember him saying that and I thought to myself, 'It's not that the episodes are getting better, but it's a cumulative effect.' People say now that when you get to Episode 4, it works. It's not that Episode 4 is good. The thing is, it's the whole. We're interested in what the whole story is about. No novelist that I know of has discussions where he says, 'Man, I really killed Chapter 4, I really killed Chapter 17.' That's just ass-backwards thinking."

Each season of *The Wire* is structured like a book (and it's easy to look at the five seasons as sections of one giant novel): lots of exposition and character introductions at the start, rising action in the middle, then a breakneck pace in the closing chapters. But since no American show had been assembled in quite this way before, people had to learn a new kind of viewing at the same time they were learning all these new faces, names and enough slang and terminology ("G packs," "juking the stats," "re-ups") that watching the show felt like a crash course in a foreign language.

And *The Wire* taught you how to watch it not only in terms of its structure, but its themes. It wasn't really a cop show, but a despairing sociological screed in cop-show drag. There were always cops, and always criminals, but the series used them to make various points about the rotting state of the American city—and, by extension, the broken condition of America itself.

I had known Simon a bit before *The Wire* began, mainly through our mutual friend Mills, but also as a fan of his work who had written a lot about *Homicide* the TV show. Still, I wasn't entirely prepared for what would come when I hopped on the phone with him a few weeks before the series debuted (on June 2, 2002). I was expecting a boilerplate interview where he told some anecdotes about what he had learned in the respective years he was researching *Homicide* and *The Corner* and how he had combined the subjects of the two. Instead, I got a mission statement unlike any I'd heard about another TV show.

"This is a cop show, but I don't think of it as a cop show," he told me. "It's about individuals versus the institutions they serve. This is a story where the cops work for Enron and the dealers work for Enron, and they get betrayed for their loyalty."

Um, what?

Sixty episodes later (hell, seven or eight episodes later), the show's suspicion of institutions and institutional thinking—of how the cops and drug dealers are both expected to do stupid things because that's how it's always been done—would be crystal clear. As the series was starting, though, it was hard to wrap my head around the idea that this wasn't going to be *Homicide* with rawer language. So Simon tried framing the argument through the earlier show.

Homicide, he insisted, "was a great show, but it wasn't after an analysis of what is and isn't working in modern police forces." He cited Roger Gaffney, a racist, incompetent night shift detective character on that show who kept failing up the corporate ladder, as an example of how *The Wire*'s philosophy differs from that of its NBC predecessor.

"Gaffney was not the problem of a real police department," he explained. "He was just the occasional asshole detective they'd create as a stick figure. We were more interested in the idea of systemic problems, not the idea that if you get rid of one bad cop or if somebody has their appropriate emotional catharsis, all will be well. All of the cop shows, even the good ones, are rooted in the premise that these guys may be flawed, the institutions may be bureaucratic, but basically everyone's heart is in the right place and they're still doing God's work. Having witnessed the drug trade in Baltimore very close up, neither Ed nor myself buy into the notion of [doing] the Lord's work anymore."

So even though we're introduced to McNulty's boss, Bill Rawls (John Doman), as he objects to McNulty's interest in the Barksdale crew in memorably profane fashion—flipping him a double bird, Rawls tells him, "This one over here is going up your narrow fuckin' Irish ass. And this bad boy here is in your fuckin' eye!"—it becomes clear in time that Rawls' concern isn't born out of laziness, bigotry, corruption(*), or any of the other familiar hallmarks television and movies had used to signify bad cops. Rawls isn't dumb; when Detective Kima Griggs (Sonja Sohn) is shot during an undercover operation later in the season, Rawls swiftly takes command of the crime scene and begins noticing details that his investigators missed. Nor is he, ultimately, all that "bad." He is simply the guardian of a fundamentally flawed system—one of many we'll meet over these five seasons—who has been trained that there's a specific way for everyone to do his or her job, and that anyone who goes outside that system is just making the job harder for the rest of them.

(*) The notion of corrupt cops is so ingrained in many viewers that even long after the series had made its M.O. and philosophy clear, some fans still had trouble accepting that every "bad" one we met wasn't inherently crooked. Late in the second season, we meet FBI Agent Koutris, who appears to be on the payroll of The Greek, that season's main target. Ultimately, it's revealed that The Greek is feeding Koutris intel about potential terrorists—nearly all of it bogus, but Koutris doesn't realize this. Koutris in turn helps The Greek elude arrest, not for monetary gain but because he feels foiling acts of terrorism is more important than taking a drug supplier and human trafficker off the street. Even though the show spells this out pretty clearly by the end of the season—and even though Simon has articulated it even more vocally in interviews with me and others—many viewers still have trouble letting go of the idea that Koutris is simply dirty. For that matter, Simon

says he still hears Rawls, Burrell, and many of the show's other bureau-
cratic bogeymen referred to as corrupt, when only a handful of charac-
ters (notably avaricious state politician Clay Davis) fit the traditional
definition of the term.

Rawls's biggest objection to McNulty's initial findings in the Barksdale case involves the murder of a Gerard Bogue the year before—which means an unsolved crime that already reflected badly on the prior year's stats would be revived to bring the current year's average down as well. Bogue no doubt had people who loved him and who mourn him, but to Bill Rawls, he is a statistical aggravation. It doesn't matter that McNulty's approach might ultimately take a dangerous criminal organization off the street from the top down; this simply isn't the way that Bill Rawls, or *his* boss Ervin Burrell (Frankie Faison), was taught to do things. The system runs the way it runs, and anyone who tries to run it differently—even if a different approach might prove better—is a threat to that system.

Simon liked to begin each year of the show with a scene highlighting that season's themes. The series opens with a mission-statement moment where McNulty investigates the murder of Omar Isaiah Betts, known to friends and family as Snot Boogie. As a surprisingly helpful witness (by *Wire* standards) explains to McNulty, Snot Boogie played in the local craps game every week, and every week after a few rolls, Snot would grab all the money in the pot and try to make a run for it, and someone would chase him down and beat his ass and take the money back. McNulty, being the inquisitive sort that he is—and the series' symbol of what happens when you start asking the right questions of people who think they're the wrong questions—has to interrupt his witness's narrative to ask what is, to him and to us but not to the witness, the obvious question: if they knew Snot would rob the pot every time out, why did they keep letting him play? And the witness, confused by the very premise of the question, lays out the basic message of the series:

"Got to. This America, man."

The America of *The Wire* is broken, in a fundamental, probably irreparable way. It is an interconnected network of ossified institutions, all of them so committed to perpetuating their own business-as-usual approach that they keep letting their own equivalents of Snot Boogie into the game, simply because that's how it's always been done.

As the season moves along, we see that Rawls's attitude towards preserving the status quo at all costs is the rule, not the exception, for the criminals as much as the cops. Though D'Angelo is introduced happily beating a murder rap because his uncle's top man Stringer Bell (Idris Elba) paid off a key witness, the murder of another witness(*) leads D'Angelo to start questioning the way the business works. Why, he wonders, is everyone in the drug game so quick to resort to violence when it's the violence, far more than the drugs themselves, that attracts police attention? As he tries to tell his teenage underlings Bodie (J. D. Williams), Poot (Tray Chaney), and Wallace (Michael B. Jordan), "Everything else in the world gets sold without people taking advantage, scamming, lying, doing each other dirty. Why it gotta be that way with this?"

(*) In one of the few instances where Simon didn't have full control of the product, HBO insisted that, when D'Angelo walks by the crime scene where McNulty's partner Bunk Moreland (Wendell Pierce) is studying the body of murdered witness William Gant, we get a brief flashback to Gant testifying against D'Angelo. Simon believed the audience would figure out who it was and what the closing scene meant; HBO felt it was such an important moment that the audience needed

its hand held just a little. Simon still complains about it to this day, but this is an instance where I'll side with the network executives over the writer; The Wire pilot was asking so, so much of the viewer—especially a viewer in 2002—that I don't think it's unreasonable to make a crucial plot point easier to follow than some earlier conversations.

But D'Angelo's words fall on deaf ears, because the world of *The Wire* is one where almost no one is willing to work in a nontraditional way, and the few that do tend to get punished for it. It's a world where nothing seems to work right, or to go the way we've been conditioned to expect it to after years of other cop shows and movies. McNulty succeeds in getting a Barksdale task force assembled, but Rawls fills out much of its roster with the dregs of the department; Burrell makes clear to reluctant task-force leader Cedric Daniels (Lance Reddick) that he wants something short and simple, using the exact same approach to police work that's allowed the likes of Avon (Wood Harris) and Stringer to thrive, and made the War on Drugs seemingly unwinnable. (Ellis Carver [Seth Gilliam], a narcotics cop assigned to the task force, tells his buddy Herc [Dominic Lombardozzi] that "You can't even call this shit a war" because "Wars end.")

And yet the task force, and *The Wire*, constantly surprise us. Though the Barksdale detail is seemingly filled with humps, some of them turn out to be almost shockingly valuable: "cuddly house cat" Lester Freamon (Clarke Peters) reveals himself to be a brilliant investigator who'd been exiled to an obscure clerical job for thirteen years ("and four months," he always adds) for making like McNulty and putting an investigation over the orders of his superiors. Trigger-happy, nepotism-aided Roland "Prez" Pryzbylewski (Jim True-Frost) stuns even himself by cracking the code the Barksdale soldiers use to communicate via pager. McNulty, introduced in the clichéd but sympathetic context of the Cop Who Cares Too Much, Darn It, turns out to be a toxic personality—as Bunk Moreland puts it, "You're no good for people, man"—and narcissist who started the Barksdale investigation mainly so he could prove how much smarter he was than everyone else. We meet Lt. Daniels, meanwhile, as a company man who puts his career and department politics over the work; by season's end, he cares more about the case—and has put his career at greater risk to pursue it—than anyone.

And Simon, Burns, and the rest are able to do the unexpected consistently because of that measured pace I mentioned before. *The Wire* moves incredibly deliberately, especially at the start of each season, but there isn't a second wasted. The task force, for instance, doesn't make any significant headway into the investigation until the fifth episode, but we need the previous four episodes to demonstrate the myriad ways the forces of departmental tradition and inertia are working against them—to see the investigators fail at playing by the old rules so we can recognize the need to try something different.

The slow pace also leaves lots of room for what makes *The Wire* so gripping, and so compulsively rewatchable, in spite of its bleak worldview. Given the show's philosophy and politics, there was always a risk that watching it could feel like homework or eating your vegetables. But however seriously Simon and Burns took the show's message, they also recognized that they were making a fictional drama, one they wanted people to enjoy and to keep watching. In discussing the various and high bars set by the series for its viewers, Simon once told me, "The other problem is, no easy gratifications, other than some real effort at careful characterization and humor. That was it. Without the humor, it would have been unbearable."

Fortunately, *The Wire* had humor, and characterization, and entertainment value to spare. By the time you're done with the series, it's impossible to separate the message from the story, but if you can, *The Wire* is a gripping narrative that rewards your time and patience with as much enjoyment as any other show in this book, and more than most.

Almost no one is exactly what he or she seems, for good or for ill, and it's one of the series' great pleasures to find out gradually what everyone is really about. The cast was made up of unfamiliar actors, many of them African-American. Those two categories were not unrelated: though many of the black members of the cast had previously appeared on *Oz*, good roles for actors of color were still few and far between in 2002, and Simon, Burns, and executive producer Robert Colesberry(*) had no choice but to fill the ensemble with relative unknowns who had previously only lacked a good showcase. Even the role of McNulty was originally offered to higher-profile actors than Dominic West (first Ray Winstone, then John C. Reilly); West got the part because he was good, not because he was a blank slate.

(*) Simon was initially annoyed when HBO assigned the veteran producer Colesberry to work with him and Mills on The Corner, *but quickly grew to like and respect the man. Their partnership continued on* The Wire, *where Colesberry helped establish the show's visual aesthetic, among other accomplishments. After a long career in film and television, Colesberry finally stepped behind the camera to direct the second-season finale; he died not long after, and Simon paid on-camera tribute to his fallen friend the next season with a raucous liquid police funeral for Ray Cole, the bumbling homicide cop Colesberry had played on the periphery of many episodes.*

But as with Gandolfini and Falco on *The Sopranos*, viewers' in-

experience with these actors turned to the show's advantage. Because we didn't know West, he simply *was* McNulty: selfish and
corrosive, but also (particularly when paired with Wendell Pierce
as The Bunk) inordinately charming and funny. We had no expectations for Larry Gilliard Jr. as D'Angelo, so we bought him as the
cocky, entitled prince of criminal empire we met in the first episode; we also believed it as the writers and Gilliard slowly peeled
away his layers to show a sympathetic, conflicted young man born
into one kind of life and wondering if any other was possible.

Again and again, characters showed unexpected complexities.
Late in the first season, we find out that Stringer Bell is taking com-
munity-college econ courses, trying to apply MBA philosophies to
the only major business opportunity open to him. Bubbles (Andre
Royo), Kima's junkie snitch, is revealed in time as the show's most
thoughtful, empathetic character. Omar Little (Michael Kenneth
Williams), a stick-up artist famous for his shotgun, his duster, and
fondness for whistling nursery rhymes as he robs drug dealers,
turns out to be gay, and hews to a strict moral code that brooks no
profanity and no attacks on people outside the drug game.

The no-profanity principle was not shared by the rest of the
characters on the show, thankfully. Among the things Simon
learned from his year embedded with the real Baltimore homicide
unit was the omnipresent, versatile use of profanity. In the series'
fourth episode(*), McNulty and Bunk methodically re-create the
scene of an unsolved murder with Barksdale ties, while communicating only with variations of the F-word. It's like a symphony of
cussing, and one the viewer can understand because D'Angelo has
provided a roadmap to the crime in an earlier scene. You get to the
end of the scene unsure whether you're supposed to giggle, give it a
standing ovation, or watch it again to make sure you saw what you

thought you saw. And yet it doesn't come close to an airtight case for the funniest scene the show ever did: off the top of my head, I'd be just as inclined to name Omar getting the better of Barksdale attorney Maury Levy (Michael Kostroff) while testifying in open court ("I got the shotgun, you got the briefcase. It's all in the game, though, right?"), or Stringer losing his temper while trying to conduct a meeting with his lieutenants using Robert's Rules of Order ("Yo, String, Poot did have the floor, man"), or Herc and Carver's various misadventures involving an expensive surveillance mic and an imaginary informant they named Fuzzy Dunlop.

(*) More than any forward progress in the storytelling, it's the all-"fuck" scene that tends to either sell people on the series or convince them it is 100% not for them.

The Wire could do comedy. It could do action, too. As the series went along, Omar's legend grew through a series of daring capers and escapes, including a desperate gunfight with Barksdale soldiers in the third season that evokes the last stand of The Wild Bunch. (Though the results were quite a bit better, with only one member of Omar's crew falling, and from friendly fire.)

But what The Wire could do best of all was punch you in the gut, leaving you simultaneously in tears and begging for more.

The show made us like and admire Kima, so it would hurt even more when she was wounded during an undercover operation. It made us invest in Bubbles's bid for sobriety, so we'd feel enormous regret when it didn't work out. Most of all in that first season, it made us understand and care for D'Angelo's three teenage sidekicks so we would feel devastated when Bodie and Poot murdered Wallace on Stringer's orders, then wrecked all over again when D'Angelo stared down Stringer in a jailhouse interview room, demanding to know, over and over, "Where's Wallace?"

A show with an attitude as despairing as *The Wire*'s wasn't likely to have happy endings, and yet in 2002 it was still shocking to see the toll taken by the Barksdale investigation, and the lack of rewards. Wallace dies in tears, begging his best friends to spare him. Omar's boyfriend is tortured to death. D'Angelo is guilted—by his mother—into taking a 20-year prison stretch to protect the family business. Kima gets shot. McNulty is reassigned to his least-desired position in the department, a punishment detail manning a boat in the marine unit. Avon goes to prison on a lesser charge, but Stringer is untouched, the business keeps humming, and there's a sense that absolutely nothing was accomplished—that, with the exception of Lester Freamon (who escapes department purgatory to take McNulty's old slot in Homicide), everyone involved would have been better off if McNulty hadn't opened his big mouth in the first place.

Yet the audience couldn't feel cheated by how that first season played out. It told a story with a beginning, a middle, and an end (albeit an unhappy one). It introduced a host of characters that we came to care deeply about. It was so good that we wanted to keep watching even as the show hurt us, again and again.

And just when we thought we finally understood how *The Wire* worked, it came back for its second season looking like an entirely different show.

The predictable route would have been for Lt. Daniels to reassemble the team and go after Stringer Bell again. Instead, we find Daniels, McNulty, Stringer, and many of the first season's central characters on the margins. Previously minor players like Prez's father-in-law Stan Valchek (Al Brown) drive much of the action, and the now-familiar setting of the West Baltimore drug markets is replaced by the Port of Baltimore, where a multi-ethnic group of stevedores take over for the Barksdale crew as our new target.

Even by the standards of the show's departures from expected norms in first season, this seemed nuts. Viewers had put so much time into learning all the players and terminology of the drug trade, and all of a sudden none of that seemed to matter(*). Who were all these new guys? Where were D'Angelo and Bubbs? And why did that annoying Ziggy (James Ransome) keep showing everyone his dick?

(*) The second season was actually the series' highest-rated, and no one has any illusions about why. When I ask Chris Albrecht, he laughs and says, "Because there were white people in it." Carolyn Strauss has a slightly different, but related, take: "There is a theory at HBO that it satisfied an audience in the first season that we weren't satisfying with other programming. That second season may have overlapped with another audience we were satisfying somewhere else, and we may have lost some of that original audience in the process."

But the shift in perspective at the start of the second season is the most important move the series ever made. It's the moment when *The Wire* went from a great crime novel that you shelve in the mystery section to a work of enduring literature. It's the point when you recognize that this isn't a show about cops and drug dealers, but a much broader look at the death of an American city. As Simon would grow fond of saying, the show's main character wasn't McNulty, or Avon, or Stringer, but the city of Baltimore itself(*). Though the characters at the port—specifically, union leader Frank Sobotka (Chris Bauer) and his nephew Nick (Pablo Schreiber)—add another plank to the "why the War on Drugs has been a farce" platform by showing how drugs get into the country in the first place, their main function is to illustrate the disappearance of the blue-collar industrial workforce that formed the backbone of the American economy for so long. As Frank says to his lobbyist friend Bruce late in the season, "You know what the trouble is, Brucie? We used to make shit in this country. Build shit. Now we just put our hand in the next guy's pocket."

(*) Dominic West, who has great affection for the series as well as a cheeky sense of humor, responds to my question about Baltimore being the main character by laughing and saying, "Rubbish! McNulty's the main character. I kept trying to tell [Simon], 'This is not an ensemble piece.' But he wouldn't listen. You can't have a city being the main character on a show! Fuck that! I'm the main character!" (More seriously, he acknowledges, "The star was Baltimore, and I think part of the reason I was cast is I wasn't a star. It's not about me; it's about the writing, and the writing was so good.")

Simon hadn't allowed himself to even consider a second season until HBO ordered one—"I wasn't naïve," he says; "we knew we had put a majority black cast in place, so I didn't know what the temperature would be on renewing it"—but when he got the good news from Albrecht, he knew what he wanted to do next.

"When they asked us what we were going to do if we came back," he recalls, "I said, 'Now we're going to build a city.' I remember going to Ed and saying, 'The next season has to be about the working class and the death of work. By making the death of work a part of the dynamic, it's no longer about the bad guys deciding they're going to be drug dealers because they're evil, it's about economic imperative.

"I knew the show would be a much smaller show if we didn't go there," he adds. "It would be a cop show."

Viewers got used to the stevedores in time, particularly once the Barksdale task force reassembled to go after them—and, eventually, the coalition of international criminals using them to smuggle drugs, cars, women, and more in through the docks—but now we were conditioned to understand that a given season of the show could be set anywhere in Baltimore, focus on any character, and touch on any theme relevant to the city's life.

So when the show returned for a third season with McNulty and company going after Stringer again, it didn't seem like a mere reversion to the status quo, because that investigation tied into new story arcs involving how things get done at City Hall; how a former Barksdale soldier named Cutty (Chad L. Coleman) adjusts to life after prison; and the seemingly insane but possibly brilliant plan cooked up by retiring Baltimore cop Howard "Bunny" Colvin (Robert Wisdom) to heal a neighborhood utterly ravaged by the drug war.

Colvin's scheme involves decriminalizing drugs in his district by limiting their sale and use to a handful of designated areas that, through a cross-cultural misunderstanding, come to be known as "Hamsterdam." The inspiration came from Ed Burns's belief (previously expressed in a memorable passage in *The Corner*) that open-container violations for alcohol were a minor offense that would have consumed too much police time and resources, had some enterprising wino not had the brainstorm to put his bottle of elderberry into a brown paper bag. It was an unspoken compromise that allowed cops to spend time doing real police work without making it look like they were ignoring blatant law-breaking, but, as Bunny Colvin puts it, "There's never been a paper bag for drugs." Hamsterdam will be his paper bag, and it works for a while before department brass and city politicians find out about it. The great tragedy is that individually, almost everyone in the city power structure who learns of Hamsterdam sees merit in the idea, but is too afraid of what an association with it would do to their careers to let it last.

Bunny Colvin will lose his career (and lucrative pension) over the experiment, and will later try and fail with a similar approach to reforming the city's school system in the fourth season. By the time we see him briefly in the fifth season, he's given up on fixing anything but his foster son, Namond. Bunny runs into callow Mayor Tommy Carcetti (Aidan Gillen)—who once seemed like a budding reformer before turning into the same kind of hack as his predecessors—and Carcetti expresses regret for how Hamsterdam turned out, insisting, "There wasn't anything anyone could have done with that."

Bunny looks at one of the many men who failed to match his idealism and sums up the series' despair by replying, "Well, Mr. Mayor, there's nothing to be done."

The Season 3 arc—which also involves Stringer's own failed attempt to reform the drug game by forming a co-op of dealers that would remove violence from the equation—could have been the series' last. It ends with Stringer dead, Avon back in prison(*), and McNulty quitting the Major Crimes Unit for a happier, healthier life with port cop Beadie Russell (Amy Ryan). Simon had dreamed of doing a spin-off called *The Hall* that would chronicle Carcetti's run for mayor, and then governor, alternating seasons with *The Wire* along the way, but now Albrecht wasn't sure he even wanted more *Wire*, let alone another low-rated Baltimore drama.

(*) Stringer and Avon wind up betraying each other to their respective fates, leading to an incredible scene (written, as all of the series' penultimate episodes were, by crime novelist turned screenwriter George Pelecanos; Pelecanos was later joined on the staff by fellow authors Richard Price and Dennis Lehane) where the two longtime friends—each aware of what he's done to the other, but not aware of what the other has in turn done to him—share one last moment to-

gether on the balcony of Avon's high-rise condo. "Us, motherfucker,"
Avon toasts to the partnership both know is doomed, even if neither
can possibly admit it.

Albrecht recalls telling Simon, "David, the show's over. Declare
victory here. This is great. People think the show's great. How are
you gonna top that?"

As he would to secure every renewal but that initial one, Simon
would write a long letter outlining his plans for the following season and arguing for his show's survival.

"And it would be a letter," Albrecht recalls(*). "It wasn't an
email. He's a great writer, and it was a great letter. We always appreciated the show. The attitude we had was, 'If we don't do this,
who's gonna do it?' The quality of the work certainly deserved it,
and David's passion deserved it."

(*) I spoke with Albrecht at his office at Starz, where he now works
as CEO. The door was slightly ajar throughout the interview, and
when I left, Albrecht's assistant (who had worked with him at HBO)
stopped me to say, "And those letters were always single-spaced." They
made an impression.

"Every time David's back was to the wall, he would sell it with
story," says Strauss. "That show was on death's door at the end of
every fucking season, and then he would send you the treatment,
and you'd go, 'We gotta do it, we gotta do it.'"

So Albrecht ordered a fourth season, but took enough time in
doing so that 19 months passed between episodes. Simon had a
two-season plan to conclude the series(*), with the fourth-season
finale leaving many developments—particularly the MCU's investigation into a series of murders tied to Marlo Stanfield (Jamie
Hector), who had succeeded Avon as West Baltimore's drug kingpin—up in the air.

(*) During the long wait for renewal, David Mills approached Simon with the idea of doing a sixth season about Latino immigrants coming to Baltimore in search of economic opportunity at a time when such opportunities were disappearing from urban America. Given the low ratings and the fight for Season 4, Simon didn't feel the moment was right to go to Albrecht and say, "We've got a great idea! Now there's gonna be a bunch of Latino actors!"

As the fourth-season premiere approached, Albrecht was publicly suggesting that it could easily be the last, barring the reaction from viewers and the media. So Simon and HBO's publicity arm did something that was unprecedented at the time: they sent the entire season out in advance to critics, hoping that reading an entire volume of this book at once would give them a greater appreciation for it, and would generate greater praise than previous seasons had gotten at the start.

The gamble worked. Critics had largely been slow to embrace the show in its first season, and more positive in its second and third, but still too distracted by shinier things. But seeing the fourth season—which made Namond (Julito McCullen) and his middle-school friends Michael (Tristan Wilds), Randy (Maestro Harrell), and Dukie (Jermaine Crawford) into the new central characters and showed how the school system(*), social services, the police, and even their own families had terribly failed these kids—in its entirety sent the level of praise and hype through the roof. Many critics now argued that *The Wire* was even better than *The Sopranos*. Albrecht ordered a fifth and final season only days after the fourth season debuted to a miniscule (even for HBO) 1.5 million viewers.

(*) Informed by Ed Burns's own experiences as a Baltimore middle-school teacher.

"In a way, I thought Chris was very clever," says Simon. "He didn't do it on the Monday [before the ratings came in], he did it on the Tuesday. He could go, 'Those are cute little numbers. It's renewed. Just call us HBO.' And that's, in a way, what *The Wire* added to the brand: 'This show goes on because we can't bear to kill it.'"

With one last renewal in hand, Simon and Burns got to close their book with a look at how the media has failed to communicate to the public all the terrible things we'd seen in previous years.

The media arc—involving a group of reporters and editors in a fictional version of Simon's old employer, the *Baltimore Sun*—was the least well-received of the show's major stories, as the same reporters and critics who had fallen over themselves praising the realism of the school story or the port case could suddenly see the dramatic liberties the show sometimes took once they happened in a more familiar setting(*). There were definitely flaws in the *Sun* story, primarily the use of a Stephen Glass–style fabulist reporter as a symbol of the ills of modern journalism, which played exactly like the Roger Gaffney character from *Homicide* whom Simon had been dismissive of at the start of this series. Though there were many systemic ills at the *Sun*, the amount of screen time devoted to the fabulist suggested that if the paper just got wise to his antics and fired him, all would be well and the real news would be reported on.

(*) As an example of a non-newspaper story where critics didn't notice the dramatic license being taken, Simon cites the decision by State's Attorney Rhonda Pearlman (Deirdre Lovejoy) to let Frank Sobotka go home to call his lawyer, arranging a deal to take down Vondas (Paul Ben-Victor) and The Greek (Bill Raymond)—a decision that allows The Greek to discover Sobotka's betrayal and order his murder. In real

life, someone like Pearlman would have called the lawyer for Frank rather than let him leave her sight for a moment, but "We didn't want that to happen. It wasn't the best possible drama."

But the fifth season also illustrated the cumulative power of the show and its novelistic approach. Whether we cared about the *Sun* reporters or not, we were still spending time with characters we'd known forever: McNulty, off the wagon and recklessly fabricating a serial killer as part of a crazy plan to get the overtime money needed to catch Marlo; Bubbs, struggling with his sobriety and guilt over the death of his teenage protégé Sherrod; or even more recent additions like Dukie, who winds up a junkie on the streets after being separated, one by one, from his friends.

The longer *The Wire* was on, the harder it hit, in terms of despair and of joy. It's a show that always put in the time to make you understand and care. The fourth season meticulously lays out Randy's bleak journey from sweet, enterprising kid with fantasies of owning his own corner grocery to cold, hard, bitter young man incapable of dreaming. He doesn't die, but his ultimate fate is as devastating as watching Bodie and Poot kill Wallace. The fifth season charts Bubbs's rise from rock bottom, living a solitary existence and sleeping in his sister's basement (she's been burned by him so often in the past that she keeps the door to the rest of the house locked). When Bubbs is finally able to open up about Sherrod at an NA meeting—"Ain't no shame in holding on to grief," he admits, "as long as you hold onto other things, too"— it's enough to reduce even the most cynical viewer to tears. And when we see him bound up the basement steps to open the unlocked door and enjoy a meal with his sister, it's incredible how joyful we feel, seeing him thrill to a mundane activity most of us take for granted.

Bubbs's walk up those stairs matters—just as the deaths of Wallace, Frank Sobotka, D'Angelo, Stringer, Bodie, and Omar matter, just as we despair for Bunny and Randy and Kima when things go wrong, just as we cheer when good things occasionally happen to Lester or Carver or Namond—because the show had taken care to make them matter, and we had invested the time following the characters to each point.

There are some episodes of *The Wire* that resonate more deeply with fans than others (usually the ones where beloved characters die), but there isn't one you could break out and show to a non-viewer to explain its genius, in the way that you could show "College" or "Pine Barrens" to a *Sopranos* novice, and say, "This is why you should be watching."

With *The Wire*, the whole is far greater than the sum of its parts. It isn't designed like any TV show before it, not even the other early successes of this new golden age. It isn't designed to be broken apart into bits, some parts elevated over others or consumed separately.

And perhaps as a result of that, the little show that lived in the shadow of Tony Soprano and kept getting renewed by the skin of its teeth has become, as Chris Albrecht puts it, "The show that became the most famous show ever after it was off the air," and one where there's a steady stream of new converts declaring, "I am ready to watch *The Wire*."

CHAPTER 4

A lie agreed upon…
The profane poetry of **Deadwood**

Early in the premiere episode of *Deadwood*, a dirty old prospector named Ellsworth sits at Al Swearengen's bar, contemplates a drink, and announces for all to hear, "I tell you what: I may have fucked up my life flatter'n hammered shit, but I stand here before you today beholden to no human cocksucker, and holdin' a workin' fuckin' gold claim, and not the U.S. government sayin' I'm trespassin', or the savage fuckin' red man himself, or any of these limber-dick cocksuckers passin' themselves off as prospectors had better try and stop me."

Three thoughts immediately came to mind the first time I watched actor Jim Beaver deliver that monologue:

1) The level of profanity in that speech is awe-inspiring;

2) Beyond the cussing, the speech is constructed in such a brilliant way that the words, both salty and non-salty, are arranged in just the right order: to convey volumes about Ellsworth's past and present, and about the allure and danger of the Deadwood camp, which began as an illegal mining settlement on Indian territory in the Black Hills of the Dakota territories; and

3) Only David Milch could have written it.

By some quirk of fate and nomenclature, the Holy Trinity of HBO dramas were all created by men named David: Chase on *The Sopranos* in 1999, Simon with *The Wire* in 2002, and Milch with *Deadwood* in 2004. All three had done their time in network television, and several of the shows they worked on in that more traditional environment are among the absolute best of their respective genres. And yet it wasn't until HBO freed them of the usual network constraints—intrusive creative notes, commercial breaks, words and images and morality that the FCC and advertisers wouldn't allow, and more—that they were really able to show what both they and television were capable of.

And of the three Davids, perhaps the best example of what happens when you take a great talent and remove all his filters is Milch on *Deadwood*.

Where exactly do you start with David Milch? To call him a character would be like calling the Taj Mahal a building: technically accurate, but failing to convey the grand scale. No one who has worked with Milch would ever say, "Let me tell you my David Milch story," because every day with him is a story unto itself. There is a method to his madness, and a madness to his method, and an unmistakable genius to it all.

So I could start with the story Milch likes to tell on himself about how his father, a Buffalo surgeon, first took him to the racetrack at the age of five or six, in what Milch describes as "a complicated and conflicting experience. He explained to me that he knew that in my heart of hearts, I was a degenerate gambler, but that despite my disposition to be a degenerate, it wasn't legal for me." And I could then add that Dr. Milch was eerily prescient about his young son, who would indeed grow up to have an addiction to gambling(*)—and also to heroin, and to have problems with alcohol and various other substances.

(*) The first time I interviewed him, as a starstruck rookie reporter, he took me to the track and offered to split the winnings if his horse came in. (While I was busy trying to remember what the newspaper's ethics policy had to say about this, the horse helpfully finished out of the money.) When I interviewed him for this book, his office TV turned itself on in what seemed like a random fashion; after shutting it off, Milch confessed that he had it programmed to turn on for a specific horse race. "My own television is busting me," he said with a shrug.

Or I could start with his years at Yale as a fraternity brother of George W. Bush's, and the time he claims he impersonated the future commander in chief when a reporter called the frat house for an interview. Or perhaps on how he was forced to leave Yale Law School because, as he memorably put it in a 2005 *New Yorker* interview, "There were guns. There were police. There were street lights. I got arrested. I had become involved in quite a protracted pharmaceutical-research project involving hallucinogens. It all seemed to come together. So I was asked to withdraw."

Or I could tell you about Milch's time as a protégé of Pulitzer Prize–winning novelist and poet Robert Penn Warren, who brought him back to Yale to work on a survey of American literature, and to teach, which is where he was working when college roommate Jeff Lewis reached out to him about writing a *Hill Street Blues* script. That script would ultimately win Milch an Emmy, a Writers Guild Award, and the Humanitas Prize. (He used the prize money from the latter to buy a racehorse, naturally.)

Various stories short: Milch traveled an unusual path to television, and his writing for the medium has always been fueled by his passions and his addictions, which were often inseparable.

Though *Hill Street Blues* in its first two years was a bold departure from previous cop dramas, Milch seemed determined to test even the limits that had been established by that show's creators, Steven Bochco and Michael Kozoll(*).

(*) Milch says that initially, that impetus came from Bochco, since Kozoll had departed right before Milch arrived and Bochco was eager to show what he could do without his former partner. But the longer Milch worked on the show, the more he wanted to test the boundaries on his own.

The award-winning debut, "Trial by Fury," involves the brutal rape and murder of a nun, and the way the usually upright and proper Frank Furillo uses the threat of a lynch mob to coerce a guilty plea from one of the killers. (Furillo is so troubled by his own behavior that the episode ends with him going to confession.) One of Milch's first major character inventions was Sal Benedetto, a violent, corrupt, racist cop played by Milch's frequent muse Dennis Franz. This was perhaps a bridge too far for network television in 1983, and Benedetto commits suicide at the end of that season. Two years later, after Bochco was forced out by the head of the MTM studio, Milch and Lewis were placed in charge of the show—and Benedetto was resurrected in the ever-so-slightly kinder form of Lt. Norm Buntz, also played by Franz.

In a hint of what would come on his other two signature dramas, those final two Milch-run seasons(*) saw him losing interest in do-gooder Furillo in favor of the shadier, self-loathing, unexpected heroism of Buntz, who became the de facto leading man by the end of the series. Though Milch has spent much of his career writing about cops, TV's most classic authority figure, his interest inevitably falls on the outcasts within the establishment—the ones who don't look or talk or act like we expect our heroes to, who are tormented by self-loathing, addiction, and other demons, and yet who are inevitably revealed to have their own hidden nobility and wisdom.

(*) One of the more memorable outings of Milch's tenure came from yet another David. Milch recruited Pulitzer-winning playwright David Mamet to write an episode in the final season, which Mamet agreed to on condition he could bring back a recurring character played by his then-wife Lindsay Crouse. It's a strange episode, peppered with Mamet's idiosyncratic dialogue (a distant cousin to Milch's own style of patter), and including a story where sensitive cop Henry Goldblum is forced to dig his own grave. Years later, while directing an episode of The Shield, *Mamet told me that "Milch asked me after the first day if I wanted the show. I said, 'What do you mean?' He said, 'Do you want it? We've been here for seven years, we're insane. If you want the show, we'll give it to you.'" It sounds like a joke, but both Milch and Mamet swear this offer was legitimate, and Mamet added, "Looking back, I kinda wish I'd taken him up on it."*

Buntz's ascendance on *Hill Street*, unsurprisingly, represented Milch's feelings about the show at the time.

"One of the blessings of working in series format is that you can revisit and refine," he says, "but I had already begun to feel a little constricted by the format. Those characters were expressions of those feelings of restriction."

After the short-lived spin-off *Beverly Hills Buntz* and the unsuccessful journalism drama *Capital News*, Milch reteamed with Bochco for *NYPD Blue*, which helped bridge the gap—chronologically and stylistically—from *Hill Street* to *Deadwood*.

Bochco was interested in the commercial possibilities of using nudity and profanity on network TV, but Milch saw hidden creative advantages. As he explained to me the first time I interviewed him, he believed that the concessions to Standards and Practices that they had to make on *Hill Street*—innuendo but no real sex, Mick Belker never using an insult harsher than "dog breath"— undid much of the illusion of reality that had been created by the way the series was otherwise written, shot, and performed. If we know that real cops use curse words, and if the cops on this show are using curse words that aren't really curse words, we're reminded that we're just watching a television show, and that the emotional and dramatic stakes don't really matter.

NYPD Blue gained notoriety when Andy Sipowicz (Dennis Franz again, straddling a middle ground between Buntz and Benedetto) called a female DA a "pissy little bitch," or when we saw the naked rear end of Sipowicz's partner John Kelly(*) while he had unambiguous sex with his ex-wife. But in Milch's eyes, the explicit content also gave him license to explore darker, more disturbing stories than he had on the earlier series, like Kelly explaining to his protégé James Martinez the appropriate circumstances and method for beating a confession out of a suspect, or Sipowicz quietly enduring the interrogation of a pedophile who raped and murdered a nine-year-old boy. As David Chase would later do with *The Sopranos*, Milch was using salacious material as a come-on to get people to watch the subject matter he really wanted to deal with—in this case, the emotional toll of police work, and the moral depths people can be surprised to find themselves sinking to.

(*) *Kelly was played by a then-unknown David Caruso; in* True Blue, *his memoir of that first season, Milch would blame a heart attack he suffered during production on Caruso's diva behavior.*

Though Bochco and Milch were credited as co-creators, it quickly became clear that *NYPD Blue* was Milch's show, featuring Milch's voice. Yet again, his interest quickly shifted from the classic leading-man type (first Kelly, then Jimmy Smits as Bobby Simone) to the coarser, unpredictable anti-hero played by Franz.

"I think that there is a restlessness in the spirit" of those kinds of characters, Milch says, "which is finally unconquerable, and that can be accommodated, provisionally, but never ultimately fully assimilated into society."

And, he adds, mixing in practicality with his usual philosophizing, "Those are the characters that always get the best lines."

ABC had a long battle with its affiliates and with the censors just to get *NYPD Blue* on the air, which gave Milch and Bochco an entire year to develop the series. In their partnership, Bochco had always had a stronger grasp of narrative unity and how to organize ongoing storylines, and the series' first 13 episodes told a complicated but coherent story arc involving the affair between Kelly and a uniform cop who owed a debt to the mob. Once Bochco ceded the everyday writing duties to Milch, story arcs became fewer and farther between, and even Milch would acknowledge that some paid off well, while others didn't.

With Milch fully in charge of the writing process—or, in many cases, the rewriting process—it became all-consuming. When Milch and Lewis replaced Bochco on *Hill Street*, Milch had developed a working method that he would continue to use for the next several decades: he would lie on the floor of the writers' room (Milch has a bad back, which can make sitting for long periods difficult) while a typist scrolled through each script at his instruction; Milch made changes line by line, word by word. By the early days of *NYPD Blue*, it was understood that regardless of whose name was on the script, the bulk of the words—and, almost as importantly, their order—came from Milch.

"It's a question of metrics," he says, by way of explaining why he'd comb each sentence so thoroughly. "If you believe that the rhythms and textures of writing are as much the vehicle of meaning as the literal meaning of things, you try and work on the metrics. I felt, if I was going to work in this medium, it uniquely afforded me the opportunity to work that way."

Over the course of time, the language used by the characters (particularly Sipowicz and Gordon Clapp's neurotic Detective Medavoy) would grow more stylized and contorted, in many ways sounding as if they were auditioning to appear in a 19th-century period piece like *Deadwood*. Sentences constructed in a familiar, straightforward manner were replaced with jargon mixed with clauses placed seemingly out of order, like Andy getting defensive with his estranged son Andy Jr.: "I took you for breaking balls, my not seeing you growing up." Or Andy advising someone, "Any money left, you can buy a self-improvement tape: 'Bein' nicer so other people don't wanna hit you with a brick.'"

Milch acknowledges now that the dialogue could sound "like a snake swallowing its tail," and says that the odd but memorable sentence construction "was the by-product of the way I was working. It would have been a distortion of the process of the way I was working for the characters to have spoken any other way."

The rewriting would at times continue up until scenes were about to be filmed, with Milch inventing new dialogue on the spot and hoping the actors could keep up. It was genre TV as improv, and while some actors embraced the approach (Franz would win four Emmys in the Milch years of the show), others (like Smits, who left after his initial contract was up) were frustrated by all the last-minute changes.

"What a superb actor he was," Milch says of Smits, "and it was just not conducive to the way he wanted to work."

"The most difficult part was watching Jimmy beat himself up," recalls the series' longtime lead director and producer Mark Tinker, "because he was having a hard time with the process. But he was gentleman enough to not reveal his anger(*) was at the process."

(*) Time has healed that anger for Smits, who now says, "Milch is, and always has been, a genius. And no matter what we went through, the work was always better at the end of the hours that we spent going through whatever we had to go through."

By the time Milch reached his seventh and final season running *NYPD Blue*, he was so weary that he fell behind schedule worse than he ever had in the past(*). In previous years, scenes occasionally had to be shot without a script, Milch dictating lines to the actors shortly before the cameras rolled. In the seventh season, this became the rule rather than the exception.

(*) Earlier in the series, Milch had periodically fallen off the wagon, but Milch and Tinker both assert that there was no obvious difference in the writing whether or not Milch was sober. That final season was a sober one, but it was also the most elliptical, uneven one of Milch's tenure. "By then," he says, "I was pretty much just worn down."

"Each year, we fell further and further behind," Milch says. "So, one after another of those disciplines eroded. First working with other writers eroded, because there wasn't the time to teach. By the time we were finished, we were shooting not only without a script, but on three different sets at once. It was terrible. It was such an imposition on everyone else. I regret it. I don't know what else to do besides regret it."

Yet there was no mutiny on the set, because people trusted Milch and because this method of working brought with it its own perverse thrills. As Tinker puts it, "We would all look at each other and shake our heads and say, 'Holy crap,' but there was something exciting about it, like an adrenaline junkie."

In that season's finale, Milch wanted Sipowicz—who by this point had suffered the deaths of his eldest son, his partner Bobby, and his wife, and whose young son Theo was facing a medical crisis—to enter the hospital chapel and rant about all that God has taken from him. Tinker was on set. Franz was on set. The entire crew was on set. And, as usual by that point, there was no script. Milch ambled onto the set, realized everyone was waiting on him, announced that he needed someone to take dictation, and launched into a stream-of-consciousness assault on the Almighty, sounding very much like Sipowicz. Minutes later, Franz performed it word for word.

Milch often begins his work day by praying, "I offer myself to Thee to build with me and do with me as Thou will. Relieve me of the bondage of self, that I may better do Thy will." With this prayer—part of the third step of AA—he hoped to push his own personality out of the way and channel Sipowicz, or Medavoy, or later Al Swearengen. More often than not, it worked.

That was Milch's last *NYPD Blue* episode. He was burnt out, and though he technically quit, "no one was yanking on my coattails asking me to stay." He once again tried to make a go of things without Bochco with *Big Apple*, a CBS drama about a joint NYPD/FBI organized crime task force. The series featured several once and future members of Milch's unofficial repertory company—Ed O'Neill as the Sipowicz stand-in cop, Titus Welliver and Kim Dickens as FBI agents—but the plotting felt as circuitous as the usual Milch dialogue, and like Bochco and Milch's short-lived *Brooklyn South*, it didn't seem to have a reason to exist beyond the assumption that Milch should only be writing about cops.

"CBS looked at me like a six-headed monster," he says. "They didn't know what the hell to do with me." *Big Apple* was canceled after eight episodes.

Then came Milch's greatest feat of improvisation—and one of the greatest works to ever air on American television.

Though he was now 20 years removed from his Yale teaching days, Milch was still every bit the scholar(*), and he had been diving into both the writings of St. Paul and works on the Roman Empire of that period. He was inspired to write a very different kind of cop show, set in ancient Rome—the joke in the pilot episode was going to be that the first criminal we see our two centurion heroes arrest is St. Paul himself—and dealing with the way the rise of any civilization corresponds with the rise of law and order to protect that civilization.

*(*) He was also still every bit the professor, as press conferences and even casual conversations with Milch tend to take on the air of a lecture. At a press conference for his post-*Deadwood *HBO drama* John from Cincinnati, *Milch went on an epic monologue about the writings of William James—being self-deprecating as he did so by noting, "Several of the actors have attempted to take their lives in the aftermath of my protracted speaking about William James." When he concluded, another reporter asked actor Bruce Greenwood, whose patience had visibly ebbed throughout the James anecdote, how working with Milch differed from working with some of the other producers on Greenwood's c.v. "Well," said Greenwood, "I think you probably witnessed the difference in the last 20 minutes."*

Milch took it to the only channel at that time (and probably even now) that would consider such a project: HBO. He went to lunch with executives Chris Albrecht and Carolyn Strauss, and launched into his pitch. Albrecht and Strauss loved it, but they were also cringing, because they knew something Milch didn't: they already had a show in development about that period called *Rome*.

Milch likes to say, "If you want to make God laugh, tell Him your plans," and when Albrecht suggested an alternate setting for the series, Milch improvised once again, and realized that he could tell a story dealing with the same themes in a very different period.

By God, he was going to make a Western.

He was going to tell the story of Deadwood, and how this enclave of utter lawlessness was able to appear presentable enough to eventually be absorbed by the United States of America surrounding it.

"It had seemed to me that the symbol of the cross as the organizing principle of behavior could be transliterated to the symbol of the badge, as a similar organizing principle," he explains. "It wasn't that different. If you changed the costumes, you could make that work. You also have to be a bit of a sociopath to say, 'Well, it isn't that much of a difference.' It's 2000 years; there's a *lot* of difference."

Just as Milch had immersed himself in the world of the NYPD while making *NYPD Blue*, he began poring over both historical accounts and primary documents of Deadwood in the 1870s. He wrote a script centered around three historical figures who were all in the camp at the same time (albeit briefly): legendary gunslinger Wild Bill Hickok, local saloon owner Al Swearengen, and Seth Bullock, the camp's first sheriff.

Milch was at a new network, working in a very different setting from the one where he'd had his greatest success. But he was still Milch, which among other things meant God was still laughing at his plans. Milch had been dazzled by O'Neill's work on *Big*

Apple, and wrote the fictionalized Swearengen character with him in mind. But HBO executives were reluctant to build a drama around an actor still best known as Al Bundy from *Married... with Children*. Then Milch cast character actor Powers Boothe in the role, but Boothe took ill right before the pilot was going to be filmed(*). So the role of a lifetime was awarded instead to English actor Ian McShane—who, like Dennis Franz before him, began a Milch series playing the villain, but gradually became its beating heart and most admirable, if unconventional, hero.

(*) To encourage Boothe to get well, Milch promised him he'd always have a part on the show, and created the character of Cy Tolliver—a more polished, overtly evil rival to Swearengen—for him, and kept the character around even after he had arguably outlived his creative usefulness. Milch on Boothe: "I'll just say that there are episodes in which he rises absolutely to the level of Swearengen. He doesn't do it a lot, but he does it sometimes."

Deadwood opens not on Swearengen, but on Timothy Olyphant as Bullock, completing his last official act as a cop in Montana before moving to Deadwood to seek his fortune in the hardware game with business partner Sol Star. A horse thief named Clell Watson sits in a jail cell, trying to bribe Bullock into taking him along to Deadwood, marveling at the idea of a place with no law at all, and the money he could make there if he weren't due to be executed come morning. The owner of the horse Watson stole shows up outside, drunk and surrounded by a lynch mob ready to string the man up then and there. Bullock could stand aside and let this happen, but instead emerges from the jail with his gun out, warning the mob that Watson will hang "under color of law." He allows the man to dictate a poignant farewell to the sister who won't be arriving in time to watch her brother die. As the embarrassed mob looks on, Watson spits out a defiant "FFFFUCK YOOOOU!!!!" and jumps off the stool, his neck breaking seconds later with some help from the marshal. Bullock asks if any man from the mob will deliver Watson's final words to his sister, and when one steps forward, Seth hands him both the paper he wrote them on and his badge.

It is, I would argue, the most vivid, important, and entertaining opening scene of any of the great HBO dramas—yes, even more than Tony meeting Dr. Melfi for the first time or Detective McNulty hearing the tragic tale of Snot Boogie. And like the introductory moments of those previous shows, it swiftly establishes the themes, stakes, and tone of the world we're about to visit for a few years.

To start with a basic stylistic issue, there is the profanity. In the seven-minute sequence leading up to Watson's death, there are a dozen "fucks" and two "cocksuckers," along with a half-dozen other stray curse words. By the series' later standards, this isn't much(*). But for the series' opening scene, and in a genre that was still—many decades, and many revisionist Westerns, later—associated with the squeaky-clean likes of John Wayne, Gary Cooper and James Arness, this was a shock to the system.

(*) Nor does it come close to the famous Bunk/McNulty scene from The Wire, *in which 40 iterations of the F-word are used in 3 minutes and 34 seconds.*

At the time, the sheer volume of the cursing throughout the pilot was so stunning that Milch was asked about little else when he did his initial round of publicity for the series. He defended it as historically accurate (though not all historians agreed), insisting at the time, "Without exception, what people said about the mining camps was that you could not believe the profanity. It wasn't just that they were profane, but they were almost insanely profane. There were so many instances where people were recalling they couldn't believe in a simple acknowledgment of 'hello' from one person to another, how much invective and obscenity could be inserted. The content of the words made it sound like people were furious with each other, when they were just saying 'hello.'"

There's also the sheer wordiness of the sequence. The pilot was directed by the great Walter Hill, who had several Westerns under his belt(*), and Milch deferred to Hill more than he normally does with directors. The Hill-directed version of that scene was focused much more on the threat posed by the lynch mob, but by midway through production of the first season, Milch and company had recognized that the series was, as writer Jody Worth (who had previously written for Milch on *Hill Street Blues* and *NYPD Blue*) describes it, "a talking show." So a good chunk of it was reshot to focus on Bullock and Watson's conversation in the cell, which would lay the groundwork for a series where violence occurred, but where the most powerful weapon in any man's arsenal—particularly if that man was Al Swearengen—tended to be his gift of gab.

(*) *Including 1995's* Wild Bill, *which also dealt with Hickok's stint in Deadwood, and also featured Keith Carradine—albeit as Buffalo Bill Cody, rather than in his* Deadwood *role of Hickok himself.*

And Bullock's insistence on playing executioner himself while he still has a badge is at once a meaningless distinction and a defining one for the series.

Deadwood is a show about the imposing of order onto chaos, of bringing law to a lawless settlement, and of the great grey area the camp and its people occupy as they wait to be legally absorbed into the civilized world. In this particular instance, if the law steps aside in favor of drunken mob rule, then where does that slippery slope end? If Bullock lets these men have their way, they have a fine old time stringing up Clell and perhaps look forward to their next opportunity to lynch someone who troubles them. Done Bullock's way, and with Clell given the chance to dictate his goodbyes to his sister and estranged son, it shames every drunk SOB in that crowd, reminds them of exactly what's involved when you take another man's life, and again maintains the veneer of civilization that is wholly absent in Bullock and Star's new home in Deadwood.

In Deadwood the place, there is no law at all. It's every man for himself, preferably with a gun in his hand (though for Al Swearengen, a knife tends to do), and you take whatever you can get away with taking. But in *Deadwood* the series, laws have meaning. Symbols of office have meaning. The social contract, and the unwritten obligations we have to each other, have meaning—even if many characters try their damndest to work around them.

The first season (which premiered on March 21, 2004) opens with Bullock giving away his badge; it concludes with him putting on a new one. Swearengen is introduced as a land-locked pirate; by series' end, he has pushed hard for the camp to have elections and basic government services, at times seemingly sacrificing his own self-interest for the good of the community—though Al would argue (perhaps honestly, or perhaps to protect his reputation) that the two situations are inextricably linked.

Though Milch didn't get to depict his Roman centurions busting St. Paul, he did get to incorporate Paul's writing into this version of the show, and make it into the series' mission statement. Wild Bill is gunned down by his former poker opponent Jack McCall in the series' fourth episode(*), and in the fifth, Bullock and Star attend the great man's funeral, as conducted by the joyful Rev-

erend Smith. Smith's eulogy quotes extensively from Paul's first letter to the Corinthians, particularly the section about the parts of
the body, including the idea that even with "those members of the
body which we think of as less honorable—all are necessary," and
that, "When one member suffers, all the members suffer with it."

(*) Because so many Deadwood *characters were based on real people, the series had certain historical markers it was always building
towards, and Wild Bill's murder was the first major one. Milch, knowing that Hickok and Bullock's time in Deadwood only overlapped by
a few days, wanted to bump off Hickok in the second or third episode.
Chris Albrecht, having seen the work Keith Carradine was doing as
Hickok, wanted Milch to push it to the end of the first season. In the
end, Albrecht got Milch to compromise slightly and wait until the end
of the fourth installment.*

Bullock has come to Deadwood to look out for his own interests and avoid setting others up to depend on him. He tries to
dismiss the whole speech as gibberish, but reluctantly becomes the
sheriff when it becomes clear how badly his services are needed.
When a smallpox outbreak hits the camp, it's Swearengen who or-
ganizes a plan to care for the sick and secure a vaccine, the first in
a series of actions that makes him the camp's leader in all but title.

Deadwood takes place in the darkest, dirtiest, most frightening
setting of the three classic HBO dramas of the period; it's also by
far the most optimistic of the three. *The Sopranos* comes across as
deeply cynical about humanity, while *The Wire* believes that any
innate goodness within people eventually gets ground down by the
institutions that they serve. They are shows about the end of the
American dream. *Deadwood* is about the birth of it, about selfish
loners existing on society's fringes finding ways to come together
in service of something greater than themselves—even as the more

respectable forces of civilization (as represented first by the territorial government in Yankton, and then by mining mogul George Hearst) do their best to undo all that work in the name of building their own fortunes.

In the service of this message, and with history as his guide, Milch crafted the most memorable characters, dialogue, and moments of his career.

To the initial troika of Bullock, Swearengen, and Hickok, Milch added the likes of (among many, many others) Brad Dourif as Doc Cochran, a twitchy Civil War veteran trying to provide a proper standard of care in an environment, and to a clientele, that rarely made things easy; William Sanderson as the scheming, unctuous E.B. Farnum, who carries himself like a cross between a dumb, feral animal and one of Shakespeare's fools; and Beaver as Ellsworth, who proves to be far more decent, wise, and brave than the "flatter'n hammered shit" monologue might have suggested at the start.

Milch had often struggled writing for female characters on his earlier series—"I don't understand women," he admits—but he found a way(*) into the minds of Molly Parker as wealthy widow Alma Garret; Robin Weigert as Wild Bill's self-loathing, alcoholic companion Calamity Jane; and Paula Malcomson and Kim Dickens as the prostitutes Trixie and Joanie Stubbs, one low-class and one high-class, each reluctantly beholden to their respective abusive pimps. The drama revolution in general and this show in particular were highlighted by strong male characters, but the women of *Deadwood* exist not as appendages to Bullock, Swearengen, and company but as their own entities with hopes, dreams, and vulnerabilities. (The awkward, unlikely friendship between Alma and Trixie is among the series' deepest.)

(*) It helped that several of these women battled the same demons

*he had. Of Alma's laudanum addiction, he says, "It gave me a way
into her that I would not have had," while "Trixie being a prostitute
is another form of brutalized sensibility, and that helped me to understand her."*

Discussion of all the profanity dominated early analysis of the
series, and, if anything, Milch and company grew more creative
with their cussing as time went on. (Swearengen's partnership with
Mr. Wu, the local Chinese crime boss played by Keone Young,
drew many laughs from the one English word Wu knew, "cocksucker," and the number of different meanings Al could intuit
from it.) But it was Milch's attention to language in its entirety—
his obsession with breaking down each sentence to its component
parts and tinkering until it emerged in a more durable, poetic
form—that would mark the series as special. As with *NYPD Blue*,
the stories didn't always make sense, but the words the characters
got to recite in the service of those stories were so beautiful that it
hardly mattered.

I could fill the rest of this chapter with memorable *Deadwood*
lines and still have more than enough left over to randomly sprin-
kle them into our discussion of *Lost*, *Buffy*, and *24*. But here are
three of my favorites, only one of them featuring any cursing at all.

First, Wild Bill does his best to convince Alma to leave town
after Swearengen arranges the murder of her idiot husband:

> "You know the sound of thunder, don't you, Mrs.
>   Garret?"
> "Of course."
> "Can you imagine that sound if I ask you to?"
> "I can, Mr. Hickok."
> "Your husband and me had this talk, and I told

> him to head home to avoid a dark result, but
> I didn't say it in thunder. Ma'am... *listen to the*
> *thunder."*

The second comes via Season 2's major addition: Garret Dillahunt(*) as Francis Wolcott, chief geologist to mining mogul George Hearst, who in the daytime arranges with Cy Tolliver to buy up most of the camp's gold claims on Hearst's behalf, and at night indulges in various sadistic, kinky tendencies with the whores of a local establishment called the Chez Ami. After his bloodlust leads to the murders of three whores, Wolcott begins losing patience with both the people of Deadwood and himself.

(*) Dillahunt had, in the previous season, played Jack McCall. McCall and Wolcott are so different in style and bearing as to suggest two different actors, but some viewers who did recognize Dillahunt's face in both men began questioning the symbolism behind the casting. Instead, it was just Milch's habit (like Franz on Hill Street Blues*) of using the same actor more than once if he liked them enough the first time.*

Around the same time, a miner named Mose Manuel murders his brother Charlie in order to sell their combined claim, then proceeds to gamble away much of his new fortune at Cy's casino. Consumed with guilt over his brother's death, a furious Manuel insists he wants it all back, and before Cy can cool the situation down, an impatient Wolcott—who can see some of his own guilt in Manuel's—sends things to a boil by asking:

> "Including youth, Mr. Manuel? And why not
> beauty? Not credibly restored, perhaps,
> but as a new non-negotiable term? Would

> you not have, too, your brother Charlie
> resurrected? Would you stipulate your envy
> of him be purged? Surely, you'll insist that
> Charlie retain certain defects: his ineffable
> self-deceptions, for example, which were
> your joy in life to rebuke, and purpose, so
> far as you had one. I suppose you would see
> removed those qualities which caused you
> to love him, and the obliviousness to danger
> which allowed you to shed his blood."

And third, here's Swearengen giving a pep talk to Deadwood's chief journalist, the lonely, idealistic A.W. Merrick, after Cy Tolliver's goons have vandalized his printing press:

> "Pain, or damage don't end the world—or
> despair, or fuckin' beatings. The world ends
> when you're dead. Until then, you got more
> punishment in store. Stand it like a man, and
> give some back."

This is gorgeous, evocative language—the kind that would slot Milch comfortably alongside the literary lions he wrote and taught about in his Yale days—and by far the rule, rather the exception, to the quality of the dialogue. Every script was overflowing with throwaway lines—say, Swearengen responding to a pointed query with "What a type you must consort with, that you not fear beating for such an insult"—that, if transplanted to some other series, would have easily been the most memorable turn of phrase used there.

And Milch had a collection of actors who seemed born to deliver his words. McShane in particular tore into the role of Swearengen like it was a gourmet meal, delivering one autobiographical monologue after another(*) to thin air, to a whore servicing him just below the frame, or at times to a severed Indian head he liked to keep in a box, all of the speeches spell-binding in his emotional conviction while performing them. But all involved seemed energized(**) by the opportunity to perform this material; few had been this good on-screen before, and few would be this great after.

(*) Where David Chase used Tony Soprano's therapy sessions to get him to admit things he would never say to another character, Milch preferred to have his characters address thin air, animals (Ellsworth often talked to his dog), or inanimate objects, rather than talk to each other. Jody Worth recalls Milch being fond of saying these people would rather kill a man than have a conversation with him.

(**) In the case of William Sanderson as Farnum, "terrified" might be the more appropriate adjective, as everyone who worked on the show knew how nervous he got about delivering long monologues—including Milch, who took this as an opportunity either to torture the poor guy or to force him to confront his fears and elevate his game, and wrote one Farnum speech after another for him to perform. And it worked. Worth says, "Billy was miserable, his wife would work with him on those speeches, and he would go from disastrous to great in one jump."

Beyond the interplay of the words, *Deadwood* continued to find beauty and power in unexpected, often violent moments.

Over the course of the first season, the Reverend Smith is revealed to be suffering from a brain tumor that causes hysterical fits—which Swearengen, who had an epileptic brother, can empathize with—and eventually mania, blindness, and loss of bodily control. Knowing that the real Smith died around this time, Milch set things in motion for a weary Doc Cochran to entrust the minister's final care to Swearengen. Cochran goes back to his office to pray for God to end Smith's suffering, and we see Swearengen in the unlikely role of holy agent, explaining to aspiring henchman Johnny what's involved in killing a man as he smothers the reverend to death in efficient and yet tender fashion, then tells the delirious man, "You can go now, brother," as he holds a rag over Smith's nose and mouth.

"There was a question of whether religiosity would survive in that community, or whether force would survive," says Milch. "And it was gonna be force. So we just tried to follow that out at the level of behavior, that Swearengen put religiosity to its death. But that's a kind of abstract, theoretical presentation. And these are two men, and one man is suffering, and the other man had a kind of compassion. And I thought that was a beautiful conclusion."

Early in the second season, Swearengen nearly wound up in Smith's position when Milch gave him a severe case of kidney stones, sidelining the character so that Wolcott could more plausibly take swift control over the town. What could have seemed like a gross miscalculation—confining the series' breakout, Golden Globe–winning performer to his bed, barely able to speak, for several episodes—instead turned into a riveting, if occasionally stomach-turning, story arc that revealed the degree to which Al's employees and acquaintances emotionally relied on him, in spite of (or in some cases, because of) the physical and emotional abuse he heaped on them.

As Al's condition worsens, Trixie, Johnny, and even Al's indomitable henchman Dan Dority begin to act like the world will end along with their boss's life (Trixie and Dan even make a pact to burn down the bar in the event of his death). With Doc Cochran on the verge of a surgical procedure that everyone—Doc especially—assumes will kill the patient, Al is able to use his eyes to convey his fear despite the loss of his voice and most of his facial muscles. The crew comes together to physically force the offending gleets out in a less invasive way, before all collapse in a gorgeous tableau on top of Swearengen, exhausted, relieved, and elated, and Cochran cries, "God bless, you, Al! Thank you! Thank you for saving me!"

Sometimes, *Deadwood* had no need to use the audience's tear ducts—or a single one of Milch's words—to make an impression. The series featured one of the more impressive, savage, gruesome fights ever put on screen, as Dan Dority throws down with Hearst's enforcer Captain Turner. These are two mature, solidly built men with impressive ass-kicking credentials, but when presented with an elaborately choreographed fight scene between them, Milch insisted instead on a simpler, more realistic street brawl. Towards the end of it, both characters are so exhausted that they're throwing punches from their knees and struggling to breathe. Turner seems to gain a clear advantage on Dan, but when Hearst (watching the gladiatorial combat from his balcony, opposite Swearengen on his, practically bringing the show back to its Roman roots) is too slow to signal permission for the kill, Dan escapes for a moment and eventually gets in position to *rip Turner's eye right out of the socket*, putting the veteran soldier out of his misery moments later after Al is much swifter in nodding his approval.

You might think this great work was coming from a more orderly, sane process than the *NYPD Blue* days. It wasn't.

Milch had a bigger cast, a bigger set (on the Melody Ranch studio, where Gene Autry had filmed very different Westerns decades earlier), and more creative freedom than he'd ever had before. There were no advertisers to answer to, and HBO was far more hands-off than the executives at NBC or ABC had been. And as a result, there was even less pretense of planning than there had been on *NYPD Blue*, and more improvisation. There were scripts for the first four episodes of Season 1, and after that, most of the series was written on the fly, with the cast and crew often not learning what they would be doing until the day before (if that).

As Jody Worth recalls, the *Deadwood* writers would gather each morning for a long conversation: "We would talk about where we were going in the episode, and a lot of talk that had nothing to do with anything, a lot of Professor Milch talk, all over the map talk, which I enjoyed." Out of those daily conversations came the decisions on what scenes to write that day, to be filmed the day after. There was no system to it, no order, and the actors would be given scenes completely out of context from the rest of the episode.

"A lot of the times, you come in and literally, you have nothing to shoot," Milch says. "On those days, that's when, to pretend you have a plan is an act of impiety. You have to look to the actors and take the resources that are available to you. It's like making soup. Sometimes, you've got to see what's there."

With a huge cast, a huge crew, and one of the more expensive TV sets built to that point, it would have been easy for any and all to grow nervous, if not angry and frightened, at all this work being done on the fly. But everyone trusted Milch—even the HBO executives who couldn't give feedback because there were no scripts to respond to.

"I'd never really worked with somebody who I saw adapt so readily to what was in front him," says Carolyn Strauss. If a scene wasn't working, or an actor's performance didn't match the character as written, "He was constantly dealing with not what he wished it was, but what it was. I learned a lot from him about making do with what was in front of him."

Chris Albrecht suggests that this method was "one of the ways David protects himself, because you have to wait for dailies, and I don't even know what the scene is when I see the dailies," but acknowledges, "the work was great. And I think the only rule we had at HBO back then was that there were no rules."

When *NYPD Blue* came to the end of its run, Mark Tinker—who had just presided over five sane and stable (but less dramatically interesting) post-Milch seasons of that show—jumped at the chance to reteam with Milch for the third season of *Deadwood*.

"I was absolutely eager," Tinker says, "because first of all, I felt the show was amazing, and secondly, despite all of David's craziness, I wasn't sick of how that process worked."

The way Jim Beaver eloquently describes it(*), "It's one of the joys (and terrors) of working for David Milch, having to use only the scene at hand as guide for who you are and what your attitude is. Since scenes are often filmed out of order, if you add the absence of complete scripts to the circumstance, there simply is no strong guide for one's sense of character beyond trusting the scene and the fact that David will correct you if you're on the wrong heading. It's no wonder that some actors might have difficulty with his process. But I thrilled in it. It was like going over Niagara in a barrel every morning, with all the fear intact, yet with a subdued voice in my head whispering, 'David won't let you die.'"

(*) *Every summer on my blog, I'll revisit one or two classic seasons of shows that existed before I began doing weekly episodic reviews. When it came time for* Deadwood *Season 1 in the summer of 2011, Beaver showed up, uninvited but absolutely welcome, to offer his memories of the show each week in the comments. They quickly became the high-*

*light of the discussion, to the point where I began viewing each review
as a Jim Beaver comment delivery system. The above quote is from one
of those comments; when I asked Beaver if he'd rather do a quick interview for the book, he said he didn't think he could express the sentiment any better than he had with that paragraph.*

Why, I ask Milch, did so many people put their blind trust in
him? Was it simply that the pages, even if they came at the last possible minute, were that good?

"Because the pages were good," he says, "and because I was on
the set with them trying. I don't think they ever had the sense that
I was being manipulative or holding back, or anything of the sort.
When they had doubts, we talked about them. And a lot of times,
their doubts clarified my thinking."

So the show was made up as it went along, with history continuing to provide guideposts, if not exact directions. The writers knew, for instance, that the letter Wild Bill wrote to his wife
shortly before his death—which includes the famous passage,
"Agnes Darling, if such should be we never meet again, while firing
my last shot, I will gently breathe the name of my wife—Agnes—
and with wishes even for my enemies I will make the plunge and
try to swim to the other shore."—would eventually reach her and
become a matter of historical record. They just didn't know exactly
when or how that would happen on the show, so the letter kept
being passed from person to person while they waited for the right
disposition of it.

Worth says one of the goals of those morning talks among the
writing staff was "pulling together threads that may or may not
have existed in what we had intended." With Wild Bill's letter,
they tied together many more threads than could have possibly
been planned. Farnum sells the letter to Wolcott, not because ei-

ther man cares about it, but as part of the hustle that Farnum thinks he's pulling on the newcomer—only to realize he's been beaten by a much more skilled and powerful player. Wolcott murders the whores at the Chez Ami, but Joanie Stubbs escapes to tell the tale to her confidant Charlie Utter, who once upon a time was Wild Bill's best friend. Charlie swears not to tell anyone else about this heinous crime, but can't resist delivering a savage beating to the geologist, who upon learning of his attacker's affiliation with Hickok—and in the midst of a stretch of great self-loathing following his own violent outburst—decides to give him the letter.

There's an almost Rube Goldberg quality to the way these mismatched pieces suddenly fit together perfectly, and powerfully. And the Utter/Wolcott fight was itself largely planned on the day of filming; Milch knew there would be a fight, but not exactly what started it, nor how it would go. Dayton Callie, who played Utter, recalls that Milch simply "told me to 'do what you do when you fight.' It wasn't pretty."

Given history, a logical endpoint for the series seemed to be the fire that burned down much of the town (including Swearengen's saloon), which took place three years after the murder of Wild Bill. That gave Milch roughly four seasons worth of story to play with, and he made the most of what he had while he had it.

That first season told the story of Bullock and Swearengen coming to realize the responsibility they each had to this community, and of Alma Garret emerging from a laudanum stupor to deal with the wealth, power, and responsibility that were suddenly thrust upon her when her husband Brom was murdered right after buying a rich gold claim. The second season brought the forces of America and capitalism to Deadwood, with Wolcott and the politicians from Yankton looking to swindle the settlers out of their fortune, and Bullock, Swearengen, and Mrs. Garret doing what little they could to stop them.

For the third season, capitalism took absolute control, as George Hearst (played by TV veteran Gerald McRaney, doing—like so many of his new co-stars—the best work of his career) ran roughshod over Al and everyone else who stood in his way. That season also introduced Brian Cox as flamboyant actor Jack Langrishe, whose theater company arrived in the camp at roughly the same time as Hearst.

"It's seemed to me," Milch explains, "that when the bosses seem to be in charge, there's always room for art as a compensatory dynamic. I think that what we do in our society, the best of us as storytellers, present an alternative to the story the bosses are telling."

But in the case of *Deadwood*, the story would conclude abruptly, thanks to a dispute between the storyteller and his bosses.

For the title of the second-season premiere, Milch had borrowed part of an old Napoleon quote suggesting that "history is a lie agreed upon," and much of the series showed us how those lies came to be. But when it comes to the history of how *Deadwood* ended and Milch and much of the cast and crew wound up making *John from Cincinnati*(*), agreement isn't so easy to come by.

(*) There's practically a whole book in the many ways that John—*an inscrutable but occasionally riveting series that mixed surfing with metaphysics—went awry, but it may have been a case of Milch finally needing more limits than he had. "One of the things with David is that there are parameters," says Strauss, who notes that he could make* Deadwood *the way he did because it was all written and produced on the same confined space on Melody Ranch, so he could bounce easily from idea to idea, task to task.* John—*which filmed in multiple locations in Southern California—didn't provide him enough focus.*

Albrecht, meanwhile, suggests that it didn't matter that the show was hard to understand: "It was the show people hated, because they blamed it for Deadwood *being canceled."*

Albrecht, for instance, insists that HBO having to share ownership of the show with Paramount (where Milch had signed a production deal before creating *Deadwood*) had nothing to do with the decision; Strauss says the desire to do a Milch show wholly owned by HBO was a major factor. Albrecht and Strauss agree that they had talked about *John from Cincinnati* with Milch before any *Deadwood* decision was made; Milch insists *John* only entered the conversation after *Deadwood* was officially done.

Milch remembers that "Carolyn came to me and said Chris would like to do either 4 or 6 episodes of the next season. It was kind of out of the blue. There was a good deal of back and forth. I said to her, 'Does he just not want to do the show?' She said, 'Well, on balance, he would rather not do the show. The numbers have dwindled.' The numbers weren't bad, but weren't what they had been. So I said, 'Well, if you're gonna cancel it after four, cancel it now. I don't want to be in that atmosphere of negativity for that protracted period of time.'"

Albrecht in turn says that he had suggested doing perhaps 6-8 episodes of a fourth season to Milch, and even offered to do up to 10 or 12 if that was what Milch really wanted; he gave Milch the weekend to make a decision. In this version, Milch knew Timothy Olyphant was on the verge of buying a house under the assumption he'd have another year's *Deadwood* salary to pay for it, and immediately called Olyphant to tell him the show had been canceled. Olyphant called his agent, his agent called the trades, and they in turn called Albrecht to inform him his show had been ended by its creator.

"I think the lesson, for me, in that situation, was you need to think through all of the ramifications before you include a creative person in a business decision," Albrecht says. "That was an unnecessary hiccup, but it wouldn't have happened had I really thought about the different scenarios and said to David, 'Here are your choices. This is what I'd like to do, here's option 2, what would you like to do?' Not have him figure out the different scenarios."

Whatever the sequence of events, and the motivating factors behind them(*), one part of the history is not in dispute: suddenly, before Milch, the actors, and the audience were ready for it, *Deadwood* had ended. There was talk of allowing Milch to wrap the series up with a pair of movies, but it always struck me as a way to placate the angry fans, not anything that could realistically happen. This was a huge cast, released from their contracts with the cancellation, and many of them (McShane and Olyphant in particular) were in huge demand in the industry due to their work on the show; there was never a way to get enough of them together at the same time. Milch says he came close as recently as early 2012, but as with all the previous attempts, it didn't quite happen.

(*) *Strauss was more vague on her memories of that period. Albrecht's take on things has long been a matter of public record, so I told her Milch's account of the conversation he had with her and asked if it was a fair representation of what they discussed and the tone of the discussion. "Probably," she said.*

In hindsight, knowing about the steep uphill climb towards those sequel movies, would Milch have rather just made a fourth season, even under a cloud, and even if it was only four to six hours long?

"I would rather have done them now," he says. "The demoralization, which I knew would ensue as a working atmosphere, was something I was not looking forward to. Let me be very clear: it was never my idea to end the show. That idea came from on high. But once it was clear that the show was going to end, the idea of doing the four episodes did not have an appeal for me. I thought there was a good chance that we would do the movie, but gradually, it was like sand. It washed away. I'd still love to do one."

Because it was well known that Milch had intended at least four seasons and only got three, *Deadwood* is looked on as the great uncompleted masterpiece of this period, but I've never quite seen it in that way. The third season leaves some dangling threads (Langrishe and the theater company never amounted to much, for instance), but it goes a long way towards completing the story of both the season and the series. George Hearst's victory over the forces arrayed against him is absolute, even as the camp itself holds its first elections, which we'd been told repeatedly were the most crucial step on the road to annexation. The community is completed, capitalism wins all the money but doesn't crush all the spirits, and we're left with the perfect closing image: Al Swearengen on his knees, scrubbing away the blood of a whore he murdered to appease Hearst, assuring Johnny that the girl didn't suffer much. As Johnny leaves the room, Al mutters, "Wants me to tell him something pretty," and returns to the blood—the symbol of one more lie agreed upon on in the history of this violent place, and of the human cost of wealth, respectability and civilization.

The end.

I had always viewed the rightness of that final scene as an accident—Milch concluding the series without realizing it. But when I interviewed him following the abrupt end(*) of the horse-racing drama *Luck*, he admitted that he had seen the cancellation writing on the wall, and that Swearengen's final line "was as close as I felt I could come to a concluding speech."

(*) Luck started as Milch's dream project and ended as a nightmare. He finally got to dramatize the racetrack world he so adored, but got aced out of his own show to a degree by director/producer Michael Mann, who had enough power to override Milch's usual pattern of last-minute rewrites. Perhaps because Milch wasn't working via his usual process, the series was just starting to find its creative footing at the end of the first season—only to see the plug pulled early in second-season filming after the nightmare of multiple horses dying during production.

Deadwood had always tried to balance a belief in the fundamental decency and generosity of people with a more pessimistic, *Wire*-esque view of the institutions these people strived to be a part of. By closing the show on that despairing note, Milch feels he didn't get to more properly balance the themes.

"I think that there comes a fallen time, and then that time must again be reclaimed," he says. "And we didn't get to that. There is a time when the Hearsts of the world will dominate, but I don't feel that's necessarily the end of the story. That's why I always wanted to do two more movies about Deadwood. They beat him. There was a legal case against him and they beat him for dirtying the water. But there was an entropic process that was operating there where the show was winding down a little bit, and that's how he came to have this tendency to some extent."

But if the story didn't end the way anyone would have wanted it to, those three seasons represented the best work that Milch and most of his collaborators had ever done, and a joyful work environment despite all the chaos.

"I remember, I used to get out there at 5:30 in the morning," says Milch, "and there was an owl always circling up above. I always felt he was saying, 'Well, are you gonna fool 'em today?' That's really what collaborative art can be. Everybody suddenly began to realize that with all the difficulties, what we were doing was very, very special. It was like getting great musicians to do solos. It was an awful lot of fun."

CHAPTER 5

I'm a different kind of cop...
The Shield *takes anti-heroism to the limit*

"Have you watched *The Shield* yet?" Diane Werts asked me. I told her that I hadn't, and that I wasn't even sure what *The Shield* was.

"Check the closed-circuit schedule for tonight," she said with a grin. "You're going to want to see it before FX's panel tomorrow."

This was January 2002, in a ballroom at the former Ritz-Carlton in Pasadena, one of the most frequent homes to the semi-annual Television Critics Association press tour. Diane at the time was a TV critic for *Newsday*, one of the TCA veterans who had taken me under her wing when I showed up on the tour six years earlier as a 22-year-old kid with no idea how any of it worked. So when Diane told me to watch something, I listened, and that night I parked myself in front of the TV in my room and waited for a closed-circuit screening of a show I had never heard of, on a channel I mainly watched for *Buffy* and *NYPD Blue* repeats, with no details beyond its title.

When the screening started, *The Shield* revealed itself as a cop drama, one of my favorite genres. It also featured several actors I knew and liked, including Reed Diamond from *Homicide*, CCH Pounder from *ER*, and Michael Chiklis, who had lost a lot of weight and added even more swagger since his days as *The Commish*.

But every time I began to feel comfortable with either the genre or the actors, *The Shield* threw me a curve. In the opening scene, the anti-gang strike team led by Chiklis's Vic Mackey chases down a drug dealer, beats him up—"That's for running, asshole!" barks Vic, using a bit of profanity I hadn't heard on non-pay cable TV since the early days of *NYPD Blue*—and pockets the baggie of drugs the guy had taped to his privates. Cut to Pounder and Jay Karnes as detectives Claudette Wyms and Dutch Wagenbach, standing over the body of a naked female murder victim and bantering about the size of the woman's chest; when the cops realize the woman's daughter is missing, Claudette mutters, "Oh, shit."

As the scenes rolled on, and the raw content continued, I wondered exactly how FX was going to get away with this. HBO could, but HBO didn't have advertisers to worry about offending. *NYPD Blue* had broken down some barriers about language and sex on commercial TV, but ABC had to fight a lot of battles with advertisers, the FCC and protestors, and no one else had really followed that show's example(*). Was FX, of all channels, going to take up that fight?

*(*) Post–*NYPD Blue, *you would occasionally find another broadcast show using one of George Carlin's Seven Words You Can Never Say On Television—in the* ER *episode depicting the end of Mark Greene's battle with cancer, for instance, he falls trying to get out of bed on his own and screams, "Shit!"—but* NYPD Blue *overall proved to be more of a historical anomaly than a trend-setter in that area. After Justin Timberlake accidentally revealed Janet Jackson's nipple to the*

world during the Super Bowl halftime show in 2004, the FCC started cracking down so hard on indecency that network TV content actually became tamer in many ways than it had been in the glory days of Sipowicz and Simone.

But it wasn't just the language that seemed unusually rough. Dutch and Claudette's search for the missing girl leads them to her crackhead father, who admits he sold her for drug money to a pedophile, who in turn traded her for "a girl to be named later"—"You know, like the kind of trades ball teams make?" he explains—to a fellow pedophile whose tastes went more towards a girl that age.

When the detectives get nowhere in interrogating the second pedophile, Vic is brought in to speed up the process. He enters the interrogation room, silently opens a paper sack and takes out a bottle of whiskey, a phone book, a box cutter, a cigarette lighter and other torture implements. Feeling cocky, the pedophile asks, "Your turn to play bad cop?"

"Nah," says Vic. "Good cop and bad cop left for the day. I'm a different kind of cop."

And Vic proceeds to prove this point, first by graphically offering to let the man have his way with Vic's daughter Cassidy—and acting offended when he declines the offer—and then punching him in the throat to establish in no uncertain terms who's in charge now.

TV had seen plenty of brutal interrogations before, on *NYPD Blue* and also on '70s shows like *Starsky & Hutch*, but never before had there been the suggestion that the cop asking the questions was every bit as sick, twisted and possibly evil as the criminal giving the answers. And even then, it wasn't clear how much *The Shield* was hedging its bets. Vic was corrupt, but he was also the one brought in to save the little girl, and the series seemed to be setting up an ongoing, *Wiseguy*-style storyline in which Diamond's Terry Crowley goes undercover in the strike team to get the goods on Vic. Vic might be a bad guy, but we were being presented with a good guy who would have the opportunity to take him down.

So as the pilot climaxed with the strike team prepared to raid the home of another drug dealer, I felt I had finally figured *The Shield* out. FX was aping bits of both *NYPD Blue* and *The Sopranos*, but ultimately we would get a classic hero-vs.-villain storyline.

Then Vic shot Terry in the face.

And whatever expectations I had for the show, for FX, or for what could be done on television outside the protected precincts of HBO died right along with him.

The Shield couldn't have existed without *The Sopranos*. Everyone involved in its unlikely origin story—including creator Shawn Ryan and FX executives Peter Liguori and Kevin Reilly—have honored and would continue to honor the debt Vic owed to Tony Soprano. But in proving that you could do an HBO-style show away from HBO, *The Shield* was one of the most important series of the revolution.

The Sopranos, The Wire, Six Feet Under, and *Deadwood* supported HBO's slogan of the era: "It's not TV. It's HBO." Great as some turn-of-the-century network dramas were (say, *The West Wing*), there was a clear demarcation between them and what was happening on HBO, and one that went far deeper than nudity and foul language. There hadn't been television drama like this before, and you couldn't find it elsewhere.

But HBO didn't keep its "art-house theater of television" monopoly for long. The revolution eventually spread far and wide, starting with an obscure cable channel suffering from what seemed like a perpetual identity crisis.

FX had launched in 1994 under the tagline "TV Made Fresh Daily." At the time, it mixed repeats of old shows like *Batman* (the only reason I knew it existed at first) with a bunch of laid-back daytime shows where people talked about pets, collectibles, or why Tom Bergeron—co-host, along with Laurie Hibbard and a scruffy-looking puppet named Bob, of the channel's first flagship series, *Breakfast Time*—was just so gosh-darned affable. Besides providing early work for Bergeron and Jeff Probst, the shows of that period were most notable for inviting viewers to participate via this crazy newfangled thing called the World Wide Web.

But the identity a cable channel starts off with is only occasionally the one it finds success with. Once upon a time, TLC stood for The Learning Channel; then came *Trading Spaces*, and after that, Kate Gosselin. A&E began life as a place for highbrow arts and entertainment programming; now it's known for *Hoarders*. While ideally you start with a brand and find shows to match it, more often than not cable channels seem to stumble upon hits and then reshape their brand, and the rest of the lineup, to fit them.

The studio shows were modestly rated at best, and their audiences were largely female. When FX's parent company News Corp. signed a series of sports rights deals that gave them more programming than they had room for on either the Fox broadcast network or Fox Sports Net, it was decided that FX would handle some of that overflow, and would need different, more male-skewing programming to provide the best possible lead-in for baseball, football and, eventually, NASCAR.

Exit "TV Made Fresh Daily," enter "FX: Fox Gone Cable," an era where the non-sporting hours on the schedule were dominated by repeats of programming from the Fox network and Fox's TV studio, 20th Television. If you wanted to watch *M*A*S*H* at 3 in the afternoon, or revisit the early days of *NYPD Blue* and *The X-Files*, FX was the place to go.

In 1998, Peter Liguori took over FX with a mandate to create original programming that would also be compatible with the sporting events, while attracting more attention than what FX was getting from its drama repeats. There were a lot of failed experiments over the next few years, from a variety show with Penn and Teller to a talk/quiz show called *The Test*, hosted by Jillian Barberie.

The only real success of that initial wave of Liguori shows was 2000's *Son of the Beach*, a *Police Squad!*–style parody of *Baywatch* created by and starring the very pasty, very middle-aged Tim Stack as the world's coolest lifeguard, Notch Johnson. It was an often funny, always raunchy comedy, but more important to its fortunes than its quality was its producer: Howard Stern. Stern shills unapologetically for his own projects, and he talked about this one constantly on his radio show; this even helped FX finally get a spot on Manhattan's Time Warner Cable after years of being shut out of the city where all the "TV Made Fresh Daily" shows had been produced.

Liguori brought in a new president of entertainment, Kevin Reilly, a former development executive who had been involved in the early stages of *Law & Order*, *Homicide*, *ER*, and even *The Sopranos*. The two men struggled to distinguish FX while doing good work, and recognized that even if they could produce a broadcast-network-quality show, they would still be everyone's seventh or eighth choice at best in any given time slot. Liguori had once worked at HBO, Reilly at NBC, and they began to realize they could find some kind of middle ground, content-wise, between the visibility of one network and the permissiveness and artistic ambitions of the other.

They could, if they found the right show, become the HBO of basic cable.

And the right show took a very unlikely route that began with Don Johnson cruising the streets of San Francisco in a yellow Barracuda and ended with Vic murdering Terry.

The Shield came about almost by accident. It was never intended to be a series, simply a writing exercise by a young producer named Shawn Ryan who was looking to branch out.

Ryan's first big break in television was as a staff writer on *Nash Bridges*, a breezy, formulaic CBS cop drama starring Cheech Marin and a post–*Miami Vice* Don Johnson. *Nash Bridges* was run by TV vet Carlton Cuse (we'll get back to him in the next chapter), and he taught Ryan the fundamentals of episodic television writing: how to transition between your A-, B-, and C-stories, for instance, or when you could get away with inserting humor into a serious moment and when you couldn't.

With that education completed, Ryan was interested in doing something more ambitious. He got a development deal at Fox Television Studios, a News Corp. company that mainly produced sitcoms, and the plan was for him to create a half-hour comedy. He spent eight frustrating months unsuccessfully trying to build shows around ideas he heard one of the networks might be interested in. Then, in the spring of 2000, a studio executive named Lisa Berger asked Ryan the million-dollar question:

"What would you like to write?"

Ryan went home and thought very seriously about his answer, and about some of the frustrations he had on *Nash*, where the writers' first, second, and third priorities was to make Don Johnson look good. ("The only mistakes he could make," Ryan recalls, "would be that he could never quite make it work out with whatever beautiful woman he was bedding that week.") *Nash* filmed in San Francisco, and Ryan had gone on many ride-alongs with the SFPD, often seeing incidents that would be perfect fodder for a cop show—just not the cop show he was working on. In the '90s, Ryan had loved *NYPD Blue* and *Homicide*; the latter was gone, and the former was far from its glory days.

"There wasn't really a cop show on the air that was fresh and new and would excite me," Ryan says today. "So I asked myself, what would I want to watch? And I never gave a thought that it would get made."

Because of that belief that this was just a creative exercise, Ryan held nothing back. Inspired in part by the LAPD's Rampart scandal of the late 1990s, he wrote a script about a revered, highly decorated cop who was as big a crook as any gang-banger he locked up, and who in the closing moments would execute the innocent cop who had been sent undercover to investigate him.

Ryan turned it in to the execs at Fox Television, got a few compliments (and fewer script notes), and assumed that was that. But even though these weren't people specializing in drama, they knew they had something interesting here, so they decided to send the script around town—including to their corporate partners at FX, whom they had heard were looking for something with a hard edge.

To Ryan's surprise, Reilly called him up and said that not only did they want to make what was then called *The Barn* as a pilot, but they wanted Ryan to executive-produce it. Ryan had jumped from *Nash Bridges* to the *Buffy the Vampire Slayer* spin-off *Angel,* and after securing permission to get out of his contract from bosses David Greenwalt(*) and Joss Whedon, he began assembling a cast and crew to make his creative-writing exercise a reality.

(*) As Ryan recalls it, the first conversation with Greenwalt didn't go as he expected, with Greenwalt bluntly telling him they weren't sure if they wanted to bring him back for another season, because his scripts to that point had been uneven at best. So Greenwalt gave his blessing, and Ryan turned in his final Angel script: "Belonging," which kicked off a season-ending arc involving the home dimension of demonic karaoke host Lorne (it makes sense if you watched Angel, people; trust me). It was so well-received by the staff that Greenwalt actually got mad that he had let Ryan go, telling him, "You're lucky you asked before you turned this in."

Ryan knew how to write a TV show, but not the nuts and bolts of producing it, week in and week out. So he recruited Scott Brazil(*), who had directed several *Nash Bridges* episodes, and more importantly had spent years as a director and producer on *Hill Street Blues*. They hired Clark Johnson—who had played Reed Diamond's partner on *Homicide*, and had been doing interesting work behind the camera for several years(**)—to direct the pilot, and it was decided that given both the lean budget and the raw subject matter, the best approach would be a kind of guerilla filmmaking, with lots of hand-held cameras and the kind of seedy Los Angeles locations that hadn't been seen in hundreds of previous movies and TV shows before.

(*) Brazil died midway through the series' run of respiratory complications from ALS.

(**) In the same period, he directed the pilot of The Wire, *and would return to both shows for their respective finales.*

An even bigger risk than the visual style was the man they chose to play Victor Samuel Mackey.

A 23-year-old Chiklis had become briefly famous after getting cast as John Belushi in the biopic *Wired*. The movie flopped, but it led to some TV work, including an offer to play Tony Scali, the hero of Stephen J. Cannell's *The Commish*. Chiklis was in his twenties, Scali in his forties, but Chiklis thought it would be an exciting acting exercise to put on some weight and play older. What he didn't realize until the show had been around for a few years was that, as he put it to me years later, "You could find yourself at the end of your run and people all over America, particularly in Hollywood, believe you're a fat 50-year-old guy."

He was typecast as that middle-aged fat guy when *The Commish* ended, playing Curly in a made-for-TV movie about the Three Stooges, and the stay-at-home dad hero of the witless sitcom *Daddio*. He had done one *Commish* reunion movie to pay some bills, but when he was offered another, "I knew that if I did it, my career would be over. My chance to do any more meaningful work, to show that I could do other things, would be gone."

His wife pushed him to instead go to the gym and not take a job until it was one he wanted. So Chiklis started exercising, dropped more than 50 pounds from his *Commish* weight, and surprised everyone in the room when he went in to audition for Vic Mackey.

The audition almost didn't happen. As Reilly says, Chiklis's representatives wanted an offer without sending him in to read first.

"You have to remember," Reilly explains, "now everybody thinks of cable as a place to go do Tiffany series, but we broke the ground on that. This was going to FX—a network that nobody had ever heard of, we didn't have ratings, had never produced a major original show. Michael had a career. He had done a network sitcom the year before, and was paid handsomely to do it. So this was a big move for him, and a pay cut. They were looking for me to offer it to them, and I said, 'I'm not doing it.'"

Reilly started pushing for Eric Stoltz, who was both a bigger name at the time and, as Reilly puts it, "an actor of quality." Ryan wasn't sold on Stoltz for the part, and Stoltz's representatives dragged their feet long enough for Chiklis to go against the advice of his reps and do an audition.

"I got so furious," recalls Chiklis now, "because I wanted to read for it and [his representatives] were adamant: 'You're a network television star. This is a little cable network. They don't even have any original programming. There is no way you're going to go in there and compromise yourself that way.' And I said, 'Have you read this? This role is a potentially life-changing opportunity.'"

"I said, 'I'm not going to stop him from reading,'" says Reilly, "and that's all she wrote. The audition blew us away."

Ryan had written the character with a Harrison Ford type in mind. Johnson remembered Chiklis as Curly and didn't even want to see him. Reilly still thought of him as Tony Scali. But Chiklis strutted into the audition room looking lean and mean, and nailed every beat of the script—especially the interrogation of the pedophile.

"You could see him getting worked up," Ryan told me midway through the series, "and by the time he got to that punch, he leapt out of his chair, and the casting associate who was working the camera just jumped back. He had totally scared her."

He got the job, and the rest of the cast was filled out with a mix of veterans like Pounder, unknowns like Walton Goggins (as Vic's sidekick Shane Vendrell), and Ryan's best friends Jay Karnes (as Dutch) and David Rees Snell (as strike team member Ronnie Gardocki, a role that had no dialogue in the pilot but turned out to be among the most crucial by the end of the series). They filmed the pilot, sent it to FX, and waited… and waited… and waited some more, as Liguori and Reilly chose between *The Barn* and *Dope*—a *Traffic*-esque story connecting a disparate group of people's lives to a kilo of heroin.

Dope had Jason Priestley doing his first TV series since *Beverly Hills 90210*, which in 2001 was more impressive than getting Michael Chiklis into his first TV series since *Daddio*. FX had developed *Dope* in-house, whereas *The Barn* script was an outside submission; *Dope* producers Chris Brancato and Bert Salke were friendly with Liguori, and Salke had worked for News Corp. president Peter Chernin. To Ryan's eye, the game seemed rigged in *Dope*'s favor, but instead Liguori and Reilly picked *The Barn*— which would be renamed *Rampart* and then, after the LAPD complained, *The Shield*.

"There was some debate inside the building over whether *Dope* was the more bold of the concepts," Reilly admits. "'HBO for basic cable' was our mantra from inside. If we led with a cop show, would it just feel too familiar no matter what we did? But I thought there was always room for the next great cop show. I thought that the writing of the characters and the tone of the cop show in and of itself felt unique. And then on top of it, there was an anti-hero in the lead; nobody had ever done that with a cop on television, to the extent of putting a bullet between the eyes of one of his co-workers.

"At the end of the day," he adds, "*The Shield* was just that good, and *Dope* was good but not great."

Ryan got the good news on August 30, 2001. Twelve days later, the Twin Towers fell, and there was a fear that the time was no longer right for a cop show whose central character could most charitably be called an anti-hero. But *Training Day*—starring Denzel Washington as a famous, corrupt LAPD cop with more than a passing resemblance to the Vic Mackey character—hit theaters in October and was a big enough hit to smooth over any of FX's concerns.

The only thing left was to sell the show. While FX, like HBO, didn't have to answer to the FCC, it did have to sell time to advertisers. So Liguori and the FX sales team assembled a meeting of 18 of the top media buyers in New York to screen the pilot. John Solberg, FX's longtime head of publicity, was in the back of the room, and after Vic shot Terry and the lights went up, he heard one of the media buyers turn to a colleague and say, "That may be the best show I've seen since *The Sopranos*, but can you sell products with it?" Liguori stood up and asked the audience how many of them would buy ads on *The Sopranos* if they could, and noted that FX had something very close. Solberg, thinking about the conversation he'd just overheard, groaned.

But FX sold enough ads to get the show on the air. *The Shield* debuted on Tuesday, March 12, 2002 at 10 PM, in the hallowed *NYPD Blue* time slot. (That spring, ABC was airing *NYPD* an hour earlier, so Sipowicz and Mackey didn't go head-to-head at first.) The premiere's ratings were bigger than anyone had expected: 4.8 million viewers, the most for a scripted show in the history of basic cable.

The reviews were mostly enthusiastic, if often surprised. The *New York Times*'s Caryn James called the show "a mix of daring accomplishment, obvious cop-show strategies and orchestrated envelope pushing." The *Chicago Tribune*'s Allan Johnson dubbed it "a fascinating, if sometimes uncomfortable, series." In *Newsday*, Diane Werts said that with Terry's murder, "the show suddenly becomes flat-out brilliant." Many of the write-ups invoked HBO in general and *The Sopranos* in particular.

As with the advertisers Liguori had screened the pilot for, not every critic was immediately happy with the show. Several objected to what they perceived as the glorification of Vic Mackey. Salon.com, for instance, dubbed it "a cop show George Bush could love."

Ryan always said he wanted to let the viewers make up their own minds about Vic, who could rescue a kidnapped girl but also murder a fellow cop, or who could dive into a swimming pool to save a drowning baby but extort and enable drug dealers in order to build up his "retirement fund." And it was that ambivalent attitude, and the lack of a dominant good-guy figure to match him— Terry died in the pilot, Captain Aceveda was always portrayed as a politician first and a cop second, Claudette mostly left Vic alone to work cases, and Dutch was often the butt of jokes—that was among the show's boldest (and, to some viewers, most confounding) moves.

The Sopranos had invited its audience to empathize with a character who was traditionally the villain. *The Shield*, on the other hand, took a classically sympathetic figure and made him into someone you could view as a hero, a monster, or something in between. The idea of the cop who doesn't follow the letter of the law in his pursuit of justice (see: Dirty Harry Callahan, Martin Riggs, and Andy Sipowicz, to name three) was so familiar that it was almost shocking to see it pushed as far as *The Shield* did. It took the cliché and showed it for what it probably was. While there are surely many police officers who bend small rules without breaking the big ones, it's not hard to imagine a Dirty Harry beginning to believe too deeply in his own legend.

The September after *The Shield* premiered, Chiklis won the Emmy for best actor in a drama series. Though it happened in a year when James Gandolfini wasn't eligible(*), Chiklis's win, along with the reviews and the ratings, validated Liguori and Reilly's plan to apply the HBO formula to basic cable. They had broken down a barrier, much the same way that Vic famously crashed through a wooden fence while chasing a suspect in the first-season finale, and proved that HBO didn't have exclusive rights to this kind of show.

(*) Even without Gandolfini in the running (The Sopranos had been off the air during the eligibility period), Chiklis still beat Martin Sheen, Kiefer Sutherland, and the two leads from Six Feet Under. That's an impressive win for anyone, and especially for someone who thought his career was over only a few years earlier. But where the Emmys are usually driven by complacency—if you've been nominated in a category before, and especially if you've already won it, it's a safe bet you will keep being nominated for years—Chiklis received only one nomination for the rest of the show's run, and the TV Academy largely ignored The Shield after that. It felt as if the win prompted many more voters to watch the show, and when they actually saw a few episodes, they were so horrified that they tried to pretend like Chiklis's win had never happened. Glenn Close got nominated for her work in the fourth season, and odds are usually in favor of any movie star working in TV, yet Close somehow lost to Patricia Arquette from Medium. It took Close transitioning to a classier FX show, Damages, before she finally took home the hardware.

And having proved that it could be done, FX kept right on doing it, introducing one or two new dramas each year that pushed the boundaries of graphic content and ambiguous morality: *Nip/Tuck*, about the big fantasies and ugly realities of the plastic-surgery industry; *Rescue Me*, about a New York firefighter haunted by memories of 9/11; and *Sons of Anarchy*, a mash-up of *Hamlet* and motorcycle-club melodrama from one of Shawn Ryan's top *Shield* lieutenants, Kurt Sutter, to name just three of the most successful products of post-*Shield* FX. Not every experiment worked; Iraq war drama *Over There* only lasted a season, for instance, and even Ryan failed—commercially, but definitely not creatively—when he returned to the channel in 2010 with the marvelous but under-watched private eye drama *Terriers*. But enough of them worked to keep the machine humming along.

And other networks quickly followed FX in trying to make their own HBO-esque dramas. The season after *The Shield* debuted, NBC tried out a pair of ambitious new series: *Boomtown*, an L.A. crime *noir* in which every story was told from multiple angles, often out of sequence; and *Kingpin*, the violent saga of a Mexican drug lord. Neither lasted long, but both came from writers with HBO on their resumes (Graham Yost from *Band of Brothers* and David Mills from *The Corner*), and at a time when NBC chairman Bob Wright was publicly questioning how the broadcast networks should respond to HBO.

When HBO was first making its splash with *The Sopranos* and *Sex and the City*, fellow pay cable channel Showtime was offering up its own edgy content, but with programs designed to target specific minority groups, like *Resurrection Blvd.*, *Soul Food*, and *Queer as Folk*. In the years following *The Shield*, Showtime would go stronger at its rival, including a mob drama of its own (*Brotherhood*), a splashy terrorism thriller (*Sleeper Cell*), a well-oiled machine designed to produce Emmy-winning dramedies like *United States of Tara* and *Nurse Jackie*, and the channel's signature series *Dexter*, in which the hero is a serial killer we like because he only targets *other* killers.

Liguori and Reilly's success in the News Corp. minor leagues, meanwhile, inevitably earned them bigger jobs on bigger stages, where they tried to apply the FX formula when they could. Reilly returned to NBC as president of entertainment and was one of the few creative bright spots in a dark, dark period for that network; among the shows he green-lit was *Friday Night Lights*, a high-school-football drama whose frankness about sex, race, class, teen drinking, and more put it very much in the cable mode. Liguori took over the FOX network, and hired Reilly as entertainment president after NBC fired him. FOX under Reilly's watch was by and large more creatively adventurous than the other broadcast networks, and one show in particular, 2010's *Lone Star*—about a Texas con artist torn between two lives (and women)—was explicitly viewed by its creator, Kyle Killen, as an experiment to see whether a drama with a cable-style anti-hero could work on the home of *American Idol*(*).

(*) Spoiler: It didn't. Lone Star was canceled after only two episodes had aired, and its premiere was so low-rated that few would have blamed FOX for pulling the plug after only one week.

The Shield premiered a few months before USA debuted *Monk*, a much more traditional mystery show starring Tony Shalhoub as a police consultant with a laundry list of phobias. That was an even bigger hit for USA than *The Shield* was for FX; between them, the two shows made it clear there was an appetite for original scripted programming on basic cable, which various cable networks then rushed to feed. Most of those shows (*Burn Notice, The Closer, Army Wives*) were closer to *Monk* than to *The Shield*, but because so many of them were being made, there was room for every channel to experiment, whether it was Sci Fi with *Battlestar Galactica* or TNT with the quiet, character-driven *Men of a Certain Age*. And eventually AMC made a reputation for itself as something other than the second-best classic movie channel with a pair of shows that would have fit comfortably at either HBO or FX: *Mad Men*, and *Breaking Bad* (which was originally developed at FX).

John Landgraf, who succeeded Reilly as FX's entertainment president and has kept the drama pipeline open (while also moving the channel into the comedy business), says of *The Shield*, *Nip/Tuck*, and *Rescue Me*, "If FX hadn't had the great fortune to put three very commercially and creatively successful shows in a row on the air, then the whole of the business could have gone away. The fact that we achieved so much success on three successive shows caused this rush in the marketplace. Not only did Turner then rush into the market—following both us and USA—but then A&E and others tried to get in. And AMC will tell you directly that they just took a page from our playbook and chased after that very same model."

And while *The Shield* was inspiring big changes all over the dial, Shawn Ryan and company were busy just making the show itself, and keeping the quality as high as possible. Though there were a handful of episodes in the seven-season run that didn't work (notably "Co-Pilot," a prequel episode attempting to squeeze too much unseen history into an hour), *The Shield* proved one of the most consistent of all the revolutionary dramas. Fans may prefer one season to another, but there isn't a season or major story arc that sticks out like a sore thumb as with nearly every other great millennial. (*The Sopranos'* fourth season, for instance, had great individual moments and episodes—Ralphie's death, Tony and Carmela's separation—but never really cohered the way the others did.)

Somewhat improbably, it was Ryan's *Nash Bridges* education that kept *The Shield* so great for so long. Because it had a murderous, drug-dealing cop as its protagonist, *The Shield* would never be mistaken for a conventional police drama—and yet many *Shield* episodes shared a formula (if not a need to flatter the leading man's ego) with the ultra-conventional *Nash*.

"The show is pretty similar structure-wise to *Nash Bridges*," Ryan told me after I had watched the series finale. "The execution may be different, but on *Nash*, I got very good at breaking stories and balancing, 'Nash is over here in the A story, Joe is in the B, and this is how they intersect.' I always loved that way of storytelling. I felt like the strike-team stories had the impact they had because they weren't taking up an hour of story with them. I see a lot of procedural stories on TV where they have the one case they're trying to solve for the hour, and there are always scenes that drag, which you need to fill out an hour of television but aren't interesting. We always looked at it as, what's the fewest number of beats we need to tell the story?"

So by mixing together stories about Vic's criminal activities, whatever the strike team's actual case was that week, the slightly more conventional (if usually kinky) murders Dutch and Claudette were trying to solve, incidents involving beat cops Dani and Julien, Aceveda's political ambitions, and more, *The Shield* never had to dwell on any one plot more than was absolutely necessary. Inevitably, one or more of the standalone stories would wind up complicating whatever Vic and Shane were up to at the moment, and the writers and actors put in the time to make the supporting characters feel like more than just Vic's foils.

Where *The Sopranos* and *The Wire* got to take advantage of HBO's lack of commercials by telling denser stories at a more measured pace, Ryan found a way to turn the FX ad breaks into a plus. Tradition in commercial dramatic television dictates that you want the strongest scene possible leading into the commercials, so that viewers will come back when the ads are over. (Or, even better, so they won't change the channel at all to avoid the risk of missing what comes next.) But where most shows build to those act breaks, Ryan instructed his writers to treat every single scene as a potential act break. The goal initially was to give him license to edit each episode in whatever order he liked best, but in doing it that way, everyone realized that they were giving the show a relentless pace and tone. You didn't so much watch *The Shield* as get beat up by it for an hour before it went off to grab a few beers and find a pimp to hassle.

In terms of language, the show never really pushed beyond what had been in the pilot(*), but Dutch and Claudette's pedophile case in that episode would prove fairly mild compared to what came later. Among other particularly nasty, graphic stories and images, Vic branded the face of a gang leader against a hot electric stove, Dutch strangled a stray cat to better understand the mind of a serial killer, Aceveda was raped by two gangbangers, and writer Kurt Sutter—whom Ryan would jokingly credit/blame for the show's most twisted material—spent several episodes playing an Armenian hitman who chopped off his victims' feet to satisfy a fetish. The cast was game for nearly all of it, and after a few episodes, Chiklis began calling out, "*The Shield*: It's so wrong!" as a catchphrase whenever they were filming something particularly vile.

(*) Again, basic cable channels aren't governed by the FCC, but they do have deals with their advertisers—and in some cases with the cable companies that carry them—that leave certain words off the table. So Claudette could say "shit," but no one could ever say "fuck." Every now and then, Ryan would try to get special dispensation—two of Vic's kids were diagnosed as autistic over the course of the series, and in one episode, Ryan wanted Vic's wife Corrine (played by Ryan's wife Cathy) to vent her frustration by screaming, "Fucking autism!"— with no success. That barrier remains in place throughout basic cable,

though AMC executives have on occasion allowed both Breaking Bad *and* Mad Men *to have characters drop an F-bomb where you can clearly read their lips, but where the sound drops out. As* Breaking Bad *creator Vince Gilligan once told me, writers try to be as creative as possible in their use of language, but every now and then you have a circumstance where only the one word will do.*

The goal for any of those storylines was never pure attention seeking, but Ryan was always worried about viewers feeling like they had seen something before—whether on another cop show or on *The Shield* itself. There's a fairly steady narrative progression in the first three seasons, as Vic eludes arrest for Terry's murder and slowly builds the retirement fund, then as the strike team attempts to rob a train carrying a shipment of money from the Armenian mob, and then as guilt, paranoia, and the Armenian mob's understandable desire to get its money back turn the members of the strike team against each other.

But after Lem, the big-hearted strike-team member played by Kenneth Johnson, burned up most of the money-train cash in a furnace at the end of the third season, Ryan began to fear that viewers had become too used to the show. So for the fourth season, he recruited Glenn Close to join the cast for a season as the new district commander. It's become commonplace now for established movie stars of that level to do long guest arcs on cable dramas— or in the case of Close (who segued from *The Shield* to *Damages*), Holly Hunter on *Saving Grace*, and Laura Linney on *The Big C*, to star in their own TV series—but at the time, it was a huge deal. Even more than Chiklis's Emmy, Close's presence gave *The Shield* credibility, and Ryan says it also forced the writers "to think even more about character, and more about writing something that's about great work rather than shock value."

As Close's Captain Rawling exited the series, Forest Whitaker entered it as Internal Affairs cop Jon Kavanaugh, the series' first legitimate (if obsessive) threat to Vic's power and freedom. Whitaker's presence shook up the series, as the stories Kavanaugh generated forced several characters—and actors—to seriously step up their games. Kevin Reilly had asked Ryan to fire Walton Goggins after the pilot was filmed; Ryan argued successfully for his guy, and by the time Season 5 ended with a tearful Shane killing Lem with a grenade to keep Kavanaugh from breaking him, Goggins had more than justified his boss's faith. As a result, the final two seasons didn't need a Very Special Guest Star: with Goggins now playing at Chiklis's level, there was no conflict the show could create that would be bigger, or hit harder, than Vic vs. Shane, mentor against protégé, brother against brother.

Because the series had built for years to this showdown—it hadn't removed Shane early, in the way that, say, *The Sopranos* had bumped off Tony's most interesting nemeses long before the end—and because it had managed to stay so consistent throughout its run, *The Shield* is not only lacking a sore-thumb season; it's the only one of the great millennial dramas whose last season many fans would be likely to name as the show's best.

Wire fans by and large didn't like the Season 5 newspaper and fake serial killer plots. Many *Sopranos* fans cringe if you mention Vito in New Hampshire or Christopher's heroin problem. The most charitable thing a *Deadwood* fan would say about Season 3's theater-company scenes is that they were setting things up for the fourth season we never got. But ask a *Shield* fan about that final season—about Vic and Shane maneuvering to kill each other, Shane turning fugitive, Vic figuring out a way to get immunity for *everything* he ever did (and almost cheerfully confessing(*) all his past sins to his horrified new federal boss), Shane murdering his son and pregnant wife before committing suicide, and then Vic alone in an ill-fitting suit in a paper-pushing job, having lost and/ or betrayed everyone he ever cared about—and chances are they'll say that what ultimately made *The Shield* great was that it ended great.

(*) There's this incredible moment in the series' penultimate episode where the camera just sits on Chiklis's face as Vic prepares himself to confess. It's only about 40 seconds, but in TV time—and particularly on a TV show that had always moved at such an unyielding pace—it feels like an eternity. Both that episode and the series finale take advantage of our familiarity with the series' rhythms to pause occasionally (on Vic studying crime-scene photos of Shane's dead family, or Vic wrapping up that first day in the new job), and force us to watch the ugly, conflicted emotions washing over Vic's face as he realizes he has destroyed or chased away everyone he's ever loved.

The Shield, like the FX brand it reinvented, was always designed as a cross between HBO and broadcast TV, between Tony Soprano and Andy Sipowicz. So it's fitting (if coincidental, according to Ryan), that the final scene of *The Shield* also involves a blackout, as the lights in Vic's new office turn off automatically at night, but that the ending ultimately isn't as inscrutable as what does or doesn't happen to Tony in that diner. The lights go out, but we still see Vic, deep in thought over all he's lost, before he smirks, picks up his giant off-duty gun, and heads out into the night. We don't know where he's going, whether he'll ever be able to rebuild even a shred of his reputation or find his wife and kids (who have gone into witness protection to get away from him); nor do we know how much blame Vic ultimately accepts for everything that's happened to him and those around him. But we know he's out there, alive and free, and that he's spent seven seasons escaping one seemingly fatal trap after another.

When the lights went out in *The Sopranos* finale, we were left wondering exactly what just happened. When the same thing happened at the end of *The Shield*, we were only left wondering what might happen next.

CHAPTER 6

Do you want to know a secret?...
The perfect storm of **Lost**

The story of *Lost* makes no sense.

And by that I don't mean the story on the show—though this is the point where you can feel free to insert jokes about the numbers, the outrigger shootout, or the reasons why Walt was "special"—but the story of how *Lost* itself got made.

The creation of *Lost* defies nearly everything we know about how successful television shows—or great ones—are made. The idea for *Lost* came not from a writer, but a network executive. The first writer on the project got fired. The replacement creative team had a fraction of the usual time to write, cast, and produce a pilot episode. The executive who had championed the show was himself fired before it ever aired. One of the two creators all but quit the moment the pilot was finished. Nearly every creative decision at the start of the show was made under the assumption that it would never succeed. Everyone believed it was too weird, too dense, too unusual to work. And it may have been. But it worked, anyway.

Lost, a show thrown together in a rush and snakebit by top-level turnover, was an enormous hit right from the start (it's the highest rated of any series discussed in this book). It was among the most thrilling, surprising, memorable dramas in the history of American network television, and at its best could go toe-to-toe with much of what was happening on cable during this period.

And more than any other classic of the era, its success was a long shot paying off big. *Lost* as we know it was made in the only way it could have been made, and it arrived at the only time when it could have succeeded.

In the summer of 2003, Lloyd Braun was in the middle of a rocky tenure as chairman of ABC Entertainment. A few years earlier, ABC had geared its entire primetime schedule around the hit game show *Who Wants to Be a Millionaire*, in the process making it impossible to grow new scripted hits; the *Millionaire* phenomenon inevitably fizzled, and the network was still recovering.

On vacation with his family in Hawaii, Braun watched his network's broadcast of the Tom Hanks movie *Cast Away*, then went down to the beach to watch the sunset and meet up with his wife and kids. As he waited, he began pondering the idea of doing *Cast Away* as a TV show, but couldn't figure out how to make it work with only one actor and one volleyball.

"And then the notion of *Survivor* popped into my head," recalls Braun. "I don't know why. And I put it all together: What if there was a plane that crashed and a dozen people survived, and nobody knew each other. Your past was almost irrelevant. You could reinvent who you were. You had to figure out—how do you survive? What do you use for shelter, for water? Is it like *Lord of the Flies*? How do we get off the island, how do you get home? And I start to get very excited about the idea, and I start thinking about the title *Lost*."

Braun had liked the name ever since he saw it attached to a

short-lived NBC reality show, and kept it filed away in his head, waiting for the right idea to pair it with. Now, he had that idea—and not much more.

He returned to the mainland and headed to an ABC corporate retreat, where executives had been instructed to pitch one series idea. Braun had another one all ready to go, but as he sat there waiting for his turn, "I was thinking of the original idea and thought it was lame. So I said, 'To hell with this, I'll pitch *Lost*,' knowing it was probably too high-concept for the room. And I did pitch it, and it was dead silent after I pitched it."

The only executive who showed any interest was Braun's head of drama development, Thom Sherman, and the two resolved to make it "our little baby," as Braun puts it, for that development season. Others were aware of it, but no one understood why their bosses were so obsessed with it.

Sherman hired a writer named Jeffrey Lieber, and as Lieber worked, Braun became infamous around the ABC offices for hovering over the idea's progress: "All year long, it's starting to become a running joke: All I'm asking about is this project."

Braun got a pile of pilot scripts from that year's development batch around Christmas, and quickly thumbed through looking for Lieber's. He found the first danger sign on the cover page: Lieber had changed the title to *Nowhere*. As for the script itself, Braun's gentle in saying that it "did not live up to my expectations, and I felt, in fact, fell prey to many of the concerns that many people had when they first heard the idea. I was very disappointed."

Given how late they were into the development season (which typically takes 8 or 9 months from summer to early spring), Sherman suggested they shelve the idea and try again next year.

"I said, 'Thom, there's no next year for us,'" says Braun, who knew the kind of thin ice he was on thanks to the network's recent performance. "At that point, it was clear to me that I didn't think any of us were going to be surviving. This was the time to take a shot at a show like this."

Lieber was out(*), and Braun turned to the one writer he suspected could do something with this on such short notice: J.J. Abrams.

(*) The Writers Guild of America later ruled that Lieber's work on the original script merited him a co-creator credit. In a 2007 Chicago Magazine feature, Lieber said his royalties from that credit were netting him in the "low six figures" annually.

Abrams had come to ABC two years earlier with *Alias*, an addictive spy drama starring a young Jennifer Garner. ABC thought so much of the show, and Abrams, that *Alias* had been chosen to air after the Super Bowl the season before.

Abrams was smart. Abrams was creative. Abrams was also very, very busy, in part because of Lloyd Braun. Earlier in that same development season, Braun had asked Abrams, as a personal favor, to develop another pilot, a bounty hunter drama called *The Catch*. When Braun approached him about doing a *different* pilot as a favor in the same season—while also dry-docking *The Catch*, after he'd spent a lot of time on it—Abrams laughed at the request, but reluctantly agreed to think on Braun's idea overnight.

"He comes in the next day and says, 'I hate you,'" Braun recalls. "'Well, why?' 'Because I haven't been able to stop thinking about this thing all night.'"

Abrams told Braun that there wasn't quite enough there for a series, but suggested that "The island has to be a character in the show, and something's wrong with the island." Braun agreed, so long as Abrams promised to keep things in the realm of "scientific fact" and have an explanation for everything.

Even with *The Catch* delayed until the next season, Abrams was still too busy to handle Braun's passion project on his own, especially starting in January at a time when other pilots were already beginning to cast and film. Enter Damon Lindelof, a young writer who wanted nothing more than to get a job on *Alias* and had been, as he puts it, "stalking" ABC drama executive Heather Kadin to help him make it happen.

Kadin called Lindelof up with a "good news, bad news" proposition: she had a way for him to finally meet Abrams, but it was in the context of a project few executives at ABC seemed to understand or believe in. Lindelof says Kadin told him, "'Impress J.J. at the meeting, and you will get a job on *Alias*. Forget about this pilot.'"

But in order to impress J.J., Lindelof needed some good ideas for the pilot. He read Lieber's script and realized, "The biggest problem with the show was the audience would want the characters to get off the island. How do we defuse that desire?" He wanted to fill the cast with characters who would have no interest in going back to their old lives, and further sate the audience's appetite for mainland stories by featuring flashbacks to those old lives in each episode.

Lindelof brought those two ideas to Abrams, who shared his own thoughts on making the island a character. Abrams proposed, for instance, that the castaways would discover a hatch in the middle of the jungle, spend the whole first season trying to get it open, and that the hatch in turn would reveal more about the island in future seasons.

The ideas, and the men proposing them, meshed well together.

Abrams had been getting grief from ABC over *Alias* and its focus on the works of a Da Vinci–like figure named Rambaldi—"This was the climate at the time," recalls Lindelof. "Serialization was bad, and mythological storytelling was worse"—but Lindelof also loved the Rambaldi storylines, and they decided to steer right into this particular skid.

"J.J.'s whole attitude was not defiant," Lindelof says. "It was the idea that we had the luxury of pitching them exactly the show that we wanted to make, and if they didn't want to do it, so what? Every other pilot was already cast—deep into casting. We have a week to basically cook the most ambitious, expensive television show ever, and if they want to make it, great. And if not, no worries."

There was no time to write a full script, so Braun asked them to write a detailed outline that he would use to decide whether to go forward. He read it on a Saturday morning on the way to the home of his friend Marc Gurvitz, a veteran talent manager, and decided, "This is one of the best shows I have ever read. I walk into Marc's house having just read it, and I go, 'Marc, you see this thing? *ER.*' And I throw it down on the table."

Lost was a go, on an absurdly accelerated schedule.

"We were shooting this thing in the end of March," says Braun, "and I didn't even call J.J. until January. This whole thing was done in 6-8 weeks. Never ever have I heard of anything like it in the TV business."

By this time, most of the usual suspects from the casting pool had already committed to other pilots. This turned to the producers' advantage, as they decided to fill the seats on Oceanic Flight 815 with a collection of mostly unfamiliar—and ethnically diverse—faces: Daniel Dae Kim and Yunjin Kim as Jin and Sun, an estranged Korean couple who appeared to speak no English; Harold Perrineau and Malcolm David Kelley as Michael and Walt, an African-American construction worker and his estranged son; Naveen Andrews as Sayid Jarrah, a former member of Iraq's Republican Guard; Jorge Garcia as Hugo "Hurley" Reyes, a heavyset everydude who tended to ask the same questions the audience had; Josh Holloway as Sawyer, a charming grifter; Terry O'Quinn (fresh off a recurring *Alias* role as an FBI official) as mysterious survival expert John Locke; Dominic Monaghan as junkie musician Charlie; Emilie de Ravin as pregnant young Australian Claire; and Ian Somerhalder and Maggie Grace as spoiled rich stepsiblings Boone and Shannon. It wasn't a cast that looked like any other on television, and was one of many signals that people who tuned into *Lost* would be seeing something unique.

At the center of the pilot would be two characters: Jack Shephard, a doctor who quickly falls into a leadership role among the castaways; and Kate Austen, a young woman whose fiancé had been in the back of the plane when the fuselage split in two, and who has no idea if he's alive or dead. In the vein of Alfred Hitchcock's *Psycho* (or even the pilot of *Oz*), they planned to pull the rug out from under the audience by killing Jack midway through the first episode(*), forcing Kate to take charge. After this sudden demise, viewers would realize no one was safe. Lindelof says Steve McPherson, then the head of the ABC studio, made a convincing counter-argument that it would teach viewers not to trust the show, and the writers ultimately agreed with him.

(*) To further elevate Jack's status for the viewers, actor Michael Keaton (who was at a point in his career where starring in a TV show would seem plausible) was approached for the role, and Abrams and Lindelof planned to make the media into accomplices by asking everyone at the TV critics press tour that summer to please keep Jack's death

a secret from their readers. Once McPherson got Jack a stay of execution, Keaton had no interest in a long-term job, and Party of Five *alum Matthew Fox was cast as a younger Jack. Unknown Canadian actress Evangeline Lilly would play Kate.*

So Jack lived (his death scene would go to Oceanic 815's co-pilot), and when Abrams and Lindelof realized Kate wasn't dynamic enough, her backstory was changed to make her a fugitive from justice (the separated lovebirds angle would go to Rose and Bernard, an older couple who appeared sporadically throughout the series).

At the same time they were sketching out the cast of characters, Lindelof and Abrams were grappling with Braun's request for only "science fact." The two men were fellow travelers in the nerd community and wanted to add some of their favorite things to this show, but they also didn't want to scare away a mass audience with too much sci-fi, too soon.

Just as *X-Files* had hidden its aliens and monsters in cop show drag, *Lost* would take its time getting to the bizarre stuff. In the final version of the pilot, the smoke monster doesn't make its first appearance until midway through the first hour, and it doesn't attack anyone until the end of that hour—and even this debut is only audio (we wouldn't get a look at it until the end of the first season). By then, Lindelof and Abrams had offered viewers plenty of opportunity to get to know the central characters, to see them dealing with an extreme and yet familiar situation with the plane crash, so that by the time Smokey is heard rumbling through the jungle—"That was weird, right?" quips Charlie—it's just one element of a larger human mystery, rather than the thing that defines the show. In their talks about the hatch, they had conceived of a scientific research group known as Medusa Corp. conducting electromagnetic experiments across the island, and the hope was to keep things vaguely plausible.

As Lindelof puts it, "When we talked about the show being set in a Crichton-esque reality—nobody thinks of *Jurassic Park* as science fiction, because they ground it in actual science—we thought we were telling the truth."

That the *Lost* pilot was produced with such haste isn't apparent in the finished product. The two-hour episode (which ABC ultimately split in half and aired over two weeks) cost a reported $13 million—Braun doesn't remember the exact figure, but says, "It came in under budget"—which was a bargain for a movie, even in 2004, but one of the biggest prices ever paid for a TV pilot. Abrams had grown as a director during his time on *Felicity* and *Alias*, and all his talents as a crafter of suspense are on display throughout.

We begin with an extreme close-up of a man's eye opening, then see him lying on a jungle floor, wearing a suit, unsure of where he is and what's happened to him. A yellow Labrador trots past, and as Jack gets up, his memory begins to return. He picks up speed, racing through the bamboo until he arrives at a beach that in one direction looks like paradise, and in the other is littered with flaming airplane parts, corpses, and a group of dazed, bloody, terrified survivors. Jack sprints from person to person, trying to save as many lives as he can (though he's too late in warning one man to step away from the jet engine before it sucks him in and explodes), and by the time he can finally catch his breath at the 7-minute mark, we are completely absorbed in this adventure, this man, and the questions of how these people got here and what they'll do now.

That riveting opening sequence is no misleading tease of what was to come. There are plenty of slower, chattier moments throughout the pilot (most of them intriguing in their own right because Abrams and Lindelof had spent so much of their limited time crafting these characters), but there are several other exciting action set pieces, including Jack, Kate, and Charlie barely surviving an attack by the monster while looking for radio equipment (or, in Charlie's case, heroin) in the cockpit wreckage, or Sawyer gunning down a charging polar bear(*) that has absolutely no business on a tropical island. We close on another unsettling note, as Sayid and Shannon discover a distress signal, recorded in French, that's been playing on a loop for more than 16 years—prompting a mystified Charlie to ask the question on every viewer's mind at that moment: "Guys, *where are we?*"

(*) Initially, the writers had discussed a wild boar attack, but Abrams wanted the animal to hint at the unique properties of the island, and suggested some kind of genetically enhanced creature. Producer Sarah Caplan felt that could make viewers mistake the creature for the monster, and suggested they just pick an animal that wouldn't belong there. In Lindelof's memory, he and Abrams replied, "It should be a polar bear!" at the same moment.

The development process had been tumultuous and rushed. It had cost more than any TV pilot had before. And it was, to everyone's surprise, worth every penny and bit of stress, because it was great.

It was, unfortunately, too late to save Lloyd Braun, who was fired in April and replaced by Steve McPherson(*). This had been Braun's baby, but McPherson put *Lost* on his first schedule anyway.

(*) As a way to thank Braun and make his connection with the show permanent despite the firing, Abrams invited him to be the voice who says, "Previously, on Lost…" at the start of each episode. Braun agreed on the condition that nobody ever know, but several years later Howard Stern figured it out and publicly identified him.

Now there was another wrinkle: Abrams was stepping away

from any and all *Lost* responsibilities(*) to direct *Mission: Impossible III*. Lindelof had spent a few years writing for *Nash Bridges* and *Crossing Jordan* but had no experience running a show, so he turned to a man who did: his former *Nash* boss Carlton Cuse.

(*) Abrams later came back to co-write the third-season premiere with Lindelof, but after the pilot, all credit (and blame) goes to Lindelof and then (starting with Season 1's "All the Best Cowboys Have Daddy Issues") to Lindelof and Cuse.

Cuse had remained Lindelof's friend and mentor, and as Lindelof found himself "on the verge of a nervous breakdown" after producing the early episodes on his own, he asked Cuse to come on as co-showrunner. Lindelof showed Cuse some episodes and scripts in advance, and Cuse says, "My brain was completely activated by *Lost.*" He approached his agent to find a way out of the development deal he had recently signed with a TV studio.

"My agent said, 'Are you crazy? That show's not going to go anywhere,'" says Cuse. "I really believed it could be something. I really thought it could last. The good thing was there were not many people who did believe that at the time, so my agent got me out of my deal."

With the network in dire need of fresh, popular blood, ABC's marketing team that year decided to take an unusual approach to the new season. Where networks traditionally will spread their marketing time and money across all the new shows debuting that fall, virtually all of ABC's promotional resources went to three shows: *Lost*, the comic soap opera *Desperate Housewives*, and *Wife Swap*. Even if you weren't watching ABC that summer (and not many were), it was hard to escape the billboards, bus ads, radio plugs, and other stunts (like leaving "I'm Lost..." messages in bottles on beaches that summer) for those shows.

The promotional blitzkrieg worked. *Desperate Housewives* opened to more than 21 million viewers, and *Lost* (on September 22, 2004) to 18.6 million.

How did Lindelof respond to this instant success? "Terror, depression, anxiety attacks," he recalls. "I'm not exaggerating. Everybody who was around me at the time knows I pretty much wanted to die, and knowing that wasn't going to happen unless I took matters into my hands, I just wanted to quit. But there was literally no one to quit to."

Cuse says, "I remember [Lindelof] coming in with the ratings after the opening episode, and he looked completely miserable. He said, 'Does this mean we have to keep fucking doing this?' If you're a producer in television, this is like getting a winning lottery ticket: having a show that's not only critically acclaimed but gets big ratings. But it was daunting to have to sustain this thing."

As the show continued to be wildly popular in those early weeks, Lindelof says, "I was completely and totally creatively crippled by people saying two things: 1) 'How are they going to keep this up?' And I had no idea. 2) 'They better have really satisfying answers to all these mysteries.' And I was like, 'We have satisfying answers for all the character ones.'"

While Lindelof and Abrams were racing to finish the pilot, the studio set up a think tank of writers that included future *Lost* staffer Javier Grillo-Marxuach. Their job, he says, was "to brainstorm elements that would become the show's mythology, as well as the character backstories that would become the majority of the flashbacks for the first season."

It was in those early brainstorming sessions, often involving the show's creators, that many of the fundamental *Lost* elements were conceived. Early on, for instance, Lindelof pitched the idea of the island as what "a nexus of conflict between good and evil," Grillo-Marxuach says. (If the show wasn't a success and had to end after only one season, they would have built to a battle between the castaways and the monster.)

Abrams had pitched the idea of the hatch early on, but Lindelof was reluctant to feature it on the show at first because, as Grillo-Marxuach recalls, "Damon came up with this one hard and fast rule that he lived by for the entire first season: he would not put anything on screen that he didn't feel confident he could explain dramatically." One day, Lindelof wandered into the writers room with the idea that inside the hatch was a man who had to press a button every 108 minutes or the world would end; the other writers liked it enough that the hatch would make its first on-screen appearance in the 10th episode.

That mixture of planning and last-minute inspiration would continue to categorize much of the first season. The show's fourth episode, "Walkabout," was pitched and plotted out as a *Death of a Salesman*-esque tale of how island adventurer Locke was a sad office drone in the real world, until Lindelof decided at the last minute to throw in a twist ending revealing that Locke had been in a wheelchair in all his flashbacks, and that the island had somehow healed him. (The end of "Walkabout" would become for *Lost* what Febby Petrulio's murder in "College" was for *The Sopranos*.)

"I don't want to be elusive," says Lindelof, "because being elusive is basically admitting you were up to shenanigans, or conveys a level of dishonesty. What I will say is, I personally believe that it's hubris to plot out what the second and third and fourth seasons of a show are. You have to have a sense of where you want to go, but at the same time, you have to put your eye on the ball and write the season that you're writing."

After the first season, Lindelof and Cuse brought the writing staff to a minicamp where they tried to sketch out the mythology in greater detail. It was here, for instance, where they decided on the idea that there was a mysterious figure named Jacob who had been recruiting people to come to the island, though the name Jacob wouldn't be uttered until the third season. (It was also at this minicamp where Medusa Corporation was rechristened, by staffer Craig Wright, as the Dharma Initiative.)

"The first season of the show was like putting out an apartment fire with a garden hose," says Cuse. "We had some general ideas of what we were going to do, but we were making the show episode to episode. That first writers' minicamp was really engaging. We started figuring out the whole mythology of what was going on in the island, started talking about the Dharma Initiative, what their history was, who else was on the island. We finally had the time— we didn't have to deliver next week's episode—so we built the iceberg for the show, knowing only the top 15 percent was going to end up on the air. We constructed a whole mythological world. Obviously, we didn't have everything plotted out."

As it turned out, a deeper understanding of the mythology wasn't crucial to the first season, when Lindelof and Cuse had so much to reveal about the characters, and could get so much dramatic mileage out of showing them simply battling for survival. Locke's paralysis—and the island's ability to heal it—was the big revelation, but there were plenty of others deserving their own exclamation points: *Hurley won the lottery! Sun secretly knows English! Boone and Shannon had sex?!?!* The flashbacks flowed seamlessly into stories about the island, like Locke and Boone discovering the hatch; Michael and Jin teaming up to build a raft to get back to civilization; or Sayid encountering Danielle Rousseau, an insane

Frenchwoman who claimed to have been living on the island for years, always staying one step ahead of "the Others."

Given the environment in which that first season was made, it's remarkable that the episodes were as good, and coherent, as they were. Viewers may have preferred some characters' stories to others (I never much cared about Kate, for instance, whether on her own or in a love triangle with Jack and Sawyer), but that was a minor issue considering how deep the roster was, and how high the level of execution was for the individual stories. *Lost* had a little bit of everything—mystery, science fiction, comedy, tragedy, deep characterization—not out of an attempt to pander, but because Lindelof and Abrams had tried to cram in as many of the things they loved about popular culture as they could into one improbable pilot.

Lindelof's decision to give the characters reasons to stay on the island opened a rich vein of material about regret and redemption. The island provided a thriller format to sustain the tension, while the flashbacks functioned as tragic short stories about people whose lives hadn't turned out as planned. We saw the rise and fall of Sun and Jin's romance, as his attempts to please her domineering father wound up turning him into a cold, unlovable brute. We saw how Sawyer's name and career had been perversely inspired by the murder-suicide of his parents due to the work of another con man. We saw John Locke rail over and over about his special destiny, when instead the only time when his life wasn't horribly ordinary was when it was tragic.

The season finale, "Exodus," tied together all the major narrative strands while spotlighting the technical genius involved in making the series. Lindelof, Cuse, and director Jack Bender (who had ably continued the style Abrams established in the pilot) put together one thrilling sequence after another: the castaways gather on the beach to help Michael, Walt, Jin, and Sawyer launch the raft (accompanied by a gorgeous orchestral piece from the show's Emmy-winning composer, Michael Giacchino); Rousseau goes on an expedition to the Black Rock, a pirate ship stranded in the middle of the jungle, in search of dynamite to blow the hatch open; Jack saves Locke from the monster's clutches; and the raft encounters another boat, but just as Michael and company are ready to celebrate their rescue, the captain tells them, "We're gonna have to take the boy," and sends his men over to abduct Walt.

The three-hour episode, aired over two weeks, captured everything that was exciting, moving, and funny about *Lost*. And in its final minutes, it captured everything that could be frustrating about it, too.

The show had spent half the season teasing viewers about what could possibly be inside the hatch, and on Locke and Boone (before he became the first of the main characters to be killed off) trying to get it open. As "Exodus" built to Locke blowing the hatch with the ancient dynamite, every viewer who had speculated on this particular mystery could feel his or her pulse quickening. *At last*, we all thought, *they're going to answer this.*

Suckers!

Instead, the episode, and season, closes on the image of Locke and Jack peering into the hole they've just blown open, and the camera zooming down a deep metal shaft to reveal... nothing, save that the ladder to the surface was broken.

Lost, ladies and gentlemen! You've been a great audience! See you in the fall!

As would happen again five years later, the reaction to what happened at the very end overwhelmed nearly all talk of what had come before, whether in that episode or in the series to date. We had been promised answers, we felt. We had wanted to see what was in the damn hatch, and they had refused to show it to us.

We were not pleased(*). And Cuse and Lindelof had not antici-pated just how displeased we would be.

(*) In my review of the finale, I recalled a conversation I had had with Lindelof and Cuse at the January TV critics' press tour, where they had promised answers, but not a timetable for them. I wrote, "I realized that then, as now, they were playing a very expensive game of three-card monte, with the show's secrets as a red queen that somehow never gets turned over, no matter how long you stay at the table."

"We weren't surprised that people would be frustrated," says Lindelof. "We were surprised that people would be *angry*. There's playful frustration: 'Oh, you scamps!' And what we experienced was, 'How dare you? How dare you make us wait all this time?'

"And the reality is," he adds, "I would not change a thing. I would go through that tenfold. That summer was so amazing. I have never been through anything like that in my life. My wife and I would be out eating breakfast together, and people would be at the table next to us going, 'What do you think's in the hatch?' The fact that that would have only lasted a week versus three months; that sense of anticipation and excitement, and I was one of only ten people on the planet who knew the answer to this question, it was pretty cool."

The idea of going inside the hatch in the first season had never even occurred to Lindelof and Cuse. While some fans loved "Exo-dus" unconditionally, there was enough very vocal anger(*) over the ending that they realized they would have to significantly widen the lines of communication with their fan base.

(*) In the middle of this section of our interview, Lindelof quips, "Something tells me there's not going to be a lot of fan anger in The Wire chapter. 'Oh, the newspaper story wasn't as good as Season 4!'"

"We realized we couldn't be David Chase here," says Lindelof. "We would have to communicate with the fans directly and indirectly. We went to Comic-Con, and we were very well received there, but nobody who went to our panel got to find out what was in the hatch. David Chase didn't have to explain his intention, because his intention was artistic. Our show required Mommy and Daddy to come out and say, 'Don't worry, we know what we're doing, everything's under control.' That's how it started. Then it morphed into, 'You can yell at us. We'll take your abuse. We understand what you're frustrated about.'"

Comic-Con appearances—featuring surprise cameos by members of the cast, as well as bonus videos (like a never-before-seen Dharma Initiative orientation film) offering clues to the show's mythology—became an annual tradition, and an easy way for Lindelof and Cuse (a duo some fans began referring to as "Darlton") to publicly engage with their audience. Early in the second season, ABC launched an official *Lost* podcast, featuring interviews with the actors and a weekly segment where Lindelof and Cuse answered fan questions(*), confirmed or debunked theories, and teased upcoming developments, all the while bantering like a vintage comedy duo playing a lounge in the Catskills.

(*) In the very first podcast, they address the old standard about how much of the series had been mapped out in advance. In the process of discussing what they do and don't know, Cuse jokingly asks Lindelof, "You're not going to tell them about the time travel, are you?" Either they didn't know at that point that they would devote an entire season (the fifth) to time travel, or that's one bold, early clue for those paying attention.

And as hard as Lindelof and Cuse worked to engage with their fans, the fans were already plenty engaged. *Lost* had come along at the exact right moment, technologically speaking.

On the one hand, the broadcast networks still had enough market share that a show this strange had the potential to become as big a hit as it did (it averaged close to 18 million viewers a week in its third season), and to sustain the kind of budget that brought the island and its secrets to life.

On the other, the technology we used to watch and engage with our TV shows had advanced to the point where we could fully understand and enjoy the show. DVD box sets and DVRs made it simpler for fans to catch up—or to go back and re-examine episodes that made them either excited or confused. High-definition television sets had become affordable enough that viewers could truly appreciate the beautiful work Jack Bender and his crew were doing in Hawaii.

Mostly, though, there was the internet.

Lost didn't invent internet discussion of TV shows—Usenet newsgroups had been around since the '80s, and TV fan sites like my *NYPD Blue* page and Dawson's Wrap (which turned into Television Without Pity) began appearing by the mid-to-late '90s—but the show and its fandom may have perfected the art. By the time *Lost* debuted, the internet was a fact of American life, and provided a venue where hardcore nerds and more casual fans alike could discuss the cursed numbers on Hurley's lottery ticket, the statue of a four-toed foot Sayid glimpsed in the second-season finale, and every other piece of island lore.

"What we never could have anticipated," says Cuse, "was that the show would debut just as social media came into existence. So there was this unforeseen confluence of events where we were making a show that was perfect for discussion and debate, just at the moment where the internet was evolving into a place where people were forming communities where they could have those discussions and debates."

The fans had come to *Lost* first, and then turned to the internet to discuss it, but those online communities in turn made it easier to stick with a show that otherwise might have been too challenging without some extra brainpower to swap theories with.

I ask Cuse if the show could have been so successful for so long without the state of technology circa 2004, and he says, "I don't think so. The audience component created a buzz around the show, which made people want to watch the show. It created a sense that if you wanted to be in the know, you had to be watching *Lost*. A few years earlier than that, no one was making serialized shows. The networks were all convinced that if someone fell out, there was no way to get caught up. But now you could watch the DVDs of the show, and the social media component really created a buzz about the show, which made them say, 'Hey, I want to be in on that.' If it had happened a few years earlier, it would have been a cool show, but a small genre show, where Damon and I and our fellow geeks would have enjoyed it and everyone else would have given up."

Those venues not only amplified fans' fascination with *Lost*, but also their frustrations with it. The audience was mollified when the second season immediately took us inside the hatch and showed us what turned out to be a half-forgotten Dharma Initiative outpost called the Swan, manned by a frantic Scotsman named Desmond Hume(*) who (as Lindelof had brainstormed back in season 1) insisted that you had to enter a certain sequence of numbers— Hurley's numbers, in fact—into a computer every 108 minutes in order to save the world. They were less enthused with that season's major cast addition: "the tailies," passengers in the tail section of Oceanic 815, who had had an even rougher go of things on the island than Jack's group, and who were led by belligerent cop Ana

Lucia (Michelle Rodriguez). Some of the tailies would became fan favorites—notably African crime lord turned holy man Mr. Eko (played by *Oz* alum Adewale Akinnuoye-Agbaje)—but Rodriguez would be the first (but not the last) new addition to the cast whom fans would loudly reject.

(*) As Desmond, actor Henry Ian Cusick would join the cast full-time the following season, and it was Desmond's special abilities—his consciousness could move back and forth through time, and provide glimpses of the future—as much as anything else that pointed the way towards the much more overt, unapologetic sci-fi qualities of the second half of the series.

The open dialogue Lindelof had sought to establish with the fans had its drawbacks. Midway through the second season, Sayid and Rousseau discover a man trapped in one of Rousseau's nets, claiming to be a Minnesota balloonist named Henry Gale and played by character actor Michael Emerson. Sayid, convinced Henry is with the Others who kidnapped Walt, brings him back to the Swan station to torture information out of him. In time, Sayid's instincts are proven correct, but not before Henry—who turns out to be the Others' leader, Benjamin Linus—has played a series of mind games on Sayid, Jack, and Locke, and been violently liberated by Michael, who murders Ana Lucia and her friend Libby as part of a deal to get Walt back(*).

(*) Because the early seasons of Lost *took place over a compressed period, while Malcolm David Kelley continued to age in real time, Walt and Michael were written out of the show after the second season. (Both returned later.) I had always figured that Kelley's growth spurt was the ultimate example of Abrams and Lindelof assuming the show wouldn't be around long enough to have to deal with such a problem, but Lindelof says they had factored that in. The original plan included*

a big time jump between the events of Season 1 and Season 2, which would have explained why Walt kept getting taller; midway through the first season, Lindelof realized the story they were telling wouldn't allow for such a jump, and the kidnapping story was a way to keep the character around a little longer before puberty fully took hold.

The fans instantly loved to hate Ben, as they were meant to, but it had been fairly well-publicized that Emerson had originally signed for only a handful of episodes. As Ben stuck around, and became even more prominent in the Others-centric third season, some fans began pointing to the character as "proof" that Lindelof and Cuse had no plan at all, and were simply making everything up as they went along.

As Lindelof explained to me a few years later, the answer was more complicated than that. Yes, Emerson had only been signed for a few episodes, and yes, his performance had been so good that Cuse and Lindelof had turned that character into the head Other. But they had always planned for a character like Ben to be at the center of the third season, viewed "Henry Gale" as a contender for the job, and were dazzled enough by Emerson's performance to give it to him. But that wasn't a simple argument to make, especially to people who wanted to be skeptical.

Early in the third season, Mr. Eko died abruptly at the hands of the smoke monster. To head off anger at the death of a popular character, Lindelof and Cuse explained that the actor had asked off the show because he didn't like living in Hawaii.

"That was something Carlton and I debated whether to reveal," says Lindelof, "because that breaks the illusion that we have this binder that details everything that happens."

"Darlton" had a larger problem than fan complaints and conspiracy theories, though. Every TV show has people complaining about it on the internet; it's half of what the internet is there for, seemingly. (The other half: porn.) What no one could have predicted was that the fans would use the internet to try to collectively solve the show's mysteries—and that they would be so successful at it.

Cuse remembers introducing an online game that would keep fans occupied and engaged with the show during a hiatus period: "We thought it would take the audience weeks to figure it out, but instead, they did it in a couple of hours. We thought, 'Well, so much for that!'"

"We never made peace with it; it was always frustrating," says Lindelof. "The show was being crowd-sourced, like the greatest code-breakers in the world were getting together to try to figure this stuff out."

Once upon a time, mystery fans had to solve puzzles on their own; now, you not only didn't need to be the one to solve it, you didn't even need to be hanging around on the website where someone else had solved it. An Ana Lucia flashback episode in the second season showed Jack's father, Christian, visiting a blond Australian woman. Not long after it aired, I saw someone on the Television Without Pity message boards passing along a theory they had read on a different site suggesting that this woman was Claire's mother, that Christian was her father, and that Jack and Claire were unwitting half siblings. I hadn't connected those dots myself, but the theory immediately made sense to me. When I interviewed Cuse that summer, he mentioned Christian Shephard, and I said, "And he's Claire's father, too, right?" Cuse looked like he was about to have a heart attack.

The advantage the show had at its best was that it could be so compelling irrespective of the mysteries. It wasn't a huge leap, for instance, for viewers to deduce that Locke's hustler father Anthony Cooper and the con man who destroyed Sawyer's family were one and the same. As with Claire's parentage, it was a theory I knew and believed in long before it was revealed on the show itself, in a Season 3 episode called "The Brig." Yet the performances by O'Quinn, Holloway, and guest star Kevin Tighe in that episode—which climaxes with Sawyer strangling Cooper with a rusty chain in the hold of the Black Rock—were so riveting that the lack of surprise was ultimately irrelevant.

Whereas the other dramas of the Steve McPherson regime were gradually homogenized until you could predict everything that would happen on one show simply by watching another for a few weeks, *Lost* mostly dodged that type of network interference, at first because no one believed in the show, and then because it was too successful and unique to mess with.

"I don't think that *Lost* was really in Steve's wheelhouse," says Cuse. "It was the vision of Lloyd Braun, who desperately wanted to make this thing and greenlit it ahead of being fired. Steve inherited it, but I don't think he believed the show was going to work. A lot of executives followed that lead, so we were left alone to do what we wanted to do, which was really an incredible blessing for us. There is an enormous pressure in network television to sand off the rough edges in things, and those rough edges are usually the best parts of a show. Because no one initially believed in the show's success, we weren't really forced to make those changes."

Cuse and Lindelof were allowed to show their main characters as people who had done very bad things on the mainland (Kate and Sawyer had both murdered people) and had unappealing character traits (Jack and Locke were both stubborn and myopic in their attempts at leadership). They were able to use storytelling devices that had previously been seen as too demanding (Jin/Sun flashback stories were presented in Korean with English subtitles; Cuse says an ABC executive sarcastically called one of those "The best episode of television I ever read"). They didn't provide easy answers(*) or instant gratification, and they filled episodes with Easter eggs and other clues that would mean nothing to viewers who were less than fully engaged with the show and its mythology.

(*) Cuse, like David Chase, grew up obsessed with European film, and also enjoyed asking, "What did Fellini mean?" He cites the oblique narratives of Twin Peaks *and* The Prisoner *as a big influence on* Lost, *and says, "We talked a lot about how we should incorporate intentional ambiguity into the show."*

"All these things occurred to us," says Cuse, "but weren't things that had been done on other shows. And those were the reasons people embraced *Lost*."

The one area in which ABC flexed its muscles was against Lindelof and Cuse's desire to give the show a finite run, thereby parceling out the mythology accordingly and not overstaying their welcome. That desire ran counter to network television's classic business model: you stay on the air for as long as there's money to be made, and if a show peters out creatively by the end, so be it.

"Everything we talked about with the future of the show was mitigated by the fact that they didn't want to end it," recalls Lindelof. "There was tremendous pushback anytime we wanted to introduce any larger mythological elements that might answer things. And Carlton and I began to get very depressed, and hamstrung creatively, almost to the point of 'Let's stop talking about how we'll end the show, and they won't let that happen, so we're leaving.'"

They began plotting that exit strategy in the third season, hiring *Alias* producer Jeff Pinkner to succeed them in the event that ABC wanted *Lost* to keep going, and going, and going...

"We said to ABC, 'Look, we understand that you may want to continue the show in an open-ended fashion, and that's okay. We just don't want to be the guys to do it,'" says Cuse.

As these discussions continued, Lindelof and Cuse were running into the show's first sustained creative rough patch. They'd had episodes and characters that didn't click before; suddenly they had a lot of elements floundering at once. The season opened with Jack, Kate, and Sawyer being held prisoner by Ben and the Others, and introduced a pair of new characters, Nikki and Paulo, who would be the show's answer to fan questions about why we only ever paid attention to a dozen or so of the Oceanic 815 passengers. The fans didn't love so many episodes in a row of Kate and Sawyer locked in polar bear cages, and they *hated* Nikki and Paulo(*). The writers were also running out of fresh ideas for the flashback storylines, a drought that culminated in "Stranger in a Strange Land," an episode that spent its time on the mainland answering a question no one had ever asked: where did Jack get his tattoos?

(*) It turns out the creative team didn't like them, either, and midway through the season, Nikki and Paulo were buried alive. "Nikki and Paulo were hated by the fans," says Cuse, "but we had already decided that was a bad idea. People thought it was gladiatorial—that they said they hate them and, thus, they were buried alive—but we were working on episodes far enough ahead that the fans wouldn't have been able to influence the show that quickly."

"Stranger in a Strange Land" is such a mess that, in hindsight, one might ask whether it was planned that way—had the writing staff conceived of a flashback story so tedious, so obscure, that it would force ABC to recognize that Cuse and Lindelof were right about the show's current course?

Cuse and Lindelof each insist that it wasn't conscious, but Cuse admits, "If you look at the first batch of Season 3 where our heroes are locked in cages, I don't think that's accidental."

The wave of fan and critical dissatisfaction couldn't have come at a better time for Cuse and Lindelof's purposes, since it coincided with the debut of NBC's *Heroes*, a superhero drama created by Lindelof's former *Crossing Jordan* boss Tim Kring. *Heroes* had, like *Lost* before it, managed to appeal to both the fanboys and the mainstream, and had done it while offering a steady stream of explanations for every mysterious thing it introduced. Lindelof and Cuse couldn't say when they would answer any big questions, because they didn't know; meanwhile, Kring was getting a ton of good press(*) by promising to resolve the initial major *Heroes* arc at the end of the first season.

(*) Midway through that season, I wrote a column—which I would apologize for a few months later—modifying my old card game metaphor: "At their respective bests, Heroes *isn't remotely in the same zip code as* Lost. *But after two years and five weeks of being teased, taunted and tricked about what, if anything, is happening on that wacky island, there's a definite comfort level to watching a show that lays its cards on the table in a timely fashion."*

"*Heroes* was a big factor in *Lost* getting its ending," says Lindelof, "because everybody was talking about how awesome *Heroes* was. Particularly how *Heroes's* design was not a mythological construct, it wasn't about mysteries, it was doing huge ratings, and everybody was saying, 'Why can't *Lost* be more like *Heroes?*'"

The combination of *Heroes's* instant success and *Lost's* recent stumbles forced McPherson to see things the producers' way, and negotiations began for a fixed end date. Lindelof and Cuse wanted the show to conclude after only five seasons, McPherson wanted eight, and ultimately they compromised on six; the deal was announced with a few weeks to go in Season 3.

With negotiations still ongoing, Lindelof and Cuse began figuring out the shape of the rest of the series. They had recognized even before "Stranger in a Strange Land" that they were running out of compelling flashback material, and they also knew that, at some point in the storyline, several main characters would get off the island, then realize they had to return. And that led them to the show's most mind-blowing moment since Locke's wheelchair at the end of "Walkabout," and the series' best episode since "Exodus."

We began the Season 3 finale, "Through the Looking Glass," with a bearded Jack on another airplane, drinking too much, yelling at people and being the same pig-headed boor I had slowly come to dislike over the last two seasons. As he had a humiliating encounter with his ex-wife, I began wondering exactly where this story fit into Jack's pre-crash timeline, but mainly I was eager to get back to the island, where Jack was mounting a plan to defeat the Others and get rescued by the crew of a freighter allegedly sent in search of Desmond by his lost love, Penny. The action tied together several long-running threads in exciting fashion. Hurley, for instance, had spent an earlier episode fixing up an abandoned Dharma Initiative van, and here used it to be an unlikely hero in rescuing Sayid, Jin, and Bernard from being executed on Ben's orders. Desmond had recently been saving Charlie's life, over and over, based on his precognitive flashes, but knew Charlie would have to die in order to ensure everyone's rescue; in the end, Charlie sacrificed himself inside a flooding Dharma station, even as he warned Desmond that the freighter was (as he scrawled on his hand in his dying moments) "NOT PENNY'S BOAT."

This was a reminder of why I'd stuck with *Lost* through polar-bear cages, tattoo histories, characters constantly failing to share information with each other, and all the other missteps—and why, for that matter, I could accept yet another flashback to Jack Shephard making an ass of himself as the cost of doing business with this wonderful show. *Lost* at its peak could play on your adrenal glands, your tear ducts, and your funny bone, all within the space of a few minutes, and "Through the Looking Glass" was doing all of that, over and over.

And then, just as Jack on the island had made contact with the freighter and arranged for what seemed like an easy rescue mission, we returned to a distraught Jack on the mainland, arranging a mysterious late night visit with...

Kate.

Whom he had never met before coming to the island.

And as Kate walked away from the rambling, manic doctor, he screamed, "We have to go back, Kate! *We have to go back!*"

Flash-forward. Not flashback.

And a whole new ballgame.

Almost instantly, the roles reversed between *Lost* (coming off one of its best, boldest episodes ever) and *Heroes* (which had spent its entire first season building up to one guy beating up another guy with a parking meter). Now it was *Lost* that knew exactly what it was doing, and it was *Heroes* wearing a suit made of the emperor's finest new clothes. And it was a position that Cuse and Lindelof would work very, very hard not to give up over the final three seasons.

"I think that part of writing it was actually enabled by all the shit we were (justifiably) eating for the first half of that season," says Lindelof, "and yes, the rise of *Heroes*, which every critic was embracing as 'the anti-*Lost*' because it had mastered the questions/answers ratio, etc. We had no reservations about doing the flash-forwards—we had creatively committed to them almost a year earlier—but the idea of Trojan horsing the idea as a disguised flashback of yet another Drunken Miserable Jack story was emboldened by how far we had been perceived to have fallen. Was it a Hail Mary? Not quite. But we knew that we had lost enough trust that if we didn't come roaring back with boldness and confidence, we would be screwed."

Shifting from flashbacks to flash-forwards that slowly but surely revealed who else had escaped the island (Hurley, Sayid, Sun, and Claire's baby son, Aaron), and intercutting those stories with the tale of how they'd escaped (and why others didn't), completely reinvigorated the series. No more spending weeks on end in cages. No more scratching for some unexplored minutiae from Jin and Sun's crumbling marriage or from Kate's fugitive days. No more running in place because the writers didn't know how many episodes they had left(*).

(*) Though even that didn't go entirely according to plan. The final seasons were supposed to have 16 episodes each, but thanks to the Writers Guild of America strike and other wrinkles, the fourth season had only 14 hours, the fifth season wound up needing 17 hours to fit everything in, and the sixth season was more than 18 hours.

Lindelof and Cuse now had specific stories they wanted to tell, and the proper time and preparation to tell them. Season 4 had the flash-forwards and the escape of "the Oceanic Six." Season 5 was the time travel season, with the island, or the castaways, or both, bouncing back and forward through time, filling in a lot of island history along the way. The final season began with two parallel narratives: Jack and company trying to get off the island one more time, and some kind of alternate timeline—what everyone began referring to as "the flash-sideways universe"—where Oceanic 815 made it from Australia to Los Angeles without incident, and where many of the characters' lives were either very different (Sawyer was a cop) or simply much happier (the lottery win only brought Hurley good luck). Even when it revisited familiar territory, the series no longer seemed in danger of repeating itself.

These final seasons used what we had come to know about these characters and this crazy island to magnify the feelings we had about them. Season 4 gave us the swooningly romantic "The Constant," in which the only thing that could save Desmond's life in the present when he became unstuck in time was hearing Penny's voice on the phone—if only Desmond in the past could get her to give him the number. Season 5 gave us "Jughead," in which brilliant physicist Daniel Faraday had to prevent a hydrogen bomb from destroying the island in the 1950s; the charming "LaFleur," in which Sawyer and the characters left behind by the Oceanic Six found themselves trapped in the mid-'70s, and joined the Dharma Initiative to pass the time; and the tragic "The Life and Death of Jeremy Bentham," in which John Locke's tortured existence seemed to come to an end at the spiteful, envious hands of Ben Linus. Season 6's "Ab Aeterno" took us back to the 19th century to learn the tragic, terrifying origin story of Richard Alpert, the Others' immortal liaison with the enigmatic Jacob.

Lost wasn't suddenly flawless; even with more concrete planning, there were too many moving parts for things to run smoothly all the time. The non-sideways episodes at the start of Season 6, for instance, finally took us inside "the temple," an oft-discussed base for the Others run by the cryptic Dogen, played by Japanese actor Hiroyuki Sanada; and his translator Lennon, played by John

Hawkes (one of a half-dozen *Deadwood* alums to guest on *Lost*, which also employed *Deadwood* writer Elizabeth Sarnoff). The temple episodes dragged—Lindelof says they realized after the fact that it was much too late in the series to be introducing significant new characters—and the writers cut bait on the idea early, letting the smoke monster (working in concert with Sayid) kill Dogen and most of the temple residents.

Reflecting on the unpredictability of adding new people to the island, Lindelof says, "God, we wasted fucking John Hawkes! How did that happen?"

The final seasons also confirmed some of Lindelof's early fears about the viewers' desire to see all the mysteries solved. Whenever we got a character-based resolution—say, Ben tearfully expressing regret for his actions and realizing that he's thrown in his lot with the monster "Because he's the only one that'll have me"—it played like gangbusters. But when the show answered some long-standing question about the island—that, for example, the whispers in the jungle came from the spirits of dead people who couldn't move on—it was often greeted with a shrug (because it was a theory many people had long since guessed or heard about) or irritation (because it bore so little resemblance to people's theories). It was a no-win scenario.

The relationship between the fans and the show's mythology came to a boil late in Season 6 with "Across the Sea," an hour set thousands of years in the past, detailing the origins of Jacob and his ancient rival (and, it turned out, brother) the Man in Black—who would become the smoke monster and, by the final season, take the form of the late John Locke—and explaining that the source of the island's magic, and the prize being fought over for centuries by the forces of good and evil, was a golden pool of light.

It was an episode loaded with answers to questions fans had asked for years, and that, in its script stage, made Lindelof think, "It's just going to blow the doors off of people." Yet it was as hated as anything *Lost* had done since introducing Nikki and Paulo.

The reasons for that loathing varied. Some viewers resented spending an episode so close to the end (and the week after an emotional hour in which Sun, Jin, and Sayid had all died) on material irrelevant to the characters we cared so much about. Many viewers thought the golden pool of light was a ridiculous explanation for the island's unique properties. Some (including me) found the episode an unintentional metaphor for the series itself; so much of the conflict between the two brothers came about because their mother failed to tell them everything about the island, just as many *Lost* viewers grew impatient with the show's stinginess with answers.

Lindelof admits that "I was swayed by the audience reaction to it and came to feel like it was one of the most fundamental mistakes we made in the series." The problem, as he sees it, wasn't that the episode provided a lot of information—had they not done that, they'd have taken even more grief from the fans after the finale—but "we were giving it to the audience but not the characters."

And then there was the finale—titled simply "The End"— which was *Lost* in microcosm. Some parts worked spectacularly well; in others, the show's reach seemed to exceed its grasp. Some fans were moved by how this six-year journey had ended; some told Lindelof and Cuse the finale made them regret having watched the show at all.

Fans had bandied about many theories about the nature and purpose of the sideways universe all season—and debated whether that universe was a good use of time so close to the finale, versus plotting the "real" versions of the characters. "The End" revealed the sideways not as an alternate timeline nor a trick of the Man in Black, but as a place in the afterlife where the island's key residents waited until they could all reunite, remember their lives, and move on together into the beautiful white light.

"We wanted to talk about Purgatory," says Lindelof. "That was something that was really interesting to us, in the original design of the pilot." In Season 1's "Tabula Rasa," Jack had told Kate, metaphorically, "Three days ago, we all died. We should all be able to start over." Now they would address the idea head-on.

In the sideways, we would get to see versions of the characters that evoked who they had once been: Jack as a well-meaning hero; Locke as a serene font of wisdom; and even long-dead characters like Charlie, Boone, and Shannon treated with nearly the same significance as those who made it to the final episodes. We would see them finally in death make peace with the demons (Jack and Locke's father issues, Hurley's bad luck) that they couldn't quite conquer in life. And as the characters each remembered their lives throughout "The End," we were treated to one well-earned tug at the heartstrings after another(*).

(*) *I've always been partial to Sawyer finding his Juliet at a hospital vending machine and being overcome with memories of how they were violently torn apart at the end of the fifth season, but all the reunions worked beautifully.*

The disclosure of the true nature of the sideways didn't universally justify the time spent there that season, as many fans rejected the idea for various reasons. Though the island itself turned out not to be Purgatory (a popular fan theory from the early seasons), the show had always treated it as a place where the characters could work out their issues; why would they need to wait until death to finish that job? And, as had happened the year before with the *Battlestar Galactica* finale (more on that in a few chapters), some fans simply didn't want their science fiction mixed with matters metaphysical.

But the individual reunions were touching, and the material taking place in the present day on the island lived up to the visceral, heart-wrenching standard of previous finales like "Exodus" and "Through the Looking Glass." The golden pool of light may have itself seemed silly, but it forced the characters to act. Jack and the monster wearing John Locke's face were fighting to the death; that was what mattered, not what they were fighting over. Again there was thrilling action (Jack and Locke throwing down on a rocky cliff). Again there was pathos (a tearful Hurley reluctantly agreeing to succeed Jack as protector of the island, then offering Ben a chance at reform as his second in command). Again there were last-minute escapes (Sawyer, Kate, and a handful of others leave the island in an airplane right before the runway collapses), and characters who didn't make it. In a moment taking the series full circle, scenes of the sideways characters preparing for the final reward together were intercut with a dying Jack lying down in the same field where we had found him six years earlier, Walt's dog Vincent again providing his only company, his eye finally closing.

"If you didn't get what was going on in the sideways," says Lindelof, "then the show would live on in its death in the same way it did in its life: with a degree of controversy, and ambiguity, and mystery and all those things that completely and totally captivated me about *The Sopranos* finale at an entirely different level. We made our peace with the fact. But again, I don't think we were prepared for the level of vitriol."

Some fans were angry about the truth of the sideways. Some felt Lindelof and Cuse hadn't answered enough questions—even though both men had entered the final season warning everyone who would listen that this would happen.

For several years after the finale, Lindelof would take to Twitter to therapeutically quote the nasty things some fans say to him about the finale—usually involving the phrase "Thanks for wasting six years of my life," followed by profanity. (Eventually, he shut down his Twitter account for the sake of his emotional well-being, though he regretted losing a medium in which he could repeatedly joke about Justin Bieber's absurdly gaudy yellow hat. "Bieber proved himself to be much more able to be a target of brutal and constant haranguing than I did," Lindelof says now. "I celebrate him for that. And, as always, for his keen hat-fashion sense.")During the 2012 Comic-Con—while he was dealing with similar barbs about his script for the movie *Prometheus*—he appeared on a panel titled "The Art of Being Despised."

Even the finale's closing credits generated confusion and controversy. ABC wanted to pair the credits with some unused footage from the series, but virtually the only thing that hadn't been picked over by this point were images of the Oceanic 815 wreckage lying on the beach, with no people in sight. (They had been shot as a contingency plan in case the production lost access to that beach and had to start filming those scenes with a green screen.) Many viewers watched the peaceful beach pictures and assumed they meant that the characters had been dead for the entire series, and not just since they had entered the sideways reality.

"The thing that we failed to anticipate," says Cuse, "was we had done so many twists in the show, had imbued so many aspects of the show with meaning and hidden meaning, at the very end, a beauty shot of the beach couldn't just be perceived as a beauty shot of the beach."

Every success in television gets imitated sooner or later, even something as idiosyncratic as *Lost*. Over the years, every single broadcast network—including ABC several times—has tried to ape some part of *Lost* or other with shows like *FlashForward, The Event, Threshold, Invasion,* and *Surface.* None of them has come close to capturing what made *Lost* work—starting with characters who will be interesting to watch, whether the secrets are answered in a timely fashion or not.

"They were all mythology," Lindelof says of the copycats, "and I think mythology is hard to wrangle. I feel sorry for those shows. *Lost* kinda screwed them, not because it was awesome, but because people were already cynical about them when those shows came along. Some people were like, 'I've already fallen for this guy. And I'm not sure about him. And I'm certainly not going to date *him*.'"

And none of those shows have had the insane, un-Hurley streak of good luck that was associated with every step of *Lost's* creation.

"If we sat down," says Cuse, "and said, 'Let's literally try to create another *Lost*,' I don't think we could do it. There's this weird alchemy that's a part of television shows. *Lost* had it in spades. Everything aligned, everything worked. It was the right show at the right time. It struck a nerve."

Lloyd Braun, who had come up with the idea and pushed for it to become a reality despite a lot of collegial skepticism, never got to enjoy the fruits of his labor. But he did take great pride in what Abrams, Lindelof, and then Cuse did with his brainstorm.

"When I look at that entire series, I think what those guys did, it was brilliant television—groundbreaking television. They took a crazy network executive's idea, and they turned it into something amazing."

CHAPTER 7

She saved the world. A lot...
Buffy the Vampire Slayer
gives teen angst some fangs

So there's a girl. She's walking down an alley. It's dark, the music is ominous, and everything we know about pop culture tells us she's going to be monster food in about 30 seconds.

Only there's a guy. He's a third-generation screenwriter, an absolute sponge for pop culture, and he likes nothing more than using our own expectations about how these things work against us. What if, the guy wonders, the girl isn't the victim, but the hero? What if the monster needs to be afraid of *her*?

And by upending that one expectation at the heart of *Buffy the Vampire Slayer*, Joss Whedon set out on a path to keep surprising us: by turning a dumb and forgettable movie into a brilliant and beloved TV show, by proving that a writer could demonstrate more artistry on the small screen than he had on the big one, by giving a fledgling, largely ignored network an identity, and by proving that cable wasn't the only part of television in this period(*) where creators were given freedom to be innovative.

(*) Technically, Buffy *debuted on March 10, 1997, two years be-*

fore The Sopranos *(and four months before* Oz*), but it was so great—and its evolution parallels so much of what was about to happen on cable—that I had to include it in the book.*

We start with Whedon, whose grandfather John had written for *The Donna Reed Show*, and whose father Tom had an eclectic resume that included *The Electric Company* and *Golden Girls*. When your father and grandfather are cops, you tend to become a cop. Joss Whedon became a sitcom writer, getting a staff job on the second season of *Roseanne*. Around the same time, he wrote a screenplay as a reaction to all the horror movies he had seen where the cute girl dies violently in an alley. As he explained to *Entertainment Weekly* in 1997(*), "I thought, I'd love to see a movie where [she] kills the monster."

(*) Whedon declined to be interviewed for this book, citing an overwhelming schedule. Any quotes from him in this chapter are from previous interviews I did with him, or from other sources that I'll credit as we go.

Though the title *Buffy the Vampire Slayer* suggested something goofy, Whedon was aiming higher. He liked the idea of monsters as metaphors for the pain and anxiety so many of us deal with in high school, and he wanted the movie to tell the story of a shallow, superficial girl who learns that she has real power, and with it (as another iconic superhero would tell you) great responsibility.

Fran Rubel Kuzui, who directed and produced the 1992 *Buffy the Vampire Slayer* movie, wasn't interested in metaphor or emotional complexity. The film, starring Kristy Swanson as Buffy, is exactly what you would expect from the title—no more, no less. There are some snappy one-liners here and there, but it's all played as a joke.

"I think *Buffy* the movie could be considered disappointing for

[Whedon], because it was too camp," says David Greenwalt, who would be Whedon's partner in the early days of the *Buffy* TV show before co-creating the *Angel* spin-off with him. "Joss does a lot of things. He does funny, he does serious, he does break your heart, but it's never camp. That was the way the person decided to direct the movie."

Buffy came and went from theaters, and though Whedon struggled to get his own screenplays produced after that, he began finding steady, lucrative work as a script doctor, sometimes getting screen credit for his rewrites (he was Oscar-nominated for *Toy Story*), sometimes not (Graham Yost, the credited screenwriter of *Speed*, says Whedon wrote nearly all of the dialogue in the final cut). He couldn't fix every film (no one could fix *Waterworld*), but Whedon's touch was golden enough that no one in the business seemed to remember that silly vampire movie he had written.

Well, almost no one. Gail Berman was an executive with Sandollar Productions, an independent production company that made both movies and TV. When Berman first arrived at Sandollar in 1991, she began going though scripts looking for projects the company could make. She found Whedon's *Buffy* script and became convinced there was a television show in there. Her colleagues told her it was already being made into a film, and when Berman suggested they might be smart to lock up the TV rights now, no one agreed. The movie bombed, and that was that.

Then in 1995, Berman saw *Clueless*, which didn't have any vampires or demons in it, but which had found success as another story of a popular high school girl with more wit, substance, and ambition than you might have expected from the poster. Now *Buffy* was on Berman's mind again, and she thought the property would be an easy sell for the budding market for syndicated drama that was about to welcome *Hercules: The Legendary Journeys* and then its spin-off *Xena: Warrior Princess*.

Kuzui, who owned part of the rights to the character, agreed to let Berman find a writer to adapt the idea for television. Whedon's deal gave him right of first refusal on such a project, so Berman reached out to him as a formality—"He was working on big movie projects at the time," she explains, "not working in television"— explaining to Whedon's agent that Whedon just had to say no so they could move on.

"But a couple of weeks later," Berman recalls, "I got a call from the agent, and he said, 'I talked to Joss about it, and the funny thing is, he is interested in it(*). Why don't you guys get together and see if there's something you find intriguing?'"

(*) In that 1997 Entertainment Weekly *interview, Whedon said, "When I said I was doing* Buffy, *my agent went 'Aaaaaaaaaggghh-hhh!!' He begged me, 'Don't do it.'"*

Berman immediately got on Whedon's good side by praising his script and explaining she had read it before she saw Kuzui's movie.

"I got what he was going for," says Berman, "and the metaphoric resonance that he thought this character could have about high school, and young adulthood. And we just hit it off."

At the time, Greenwalt says, "Nobody thought anybody would come from movies to television; people usually tried to move the other way. And what they didn't understand is that Joss is an artist, and money is not important to him, and what's important to him is making a good product. And here he had a chance to do it right."

With Whedon unexpectedly attached to the project—in part because he wanted to get into directing, and Berman was on board with him directing the pilot—Berman saw *Buffy*'s ceiling go from syndication to network. She thought for sure Fox would be interested, but they passed. Then she thought she had a good shot with NBC; they passed, too.

"At that point," she says, "the WB was the next logical choice for a young-adult show."

The WB, like its then-rival UPN, had launched in January of 1995 in an attempt to prove there was a market for a fifth broadcast network. The WB's advantage over UPN, it seemed, was that it had some of the chief executives who had been in charge when Fox had launched nearly a decade earlier in an attempt to prove there was a market for a *fourth* broadcast network. In the early going, the WB had leaned on sitcoms with African-American stars like Robert Townsend and the Wayans brothers, but WB executive Susanne Daniels says they were looking to "broaden" the network's audience as they began developing shows for the 1996-97 TV season.

Enter Joss Whedon and Gail Berman, with a pitch for a show that Daniels didn't expect to like.

"I had a slight bias going into it," says Daniels, "which is that I really didn't like the movie. I thought it was a B as a movie; it was just okay. I was a fan of Joss's writing and of Gail Berman, but I was wary of the pitch, because it was based on the movie. What I was struck by in the pitch was how it was such a fresh and improved take from the movie, and the emotionality that Joss was bringing to Buffy's story and backstory and where it was going. I will tell you that because of all of the changes, I really didn't want to call it *Buffy the Vampire Slayer*. I wanted to just call it *Slayer,* largely because I wanted the title of the show to reflect the significant changes and improvements from the movie that Joss had made. But I lost that battle(*), which I still believe to this day in some ways limited the growth potential of the audience that we could have had."

(*) Berman says they hated the Slayer *name: "It sounded like a bad metal band!"*

Buffy the movie had largely been a solo adventure, while the TV show would be an ensemble story about the surrogate family Buffy creates among her fellow high school outcasts: stuffy librarian (and secret demon expert) Rupert Giles; wisecracking geek Xander Harris; and sweet, vulnerable nerd Willow Rosenberg. But Buffy was the most important part, and the most difficult to cast. Sarah Michelle Gellar, coming off a Daytime Emmy–winning role as bitchy teen Kendall Hart on *All My Children*, had come in to read for the role of mean girl Cordelia Chase, a stand-in for the kind of superficial brat Buffy used to be. With the producers at their wit's end trying to find someone who could play all the different sides of Buffy, someone—accounts differ as to whether it was WB entertainment president Garth Ancier, WB casting chief Kathleen Letterie, or 20th Century Fox Television president Peter Roth—suggested they try Gellar in the part. Gellar nailed it.

Buffy was the last show the WB had ordered that year, so there was only money left in the budget to produce a 25-minute pilot presentation—just enough to give the WB an idea of what the show might look like, but not enough that the finished product could be put on the air. Whedon wrote the script and, after some debate among the WB's executives, got his first turn in the director's chair.

Whedon has fought to keep the presentation from being officially released as part of any DVD set, but it's floated around the internet for years. It's a very rough sketch of what the series would be, and not just because actress Riff Regan plays Willow (Alyson

Hannigan would play her in the series), while familiar character actor Stephen Tobolowsky has a small role as the school principal (Ken Lerner would replace him). Whedon's gifts for banter and self-aware humor are already evident—as Giles begins the *de rigueur* monologue about Buffy's destiny as the Slayer, she quips, "Wow, you're going to give the speech and everything"—and he gets a performance from Gellar close to what she would do on the series. But the action-packed climax, in which Buffy saves Willow from a group of vampires (and Willow in turn saves Xander), is clumsily staged at best, and doesn't in any way suggest that its director would one day be responsible for a $1.5 billion summer action movie.

"It's probably not his greatest work," acknowledges Berman, "but I'll tell you one thing: I thought it was awesome."

"I thought that he had captured a distinct and exciting lead character, and not a lot else," says Daniels. "Sarah Michelle Gellar shined in his pilot presentation as Buffy, and was endearing and fascinating and someone I wanted to go on a ride with, and see what was going to happen with the character and how. And I thought he had established an intriguing world, but I also thought it was messy."

"The pilot was not great," says Garth Ancier. "And we had some better pilots that year. The discussion was, 'Do we make our bet on another show from Stephen Cannell? Or do we make our bet on Joss, who we believe in as a writer, even though this pilot will have to be thoroughly trashed?' So we bet on Joss."

The WB ordered *Buffy* to series for mid-season, but wanted some veteran support around the relatively untested Whedon. Charles Martin Smith directed the revamped premiere episode, and veteran TV writer David Greenwalt(*) was brought in to help run the show.

(*) Greenwalt was coming off of Profit, *a strange, short-lived, criti-cally acclaimed Fox drama that in hindsight seems to have been sent back in time from an FX development season circa 2006.*

"We met, and it was kind of a love affair from the get-go," says Greenwalt. "He's the only honest-to-God genius I have ever met. Joss was amazing, and he was young, too. He had just invented this whole language that he used for the kids to speak in. He fig-ured if he tried to be hip to how 'kids actually spoke,' it would grow stale. I was 'the old guy' brought in to teach the new guy how to run a television show, and I learned way more from him than he learned from me."

That dialogue—Buffy and friends were fond, for instance, of adding "y" to the end of verbs to make adjectives, like Buffy ask-ing, "Who are we to be all judge-y?"—became infectious among the staff.

"I knew that life was going to be interesting when I heard David Greenwalt speaking in Joss-speak," says Berman. "David was brought on to be the co-showrunner, but the guy was more experienced than Joss. And what I found was people, including David—and I mean this very lovingly—sitting at the altar of Joss, starting to pick up his expressions and the way he spoke, and the various interesting verbiage he created. That was so interesting to me that Joss was such a presence that it became the student being the teacher to everyone."

The student and the teacher both had a lot of learning to do in that first season.

To avoid running out of vampire stories, Whedon had posi-tioned the show's Sunnydale High School directly over a "Hell-mouth" that was constantly spitting up all manner of supernatural nastiness. He wanted each *Buffy* monster to work on two levels, as both an opponent for Buffy to defeat and a reflection of an arche-typal problem of adolescence.

As Jane Espenson, who joined the writing staff in the third sea-son, explains, "Joss's first step is always, 'Why are we telling this story? Why does it have to be told now?' It would come from a place of 'Let's tell a story of the high school experience. We're going to tell a story of loneliness and isolation, and it's going to re-late to Buffy, because that's what Buffy is going through right now.' 'What's the Buffy of it?' was always a huge and primal question."

An early episode called "Witch" reinvented the familiar story of a mother trying to relive her youth through her daughter by mak-ing it literal, with the mother using magic to swap bodies so she could go out for the cheerleading squad. "The Pack" took the pred-atory mentality of the school's most popular clique to its violent conclusion by making them (and, in a twist, Xander) possessed by the spirit of a wild animal. In "Out of Mind, Out of Sight," a Sunnydale student is ignored for so long that she literally turns invisible and begins attacking everyone who failed to notice her.

The ideas were there, but the execution was spotty at first. The show never had a big budget, but in the early days it was made on the extra-cheap(*). The praying mantis monster from Greenwalt's first script, "Teacher's Pet," looks like a joke, and many of the other monsters had makeup indistinguishable from the rudimentary prosthetics the vampires used. There are also tonal issues—in the early going, for instance, the show and its characters don't seem to know how seriously to take the weekly deaths of innocent teenag-ers—and some of the supporting actors have a lot of growing to do. (As Buffy's good-guy vampire love interest Angel, David Boreanaz is so stiff in his early appearances that it's hard to imagine him car-rying the role at all, much less five seasons of an *Angel* spin-off and then 10 seasons and counting of the Fox mystery *Bones.*) Some episodes ("Nightmares," in which the worst fears of Buffy and her friends come to painful life) work quite well, while the less said of a few others (like "I, Robot... You, Jane," in which Willow is menaced by a demon that's been uploaded to the internet), the better.

(*) For budgetary reasons, the first two seasons were filmed on 16mm film rather than the more conventional 35mm, which meant any night scene—a staple of a show about vampires—looks incredibly grainy.

Through those early growing pains, *Buffy* still had Gellar, who was everything a show with this many disparate flavors could ask for: tough, vulnerable, funny, and versatile. (She would, unfortunately, never find the love from primetime Emmy voters that she had in daytime; the Emmys in general don't know what to do with sci-fi and fantasy.) It had Whedon's dialogue, and also his flair for knowing exactly how and when to have some fun at the expense of our expectations. The story arc of the first season involves a powerful vampire called the Master trying to escape the Hellmouth; in the season finale, he triggers an earthquake and delivers the requisite speech about the evil he's about to rain down on earth, then pauses to guess—like any self-respecting Californian—what the quake must have registered on the Richter scale.

Years later, when Whedon was working on the Fox show *Dollhouse,* I asked him about his fondness for subverting clichéd scenes like that.

"I'm not interested in breaking the fourth wall very often," he said, "but at the same time, there are certain genre expectations, and the bad guy will come from the shadows and take too long to say the thing. And you just lose patience, and so my characters do, too. Someone is going to set up an expectation for a scene that you have to subvert. If everyone knows exactly what scene they're in every time, then they've watched it already. With TV, you're serving both masters. On the one hand, you want people to know what they're signing up for. On the other hand, you want them to sign up that they don't know."

That earthquake gag comes at the start of the first-season finale, "Prophecy Girl." Whedon was again directing, and he was about to demonstrate—as he would throughout his TV career—a dramatic, rapid gift for self-improvement. All the amateurish staging and tonal clumsiness from the pilot presentation are gone. "Prophecy Girl"—the title comes from Giles's discovery that Buffy's death at the Master's hands has been foretold—is a confident, powerful piece of work, never more than in the moment when Buffy tearfully refuses Giles's appeal to her sense of responsibility by saying, "I don't care! I don't care. Giles, I'm 16 years old. *I don't want to die.*" Buffy does die, briefly, but returns to life (thanks to timely CPR from Xander) seemingly more powerful than ever, and if you want to read that as a metaphor for Whedon's experience with the character from the movie until that point, well… he'd earned that by this episode.

Daniels thinks Whedon had a very short learning curve: "He was on the set every minute of every day that season. He just learned what he needed to learn. He got it. He's a quick study and he's a genius, so he figured it out. That's all. And he did a kick-ass job! It was so great!"

"Prophecy Girl" was a breakthrough, not a fluke. *Buffy*, particularly in its second and third seasons, was a classic—not just of sci-fi/fantasy TV, not just of teen drama, but for TV drama, period. Whedon and company had found a way to tell high school stories that had enormous power, whether or not you were the same age as

Buffy and Willow. The metaphoric resonance of the monsters grew deeper, and the writers began to recognize that those stories should not only reflect a familiar problem of adolescence, but something specific to one of the regular characters.

Other high school series—*My So-Called Life* and *Freaks and Geeks*, to name two of the best—had dealt astutely with the confusion, pain, and isolation that come with adolescence, but they were almost *too* painful at times. The vampires and other beasties gave the audience license to experience the emotions of each issue, without feeling like they were reliving the worst moments of their own teenage years.

"I didn't understand or realize the power of genre television," says Greenwalt, "that people can really project onto the characters and at the same time feel one step removed from them, and feel almost more emotion than in a 'regular story.' We'd get letters from people—I got one from a woman who was an agoraphobic, and she said the previous night's episode had given her the courage to leave her house. I had never gotten a letter like that in all of my work."

Buffy simply got better at what it was doing, from technical matters (the special effects didn't look quite so cheap, and the transitions between Gellar and her stunt double weren't so blatant), to pop-culture references (Buffy's friends began referring to themselves as "the Scooby gang" after the *Scooby-Doo* comparison had become obvious to everyone watching) to acting. David Boreanaz grew so much as a performer that Whedon felt comfortable turning Angel into the chief villain (or, in Joss-speak, "big bad") of Season 2.

The show would tell more ambitious stories than the one in "Surprise" and "Innocence," the two-parter where Angel turns evil, but never a more quintessentially *Buffy* one. On her 17th birthday, Buffy barely escapes from a nest of vampires with help from Angel, and in the flush of survival, the two finally consummate their relationship. Unfortunately, the pure happiness Angel feels in that moment voids the spell that had given him his soul back, and he becomes obsessed with destroying the world—and Buffy's spirit right along with it.

In a shattering scene in "Innocence," Buffy returns to Angel's home to talk about their night together, not realizing what he's become.

"You've got a lot to learn about men, kiddo," Angel says, relishing her pain and confusion.

"Was it me?" Buffy asks. "Was I not good?"

"You were great," he tells her. "Really. I thought you were a pro… Lighten up. It was a good time. Doesn't mean like we have to make a big deal."

Angel walks out smirking, having hurt Buffy more deeply than any fight with a demon could have.

"It's such a metaphor for the guy turning into a jerk overnight and not calling her after they have sex for the first time," says Greenwalt. "We knew that was powerful, but we didn't realize how powerful."

By the time Season 2 culminated with Buffy consigning her boyfriend to Hell to save the world (spoiler: he got better), *Buffy* had cemented its position as a deep, significant piece of work. The show inspired a cottage industry of scholarly books with titles like *Fighting the Forces: What's at Stake in Buffy the Vampire Slayer?* or *What Would Buffy Do: The Vampire Slayer as Spiritual Guide*.

Espenson and several other writers arrived for the third season to find a well-oiled machine run by Whedon and Greenwalt.

"The show was changing," Espenson recalls. "It was going from being Monster of the Week to much more arc-driven and much deeper emotionally. But I think that had to do with the show coming of age, not Joss learning stuff. He talks now about stuff that he's learned, and obviously as a director, he was very new and inexperienced and is now the number one director in the universe. But when I came in, I saw a confident person who knew exactly what he wanted to do. I didn't see a lot of youthful hesitation in Joss. I saw someone who knew when the story was right, who knew what shots he wanted. I'm sure he'd say there was growth, but boy, I saw a fully baked cookie when I was there."

Though no other big bad could quite equal the resonance of Buffy versus Angel, Season 3 came close with its introduction of Broadway actor Harry Groener as Richard Wilkins III, the mayor of Sunnydale, a paternal, polite, fastidious '50s throwback who just happened to want to turn into a giant, immortal snake demon. As Buffy and friends moved through their senior year at Sunnydale High, they went through end-of-adolescence rituals like prom(*) and graduation. The characters began grappling with their place in the series: Angel is haunted by the ghosts of all the people he'd killed during his evil periods, while Xander has a wild, secretly heroic night after he feels he's become a fifth wheel to the more powerful Scoobies.

(*) The highlight of "The Prom," written by longtime Buffy *writer/ producer Marti Noxon, involves the other students finally acknowledging that they've known Buffy's secret identity all along, and that they appreciate her having saved as many of them as she did. The speech where Buffy is presented with the award for "Class Protector"— it opens with the lines, "We're not good friends. Most of us never found*

the time to get to know you. But that doesn't mean we haven't noticed you"—plays like many a teen outcast's fantasy of finally being recognized and welcomed by their peers.

This classic stretch came out of Whedon and company successfully unlocking the series' secret formula; that they had been given the autonomy to do it also helped. The WB of the period was very trusting of Whedon, whose creation had finally given the network an identity. Now it was the network with cool dramas for teens and young adults, as well as a place where talented but inexperienced creators could learn their craft in a nurturing network environment. The season after *Buffy*, the WB debuted *Dawson's Creek*, a high school drama from *Scream* screenwriter Kevin Williamson, and the season after that introduced *Felicity*, a college series cocreated by a young writer named J.J. Abrams.

None of this was done by design—Garth Ancier laughs at the suggestion and says, "There's no such thing as a master plan in this business"—but rather, as Susanne Daniels puts it, "It was about, in each case, finding a person who I believed had a strong voice, a distinctive point of view, who was bringing something original to the table, and I was just bowled over by their talent."(*)

(*) Daniels also notes that even though the WB was giving on-the-job training to Whedon, Williamson, and Abrams, the creators were surrounded in each case by TV veterans: Berman and Greenwalt on Buffy, or Paul Stupin on Dawson's Creek.

"Basically, they had to compete," says Gail Berman. "And one way for them to compete was to be an alternative place. Giving people a reason for showing up at their door was important, so they had to play a little bit differently than anyone else."

Part of doing things differently was taking a gentler hand with the creative types than at one of the larger broadcast networks, where executives were issuing constant notes and demands for how storylines should go.

"Did we give notes? We certainly gave notes. Joss will tell you that," says Daniels. "But we really did have a philosophical approach, both Garth and myself, that we wanted to get into business with people we trusted, and let them do their thing."

"I think in a way the WB at the time, and Joss's stuff there in particular, was a bit of a forerunner to what would later happen at HBO and FX and elsewhere," says *Angel* writer/producer Tim Minear. "Certainly it was Shawn Ryan with *The Shield* which gave rise to what would happen on basic cable. And Shawn was on *Angel* before he went off to do that pilot."

"I have rarely seen that level of non-interference from the network," says Espenson. "There were very few notes calls. I wasn't in on those calls, but I don't ever remember Joss changing things against his will."

There would be disagreements and discussions, but the only major executive intervention during *Buffy*'s WB tenure came late in the third season. Espenson had written an episode called "Earshot," in which Buffy temporarily gains the power to read minds and discovers that someone in the school is plotting to kill everyone. She finds nerdy student Jonathan assembling a rifle in the school clock tower, but discovers he was planning to commit suicide; the homicidal thoughts were coming from Sunnydale High's deranged lunch lady as she prepared to poison the cafeteria food. The Columbine High School massacre had happened a week before the episode was set to air in late April of '99, and the WB shelved "Earshot" until the following September for fear it was too evocative of this real-life tragedy.

"This was the right move for many reasons, but people always assume that I would be upset," says Espenson. "The truth is that the episode was not intended to be viewed in the environment that the incident created. Episodes like that are effective because the humor is disarming so that the point can land. In the week after a shooting, the humor is not going to work. In fact, it's going to be off-putting."

The WB also chose to delay the Season 3 finale, in which the mayor finally achieves his dream of becoming a giant snake demon and attempts to devour all the graduating seniors, from May until July of that year. This was a less clear-cut case of sensitivity—yes, teenagers are in danger, but from a *giant snake demon*—but the network attitude was better safe and sensitive than sorry.

"There was very little discussion" about delaying the two episodes, says Daniels (who by this point had succeeded Ancier as WB president). "That just felt like something we had to do. That was an awful time, and we didn't feel right about airing that after that tragedy. We just all agreed that timing is everything and that was not the time."

Buffy and her friends did graduate, even if it happened later than planned, and even if Sunnydale High got destroyed in the process of saving its student body. Though teen dramas are understandably hesitant to send their characters beyond the walls of high school(*), Whedon wasn't interested in running in place for as long as Gellar, Hannigan and Nicholas Brendon looked vaguely plausible as teenagers.

(*) Beverly Hills, 90210, which filmed its exteriors at the same local high school as Buffy, even made most of its characters repeat their junior year without acknowledging that it had happened, just to delay graduation as long as possible.

"There may have been some discussion of keeping them in the high school element," says Greenwalt, "but Joss had a firm resolve to let them graduate and move on with life, and for us to live up to the challenges of what happens when you keep moving forward as opposed to being like an animated show, and keeping them in suspended animation."

"We knew we had to leave high school," says Espenson, "but we also knew that the 'high school is Hell' metaphor was perfect. College is not Hell. College is fun. So that was obviously going to be a challenge. But real life can be hellish in its own way, so we leaned into that."

Like many of the popular kids the Scooby gang disliked, *Buffy* peaked in high school. The post-graduation seasons aren't as thematically pure, nor as consistent, as Seasons 2 and 3, but they have plenty of great moments and stories. Season 4, for instance, actually does quite well with the transition to UC-Sunnydale—where Willow blossoms (and realizes she's gay), while Buffy struggles to fit in—and any stumbles that year are due to the series' least interesting big bad, a part-man, part-machine, part-monster military hybrid named Adam.

And it was in those later years that Whedon rolled out a string of timeless episodes that seemed designed to stretch his limits as both writer and director.

Buffy had gotten so much praise for its dialogue that Whedon attempted to do an episode without it. This gave us Season 4's "Hush," in which a group of fairy tale monsters called The Gentlemen render the Sunnydale population mute, enabling them to carve out their victims' hearts without all that pesky screaming. "Hush" is a gorgeous, chilling homage to silent horror movies (The Gentlemen even look a bit like Max Schreck in *Nosferatu*, if he'd had better tailors), and yet Whedon finds ways to incorporate his sense of humor without the characters being able to say a word. (Buffy's attempt to mime stabbing a monster winds up evoking a less Slayer-y activity.)

Whedon concluded that season with "Restless," an abstract episode that puts viewers inside the unsettling dreams of Buffy and the Scooby gang after a long night of monster-fighting. The episode aired only a few weeks after "Funhouse," among the more dream-intensive *Sopranos* outings, and it's just as artful and technically impressive as its HBO counterpart, if not more so. Season 5's "The Body" kills off Buffy's mother Joyce, not via vampire or werewolf or demon, but with a mundane brain aneurysm. It's an episode stripped of all incidental music, mostly devoid of jokes and monsters—a sober, devastating hour about the emptiness of death.

In Season 6, Whedon presented "Once More, with Feeling," a tribute to Technicolor movie musicals in which a demon curses all the residents of Sunnydale to sing about whatever they're feeling, whether important (Xander expresses concern about his impending nuptials) or not (a random citizen leads a production number about how his dry cleaner got rid of a mustard stain). TV shows doing musical episodes was nothing new, but they tended to feature the actors singing pre-existing songs with a tangential connection to ongoing storylines. Here, Whedon wrote all the songs himself in a variety of styles (Sondheim, rock opera, contemporary pop, and even a nod to Fred Astaire and Ginger Rogers), and made sure they would reflect exactly where the characters had been and where they were going.

"This is the reason I hate and love Joss Whedon," says Greenwalt. "When I met him, he had a keyboard, and he knew a few chords on the keyboard. And some few years later, he writes the

musical for *Buffy*—writes the book, writes the lyrics, writes everything. And it's a fantastic musical that, in my humble opinion,
could have been on Broadway. How he progressed, in that amount
of time, while running television shows, is just a complete mystery
to me."

In the DVD commentary for the episode, Whedon laments
the fact that it ran eight minutes longer than a normal show, "Because I didn't want to say, 'Look! We're better than a TV show!'
I wanted to say, 'You can do all of this in an episode of television. It just depends on how much you care.' And because I think
one of the other things about musicals is everybody saying, 'Oh,
look! We're taking you outside the world of television. We're better than the world of television.' Which of course drives me crazy.
I love TV. I love what you can do with it. And to be able to go
this far emotionally, and be this silly on a regular old episode of
television—albeit eight minutes over—is a way of saying, 'This is
just an episode. This is just what we do. It's not better, it's just TV
in all its glory.'"

Whedon was, by this point, working on three series at once:
the sixth season of *Buffy*, the third of *Angel*, and a pilot he had
in development at Fox called *Firefly*. Tim Minear says that in the
early days of *Angel*, that show's writers would joke that "*Buffy* gets
fresh Joss, and we get shit Joss, but shit Joss isn't stupid, either."
Whedon had the ability to move efficiently between the shows
and, as Minear puts it, "come in and say, 'Okay, that's great. Move
this here, do this, and do that,' and you're off and running." Fans
would speculate on which show was getting the bulk of Whedon's
attention—and try to blame other producers for storylines they
found less than satisfactory, absolving Whedon in the process
(Marti Noxon became a frequent scapegoat in the later *Buffy* sea-

sons)—but Minear insists that "One hundred percent of him was in each show, in a weird way. He didn't let anything go under the bus. It's not like he checked out of *Buffy* or checked out of *Angel*."

Buffy had shifted from the WB to its rival UPN after the fifth season, a rare TV free agent switching teams for a more lucrative contract(*). The WB era ends on the perfect note: Buffy sacrifices herself to prevent another apocalypse and save her little sister Dawn, and we close on a tombstone that reads, "Buffy Anne Summers, 1981–2002. Beloved sister, devoted friend. She saved the world a lot."

(*) Daniels left the WB as a full-time executive not long after that decision was made—"That felt like the end of the world to me," she says, having disagreed strongly with network chairman Jamie Kellner's refusal to meet the studio's demands—and in her book Season Finale: The Unexpected Rise and Fall of the WB and UPN, *she writes, "In hindsight, it's clear that the deal signaled the end of the WB's ascent."*

The Buffy who was reborn on UPN was a more guarded, angry character (it turned out her friends, in resurrecting her, had yanked her out of Heaven rather than rescuing her from Hell) who spent the final two seasons dealing with more adult problems(*), including a self-loathing, at times sadomasochistic sexual relationship with reformed villain Spike.

(*) Some of these stories showed the limitations of the monsters-as-metaphor approach once the characters were no longer teenagers. A Season 6 episode called "Wrecked" finds Willow hitting rock-bottom in her addiction to witchcraft by hanging out in what looks very much like a magical crackhouse. Usually, Buffy episodes play with more depth than a one-line plot description would suggest; this is not one of those times.

Meanwhile, *Firefly*—a sci-fi/Western mash-up about an outlaw spaceship crew operating on the fringes of a new solar system—should have been a happy reunion with Gail Berman, who by this point was Fox's president of entertainment. Berman says that once she stopped being a hands-on *Buffy* producer, "I spent every day of my life" pondering when and how she and Whedon might work together again.

Instead, it was, as Minear (who produced it with Whedon) bluntly puts it, "demoralizing." Fox executives(*) refused to air the two-hour pilot as the first episode and scheduled the series in a dead-end Friday timeslot. *Firefly* was the first (and, to date, only) Whedon series to come out of the gate fully formed, but on a network that didn't seem to want it.

(*) "I obviously had a boss at the time," Berman says delicately (during this period, she reported to both Fox entertainment chairman Sandy Grushow and News Corp. president Peter Chernin), "and I obviously didn't want to be disappointing to Joss, having been his partner for a long time. It was all done on eggshells."

Still, the fans who did watch the 14 episodes made before cancellation took to it even more deeply than they had *Buffy* or *Angel*, because this show needed their love and protection in the way the others didn't. Like Trekkies many decades before, the fans (dubbing themselves "Browncoats" in tribute to the losing army main character Mal Reynolds had fought in before the events of the series) began organizing conventions and loudly agitating for the series to continue somewhere else. Whedon was able to use that passion to convince Universal to let him make a *Firefly* movie, called *Serenity.*

"I know there's this meme that the DVDs sold so well that Universal looked smart enough to know they had a thing there," says Minear, "but it had nothing to do with DVD sales, and everything to do with Joss's force of will. Universal wanted to be in business with Joss Whedon, and they saw it as a way to do that."

With *Serenity*, Whedon found himself back in the movie business he'd been comfortable walking away from nearly a decade earlier, only now he was the one in charge. The movie—which peaks with a 20-plus-minute action sequence that includes a pitched space battle, a harrowing crash landing, an Alamo-style last stand for the Serenity crew and an elaborate one-on-one fight between Mal and a government assassin—demonstrated all the technical skills Whedon had learned on television, without losing the devotion to character, theme and humor that had marked those shows as special.

"I was actually very happy for him that he got it to happen," says Berman. "This is the thing about him: He wanted *Buffy* to be the vision he had for it, which is why he went ahead and did the television show. He wanted *Serenity* to be a vision that he had had in the show but could pull off better in a feature. For him, it was about being true to his vision and ultimately getting to do it, which is pretty awesome for him. I was happy for him that he had the opportunity. By this point, he was very, very angry at me, so it wasn't like I was communicating with him anymore at that time."

Whedon had gone almost overnight from having three TV shows on the air simultaneously to having just *Angel*, and that would end the following season. Fox canceled *Firefly*, and *Buffy* concluded its run after its seventh season, in which Buffy trains a group of young women who are all potential future Slayers. In the climactic battle against thousands of vampires, Buffy and Willow take the series' theme of female empowerment to its conclusion by finding a way to activate the powers of every potential Slayer at once.

"In every generation, one Slayer is born," Buffy explains, "because a bunch of men who died thousands of years ago made up that rule."

Good triumphs over evil one more time, and the Hellmouth permanently closes (though Giles explains there's another one in Cleveland), taking the entire town of Sunnydale down with it. Buffy and most of her loved ones survive, and their stories have continued in a series of comic books often written by Whedon, Espenson, and some of the show's other writers. (*Angel* and *Firefly* inevitably got their own comics, too.)

Whedon could have returned to movies full-time. Instead, he was inspired to build a new TV show around frequent *Buffy* guest star Eliza Dushku: *Dollhouse*, about a woman who agrees to have her mind wiped so she can get a new personality and skill set each week to service the needs of wealthy clients.

As Whedon was getting *Dollhouse* on its feet, I asked him why he would do another series when so many opportunities had reopened to him in movies.

"What draws me to TV even more than movies," he said, "is you get the time to tell a story about a person. You're tracking a person over the course of their life, and you're dealing with a person. An actor is giving you seven years of their life. That's a lot of it. You're dealing with an actual life. You're not just dealing with the characters, you're dealing with a human being, a number of them. What I'm interested in talking about comes from the characters, and to an extent, sometimes comes from the actors as well. You're informed by the voice of the person who's playing them if you're listening at all. It just happens. I think there's a difference between trying to create plot twists and trying to develop characters. And that's the hard line to walk. Is this really the next step for this character, or this just a way to say, 'Boo'? I try to stay away from 'Boo.' I've been accused of 'Boo,' because God knows, I'll throw people a curve, because that's life. But for me, it is really about, let's just turn somebody over in your hand like a rock, and examine them over and over, because there's always something more to say about them. And that's different from just stringing it out."

Dollhouse ran into many of the same problems with Fox that *Firefly* had (Friday timeslot, creative interference) and was canceled after two partial seasons. There was less garment-rending from the fans this time, because *Dollhouse* tended to work only in fits and starts; "There was probably a flaw in the DNA of the idea," admits Minear.

By then, the WB and UPN had also been canceled. Though the WB had done well at grooming a new generation of creators and stars (Michelle Williams, Katie Holmes, Keri Russell, Jamie Foxx), and UPN had done some interesting experiments of its own(*), there wasn't enough audience to sustain either one with the other as a competitor—particularly since UPN had become more overtly WB-like after its acquisition of *Buffy*. In 2006, the two networks merged into the CW, which in theory should have inherited the best attributes of both its parents, but initially seemed to embody the most cynical reading one could have made about the WB in the late '90s: shows about young and pretty people, without much thought put into most of them.

(*) Veronica Mars, *a teen* noir *drama about a high school outcast who doubles as a private detective, was the UPN equivalent of* Buffy, *and its first year did as good a job of telling a season-long mystery as any network drama I've seen.*

When *Dollhouse* was canceled, it wasn't clear what Whedon would do next. Espenson sums up the hope at the time of many of his fans by saying, "I felt that if some high-class cable outfit just gave Joss total control over some dream project of his, that he would have a runaway success. No question."

Whedon did in fact take a lunch meeting with FX after *Dollhouse* ended, but the business had bigger plans for him involving Captain America, Iron Man, and the rest of *The Avengers*. And on an even grander scale than *Serenity*, Whedon got to showcase everything that had been great about his TV work. There were clear character arcs for all six Avengers (though his interest was unsurprisingly most drawn to the quippy Iron Man and warrior woman Black Widow), and the action sequences never lost sight of either those characters or Whedon's convention-puncturing sense of humor. (In one of the movie's most crowd-pleasing moments, the Hulk interrupts a monologue by Loki and begins thrashing him around the room like a rag doll, ultimately depositing the broken villain on the floor before rumbling, "Puny god.")

Suddenly, Whedon wasn't the guy with the adoring little cult audience. He was the guy with the universally praised summer blockbuster film.

"I was always shocked when a Joss project *didn't* generate a billion dollars," says Espenson, "because I was always tap dancing around with excitement waiting for the public to get electrified by whatever the project was—including *Dollhouse* and *Firefly*. When I realized what *The Avengers* was, I knew it would turn out great, but I didn't really know if the general public would find it, or just the tuned-in, really smart, Joss-ready ones."

Everyone found it, and the film's massive success feels in many ways like those final episodes of *Buffy* Season 3, the nerds and the popular kids coming together. And as a result, Joss Whedon can pick his projects, big (he's directing the *Avengers* sequel), small (he continues to churn out *Buffy* comics, and directed a low-budget version of *Much Ado About Nothing* starring many actors from his shows), and in between (he's developing an *Avengers* spin-off series for ABC, based on Marvel's *S.H.I.E.L.D.* spy franchise, to be written by Whedon, his brother Jed, and Jed's wife Maurissa Tancharoen). He's not naïve—in the summer of 2012, he told Vulture that ABC might be very supportive of *S.H.I.E.L.D.*, "and then decide, 'Eh. Yeah, it's [airing on] Friday.'"—but he's come a very long way from the guy who wasn't allowed to direct the first episode of his own show.

"He has done something that very few people are able to do, which is create total visions," says Gail Berman. "One was incredibly successful, one was less successful but has an enormous fan base. He created franchises that carry on in comic books, with audiences at his feet. There isn't an artist I know or a writer-director that doesn't have missteps along the way, but if you actually work with him and you know the way his mind works, it was just a matter of time for him to get this opportunity. Obviously he did a great job with the movie, and deserves all the success that comes his way. But in the '90s, when I first met him, he just had that thing. It's not often that you see it. It's a rare gift."

CHAPTER 8

Tell me where the bomb is!...
24 *goes to war on terror, boredom*

Every decade has iconic action-film heroes to choose from—
John Rambo or John McClane in the '80s, the good Termi-
nator or Neo in the '90s—and the '00s offered no shortage of
potentially defining ones: Captain Jack Sparrow, Batman, Spider-
Man, and all nine members of the Fellowship of the Ring. (Okay,
maybe not Boromir.) These all were, in one way or another, escapist heroes operating in fantastical worlds, which isn't surprising
given the harsh realities of that decade.

Me, I'll take Jack Bauer over any of those guys. The snarling,
bloody, paranoid hero of Fox's *24* may not have transported me to
some far-off land where I didn't have to think about the dark state
of current events, but that was exactly why I liked him.

24 wasn't initially designed as a ripped-from-the-headlines
drama. But when life horrifically imitated art on September 11,
2001, *24* was in a perfect position to reflect and deal with our terrifying new world.

The idea for *24*—an intensely serialized real-time drama, each season covering 24 hours in Jack's dangerous life—came from a very mundane, mathematical place.

"I was standing in my bathroom one day," recalls the show's co-creator, Joel Surnow, "thinking about how for the rest of my life, I'm going to have to do 22 episodes a year. I'm basically a journeyman TV writer, so it's 22, 22, every year of my life is 22. And I thought, 'What if it was 24? Could you do a whole show that spanned one day?'"

He called his friend and frequent collaborator Robert Cochran, with whom he had developed USA's *La Femme Nikita*, and asked what he thought of doing a TV show in real time.

"He said, 'I think it stinks,'" says Surnow, "so I hung up the phone and I didn't think about it."

Surnow couldn't let go of the idea—nor, it turned out, could Cochran, so a few days later the men found themselves brainstorming ideas at a local IHOP. They had no particular genre in mind; they were simply considering the scenarios you could apply a 24-hour real-time format to, like the day of a young couple's wedding(*).

(*) Years later, ABC would actually try this idea with Big Day, *a short-lived sitcom told mostly in real time. Let's just say Surnow and Cochran were wise to go a different route.*

"The key that we realized, very quickly," says Surnow, "is that for real time to work, it should be a race against time. We asked what would keep someone up for 24 hours. And then we asked, 'What if there's a presidential candidate in town and we know he's going to be assassinated?' And if the same federal agent who has to stop the assassination has his daughter go missing at the same time, then you're not going to bed."

Surnow and Cochran took the idea to FX, but were told the idea might be too expensive for the channel to produce. The next stop was Fox, where they were friendly with executives David Nevins and Craig Erwich. Nevins's interest was piqued by the real-time concept, even more when he heard the assassination idea.

"There was no studio and no production company," recalls Nevins, "and I said yes in the room because I was skeptical that it could come back and work, but it was worth the price of the script to find out."

The script—which introduces Jack, wife Teri, daughter Kim, Jack's colleagues at the Los Angeles field office for the fictional Counter Terrorist Unit (better known as CTU), presidential candidate David Palmer, and a beautiful assassin named Mandy—was worth the money, says Nevins's boss Gail Berman, who calls it "The fastest page-turner I've ever read. Couldn't have been more exciting or better executed."

Despite the excellent script, Nevins says some of his colleagues worried that *24* would be "too plot-driven" and not focused enough on the characters.

"Once we added Kiefer Sutherland," he says, "the character questions went away."

Sutherland was 34, though he had a daughter only a few years younger than Kim Bauer. He was a second-generation movie star, coming of age in the business at the same time as Julia Roberts, Charlie Sheen, Kevin Bacon, and other famous co-stars, but he tended to have his greatest box office success in ensembles, or in straight-up supporting parts, than when he was cast as the lead. After playing a string of creepy villains, Sutherland reluctantly agreed to give television a try, playing the Kevin Spacey role in an adaptation of *L.A. Confidential.*

"It was a terrible pilot," says Berman, who'd been an executive at Regency Television, which produced it. "But Kiefer was in it and he was amazing, and we had convinced him to do that pilot, so I had a relationship with him, and I thought he would be fantastic for Jack Bauer."

Surnow and Cochran had written an older, funnier Jack Bauer, along the lines of Bruce Willis in *Die Hard*. Sutherland was not that.

"We might have thought of this guy who might crack wise a little bit," says Surnow, "but Kiefer brought such a power and seriousness to it that that kind of smart-aleck remark that you would see in a lot of action movies just didn't play. He made it more serious and more intense and we had to write to that. He took our idea to its ultimate iteration, which was, if this is going to be intense, then I've got to play everything very straight."

Reinforcing that sober tone was director Stephen Hopkins. Surnow says they chose Hopkins to direct the pilot because he was the only candidate who seemed to understand that the *plot* would be fast-paced, "But the camera's not fast-paced. That's something that was counterintuitive to a lot of directors. It's a very static show, and it's a very expositional show, it's just set up in a way that there's built-in tension from the beginning."

Hopkins maintained the tension of the script, and editor David Thompson helped cement the series' visual style by suggesting that the many phone calls made by Jack, Teri, and others would be more interesting if you could see both parties at once. "It wasn't a split-screen; it was boxes," Surnow clarifies, and those boxes were used to tie the disparate bits of plot together in the closing moments.

The pilot offers up not just the visual style, but the sense of Jack Bauer as the world's most impatient spy—and therefore the ideal man for a thriller set in real time. Jack gets a tip about an assassination attempt on David Palmer, and that someone in CTU's L.A. field office is working for the other side, leaving him with no time to waste and few people to trust. When superior officer George Mason is stingy with information, Jack doesn't bother pleading with him, going through channels, or anything else; he shoots the guy with a tranq dart, assigns an analyst to hack Mason's financial records while Mason is unconscious, then blackmails him for the intel. With Jack just getting up to speed—and spending a lot of time on the phone with Teri as she looks for Kim (whose wild night out quickly turns into a kidnapping)—the major piece of action in the hour involves Mandy, who seduces a celebrity photographer in a passenger jet bathroom so she can steal the ID card he needs to meet David Palmer in the morning. Her mission accomplished, she parachutes out of the plane and blows it up behind her.

Fox executives loved the pilot, but opinions were deeply divided over whether 24 would work as a series. Everyone remembered the failure of ABC's *Murder One* (which told a single story over its first season, albeit without the real-time component), and research showed that even a popular drama like *ER* only got the average viewer to watch a quarter of the episodes each season. Berman wasn't one of those skeptics, and she decided to make a stand.

"This was the one where you put yourself on the train tracks, and no matter what they say, you just have to combat it and get the show picked up," she says. "They told me, 'People don't watch TV this way, men don't watch TV this way.' We said, 'They do; they're watching *Survivor* like this.' 'Well, men don't watch scripted shows like this.' I said, 'It's a male soap. They will. They are doing it with reality.' And then it was, 'Does it have to be so serialized?' So we lied and said, 'No, we could do it closed-ended.' That was just a lie. Of all the years I sat in the scheduling room, it was probably the hardest show to get ordered, to get everyone on the same page about it."

Fox ordered *24* to series for the 2001–02 season, and *X-Files* veteran Howard Gordon came in as Surnow and Cochran's top lieutenant. Berman had declined to pick up Gordon's own pilot that season, an adaptation of the comic book *Ball & Chain*; when Gordon watched *24* for the first time, he recalls saying, "She made the right choice."

Over the summer of 2001, everyone who worked on *24* grappled with the implications of real-time storytelling. Carlos Bernard, who played CTU analyst Tony Almeida, had neglected to shave the soul patch he had grown for a previous role; "We shot the first scene, and I realized, 'I'm stuck with this for 10 months,'" Bernard told me after the first season wrapped.

Berman had lied to her bosses about *24* telling standalone stories, but the format ultimately forced the writers to do it.

"The gift for a real-time show is there's only so much a character can do," says Gordon. "Even if you don't know the context of it, Kim and the kidnapper digging a hole to bury the dead friend, it takes about an hour to do that. It's not that hard. Jack has to go in and grab the device and bring it out of the building, and maybe take it to one other location. So you knew the mission for that hour. It was circumscribed by real time. It's easy to follow, and I wish people understood that [in the beginning]."

The format provided more challenges than it did solutions in the early going, particularly in the way the writers discovered it was eating up story much faster than they had anticipated.

"Our assumption was that the assassination attempt would be

in Episode 24 and Jack would foil it," says Surnow. "That would be like a movie. Because of the way the story laid out, instead of Episode 24, the attempt went down in Episode 8. We realized, it's still an eight-hour goddamn movie. We got really tired of wondering when someone was going to kill David Palmer. We had to rethink the whole way we thought of the show."

And not just from a pacing standpoint, either. *24* had been conceived in a peaceful era, when terrorist villains and exploding passenger planes seemed only slightly less far-fetched than alien invaders.

Then came 9/11.

"Everyone was in shock, like everybody in the country," recalls Gordon. "When we were able to compose ourselves from our own stunned response, we assumed it was the end of the show. The pilot hadn't aired yet, and the plane was blown up by Mandy in a very graphic way, which suddenly had a resonance that was horrifying."

"9/11, I didn't go into the office," says Nevins. "9/12, I remember going in and briefly discussing it with Gail, and we said, 'Let's wait four or five days and not make any rash decisions.' And it quickly became, 'Let's take out the explosion of the plane.'"

24 wasn't scheduled to debut until November 6 because of Fox's baseball playoff commitments, which provided the necessary time to tweak the pilot. Given where the series was in production, it was impossible to eliminate the explosion as a story component, but the shot of Mandy parachuting to safety while the plane blew up behind her was altered. Now viewers would see Mandy in a tight close-up, with only a few small pieces of flaming debris streaking behind her. The story still unfortunately evoked a national tragedy, but at least viewers would be spared the visual.

The concept had already faced great skepticism pre-9/11; now, no one knew if the subject matter was something anyone wanted to watch in a fictional context.

"There was a quick response that TV would respond with blue-sky programming from dramas, and people would need to laugh, because we were in shock," says Gordon. "We had no idea that the opposite would happen: that Jack would come to represent this ca-thartic character, not only about stopping the bad guys, but he was also the tonic for what became this terrible failure of intelligence. Our own bureaucracy didn't protect us, and Jack had to fight a bunch of bureaucrats who were indifferent or corrupt. Jack came to represent a uniquely American kind of rugged individual, fight-ing not just the bad guys, but the bureaucracies that were ham-stringing his job."

Jack didn't achieve his status as a 21st-century John Wayne in-stantly. The series debuted in third place in its timeslot among the young adults advertisers pay to reach (after *NYPD Blue* and *Fra-sier*), fourth in overall viewers, and its ratings were never very im-pressive that season. The writers, meanwhile, had their hands full trying to generate enough story—which ultimately involved Den-nis Hopper as a Serbian warlord plotting revenge against both Jack (who had tried to assassinate him) and Palmer (who had issued the order)—to make it to the end of the season. They couldn't spend much time thinking about how to insert Jack into the current geo-political landscape(*).

(*) Other TV dramas were much quicker to respond to 9/11. Three weeks after the attacks, The West Wing aired a special out-of-conti-nuity episode in which the White House went on lockdown due to a terrorist threat, which gave Josh Lyman an opportunity to lecture a visiting high school class about the origins of terrorism. A few weeks

after that, NBC's Third Watch, *about a group of Manhattan first responders, debuted a two-parter that showed what its characters were doing the night of September 10 and the morning of September 11, and then how they were all coping 10 days after the Twin Towers fell. The rapid turnaround of television production made that possible. (Though sometimes speed was not an advantage; that* West Wing *episode is viewed by all but the show's most ardent fans as patronizing in the extreme.) The first major movie to take place in a post-9/11 New York, Spike Lee's* The 25th Hour, *came out more than a year after the attacks.*

But when the season ended and Surnow and company had time to reflect, everything changed.

"Coincidentally, we called it the Counter Terrorist Unit," says Surnow. "Jack could have been an FBI agent in terms of what he did the first season. We weren't thinking of it in terms of international terrorism. But having lived through that first post-9/11 year, we got the pickup for Season 2 and said, 'We're a counter-terrorism unit, terrorism is the word of the day, and we have to be honest. We can't come up with mythical Swiss Army Ranger terrorists. So we went right into it and made Season 2 about the modern terrorist narrative: Middle Eastern terrorists coming onto U.S. soil."

Season 2 deals with a nuclear bomb hidden in Los Angeles; meanwhile, attractive blonde Marie Warner is preparing to marry Reza Naiyeer, a young Brit of Middle Eastern descent, whom Marie's sister Kate suspects of being tied to the terrorist threat. Over the course of the day, President David Palmer (he'd won the election between seasons) is pushed to the brink of war with three oft-mentioned but unnamed Middle Eastern countries thanks to the bomb, which George Mason winds up sacrificing himself to detonate over the Mojave desert.

It was, at a minimum, provocative.

"None of us set out to be handmaidens of Islamophobia," says Gordon, "but Muslim advocacy groups were incensed by a billboard Fox put up that had a Middle Eastern family on it, and the tagline was, 'They could be living right next door.' We realized then that we were potentially exploiting xenophobia. So we met with a bunch of these groups. People have unique sensitivities, and it was understandable."

As the story progressed, the writers introduced a sympathetic Muslim character, a Middle Eastern intelligence agent who would be mistrusted by Tony Almeida before proving his worth by saving Kate Warner's life, then beaten to death by three racist white men angry about the nuclear detonation. And it turned out that Reza was completely innocent; it was Marie Warner who was involved with the terrorist cell—and the bomb was provided by a group of businessmen looking to profit from a U.S. war in the Middle East, and willing to force that war by any means necessary.

"I'm not saying this as an excuse," says Gordon, "but we began to own the responsibility that what we were putting out there could be read that way. We tried to be very careful from that moment on to be sure that every Muslim wasn't a terrorist."

Surnow was a rare outspoken conservative in a liberal business. Gordon's politics leaned more to the left. Each man insists that had nothing to do with the writing of the show—"My politics really didn't enter into the storytelling at all," says Surnow—but whatever their motivations, *24* turned into what David Nevins calls "a political Rorschach test, where both the right and left can point to that and say, 'See? That proves my point!'"

Not since *All in the Family*'s Archie Bunker—famously perceived by liberal viewers as a clown the show was mocking, and by conservatives as a hero the show celebrated—had there been such a polarizing TV character, and series, as Jack Bauer on *24*. You can watch Season 2 and freak out about the idea of Islamic radicals bringing a nuke onto American soil. Or you can look at the ultimate explanation for how they got the bomb, and find one of the many leftist conspiracy theories about the U.S. invasion of Iraq (which happened midway through the airing of that season). You can be horrified as Jack guns down a man and prepares to cut off his head in order to quickly establish his undercover bona fides with a terror cell. Or you can cheer him as he kneels over the body and sneers at Mason, "That's the problem with people like you, George: you want results but you don't want to get your hands dirty. I'd start rolling up your sleeves. I'm gonna need a hacksaw."(*)

(*) "The network said, 'You're kidding with that line, right?'" recalls Surnow. "I said, 'Not only am I not kidding with that line, it'll be one of the more memorable lines in the history of the show.'" It was extreme behavior for a network TV character, but the script took some measures to ensure it wasn't too extreme. The man Jack is about to murder is an unrepentant pedophile who will be receiving full immunity in exchange for testifying against the terrorists. The world, the show wants us to understand, is better off with this man getting the hacksaw treatment.

The show averaged over 3 million viewers more per week during the second season than it had for the first.

"People loved it," says Surnow. "It felt suddenly not just like a great fictional show, but a relevant show. And we were a show about a hero, and our hero prevailed. I think there was a lot of maybe cathartic wish fulfillment in Jack Bauer. That was back when there was patriotism in this country—when it was running at a higher pitch than it has since."

Unlike George Mason, Jack Bauer had no problem getting his hands—and feet, and elbows and forehead and any other hard-impact surface on his body—dirty, early and often. The real-time format didn't give him time for legal niceties—in the pilot episode, he talks a colleague out of waiting for a warrant, establishing a pattern of shortcuts by necessity—and could justify any bit of rule-bending or -breaking, up to and including the hacksaw.

"The ticking clock scenario really occupies .0003 percent of all real-world situations," acknowledges Gordon, "and it occupied 99 percent of the dramatic context of the show."

And the dramatic context of the show very often led to Jack torturing information out of suspects. (When he wasn't busy being tortured himself, that is.) Jack Bauer wasn't Frank Pembleton from *Homicide*: he didn't have the time, patience, or verbal dexterity to talk terrorists into confessing their sins, the location of the bomb or the identity of their employers. A glower and a scream of "WHO DO YOU WORK FOR?!?!" only took him so far; past that point, it was time to start aiming at kneecaps, shoulders, and non-vital organs, or to grab hold of whatever gear was handy (hospital equipment was often very useful, and in one episode, he threatened to rip a man's stomach lining out with a towel) to burn his way to the truth.

Over time, the show's frequent use of torture as a plot device became a hot-button issue, particularly after a 2007 *New Yorker* profile of Surnow—he complains that it "tried to paint me as some lunatic right-winger"—detailed a visit to the set by an Army brigadier general who wanted to convince Surnow, Cochran, and Gordon that the torture scenes were sending a bad message both to young American soldiers and to the rest of the world, and that physical torture was ineffective.

"It was a perfect storm in some ways of circumstances and of current events and personal idiosyncrasies," says Gordon. "Joel was a public conservative. We were at war. [But] the show never was a polemic. We never sat around and said, 'Let's dramatize Karl Rove's talking points.' Barbra Streisand loved the show, President Clinton loved the show, and so did Rush Limbaugh. That's a good sign. If it benefited in some level from 9/11, that aspirational part of it, it actually was stained by Abu Ghraib and Guantánamo. Guantánamo and Abu Ghraib made you suddenly see Jack through a different lens, and we had to account for that. It was five years from 9/11, and we were in two conflicts across the world that weren't going particularly well, and America was suddenly being accused of betraying some basic human rights. So Jack, who did what every other action hero does—there weren't protests for Dirty Harry or Rambo or John McClane—people conflated Joel's politics and current events with the tropes of a show like this."

"By the time I was done with my tenure on the show, I didn't really love [the torture] myself," says Surnow, who passed off show-running duties to Gordon after the fourth season (though he continued to write episodes for several more years), "but probably for different reasons. I just thought we were dipping in the same well too many times."

Of the complaints about the depictions of torture, he says, "Maybe Bush fatigue—war fatigue—had set in, and people were looking at ways to voice their protest about the war and using our show to do it as well. Everyone's entitled to their opinion, and I had my own issues with it. The conceit we always had for the show was that Jack would do anything it takes and sometimes go too far. That was the point of the drama. We weren't saying, 'God, isn't this great?'"

The seventh season relocates the series to Washington, D.C., where Jack begins another long day by testifying in front of a Congressional subcommittee about all of the extra-legal methods he'd used during his time at CTU.

"Am I above the law?" Jack asks, contemptuous of the politicians daring to judge him. "No, sir. I am more than willing to be judged by the people you *claim* to represent ... But, please, do not sit there with that smart look on your face and expect me to regret the decisions I have made. Because, sir, the truth is, I don't."

This seemed like the series thumbing its nose at its many detractors. Instead, it was setting up a season-long arc that starts with Jack teaching his brutal methods to FBI agent Renee Walker, and ends with Jack in a hospital bed, near death, seeking absolution for his sins from an imam he had racially profiled earlier in the day. Renee asks Jack whether she should torture the mastermind of the day's events to ensure his conviction and the arrest of his co-conspirators, and Jack acknowledges he's a guy who will do anything, break any law, to save the lives of 15 strangers held hostage on a bus. But though Jack insists he doesn't regret anything he did that day, he says he also doesn't work for the FBI.

"You took an oath," he tells her. "You made a promise to uphold the law. You cross that line, it always starts off with a small step. Before you know it, you're running as fast as you can in the wrong direction, just to justify why you started in the first place. These laws were written by much smarter men than me, and in the end, I know that these laws have to be more important than the 15 people on the bus. I know that's right. In my mind, I know that's right. I just don't think my heart could ever have lived with that. I guess the only advice I can give you is, 'Try to make choices you can live with.'"

It wasn't quite *24* apologizing for Jack's behavior, but it was at least an acknowledgment of the moral complexities and emotional toll of such behavior. When Renee chooses to torture the bad guy in a later scene, it's presented as the wrong choice; when she appears again the following season, her career has been destroyed as a result of nearly killing him during the interrogation.

In 2011, Gordon and fellow *24* alum Alex Gansa would produce *Homeland*, a Showtime drama dealing with many of the same issues—an intense government agent cutting corners in the service of a righteous cause, Muslim sleeper agents, bureaucracy versus justice—but with a far more measured pace, and in a more nuanced way. Some critics suggested the series was in some way Gordon and Gansa's apology for the political excesses of their previous series.

"I would say that's an incorrect assessment, though I can understand why people are coming to that conclusion," says Gordon, "in the same way I can understand why they would think there was something to apologize for to begin with. When they cast it as an apology or a make-good, it's inaccurate. *Homeland* had the benefit of hindsight, when we were all 10 years after 9/11. We have a much more sober view of the so-called War on Terror. *Homeland* reflects that sobriety and the nuance that I don't think people would have been interested in back then, because they didn't live there. George Bush and Barack Obama are being judged under different criteria. I think they're a continuum of the same story."

The parallels between Jack Bauer's one-man War on Terror and the real thing happening around us kept *24* in the headlines. The way the writers generated improbable, thrilling storylines out of the real-time format—and the way that format allowed the series' incredible highs to exist right next to its absurd lows—kept *24* on the air for eight seasons.

It was a format that nearly got abandoned after the first season.

"This was a standing problem: We had people in the company who didn't believe in the show," says Gail Berman. "The ratings weren't setting the world on fire. There was critical acclaim, and let me assure you that the Fox Broadcasting Company gives not a hoot about critical acclaim. That would be an understatement."

So Surnow was tasked with writing a standalone, non-real-time script featuring Jack Bauer in action. Surnow doesn't even remember the details anymore—Gordon was the only person I interviewed with any recollection of the plot, saying, "I think it involved a heist of some kind, and diamonds embedded in ice"— and everyone agreed immediately that it didn't work, and that *24* would have to live in real time, or not at all.

"Let's just say it wasn't Joel's finest hour," says Gordon, "and some of it may have been intentional sabotage. We could say in good faith we had gone through the motions."

"The reason that that script was written is because Fox didn't realize yet the full potential of the show," says Surnow. "Once the show went overseas and became an international hit for them, suddenly, all our concerns melted away. We weren't going to be on the syndication model of *Law & Order*"—whose standalone episodes made it perfect for rerunning every hour of the day on one cable channel or another—"but we were going to be doing something new and making plenty of money for everybody."

Like *Lost*, *24* had come along at the right technological time. There would be no syndication money, but the show sold like hot-cakes on DVD, a new revenue stream that hadn't existed even a few years earlier. And the proliferation of TiVo and other DVRs made it easier for fans to watch every episode: just set the season pass and Jack Bauer would be waiting, ready to spit out his disgust at the world he was being asked to save once again.

In the early seasons, though, *24* had a scheduling problem. There were 24 episodes in each season of *24*, but the broadcast network TV season lasts more than 24 weeks, stretching all the way from late September to late May. Fox delayed the start of each of the first three seasons until after the World Series, but that still left several weeks off for the show per season. For the average network drama, reruns or pre-emptions weren't a big deal. For a complicated, serialized drama like *24*, it was like breaking faith with the viewer.

Midway through the third season, Fox's scheduling chief Preston Beckman began studying research that showed "a lot of complaints about the sporadic scheduling of it, and I said to myself, 'Gee, what would it look like if we could run it consecutively?'"

The model for cable dramas that began with *Oz* said you ran all your episodes in a row, but that involved a shorter run (13 episodes or fewer), which was both easier to schedule and to produce in time to air them consecutively. It was logistically impossible for a network series to premiere in the fall and air all 22-24 episodes in a row, so Beckman began looking at what he and his colleagues called "the Hebrew version of scheduling, which is you start at the end and go backwards." If Beckman wanted *24* to end in late May, and begin around the time Fox was covering the NFL playoffs, they could make it work if they aired four episodes in the first week, as a miniseries-style event.

Just as Gail Berman had had to fight to get the show on the air, Beckman had to argue for the unorthodox scheduling(*), but he was proven right in the end. The fourth season, the first under the new plan, got the show its highest ratings to that point, and the fifth season did even better.

(*) Beckman remembers at the end of one contentious meeting, "I got the old 'Well, it's your ass on the line, but fine' thing. My ass is always on the line. When it comes to schedulers, threatening them with their ass on the line is like saying, 'Have a nice day.'"

"Preston Beckman, who's a scheduling genius, pitched that idea, and it really made it an event," says Gordon. "Suddenly, the contract with the audience was sealed."

By that point, the show's actors and writers had already made their peace with a creative process that Gordon bluntly describes as "insane." The speed with which the first assassination attempt on David Palmer occurred in Season 1 made it clear there was no such thing as a long-term plan on *24*. The series consumed plot ideas like Pringles, and the best the writers could do was develop a sixth sense for when a story was about to exhaust itself, then quickly move on to the next thing.

"Do you understand the level of desperate we were at?" asks Gordon, shaking his head at the memory. "It's like driving at 65 miles per hour on the highway and you're building the highway as you're driving. On the one hand, that energy and necessity of invention fueled the show, but it was crazy. We wrapped in May and started shooting in July. You can't plot 24 episodes in that time."

The dirty not-so-secret of *24* was that the series didn't really tell one story over a season, but rather a series of smaller arcs—some clearly connected to the one before, some not—that would keep Jack moving for the full 24 hours. The bomb in Season 2 gave way to Jack trying to prevent a bogus war. Season 3 starts off with Jack trying to stop one biological threat before revealing that the whole thing was a cover for the true virus being released by a different enemy. More often than not, the plotting evoked the Bill Cosby line from his original Fat Albert routine: "Now, I told you that story to tell you this one."

"We realized that unlike a movie, where people were following a story, our viewers weren't really following a story after a while," says Surnow. "They were tuning in, watching the pin on the grenade be pulled in the first act and waiting for the grenade to be exploded."

24 needed to constantly reveal new threats, and the most useful of those often came from within. If CTU were truly competent and all its agents on the up-and-up, most of these problems would be solved within a few hours; instead, Jack's employers apparently had a horrible vetting process that allowed a steady stream of moles to get jobs there and undermine any and all progress. Because these characters were rarely designed to be double agents from the start, the writers had to study every past scene to figure out who couldn't be a mole, and sometimes realized they had inadvertently ruled everyone out.

"You have to go back and retrofit," says Gordon, "and there are a couple of things you have to squint at and go, 'If it's not perfect, it's good enough.' I'm a little too logical sometimes, and sometimes you just have to go for a moment even if it doesn't quite make sense."

The actors were even more in the dark, playing characters they assumed were good guys, but always with the chance they could turn evil when the next script arrived. At the end of the first season, Carlos Bernard recalled spending much of that year hanging in the makeup trailer with co-stars Xander Berkeley (as George Mason) and Sarah Clarke (as Jack's ex-lover Nina Myers): "We would try to come up with theories about who [the mole] could be. And we were all wrong." (It was Nina.) Even if their character did something that seemed to put them in the clear—say, Tony saving Teri Bauer's life—they knew it could always be rationalized as part of a longer con(*).

(*) One of the few CTU employees the writers never really pondered turning into a mole was Chloe O'Brian, the tense uber-hacker played by stand-up comic Mary Lynn Rajskub, who joined the cast at the start of the third season after Surnow liked her performance in the movie Punch-Drunk Love. *Chloe turned out to not only be an everlasting plot device (there was no system she couldn't crack if the story required it), but a source of dry humor and surprising emotion, particularly as the years went on and Chloe and Jack kept being the last two standing.*

There was also the problem of needing to keep certain characters out of action for a few hours, which isn't an issue on a traditionally structured show but an enormous hassle for one set in real time. Late in the first season, the writers needed to prevent Teri from alerting Jack that Kim was in danger yet again; lacking a better idea, they gave her a temporary case of amnesia.

It all goes back to Gail Berman's theory that *24* was a male soap opera. "There's a reason why, on soap operas, people are always coming back from the dead and having amnesia," says Gordon.

During the hiatus between the first two seasons, Gordon told me, "I'd hope that whatever this year's amnesia is is less egregious, but I can't make any promises."

He was wise not to promise, because that year's amnesia equivalent qualifies as one of the silliest things to ever happen on a series that would one day win an Emmy for Outstanding Drama Series: Kim Bauer, on the run in the woods, is menaced by a cougar and unable to escape it after her foot gets trapped in a hunter's snare. It was so ridiculous that some members of the creative team can't be blamed for blocking out all the details.

"Listen," says Surnow, "we had her chased by a raccoon or something. You can't be proud of everything."(*)

(*) *The writers often struggled to integrate the Kim character into that day's story, and actress Elisha Cuthbert ceased to be a regular cast member after the third season, though she continued to appear throughout the series. But Surnow praises Cuthbert's work and says Kim was necessary in the early days: "You felt the connection, and then the disconnection, with her and her father, and that all really helped us flesh out Jack Bauer."*

"I think the cougar suffered from a little bit of overreaching," says Gordon. "I don't know what movie it was, but there was a foreign art film that was referenced involving a mystical animal in the jungle, and we thought, 'Let's do that.' And it didn't turn out that way."

David Nevins, now the president of Showtime, says they use it as a watchword: "We have these conversations all the time about *Homeland*: 'Oh, is that going to be too cougar-y?'"

Yet in the middle of these improbable soap-opera twists, there was Kiefer Sutherland as Jack Bauer, always projecting a sense of danger even in the most peaceful of settings, always treating the material with deadly seriousness, always making the absurdity seem absolutely, painfully real.

"We're nothing without Kiefer's delivery," says Surnow. "He had to sell everything. He had to carry us along through the suspense; the reason the suspense worked is that you believe in Jack Bauer. He loves his wife, he loves his family, he loves justice, and all of that had to be written on his face without saying anything. That's what sold the show."

Sutherland would spend 23 or so episodes running around, screaming and punching and shooting and threatening, and then usually right at the end of each season, the writers would tear Jack Bauer apart so Sutherland could let the rawest of emotions come pouring out. The first season concludes with Nina Myers murdering a pregnant Teri Bauer and—in one of the series' defining moments—Jack cradling his wife's body, thinking back on how peacefully the day had started and softly telling her, "I'm sorry" over and over.

"We just realized that by the end of the season, a happy ending would have felt ridiculous, considering what we'd just gone through," says Surnow. "That if you don't pay a price for what happened, that it would not feel real. Ultimately, at the end of the day, there was an edge to the show that we didn't want to rub off. We wanted to keep the audience feeling that what makes the show great is that anything can happen. Killing off Teri, that was the single most relevant moment in the history of the show. It was the one that declared what the show was. The show is not a happy Hollywood ending, it is ultimately a tragedy. Bad guys get caught, but people pay a price. We were not playing by the rules that television plays by or movies play by. That seems quaint by today's standards, but back then, it was radical."

It was so radical that Gail Berman recalls that when Surnow proposed the idea on a conference call, she angrily hung up on him.

"That was hard for me," she says. "I wanted [Teri] to survive, but Joel wound up being absolutely right, and we wound up going along with his vision for it. After having that really serious moment of discussion and anger, we actually talked about it, like, 'What is the right thing for this television show?' As opposed to

'What is the right thing for television?' or 'What would people in network TV do?'"

Teri's death let the writers give Jack something of a clean slate the next season (and a reason for vengeful fury whenever the plot allowed Nina to return). The format that was so tricky in some areas turned out to be surprisingly helpful to the series' longevity.

"Early on, there was some discussion: 'Is this a one-season concept, a two-season concept?'" says David Nevins (who became head of the show's production company, Imagine Television, in 2002). "But it turned out to be a perfect long-running concept. What was seen as a detriment ended up being an asset. You could reinvent it every year."

"I don't think anybody knew this thing had that kind of legs," says Gordon, who was there from the first season through the eighth (plus a TV movie that aired during the long, Writers-Guild-strike-fueled hiatus between Seasons 6 and 7). "In hindsight, it looks like, 'Of course it did.' Because even for a densely serialized show, it was still about a good guy—a complicated good guy—trying to stop something bad from happening. That's a durable engine. I think the gift of the show is that, unlike a *Lost* or an *X-Files*—that builds on a mythology and asks questions that will inevitably have disappointing answers—we got to reset every year. The only thing we had to do was track Jack's emotional growth and make sure he was moving forward in his life, and we were honoring the baggage of the past he had with him."

When Gordon became showrunner for Season 5, "I thought we had exhausted everything and I had been left holding the bag." Instead, that would be arguably the series' greatest year, the one that finally won it the Emmy and gave Sutherland his lone Outstanding Lead Actor in a Drama Series win for playing Jack Bauer.

David Palmer (now an ex-president) was assassinated (at last); the conspiracy eventually led back to the sitting commander in chief, Charles Logan, played by character actor Gregory Itzin. Logan had been introduced the year before as the cowardly, none-too-bright VP to Palmer's successor. Like the moles, he wasn't designed as a villain, but around the eighth episode of the season, the writers feared the plot was becoming stale, and proposed making Logan a heavy.

"Greg Itzin played him as a weasel," says Gordon. "He was always a weasel. There was something that suggested a character that wasn't a weasel but a fox. We just broadened the character we had sketched."

Logan would be one of seven or eight presidents (it's complicated) to appear over the life of the series. If you paid attention to the cues about how much time passed between seasons, we were witnessing more than 14 years in the life of Jack Bauer, during which he killed at least 268 people on camera(*); worked for CTU (where he answered to a dozen-odd bosses over the years) and with the FBI; had a granddaughter; and battled terrorists and other villains in Los Angeles, Washington, New York, and (in the *24: Redemption* TV movie) the fictional African nation of Sangala.

(*) The 24 wiki has a helpful list of all the kills, including names, photos, and weapons used (or, in some cases, descriptors like "punch to the heart" and "interrupted surgery").

When last we saw Jack Bauer on *24* proper, he was staring up at a military drone camera, saying a final goodbye to Chloe, moving slowly from his latest gunshot wound, a fugitive one more time thanks to a mission that would bring down presidencies in both America and Russia. After saving our lives again and again, his only reward was a brief head start on getting out of the country and starting a new life under a new name.

By that point, he had become something of a relic of an earlier era, one that needed a hero like Jack Bauer to kick ass, take names, and ignore any inconvenient laws along the way.

The eighth and final season of *24* concluded in May 2010. For the next several years, there was talk—some of it fueled by interviews with Sutherland or Gordon, some by the modern TV viewer's inability to let any show stay dead for long—of reviving Jack and Chloe in a big-screen film. But it was the serialized format as much as Sutherland's intensity that made *24* special, and the franchise came back to life four years later in the same medium, and on the same network, where it began, with the miniseries *24: Live Another Day*, which transplanted the action to London.

Gordon and other producers told the press that doing only 12 episodes—and possibly allowing for time jumps between episodes—would limit the creative team's reliance on some of the goofier tropes required to fill 24 hours of television, and to keep every character occupied for every hour of a day. With the revised format, and a changed political climate, would this be the same old Jack Bauer?

Pretty much, as it turned out. There were nods to events in the news and pop culture (the opening storyline involves the U.S. military's drone program, and Chloe—now made up, almost comically, to resemble the heroine from *The Girl with the Dragon Tattoo*—had left the government to work for a Julian Assange figure), but Jack was the same as he ever was, and so was *24*. In half the usual number of episodes, there were still three different terrorist plots and a chance for his ex-lover Audrey (Kim Raver) to die a *second* time because, hey, *24*. The promises of time jumps didn't amount to much: all the episodes took place in consecutive hours, save for the last few minutes of the finale, which leaped ahead

12 hours to allow everyone a little rest before the final plot twist, in which Jack turned himself in to the Russians in exchange for Chloe's freedom. And even that was a rehash of the end of the fifth season, where Jack was taken prisoner by the Chinese.

Live Another Day wasn't without its charms, including Yvonne Strahovski as one of Jack's more interesting protégés. But what was once formula-breaking had by now simply become another formula, for good and for ill. The time off and the slightly tweaked structure hadn't reinvigorated the franchise, but there was a modest audience eager to see Jack doing exactly what he had done before, in exactly the same way. In a review of the miniseries' finale on HitFix, I lamented the lack of innovation; fans flooded my comments section and inbox to insist that another formulaic adventure was all they needed, or even wanted.

The franchise's future remains uncertain: in May, Fox executive Gary Newman told reporters, "We have been developing another version of *24*, but it is still fairly early in the development process, so there's just really nothing that we can tell you at this time other than [that] we are working on something." Later reports suggested any new show would feature a new male lead, with Sutherland perhaps guest-starring when available. But if another miniseries (or even sequel ongoing series) happens, I wouldn't expect much to change, even with a younger hero replacing Jack full-time.

It's an inevitability. Yesterday's music rebel is today's classic rock act, cycling through all the greatest hits for an audience that doesn't want to hear any of the new stuff. But *24*'s innovations, and the audience's willingness to embrace them, continue to be felt in the shows that followed it, even if it ultimately became as conservative structurally as it was often accused of being politically.

CHAPTER 9

So say we all...
The thinking man's sci-fi of
Battlestar Galactica

"All this has happened before, and all of it will happen again."
This is a line that, appropriately, was repeated over and over throughout the mid-'00s run of *Battlestar Galactica*. It's not an original line; the series' head writer, Ronald D. Moore, borrowed it from the opening of the Disney version of *Peter Pan*. Nor was *Battlestar Galactica* an original series; it was a remake of a short-lived cult curiosity from the late '70s, and only got on the air after several previous attempts had failed. All this had happened before, and all of it would happen again—but in a better, deeper, more socially resonant way that made it the unlikeliest, but best, millennial TV show inspired by 9/11.

Hollywood has a bad habit of remaking greatness when there's no upside in it. You cannot make a better *Psycho* than Alfred Hitchcock did, so why bother? If you're going to do a remake, you're better off picking something with a good core idea but plenty of room for improvement—something like the original *Battlestar Galactica*, which was a naked attempt to cash in on the *Star Wars* phenomenon. Created by veteran producer Glen A. Larson, the original *Galactica* told the story of an Earth-like colonial civilization that suffers a devastating attack from a race of warrior robots called Cylons. The handful of survivors board a ragtag fleet of spaceships, led by the last military vessel standing, the Galactica, its wise Commander Adama (Lorne Greene), Adama's brave son Apollo (Richard Hatch), and Apollo's roguish best friend Starbuck (Dirk Benedict). The series had a great theme song and an interesting premise—including the fleet searching for humanity's lost 13th colony, which had reportedly settled on some planet called "Earth"—but mainly used the idea as an excuse to recycle the same space-battle footage over and over for 24 episodes.

"My big criticism of the original *Battlestar* series was how this great dark idea became this silly show," says Moore, who remembers a haunting moment in the original pilot where we see the crew of Galactica reacting to news of the death of billions during the Cylon attacks—and then how that emotion is quickly undercut by a trip to a resort planet where Starbuck can gamble and cavort with beautiful women.

ABC canceled the series after only a season, then tried to salvage the investment with a cheaper spin-off called *Galactica 1980* where a couple of Galactica pilots had adventures on present-day Earth. It aired 10 episodes (one of which was just a leftover *Battlestar* script that brought back Dirk Benedict) before ABC again pulled the plug.

But sci-fi fans have a way of holding on to things, even things as derivative and goofy as the original *Battlestar Galactica*, and over the years they tried to revive the series in the same way *Star Trek* had come back to life with the movies and then the TV spin-offs. In the late '90s, Richard Hatch even produced a trailer for a proposed sequel series, screening it at comic and sci-fi conventions to an enthusiastic response, but it wasn't enough to convince Universal, which owned the rights, to let him do more with the idea.

Instead, *X-Men* director Bryan Singer and his producing partner Tom DeSanto began working on a new *Battlestar* to air on Fox, set 25 years after the events of the original series, and incorporating many of that show's actors and characters. (Hatch, for instance, would play an Apollo who had been captured by the Cylons and converted into one of their own.) In this version, the fleet had stopped looking for Earth after Adama's death, and instead settled in an asteroid belt that in time became a monument to decadence.

"The way I sold the show," says DeSanto, "was, 'What if Moses died at Mt. Sinai and the Jews decided to stay there and build Las Vegas?'"

This *Battlestar* was nine weeks away from filming when 9/11 happened, and suddenly this escapist sci-fi adventure began to feel uncomfortably real.

"Because of 9/11," says DeSanto, "our storyline, including special effects tests we had done, was very similar to what the country was going through at the time. We actually had images of Cylon Raiders going into space stations, and into Galactica in kamikaze attacks, which looked like the planes going into the Twin Towers. So everything was put on hold for 30 days."

That delay cost the project the services of Singer, who had a commitment to direct the second *X-Men* film, and eventually Fox passed on the idea altogether. But studio executive David Kissinger wasn't ready to give up on a new version of the property. He asked producer David Eick to take a crack at it, and Eick agreed, on the condition that he could find his own writer and start over from scratch.

Eick and Moore had crossed paths on a short-lived USA series called *G vs. E*, but Eick says, "I knew him as a *Star Trek* guy, and I didn't know what I wanted to do with this franchise, but I didn't want it to be like *Star Trek*."

As it turned out, neither did Ron Moore.

Moore's television career had begun with the third season of *Star Trek: The Next Generation*, and he would go on to write or co-write many of that series' most memorable episodes, including the series finale. When *TNG* ended, he shifted over to *Star Trek: Deep Space Nine*, which had and would continue to be the odd man out of the franchise. *Deep Space Nine* was set on an immobile space station rather than a starship, which allowed for more continuing storylines than the other *Star Trek* series, and the morality wasn't as black-and-white. Everyone on the Enterprise was the best of the best, and never made the wrong decision; on Deep Space Nine, the crew were outcasts who passionately disagreed with one another and were known to screw up from time to time.

David Weddle, who joined the writing staff after Moore, says the moral and narrative complexity of *Deep Space Nine* came from showrunner Ira Steven Behr, who pushed the keepers of the franchise to let this spin-off be different from the others. The series concluded with an extended war arc, and the writers were allowed to drop any pretense of standalone episodes and tell one sweeping story.

"I think that was the first time that Ron realized, 'Oh my God, the television medium has so much potential that has been untapped,'" says Weddle.

Moore attempted to stay within the franchise by moving over to *Star Trek: Voyager*, but found a series that, much like the '70s *Battlestar*, was doing its best to squander a dark, interesting premise in favor of the same-old same-old. The series dealt with a starship flung to the opposite end of the galaxy, decades away from getting home, and a crew featuring a mix of Starfleet officers and members of an IRA-like terrorist group. Rather than use the foreign setting and crew composition to make a clean break from some of the tropes that had become repetitive on *The Next Generation*, the *Voyager* writers had instead gone out of their way to make the new show as much like the old one as possible. Though the ship allegedly had limited resources and no easy way to refuel, the holodeck always worked, because those episodes were fun and easy to write. And the crew acclimated to each other so quickly that a latecomer would be forgiven for not realizing these people had once been at war with each other.

Moore "had tried to bring the sensibility of *Deep Space Nine* to *Voyager*," says Weddle, "and [*Voyager* producers] Rick [Berman] and Brannon [Braga] didn't want it. And he ended up leaving somewhat bitterly, and he wrote a manifesto on leaving *Voyager*, on everything that was wrong with the *Star Trek* franchise, how it was dying creatively, because it's a fly in amber, and here are all the aesthetic rules of the show, and we can't screw with that. One of the primary rules was that everyone was well adjusted. Nobody had any character flaws or neuroses, and the only way they could have interpersonal conflict was if they went through a space anomaly. And Ron was saying, 'It doesn't reflect the real world, and it's lost its relevance. It's become juvenile.'"

When Eick finally approached him, Moore was wary from his *Star Trek* experience, but he agreed to watch Larson's pilot episode in case it gave him any inspiration. And the tragedy that had scuttled the previous *Battlestar* remake became the driving force behind the new one.

"I watched it over a weekend," Moore says, "and when I was watching it, I was struck by the possibilities of doing that in a post-9/11 world. It was only two or three months after the attacks, and it's all about a surprise attack on an unsuspecting human population and a show about the survivors of that apocalypse. I realized it was a tremendous opportunity to do something that would have an enormous emotional resonance with the audience."

Moore and Eick were both political-science junkies, and as they began meeting over dinner to propose ideas for a reimagined *Battlestar*, Eick says, "All of our discussions were effortlessly informed by the issues of the day. We were inundated by bin Laden and Al Qaeda, and color-coded disaster warnings. I think that seeped into the discussion unconsciously. After several weeks, we put together something we were excited with."

At one of those dinners, Breck Eisner, who was supposed to direct the project, joined them. (He later dropped out and was replaced by Michael Rymer.) The men realized that they wouldn't have the budget to use CGI Cylons more than once or twice per episode, and only briefly, and Eick says "men in [robot] suits was a non-starter" because they would seem too corny for the desired dark tone. As the conversation continued, someone suggested that the Cylons had once looked like robots, but had evolved to a point where they looked as human as the creators they had rebelled against.

"It melded into a discussion about the Manson family," says Eick. "I'm a true-crime buff, and at some point, we discussed this idea of the mentality where you're thinking, 'In order to move forward, we have to kill people.'"

Soon, they had their framework. They would confront the parallels between the material and current events head-on. The Cylons became religious zealots(*) who believed their one god was truer than the Greco-Roman pantheon worshipped by the humans, and they would attack their creators for their blasphemy. The show would borrow familiar bits of 9/11 iconography, like a memorial wall in a Galactica corridor that very much resembled the ones that sprung up all around lower Manhattan that fall.

(*) In an early draft of the script, Moore had one of the Cylons say, "God is love," just because he thought it was an interesting thing for a robot to say, "And Michael Jackson—the studio executive, not the singer—sent me a note saying, 'That's fascinating. You've already got things in the miniseries that are allegories to Al Qaeda and 9/11. Why not do more with that? Play with fundamentalism and religion as part of the Cylon motivation?' And I said, 'Yeah, baby! No one's ever going to give me that note again!' So I just grabbed it and ran with it."

As Moore completed the script for a miniseries that the cable channel Sci Fi was interested in airing as a backdoor pilot (if the ratings were good enough, it would become an ongoing series), Eick began to fear that the *Battlestar Galactica* brand name was about to become a liability, promising silly space adventure when the show they were making was more high-minded. He suggested Moore write another manifesto to append to the front of the script, establishing the more adult, serious tone of the project.

The new essay, titled "Naturalistic Science Fiction, or Taking the Opera out of Space Opera," opens by declaring, "Our goal is nothing less than the reinvention of the science fiction television series," and that they wanted nothing to do with the "stock characters, techno-double-talk, bumpy-headed aliens, thespian histrionics, and empty heroics" that had become tired staples of the shows Moore had worked on in the past. Moore's template was not *Star Trek*, not *Star Wars*, not anything else from the sci-fi canon. As he explains in a section on how the show would approach its characters:

> "This is perhaps the biggest departure from the science fiction norm. We do not have 'the cocky guy,' 'the fast-talker,' 'the brain,' 'the wacky alien sidekick' or any of the other usual characters who populate a space series. Our characters are living, breathing people with all the emotional complexity and contradictions present in quality dramas like *The West Wing* or *The Sopranos*. In this way, we hope to challenge our audience in ways that other genre pieces do not. We want the audience to connect with the characters of Galactica as people. Our characters are not superheroes. They are not an elite. They are everyday people caught up in an enormous cataclysm and trying to survive it as best they can.
>
> "They are you and me."

With the manifesto, Moore was hearkening back to the roots of science fiction, which pre–*Star Wars* had frequently been as much about social commentary as about cool spaceships and robots.

"One of the things I said in the manifesto was I wanted to return to a science fiction that was about something that was socially relevant," says Moore. "The sci-fi when I was growing up, and even before me, was about big ideas. It was about things happening in our society, and it was a way to debate and examine different social and political issues through a science fiction prism. The genre had kind of gotten away from that to become almost completely escapist. It was all about popcorn, and not much else. I like popcorn as much as the next guy, but I also wanted some meat and potatoes every once in a while, wanted something to chew on, something that was more interesting and thought-provoking. That's what I wanted to do with *Battlestar*: not just make it a big, fun, silly show. I wanted it to be about where we were as a society, what were we dealing with, and really ask some hard questions."

Moore says the Sci Fi executives were "surprisingly receptive" to the manifesto. The channel was coming to the end of the run for *Farscape*, another space-based series that had been a modest success at best, and Moore's radical reinvention of the genre was coming at the right time.

"They were approaching the project from the question of 'Is the genre viable?'" Moore says, "and I was coming at it from an idea where we're really going to reinvent the form, going to shoot it documentary-style and tackle the issues more directly. It was all folded into this package of 'Here's a new approach,' and they were tired of where it had been, and they were seeing audience ratings falling off. There was a certain sense it was a tired genre on television.

"It's always astonished me in retrospect," he adds, "that the big ideas—the things that really set the show apart, the controversial aspects of the show, the political and religious themes of the show—we didn't have any debates about any of that. They just accepted that that was a given about what the show was."

Because the manifesto had been attached to the script sent to Sci Fi, it stayed attached to the copies that were sent out to actors. Edward James Olmos was the producers' first choice to play Bill Adama; when he came to meet them, he admitted he never would have read a script with that name if it hadn't started with Moore's essay.

Olmos wasn't exactly Lorne Greene, but he had a similar level of gravitas that forced you to take the material seriously, and English actor Jamie Bamber had the looks and upright bearing to work as Apollo (real name Lee Adama, as most of the character names from the original were treated here as pilot call signs). Other characters and elements of the original(*) departed from it more radically.

(*) The weekend that Moore went home to watch the original pilot, Eick was supposed to as well, "And I think I watched SportsCenter," Eick says. "In a funny way, I think that served us. One of us knew what had been done and how to correct against it, and the other one could remain objective. There was stuff you didn't want to throw out that was good about the original concept. I would only learn about it through him, because I hadn't seen it, but it created healthy debate. We weren't smoking out of the same crack pipe."

The '78 series had featured civilian members of the fleet, but mostly as straw-man opponents for whatever Adama wanted to do. Moore wanted to more thoroughly explore life in the fleet away from Galactica, and also give Adama a legitimate counterpart among the civilians. He created the character of Laura Roslin, the Secretary of Education who is the highest-ranking member of the government to survive the Cylon attack, and is sworn in as president in a scene designed to evoke the famous image of Lyndon Johnson taking the oath of office aboard Air Force One in the hours after the JFK assassination. Actress Mary McDonnell, a two-time Oscar nominee, took the part.

There would be more estrogen to come in the reconceptualization of Starbuck. Moore looked at the Dirk Benedict version and realized, "I didn't know what to do with that." There had been too many charming, womanizing rogues in pop culture for him to find a new angle, until it occurred to him to make the character female and cast actress Katee Sackhoff as Kara "Starbuck" Thrace.

"We've never seen that before," he says. Apollo would still be the straight-arrow who tried to do everything right, but "If I made *her* the rogue and gambler and one who sleeps around, the bad-ass and the black sheep(*), it just suddenly became more interesting."

(*) In one of her first scenes of the miniseries, Kara punches out Galactica's executive officer, the notorious drunk Saul Tigh (Michael Hogan). Tom DeSanto (who is complimentary of the Moore/Eick version, saying it "did a great job" of incorporating 9/11 into the story) says that in his script (which Moore and Eick never read), we see a young female pilot get in trouble for decking a superior officer—and it's Starbuck's daughter. All this has happened before...

Later, in writing a new character named Sharon Valerii (to be played by Grace Park), a Galactica pilot who turns out to be an unwitting Cylon sleeper agent, Moore decided he would give her the call sign Boomer, the name used for a '70s *Battlestar* character played by Herb Jefferson.

As word began to spread of all these changes—but particularly the gender swap for Starbuck, a figure many a fanboy had dreamed of being—the fans of the Larson series were not pleased. Many began referring to the new series as "GINO," or "Galactica in Name Only."(*)

(*) Moore would later borrow the name and, somewhat appropriately, give it a sex change by dubbing one of his characters Gina.

A few months before the miniseries was set to debut, Moore, Eick, and several actors attended the Television Critics Association press tour, a routine promotional stop for any significant new project. Sci Fi president Bonnie Hammer, Moore, and Eick spent the session insisting that this new *Battlestar* would be accessible and exciting for new viewers without alienating fans of the original.

Edward James Olmos was having none of that.

The actor, legendary within the business for always speaking his mind no matter the cost, interrupted this attempt to placate the Larson fans and announced, "I must say one thing and will say this very clearly: If you are a person who really has a strict belief in the original, I would not advise that you watch this program. It'll hurt them."

He went on to say that while the new series borrowed some ideas and character names from the original, the intent and level of reality would be very different. "And so I tell them straightforward, 'Please don't watch this program. Buy yourself the new DVDs that they are putting out of the old episodes, and whenever we come on, just put that in. Don't watch this, because it will hurt.'"

This unfortunate outbreak of candor at an event designed for positive spin prompted Hammer to lean into her microphone to quip, "Kill me now."

For the producers, though, Olmos had just performed a valuable public service.

"I knew we had nothing to fear from that, that any publicity was good publicity," says Eick. "With the *Battlestar* fans, if they hated us, they would watch it. If they loved us, they would watch it. And I also knew that was a lunchbox audience. It was a fragment of a fragment of a fraction of a ratings point. It's not like *Star Trek* or *Star Wars*; it was a little fringe kind of cult hit that didn't last into a second season. To have been reactive to whether or not we were upsetting that fan base would have been crazy. We never would have made it. If he was insulting them and getting the attention of a gazillion people who would go, 'Wow, what's this?,' great!"

"The truth, I always felt, was some of our most dedicated fans were the people that hated the show the most," says Moore. "They would write this long, detailed analysis of why it was so bad, and sometimes, they would say, 'And the third time I watched this show, it was worse than the first two times.' Well, that's a fan: these people who love what you're doing but express it with this cup of vitriol. I didn't mind. Let 'em scream and yell, and talk to the press about why it's terrible; it just brings more attention to the show."

Even the Sci Fi executives seemed okay with Olmos's outburst. Mark Stern, who was the network's vice-president of original programming at the time, says, "I thought it was fantastic. I know that the corporate mindset is, 'This is the worst! Don't tell them not to watch the show!' But first of all, it was pure Olmos. He was very calculated. I think the persona is, 'He's a crazy loose cannon!' But he was very deliberate in what he was doing, and I recognized that. I don't remember major network fallout about it. Everyone was like, 'Okay, we got it.'"

Moore faced skepticism from another quarter: his old *Deep Space Nine* colleagues David Weddle and Bradley Thompson. They reluctantly attended the Hollywood premiere of the miniseries, afraid of seeing their friend associated with a brand that Weddle remembered as "complete schlock." Worse, as they entered the theater, Moore ran over and asked them to find him after the screening to tell him what they thought.

"And we thought, 'Ohmigod, we're so fucked. What are we going to say to him?'" says Weddle.

Then the miniseries—in which the Cylons annihilate most of humanity with the unwitting help of government scientist Gaius Baltar (James Callis), a callow fop seduced by a gorgeous Cylon known only as Number Six (Tricia Helfer), then send Galactica and the civilian fleet on the run—began to play, and Moore's old colleagues had to revise their opinions almost immediately.

"About 10 minutes in," Thompson says, "David nudges me and says, 'This is pretty good.' A half hour later, we said, 'This is fantastic.'" Recalling Moore's *Voyager* manifesto, Thompson (who, with Weddle, would join the writing staff of the ongoing *Battlestar* series) approached him afterwards, "And I said, 'Ron, you did it. Everything you said you wanted to do with *Star Trek*, you've done.'"

The miniseries debuted on Sci Fi on December 8, 2003. The first night averaged a modest 3.9 million viewers. To everyone's surprise, they ticked up the second night to 4.5 million—Eick believes people who watched the first night told friends, "'Ohmigod, it's not what you think!'"—but it wasn't enough to merit a series pick-up.

"The show was dead," says Eick. "There was a conversation with Michael Jackson, the CEO of the TV studio at the time, who said, 'If you want to do it, recast the whole thing with Vancouver actors.' It was really depressing and horrible."

New life came from across the Atlantic. Studio executive Belinda Menendez cut a deal with the UK's Sky1 to pay what Eick calls "an ungodly number" to co-finance the first season, in exchange for the rights to premiere each episode before it aired in America. *Battlestar Galactica* debuted as an ongoing series on Sky in October of 2004, and on Sci Fi in January of 2005.

The miniseries had established the dark tone and documentary aesthetic Moore had promised in the manifesto. With "33," the first episode of the series, Moore wanted to make clear that his vision would not be compromised long-term. The episode takes place a few days after the events of the miniseries, with the fleet in the middle of an exhausting ordeal: every 33 minutes, the Cylons appear and attack, requiring constant readiness to make an escape each time. Eventually, Adama and President Roslin come to suspect a passenger ship of being infiltrated by the Cylons, and Apollo and Starbuck are ordered to destroy it—and the 1,300-plus passengers aboard, many of whom the two pilots can see peering out at them as they open fire.

The miniseries had done a good job of laying out the tone, aesthetic, and storylines of this *Battlestar*, but "33" was the masterpiece that made it clear the level of execution could match the ambition of the Moore manifesto.

"The Sci Fi executives saw that and said, 'Ohmigod, this is our *West Wing*,' and there were hugs and tears all around," says Eick. "And then it went to committee."

In Vancouver for production of the series' fifth episode, Eick got a call from Sci Fi and began wandering the streets as he listened to a series of demands about changing "33," or possibly dumping it altogether. He was so distracted by the call, "I found myself wandering into a heroin den in Vancouver."

Eick and Moore eventually made their case that this is what their *Battlestar Galactica* was, and that "33" had to air first to make that plain (and also so the story arcs would make sense). Mark Stern agreed, and defended the episode to his bosses in New York.

"When we saw the episode," recalls Stern, "one of the comments, which I will not attribute, was, 'They're all so dirty-looking.' And there was some discussion about airing the second episode first, and as much as I was working and arguing with Ron and David about finding the balance [between light and dark], I was having to fight the fight on the other side. I said, 'We need to air the first episode first. This is serialized. We're not doing *Stargate*. I know they're dirty and they're tired and they don't look their best, and that's just the way they've got to be.' And to their credit, New York agreed."

A compromise was reached: the passenger ship's windows would be tinted by the visual effects team so that we couldn't see all the innocent civilians about to be slaughtered. Eick was happy to make the change, because "I felt that they had made an error in their attempt to lighten it—that it was a darker, more harrowing idea that you couldn't see who was in that ship. Seeing the desperate faces of the grandpas and granddaughters was almost too treacly and maudlin. It was a much more harrowing and heavy tone to have those windows blackened."

In general, disputes with Sci Fi tended not to be about the series' reference to hot-button current events, but to smaller questions about tone.

The series' eighth episode, "Flesh and Bone," has Starbuck interrogating a Cylon named Leoben, resorting to waterboarding and other forms of torture when Leoben claims to have hidden a nuclear bomb in the fleet. At episode's end, President Roslin—who to this point in the series has been the dove to Adama's hawk—gets Leoben to admit that he lied about a bomb to save his own skin, then orders him thrown out the nearest airlock.

"We had a pretty knock-down drag-out fight about that episode," says Moore, "but it was 'How graphic was the show going to be? How much of the torture are you going to show? Is it too bleak?' There was no argument about the point of view of the characters, or what was at stake, or what we were trying to say about interrogations or the political ramifications of that, or could Laura Roslin throw him out the airlock. None of the real issues that the show is about were argued about. It was all, 'How far can we go on television?' and 'Is this just too depressing a series?'"(*)

(*) Early on, Mark Stern and other Sci Fi executives would ask Moore for the occasional light moment, like a birthday party or a sporting event or something else to suggest that life in the fleet wasn't a never-ending horror. Around that time, Weddle and Thompson wrote an episode called "Act of Contrition," where Starbuck would need to train a crop of new fighter pilots to replace the ones who had been dying. Moore added a new opening sequence, in which the celebration of a pilot's 1,000th landing turns tragic when a recon drone accidentally launches and kills 25 of the pilots. "I got a call from the network," says Moore. "'Okay, we get it. No more asking for parties and birthdays.'"

"I often reflect on the idea," says Eick, "that I don't think you could get away with it today on that network or any network. We lucked into a network that had revamped its management staff. Mark Stern had arrived right as we were getting under way with the miniseries. He was new, anxious to make his mark, there was a lot of turmoil in upper management, and there was ample and healthy distraction, which I don't think can be understated."

"A big part of the life of the show for me," says Stern, "was navigating between Bonnie and the larger New York concerns about darkness, and David and Ron wanting to basically drown babies at every turn, and trying to make sure we were trying to be true to the tone of the show, which was going to drown babies. It just was.

"There was a certain, I think, lack of perspective between Ron and David," he adds. "There was a very interesting conversation I had with Ron at some point in that first season, and we were talking about, 'What is the show about?' And Ron said, 'This is a show about people struggling and being persecuted and going through Hell,' and I said, 'Yes, it is, but it's also about a hope and a dream of coming through the other side. It's not just the struggle to survive, but it's ultimately uplifting. You want the wins as well.' It's about the balance of light and dark, and that was a shift in perspective. We kind of pulled each other in those directions. It made us nervous as a network, but we needed to go there, and they needed to understand why you're ultimately watching the show, which is not just to watch people go deeper and deeper into the morass."

As the new *Battlestar* continued down its dark path, viewers and critics stopped comparing it to the Richard Hatch(*) version, and started comparing it to the other revolutionary dramas that were appearing on cable.

(*) Though Hatch was skeptical of the remake at first, he took on a recurring role as Tom Zarek, a convicted terrorist whose prison ship is part of the fleet, and who becomes an important (if untrustworthy) member of the civilian government.

"TV started out strong and became incredibly mediocre for years, because of the networks and the desire to appeal to a mass audience and offend nobody," says Weddle. "When the audience started to fragment, the first person who grasped all the possibilities was David Chase of *The Sopranos*. We all saw that. Every writer in TV saw that and wanted to go through that door. We're all watching what other people are doing, and going, 'Ohmigod, that's amazing. We want to do that.' On *Battlestar*, we wanted to do everything we saw happening on the great HBO shows, and bring all that complexity to the sci-fi genre, because why couldn't it be as adult and complicated and disturbing and moving and all of that?"

"When we did *Battlestar*, we didn't want the *Star Trek* fans," says Eick. "And by the second season, the show seemed to be more consistently appealing, at least anecdotally, to fans of *West Wing*, *Sopranos*, *The Shield*, and the like, than to fans of *Star Trek*, *Stargate*, and

Andromeda. That, to me, is the most satisfying achievement: that the show broadened its appeal beyond that which its ghetto—its sub-genre of space opera—would dictate."

Though the series' connection to current events were clear, the writers tried to avoid making one-to-one parallels. The writers were all history buffs of one kind or another—Weddle and Thompson bonded in film school over a shared love of military history, and many of their episodes were informed by famous battles of World War II—and could see how our own history, like that of the show's humans and Cylons, kept repeating itself.

Of the miniseries' parallels to 9/11, for instance, Thompson says, "In a weird way, I didn't find 9/11 that different from the rest of history. It was the same thing as Pearl Harbor, really."

Buffy alum Jane Espenson, who began writing for *Battlestar* in the third season, says her new colleagues "had this vast breadth of real-world knowledge that isn't always the case in TV writers' rooms, where some of us only ever did TV. These guys came in with really well-developed points of view on the world, on war, on truth, on human interaction."

"Ron didn't want Laura Roslin as George Bush, and Adama as Colin Powell," says Weddle. "So constantly, he had the vision of 'sometimes, good people do terrible things for good reasons, and sometimes terrible people do great things for wrong reasons.' He didn't want the series to be political dogma or reflect our own political prejudices. What he wanted it to do was just reflect all the issues and the struggles that were coming up for America in the 9/11 years. And really, those same issues come up for every society all throughout history. He didn't want people to go, 'Oh, this is a liberal dogma show!' and turn the show off."

Every now and then, though, the writers were willing to get

more specific in their references, particularly in the series' creative high point, an arc spanning Seasons 2 and 3 in which the fleet finds an inhabitable planet they dub New Caprica, and settles peacefully on it before the Cylons arrive as an occupying force. It's an incredible string of episodes, one that not only jumps the story forward by more than a year(*), but features a mix of action (Galactica literally drops out of the sky to launch a rescue mission), psychological drama (a reborn Leoben tries to live out a twisted domestic fantasy with an imprisoned Starbuck), and politics. In the most memorable part of the storyline, Saul Tigh loses an eye under torture ordered by Cylon leader Brother Cavil (Dean Stockwell), and leads an insurgency in which humans become suicide bombers.

*(*) TV shows taking massive jumps forward in time has since become a common device (*Lost *let many of its characters age three years late in the run,* Desperate Housewives *did it as a means of escaping a bunch of tedious storylines, and each season of* Mad Men *tends to begin a year or more after the end of the previous one), but it was considered radical at the time. The series was never afraid to significantly advance characters or plots. When Thompson and Weddle moved to* CSI *after* Battlestar *ended, Thompson says their new boss Naren Shankar (a fellow* Star Trek *alum) told them, "'The character movement you make in one episode of* Battlestar *takes us an entire season.'"*

If the parallels between the humans and the United States, and the Cylons and Al Qaeda, hadn't been exact in the series' earlier days, they were clear enough that it was shocking to see the allegory shift to the Iraq war—with the roles reversed.

"That was a deliberate choice," says Moore. "I just thought it's interesting if we flip the calculus on its head. What if I suddenly tell you the suicide bombers are our human characters you've been rooting for all along, and the occupying forces are the Cylons?

How do you feel now about this situation? I wanted to flip it upside down and challenge the audience and see how they would feel, knowing what the normal conversation out in the world was, and how people felt about suicide bombers and the occupation of Iraq. I knew it would challenge some people and offend others, and I said, 'Frankly, I don't care. Let's do it and see what happens.' It was the right move for the show. It was another one of those moments where I expected to get serious pushback from the network and they never said a word about it. When we started arguing about that episode, it was about Tigh's eye, and how much we're going to see and how gross it would be, and how long was he going to be without an eye."

"I just thought it's interesting" would motivate many of Moore's storytelling decisions. Whereas David Simon would meticulously plot out years of *The Wire* in advance, Moore wrote more instinctually, often incorporating ideas he liked into scripts and figuring out their implications later.

Thompson recalls a moment in the miniseries where Number Six, a few hours before her people are about to rain nuclear weapons down on humanity, studies a baby in a stroller, snaps its neck, and walks away with a sad look on her face. When he and Weddle joined the writing staff, they brought up that scene—as well as an earlier one where Six meets a human ambassador and, just before killing him, asks, "Are you alive?"—and asked Moore what it all meant.

"And Ron said, 'I don't know. It just seemed cool for her to say,'" Thompson recalls. "And he would trust his instinct that it would lead to something, even if he didn't know what it meant."

In a subplot in "33," Boomer's co-pilot Helo (Tahmoh Penikett) is stranded back on a colonial planet that's been occupied by the Cylons, and on the run from a Number Six, he's rescued by another Sharon(*). Weddle says when they asked Moore why Sharon would do that, he again told them he didn't know. And as the writers began talking about the action, and the infanticide and "Are you alive?," they realized that perhaps the Cylons were motivated by jealousy of humans, who could breed biologically in a way they couldn't. This led to the idea that the Cylons were conspiring to have Helo and this Sharon fall in love and create a human/Cylon hybrid baby, and that many of their actions over the life of the series would revolve around fertility questions.

(*) By this point, we knew that there were 12 individual Cylon models, and that each one had many copies.

Moore and Eick have never made a secret of the fluid way the series was written—"This is not to suggest we made it up as we went," says Eick, "but there was a deliberate anarchy that was part of the DNA of how the show ran"—nor do they apologize for it.

"Part of the process of making television undercuts that kind of long-term thinking, anyway," says Moore. "You sit there and you come up with all these big plans, and you have this long, intricate mythology and how it's all going to work, and then right away, suddenly the network doesn't want to do this piece, or they don't like that story or that character, so you start making changes anyway."

Moore had wanted, for instance, to spend nearly as much time among the civilian ships in the fleet as he had on Galactica. The first episode along those lines, set on board Tom Zarek's prison ship, proved to be so expensive that they had to trim the budget of the next several episodes to make up for it, and Moore had to significantly scale back his plans in that regard.

"I could have written a whole thing about the civilians," says

Moore, "and who the characters were, and maybe there were more Cylons out there. We could have written a whole story about a Cylon who turns out to be one of the ship captains, and I get to Episode 3 and I can't afford to do that, anyway. So all that gets chucked out the window. I feel like it's nice to have a plan and an idea of a direction that you're going, and a firm understanding of who the characters are, but you've really got to be willing to swing as it happens."

That willingness to swing led to some of the series' most memorable storylines. Baltar had become a Cylon collaborator during the New Caprica arc, and though he would eventually stand trial for his crimes back aboard Galactica, Moore was in no hurry to get there. Instead, he decided to have Baltar spend some time on a Cylon base ship, to better explore the culture of the show's villains. There was just one problem: *Battlestar* had to this point revealed the identities of only seven of the 12 Cylon models, and had used many of those revelations to jolt the audience. If Baltar was on a Cylon ship for a while, the writers would have no excuse for keeping the identities of the other five a secret.

"So I sat down to write a document and explain how the base ship functioned and what Cylon society was going to be like," says Moore, "and I literally, in the moment, came up with the idea that there's five Cylons you haven't seen, and there's a reason why they're a secret, and carefully hidden. I liked the name 'the Final Five.' It preserved our ability to maintain some secrets, and it created a new mythology that had not been present in the series up until that point, and we got a lot of mileage out of it. 'Who are the Final Five?' became a whole thing. That was great, and I had no idea where we were going with it when I started."

It would be explained in time that the seven Cylons we knew

had rebelled against the five who designed them, erasing their memories and sending them to live among the hated humans. (They turned out to be a horrified Saul Tigh, his boozy wife Ellen, Galactica deck chief Galen Tyrol, Starbuck's athlete husband Sam Anders, and President Roslin's aide Tory.) That arc also allowed Moore to finally make use of Bob Dylan's "All Along the Watchtower"—which he had felt an unswerving desire to put on the show since the first season—as a song the Final Five all recalled as their memories came back, and a way to tie the story of these people to our own culture(*).

(*) *Moore told the show's eclectic composer Bear McCreary to arrange a version of the song that didn't sound like Dylan, or Jimi Hendrix, but simply like* Battlestar Galactica. *McCreary came up with a mix of Middle Eastern and hard rock that had the lyrics and melody we knew, but still felt otherworldly.*

Whether stories were planned out in advance or conceived in a half-understood Eureka moment, the work was great. The nature of the material, and the caliber of the writing and direction, brought out the best in all the performers. It didn't matter if they were pre-established heavyweights like Olmos and McDonnell or an untested commodity like Tricia Helfer, a former model with minimal acting experience who, in playing many different iterations of Number Six, proved she could do much more than look great in a slinky red dress. Saul Tigh never did get his eye back, and the writers seemed to go out of their way in the final seasons to let Michael Hogan express a staggering range of emotion with the one good eye. The Emmys didn't notice (the show picked up a couple of writing and directing nominations, but was mostly relegated to the sci-fi ghetto of the technical awards), but critics and viewers did.

Despite the obvious quality, *Battlestar Galactica* was never a big hit for Sci Fi(*), and Moore frequently worried that the network would decide to pull the plug before he had wrapped things up properly.

(*) As Battlestar *ended, the channel changed its same to the more easily trademarked Syfy, and found greater commercial success with a collection of lighthearted, earthbound series more in the vein of sister network USA.*

Beyond that, as the show concluded its third season with the identities of four of the Final Five, and the death and surprising resurrection of Starbuck, Moore realized he was running out of plot.

When Moore was forced to abandon plans to spend a lot of time among the civilian fleet, "that forced story back aboard Galactica," he says, "and it also meant that the mythology of the show started to become front and center. The ongoing story of Laura and Adama, and the mythology of the Cylons and Earth, started taking more and more hold of the narrative." If he'd been able to tell more stories about the civilians, "I think the series might have lasted a lot longer. We could have then slowed down the mythology and the overarching narrative of the show."

So Moore and Eick approached Sci Fi and asked to end the show on their own terms.

"The ratings were never amazing, absolutely, but there were also a lot of accolades, which at that point was unprecedented," says Mark Stern, who was initially reluctant to go along with the plan. "I'd never had that experience of an executive producer cancelling their own show before, so there was a certain amount of, 'You want to do what?' I think if it had been a big smash hit, there would have been more consternation about it. But when you heard the reasoning and why they wanted to do it and the fact they had a plan, and you saw the real opportunity that presented, it made a lot of sense."

The final season somehow managed to adopt an even *more* somber tone; storylines included a Cylon civil war, the Final Five cracking up over the discovery of their true natures, Starbuck leading the fleet to an "Earth" that had already been devastated by nuclear war, a mutiny on Galactica, the ship itself physically starting to fall apart, and Gaius Baltar becoming a cult leader appealing to the desperation of people who had been trapped inside dank metal cylinders for years by this point.

All the chaos builds up to a massive battle with the forces of Brother Cavil that wipes out the genocidal Cylon faction and inadvertently leads the survivors to our Earth, 150,000 years in the past. The people of the fleet decide to give up virtually all of their technology, and the resurrected Starbuck (who was responsible for the discovery of Earth) begins to suspect that she's an angel—much like the hallucinatory versions of Six and Baltar that we've been watching throughout the series, who turn out to be working for a higher power that prefers not to be called "God"—and then seemingly vanishes into thin air while Apollo's back is turned. Laura Roslin finally dies of the cancer she was diagnosed with in the miniseries, Helo and Sharon's daughter turns out to be the "Mitochondrial Eve" geneticists claim is the most common ancestor of modern humans, and then we leap forward to the present, where the spectral versions of Baltar and Six notice that humanity has once again started to build robots with artificial intelligence. All this has happened before…

It was, to put it mildly, a divisive finale—and one that, like the end of *Lost*, led its detractors to claim it had ruined all their memories of the series. Some were upset with the way the series' remaining mysteries had paid off, like a recurring vision of an opera house that ultimately didn't amount to as much as promised. Some were upset that the humans would so easily throw away all their useful technology(*) to live among the cavemen, exchanging one period of extreme hardship for a lifetime of it.

(*) "They took bags with them," says Moore. "They didn't throw it all away." He acknowledges that this particular choice was perhaps not the wisest these people could have made, but calls it a philosophical one—like back-to-nature movements in today's society—made in response to spending years on spaceships and being chased by technology run amok. "Even if it's a fool's errand, and you can argue that that doesn't make any sense, and it's a stupid way to go," he says, "I can see why it's attractive to these people."

Mostly, though, many *Battlestar* fans—like many *Lost* fans—didn't like the amount of God in the machine at the end.

"I think if you were with us from the beginning, you had to accept that this was part of the show," Moore says of the metaphysical bent of the finale. "We had declared that very early on, and all the way through the series, that there was this other element—whether you call it supernatural, divine, spiritual, or just another dimension of being—in the show from the outset. I didn't think there was any other way to wrap up the show without bringing it into the forefront and trying to grapple with it in a similar fashion. People that don't like that in the end, probably didn't like that all the way through the show. It was just one of those things that they probably chose to ignore, but it was always fundamental to what they were doing."

Some of the finale's detractors, though, felt that Moore had used God as a one-size-fits-all explanation for any story thread he didn't have a good explanation for—when in doubt, simply say, "Angels did it."

"I don't think that's fair, and I don't think that's actually what the show says," Moore says. "There were different times in the series where unexplainable things happened, and there was no way not to deal with that by the end. There were roadmaps and scriptures and prophecies and predictions, and Laura Roslin had visions. All of that meant something. If it didn't mean that in the end, if in the end, none of that came home and had some validity, then what was all that stuff? Was that just jerking the audience around and in the end saying, 'Ah, just kidding'? In the end, it had to have some meaning. God, or a being that doesn't like being called God, didn't solve things for them. They did have to figure things out, they did make decisions on their own. But there was a sense of some kind of plan, some kind of effort to move humanity in a certain direction, guided by certain people."

Moore resisted explicitly calling Kara an angel in the script (the reference comes from Leoben, who was always depicted as a religious fanatic), and Thompson says that on that subject, the explanation for what Kara truly was will depend on which of the show's writers you ask. (Jane Espenson, for instance, believes, "She is a flesh-and-blood Kara created by Cylons from the ovary they stole earlier [in the series]. She did not fade away at the end, but dropped into the high weeds and crawled away.")

"I certainly recall playing devil's advocate about it, as I usually did with everything, but in this particular case, I really didn't fight it," says Eick. "To me, it was never going to make logical, literal sense. I don't think any finale that did would have been satisfactory. The fact that this one was a little controversial and unsatisfying to some people is okay with me. I think it will pass the test of time. It's true to the origin of the show."

Thompson remembers that when it was time for the writers to craft the story for the finale, everyone got hung up on making the space-battle sequence to end all space-battle sequences, and weren't getting anywhere. The next morning, they came into the room to find a simple message from Moore: "It's the characters, stupid." From that point on, the focus wasn't on the battle (though it was ultimately an impressive one), nor on the mythology (and your mileage will vary on how well that was handled), but on the stories of these people who had struggled together for years and years.

When I think back on the *Battlestar* finale, I don't think of angels; I think of Bill Adama taking a dying Laura Roslin on a flight around the planet she would never get to call home, or effete urban snob Gaius Baltar choking up as he recalls the past he tried so hard to erase, telling Number Six, "You know, I know about farming." And in that way, this *Battlestar Galactica* recalls not some elaborate science-fiction saga, but the other multi-layered, character-driven series of this book, some (*The Shield, Friday Night Lights*) which wrapped things up in a way everyone found perfect, others (*The Sopranos, Lost*) whose endings still make fans angry when you mention them.

"How good is [*Battlestar*] and how important is it and how historic is it in television annals, that's not for me to say," Eick says. "The only thing I can say is we set out to make a space opera that would be appealing for people that hated fucking space operas. And that, I do think we did."

CHAPTER 10

Clear eyes, full hearts...
Friday Night Lights goes deep

The culture of masculinity in America means that crying is only acceptable for men in very specific situations: The birth of a child. The death of a loved one. *Maybe* your wedding day. It's also considered acceptable under certain circumstances to cry about sports, but unless it's some epochal event like the Miracle on Ice or the Red Sox breaking the Curse of the Bambino, you have to hide behind euphemisms like, "Boy, the living room sure is dusty all of a sudden."

There's also a transitive property that allows for a certain dusty quality to the viewing of sports movies. Men can't get choked up when Jack drowns in *Titanic*, but when Gale Sayers says he loves Brian Piccolo at the end of *Brian's Song*, or Kevin Costner asks his dad to have a catch in *Field of Dreams*? Let the tears fly, gentlemen.

And then there is *Friday Night Lights*, the one television show of my lifetime that no one ever apologizes about crying over, or tries to pretend that they weren't—because how could you? It is an engine built to make you cry—and laugh, and cheer, but mostly cry—and it is relentless.

Case in point: I have watched the *Friday Night Lights* pilot—which concludes with Jason Street, golden-boy high school quarterback of the Dillon Panthers, getting paralyzed by a brutal on-field hit, followed by his shy backup Matt Saracen having to take charge of the team under the worst circumstances imaginable—at least two dozen times since it first aired on NBC on October 6, 2006. There is a moment after Street's injury where the head referee asks the captains to come to midfield to discuss resuming the game, and Coach Eric Taylor has to turn to young Matt and prompt him: "Saracen, quarterback's a captain." The look of sheer terror on Matt's face as he takes the hand of running back Smash Williams gets the waterworks going for me. Every. Single. Time. And where I often get irritated at works of fiction designed to encourage tears, I can never begrudge *Friday Night Lights*, because it always comes by those tears honestly. It puts in the work, and deserves the reward.

Like *Buffy the Vampire Slayer*, *Friday Night Lights* was an adaptation of a movie, written by the same man who had done the screenplay for the film. Unlike *Buffy*, *Friday Night Lights* wasn't a do-over made out of regret over how the film turned out, but a recognition that the story was ultimately better suited for a different medium.

Friday Night Lights began life as a 1990 non-fiction book, written by H.G. "Buzz" Bissinger, a Pulitzer Prize–winning investigative reporter from the *Philadelphia Inquirer* who spent the 1988 high school football season embedded with the Panthers of Permian High School in Odessa, Texas. The book was celebrated almost everywhere in the country but Odessa, where many of the locals felt Bissinger had depicted them as vapid bigots who cared about football at the expense of all else.

Bissinger had a cousin named Peter Berg, an actor (he spent parts of five seasons playing "hockey doc" Billy Kronk on *Chicago Hope*) who had shifted into directing with the black-comic film *Very Bad Things*. In 2000, ABC debuted *Wonderland*, the Berg-created drama about a New York psychiatric hospital. *Wonderland* was so emotionally and stylistically raw that it was years ahead of its time for a broadcast network, and its dark content (including a scene where a pregnant doctor's belly gets stabbed with a syringe while she tries to subdue a patient) might make it a tough sell on FX or Showtime even today. But the series demonstrated that Berg had a distinct voice and visual style that could produce something special if he had even slightly more commercial material.

After directing the likable action comedy *The Rundown*, Berg adapted his cousin's book for the big screen, co-writing the screenplay and directing the 2004 movie version of *Friday Night Lights*. It's a beautiful, impressionistic film, telling the story of that one season for the Panthers in pictures more than in words. It creates a very real and open sense of time and place, and the unfair burdens put on these kids in a community where the locals view high school football the way Vince Lombardi viewed his Green Bay Packers: winning isn't just everything, but the only thing.

The movie was well-reviewed, and a modest success at the box office, but its director wasn't satisfied. As Berg would tell reporters at the TV critics press tour in the summer of 2006, in the book, Bissinger "was able to hit upon pretty complex issues: racism, education, parent-child relationships, celebrity, all these different issues. And in the film, we were limited. It was a 90-minute movie. And afterwards, I sat down with Brian Grazer, the producer, and Buzz and said, 'Well, you know, wouldn't it be kind of neat to be able to go deeper and to explore these issues?' And that's what brought me back one more time, because, a television series, if we're lucky, we'll have the opportunity to go deep."

Friday Night Lights the series would air on NBC, run at the time by FX alum Kevin Reilly. It was produced by Imagine Television, whose president, David Nevins, had worked with Reilly at NBC in the early '90s. Both men were fascinated by Bissinger's book, and when they failed to option it for television, "We ripped it off without getting the rights," Nevins says bluntly about *Against the Grain*, a short-lived drama about a Texas high school football coach whose son (played by a young Ben Affleck) was the quarterback.

Of Bissinger's book, Nevins says, "I just thought it had time and place, and a really clear subculture that resembled any big-city show. When it was turned so beautifully into a movie, I didn't think much about it as a television show, but it was Pete who wanted to do it. You had the great advantage of a director getting to remake his own movie. And he did a lot of things better in some ways. The production was certainly better, cheaper, faster and more authentic, because he'd already made the movie once and he got to fix certain things."

The movie had been a straight adaptation of the book, set in the late '80s and starring Billy Bob Thornton as embattled veteran coach Gary Gaines and Connie Britton as his wife. The series would be fiction, set in the present. Berg talked Britton into playing the coach's wife (now called Tami Taylor) again by promising that the TV version would give her something to do besides cheer from the stands and look supportive. For Eric Taylor, Berg pushed for actor Kyle Chandler, whom Nevins was reluctant to use because he remembered him as the handsome but lightweight star of shows like *Early Edition* and *What About Joan?* Berg was convinced Chandler had aged into someone more interesting, and was proven right.

Where Berg really earned his money was in the casting of the eight regular high school characters on the show: Street (Scott Porter), Saracen (Zach Gilford), Smash (Gaius Charles), Eric and Tami's brainy daughter Julie (Aimee Teegarden), Street's brooding best friend Tim Riggins (Taylor Kitsch) and cheerleader girlfriend Lyla Garrity (Minka Kelly), Riggins's fiery girlfriend Tyra Collette (Adrianne Palicki), and Matt's wisecracking buddy Landry Clarke (Jesse Plemons). All were unknowns; most would dazzle viewers repeatedly with the depth of emotion they could display.

"Pete is like a genius with casting," says Nevins. "He has that amazing ability to make bad actors good and good actors great. I never sat in a casting room with anybody like him. Kyle didn't audition, but [Berg] was able to see in him the quality he was looking for. He was able to change the character. I would sit with him in a room with kids who knew nothing about acting. You would see the first take, and it wasn't very good, and he would work with them and make some suggestions, and then you go, 'Oh, that guy can play Riggins.' He's unlike anyone I've ever seen with that."

In this version of the story, Coach Taylor is an untested coach promoted due to his relationship with Jason Street, the top quarterback prospect in the country. Street's crippling injury was inspired by an incident Berg witnessed while watching real Texas high school games to prepare for making the movie. The injury, and the unlikely comeback victory led by Matt Saracen, provided a clear dramatic climax to an hour of television that until that point had been more concerned with establishing atmosphere than storylines. We get a sense of the weight of expectations on Coach and Street, of the cockiness of Smash and the boozy self-destructiveness of Riggins, and hear a few phrases that will echo throughout the series—notably Coach's pre-game mantra, "Clear eyes, full hearts, can't lose."(*) But much of the pilot feels more like a *verité* documentary than a scripted high school drama.

(*) That phrase accumulated so much power over the years that both the Obama and Romney campaigns used it at different points in the 2012 presidential campaign.

"The very first cut of the pilot was gorgeous," says Nevins, "but it was essentially a 40-minute tone poem. If you look at the [final version], it still has some of that, but I imposed some structure. I tried to use the week leading up to the game to allow you to realize who the main characters are."

"It was syncopated," Kevin Reilly says of Berg's hand-held filming style. "Some would say it was choppy. It had a stripped-down feel to it. And the narrative was not a fast-moving narrative."

Berg wanted to bring *Friday Night Lights* to television, but he didn't want to run the series. Enter Jason Katims, a veteran producer with several high school series under his belt, including the '90s cult classic *My So-Called Life*. Katims was looking to develop his own show when he got the call to visit the Imagine offices and watch *Friday Night Lights*.

"And after watching the pilot," Katims says, "I thought, 'What could I possibly write or think of in the next year that's going to be a richer experience than working on this show?'"

A Brooklyn native with little interest in football, Katims nonetheless found himself absorbed in the world Berg was depicting.

"The thing that stood out about the pilot," he says, "is what I hear that people generally responded to in the show: how authentic it felt. It felt like I was in this town. It was as if somebody dropped you into this town and you were there. That's what was so exciting about it. The sense of place was so specific, and the sense of this community felt so real, and the people that were in it felt so real. That was the thing that I gravitated to."

Katims and director Jeffrey Reiner were tasked with continuing the story Berg had begun, and telling it roughly the way he had (though the show's visual style became slightly calmer under Reiner). The key for Katims (other than continuing to film the series outside of Austin, rather than trying to make Southern California look like Texas) was the decision that Street's injury not be miraculously cured in time for November sweeps.

"Once that unexpected event happened," he says, "it suggested all of these episodes and all of these questions about what was going to happen with him and his girlfriend, what was going to happen with the team. Was his backup QB going to be able to step up? How was this going to manifest in terms of the pressure on this coach, who already had such expectations put upon him even with a star quarterback? And that allowed us, as writers, to start writing to that. Once we got that train of storytelling going, the train really never stopped. One thing led to the other, led to the other, led to the other. Truthfully, we could have done another two or three seasons and had material or stories to tell."

Coach's job security comes into question immediately after Saracen loses his first game as a starter. The painfully introverted(*) Saracen, who has to care for his senile grandmother while his father is stationed overseas, struggles with his newfound celebrity, and his relationship with Coach is strained when he begins dating Julie Taylor. Street grapples with the reality that he'll never walk again, let alone be the next Peyton Manning, while Lyla and Riggins have an affair to cope with their feelings about his injury. Smash becomes the new star of the team, but feels pressures of his own that cause him to experiment with steroids; he later leads the black players in a walkout to protest racist public comments by offensive coordinator Mac MacGill. Even Tyra's ability to let go of her rage at her lousy life and find a way to get the hell out of Dillon is eventually attributed to her witnessing Street's injury; as she explains two seasons later, if such a tragedy could happen to a beloved good guy, "It made me realize that life isn't fair for anybody—not just me."

(*) The show mined a lot of tears out of Saracen's personality and situation, but also a lot of laughs, including Saracen awkwardly greeting Tami Taylor one day with, "Hi, Mrs. Coach"—a nickname that would endure among fans long past the end of the series.

If a lot of these stories seem soap-operatic on the page, it's because they were. *Friday Night Lights* was unapologetic about being a melodrama set in a macho culture. But what made each story transcend its soapy roots was the specificity the writers gave to each character and plot, and the way the unusual filming style Berg used in the pilot (and that Katims and Reiner continued) brought out the best in the cast and crew.

Where most TV shows typically film a master shot of each well-choreographed scene, then do takes featuring coverage of the individual actors, *Friday Night Lights* was shot in a much less formal manner. The sets would be lit minimally so there would be no need to pause to adjust the lights between takes. The actors would perform the scene without rehearsal, and with minimal blocking at best—a discussion of where they might move over the course of the scene, but no specific plan and no marks taped down on the stage for them to walk to. The scene would be filmed with multiple hand-held cameras at once. Because the performances weren't being filmed individually, the actors, directors, camera operators, and sound operators all had freedom to adjust on the fly and create or capture moments that might never have happened in a more practiced, conventional filming style.

"The single essential ingredient about the show was that we had three cameras shooting in this particular style," says Katims. "Through [the] majority of the filming, we would be shooting both sides of the scene at once. If it was a Tyra and Tami scene, one camera would be behind Tyra shooting Tami, the other side would be behind Tami shooting Tyra, but doing it in such a way that they weren't filming each other. It allowed the actors to have a very naturalistic way of performing. They were able to respond to each other in the moment. They didn't have to worry about matching what was done in the previous take, they didn't have to worry about overlapping with each other, because the artifice of filmmaking was taken out of the process. Normally if you shoot with multiple cameras, you're still shooting one side. This allowed you to capture both performances at once, and that allowed the actors to play off of each other. If they were to overlap, and one would say in one take something that just came to them, the other could respond in the moment."

Sometimes, this would play out as the actors improvising dialogue—Katims is fond of a moment in the series' penultimate episode when Britton decided to say "18 years..." as a spur-of-the-moment complaint about how long Tami had made her life subordinate to Eric's career—but often, it just meant the actors feeding off each other's energy, or the camera operators realizing they needed to zoom in on an actor's eyes or hands without the director telling them that's where the audience's attention would want to be focused.

The style's benefits were obvious to anyone watching at home—

even if we didn't know how the show was being filmed, we could feel what Katims describes as "the way the visual vocabulary of the show tapped into this very emotional thing." It took some getting used to for executives like Nevins, who would read the initial script and then see a rough cut of the episode that took departures from that script.

"I would occasionally call up Connie," he says, "and go, 'What happened to the breakfast scene?' We would argue about it. I would get mad that she had gone so far from the script, but I think Jason was a complete convert. He had come up with [*My So-Called Life* producers Marshall] Herskovitz and [Ed] Zwick where the words were sacrosanct, and now became a complete convert. He would say that the stuff you get was occasionally worth losing a sense of the scene. I'm rarely the stick in the mud, but I was the big stick in the mud in that dynamic. Connie, I would call her out: 'You fucked up the breakfast scene! What were you doing?'"

Kevin Reilly says, "The only thing Pete and Brian Grazer asked [in the pitch meeting] was, 'This is something special. We don't want to damage it.' I kind of knew what they were talking about. It was the personal nature of the show, the small drama of the show that made it so special. It was the scenes between the husband and wife, the scenes between those friends, the things that would choke you up. It was, in its own way, a bit of a fragile drama. And that's part of why it was never highly rated, but they didn't want to turn it into something it was never meant to be to try to chase the ratings."

NBC had scheduled *Friday Night Lights* on Tuesday nights that first season, wanting to protect a show that Reilly loved rather than start it out on a night with low overall viewership, and one where the series would have to compete with actual high school football games. But audiences never came in large numbers, in part because the perception of the show was alienating to both genders; speaking very broadly, women didn't want to watch a show about football, and men didn't want to watch a high school soap opera.

"A lot of men also said, 'If I want to watch football, I can watch football,'" says Reilly. "There was a bias going in, [but] when people actually saw what it was, they wanted to watch it. It was just a barrier to entry."

The football action was never the show's greatest strength, anyway. Of the original cast, the best real-life football player was Jesse Plemons, and Landry wasn't even on the team at first. (When he did join, it was as a backup tight end, and later as a punter and placekicker.) Katims needed a lot of outside input with the ingame strategy, and Coach comes across like an incredible molder of men, but also a horrible clock manager whose teams are forever having to come from behind in the closing seconds.

Katims agrees with Reilly that "There's nothing dramatically you could do that would replace a football game." After a few episodes, the writers gave up trying to outdo the Immaculate Reception and instead tried to turn each game into the story of a particular character, whether it's Smash trying to impress a college recruiter with his play or the team struggling at the start of the state championship game because of a rift between Coach and Matt.

And if Katims didn't know football, he sure knew character—both the teens and the grown-ups. Conventional wisdom in the TV business says that there's nothing more boring than a happy couple, which is why characters so often take forever to get together, and run into rocky patches as soon as they do. Episode by episode, season by season, the writers, Chandler, and Britton exposed that theory for the lazy falsehood it was. Coach and Mrs. Coach had their issues with one another—there was often tension in the marriage over the way the team encroached on the family, and disagreements about how to parent Julie, and later baby Gracie Belle—but there was always a clear foundation of trust(*) and respect and love between those two, and seeing them navigate this life together was anything but dull. And because so many of the kids grew up in broken homes with only one parent (or in some cases, none), the Taylors became not just an idealized couple for the audience, but ideal father and mother figures for these damaged, lonely children.

(*) *In a later season, Tami's co-worker Glenn kisses her outside a bar. On almost any other show, this would have been the starting point for some contrived drama between the main couple, if not an outright separation. On* Friday Night Lights, *it was only the source of a bunch of jokes between Coach and Mrs. Coach about how Eric had now, by proxy, also kissed Glenn.*

"What I love about Kyle and Connie and all the actors, but particularly Kyle and Connie," says Katims, "is they would never say anything if they felt it was false. That is what we owe, when people talk about that marriage and those characters, and everything they did, it's because they were so protective of that relationship and their characters. That was really such a great contribution to the show."

The teen stories, meanwhile, were presented with a candor and lack of judgment rarely seen on broadcast television, where Standards and Practices departments generally require teen sex and alcohol consumption to be presented as reckless, good only as the subject of A Very Special Episode. On *Friday Night Lights*, the kids drank the way many teenagers drink, and they had sex. Sometimes, these actions had consequences; most of the time, though, they were presented as facts of life.

"Early on," says Katims, "the network just looked at Tim Riggins and went, 'Well, Tim is Tim. Tim plays by his own set of rules.'" The writers had made it clear that Tim had a rough life (he and his older brother Billy were essentially raising each other) and emotional issues related to the abandonment by his parents, so if he was behaving recklessly, it was understood. And so long as the other characters were drinking out of red cups at parties rather than beer bottles, Standards and Practices usually let it slide.

"The irony is, it might have been harder for us if more people were watching the show," says Katims.

There weren't enough viewers to make protests likely, but besides that, the producers and the censors got along.

"Whenever we wanted to do a story about race," says Katims, "or Julie losing her virginity, or mental health, or about abortion—all of the things we covered over the course of the years—there was a trust built into the relationship where they felt we could handle these things in a way that was going to respect all the characters involved."

And that trust was earned by how smartly and delicately the series treated these topics. The storyline where Smash rebels against Mac's comments, for instance, phrases those remarks (in which he implies blacks aren't smart enough to play quarterback, and compares Smash's style of play to "a junkyard dog") in a way that are both clearly prejudiced and yet something Mac's defenders can plausibly wave away. And Mac himself is presented as ignorant but not a racist caricature.

Or take one of the series' best scenes, when Tami confronts Julie after seeing Matt buying condoms at the local drugstore.

Julie, convinced she's ready to lose her virginity and annoyed her mother is hassling her about it, laughs at Tami's use of the phrase "make love," which inspires a fabulously indignant line reading from Connie Britton as a tearful, furious Tami retorts, "Don't you do that! Don't you smirk at me right now! I am very upset! *You are not! Allowed! To have sex! You're fifteen years old!*" By the end of the episode, Tami's words about waiting until you're emotionally ready have sunk in, Julie and Matt elect not to go all the way, and she even awkwardly thanks her mom for the talk. When Julie and Matt finally do have sex late in the third season, there's another dusty mother/daughter conversation, but of a very different tone, as Tami recognizes Julie is mature enough to make this decision now, but still wishes her little girl had waited.

"I feel like that was one of the defining scenes of the show," Katims says of the initial sex talk. "It's the hardest kind of conversation to have, and to be able to do a scene like that on this show, we're able to tap into this relationship in a way that feels utterly real."

Religion is another minefield for many drama series, but it was an ingrained part of life in that community, and on the show. After the Panthers win the game in the pilot, Smash leads both teams in a prayer for Street's health, and the following episode (the first written by Katims and directed by Jeffrey Reiner) opens with most of the cast attending church services that Sunday. The spirituality of the characters was always present and treated as a positive, even if it only occasionally became the primary subject of a storyline.

"*Friday Night Lights* was a very spiritual show," says Katims. "Not just the church scenes. The football was spiritual—the coming together of the town, the worship, the belief. Coach Taylor was the most Christian character I've ever written. His struggle with the moral ambiguities of his job were directly connected to his Christianity. I wasn't raised in a religious home, or a spiritual home. So I think that aspect of the show was a little bit of a fantasy for me. In the second episode of the show, we were shooting Smash's church, this small Baptist church. It was a real church, real congregation, real preacher, real choir. Jeff Reiner and I were sitting on the floor in this tiny corner of the church watching behind the monitors. It was so powerful. By the end, these two Jewish kids from Brooklyn and Queens were ready to convert."

The first season concludes with the Panthers making it all the way to the state championship, in a contest that mirrors the structure of the final game of the book and film. But where the real-life Panthers fell short of their comeback attempt, the fictional Panthers get to win—not, as many fans assumed, as some kind of parting gift in the event of cancellation, but because Katims and the writers were trying to be hopeful about renewal.

"It was a show we desperately wanted to have come back," he says. "So we were deciding things based on what would give us the most energy going into a second season. You could argue it both ways—and we did. The natural way to think about it was if they lost it would make them hungrier and therefore would give us more of a need to see them next year. However, I felt like with the Jason Street injury, they needed a win. It felt like giving the team and the show something to celebrate was important and would help the show to go on. We also had cliffhangers embedded, like Coach's college job offer, and Tami's pregnancy."

Kevin Reilly had championed *Friday Night Lights* all season despite skepticism from his superiors. "I think some of the Powers That Be, not mentioning any names—Jeff Zucker—thought it was never going to make it past the pilot," he says. Shortly after the show was renewed for a second season, NBC chairman Zucker replaced Reilly with independent producer Ben Silverman, a charismatic deal-maker with no loyalty to most of Reilly's shows(*).

(*) The Silverman era was a catastrophe for NBC, even by the overall disastrous standard of the early years of the 21st century at the Peacock network, and as Silverman gave way to various unsuccessful replacements, Reilly took pleasure in the continued survival of shows he greenlit, including Friday Night Lights, The Office, *and* 30 Rock. *"Shows I was very unpopular in the building for developing, that they felt were the low shows that were holding them back, were [instead] the ones that stayed on by default there, and were the ones propping up the network for a while."*

That first season is among the more perfect seasons in the history of broadcast network drama—so good, in fact, that in my review of the finale, I wrote that I feared there was nowhere to go creatively but down, and that perhaps we'd all be happier if the series lived fast, died young, and left a good-looking corpse.

I just didn't realize that an actual corpse would be part of the second-season premiere.

Late in the first season, Tyra barely escapes being raped in a parking lot, and as the new season begins, her attacker returns for a second chance. Landry, who had been nursing a crush on Tyra since midway through Season 1, shows up to scare the rapist away(*), but when the man threatens to keep coming back until he's satisfied, Landry hits him in the head with a lead pipe, inadvertently killing him. Panicked, Tyra convinces Landry (whose father is a local cop) that their best course of action is to dump the body in a river.

(*) As with so many Friday Night Lights *scenes, this one was shot multiple ways. In the version originally sent to critics, the killing blow*

is struck while Landry is defending Tyra from an assault by the rapist. Landry's actions become more justifiable in that circumstance, but then the decision to hide the body makes even less sense.

That storyline seemed wildly out of keeping with the universe and tone of the show to that point, particularly in the way it thrust Landry—whose role had always been the everyman observer of the dramatic things happening around him—into the middle of this dark, overwrought idea. Everyone assumed this was a directive from the network to make the show sexier, more dangerous, and easier to promote in its second season. It wasn't. Katims and the writers had cooked it up on their own as a way to push Landry and Tyra closer together.

"I definitely think that it was that people rejected the idea of that story at a seminal level," Katims told me at the end of the series' final season. "I don't think people were really responding to the execution of it. They just didn't believe this was the show they'd signed on for. They leaped to, 'This is the network forcing a story,' which wasn't true... We told that story in a similar way as we tell other stories. It wasn't that different. I think people just rejected it from the basic idea of it."

The murder was Season 2's most obvious misstep—and the angry reaction to it captured just how great Season 1 had been (no one gets this upset when a slightly above-average show jumps the shark)—but it was far from the only one. The center of the series in its first year had been the football team, with stories spinning out of what Coach and his players were doing and how it affected the community at large. The second season, meanwhile, often kept the Panthers in the background, and the characters were flung far and wide in disconnected storylines that increased the soap-opera factor, past the point where even the actors and filming style could elevate the material: Street, Riggins, and Lyla take a trip to Mexico, where Jason ponders getting a dangerous, experimental procedure to restore his mobility. Julie dumps Matt for a hot lifeguard, and Matt responds by having an affair with his grandmother's live-in nurse Carlotta. Buddy Garrity (Brad Leland), Lyla's father and the Panthers' most powerful booster, takes in a juvenile delinquent named Santiago and encourages Eric to give him a spot on the team. Tami randomly winds up coaching the Dillon girls' volleyball team, and recruits the inexperienced Tyra as her new star player.

Right before the writers strike interrupted production of the season, Katims and his team were finally beginning to pull the show out of its tailspin. Landry and Tyra fess up to the cops, get off with little more than a warning, and both they and the show implicitly agree that the whole ugly affair will never be mentioned again. The next-to-last episode of that season features one of the show's best single scenes: Matt has been in a drunken tailspin, and Eric throws the kid, fully clothed, into a shower to sober him up. "Everybody leaves me!" Matt bellows, alluding not only to the break-up with Julie, but the departure of both his parents, Carlotta, and even Eric himself for a period at the start of the season. "What's wrong with me?" Matt's emotions are so painful and raw and obvious that all a chastened Eric can do is reply, "There is nothing wrong with you. There is nothing wrong with you at all."

Katims had recognized that the lack of football-related stories was becoming a problem, and was preparing to address it in the season's second half. Then the strike shut the business down for a few months, and unlike some of NBC's other shows, *Friday Night Lights* wasn't allowed to resume production when the strike ended.

"Every show that I've done is a bubble show," says Katims. "I'm used to it, but in my career, I have never felt more passionately about needing to have a show come back than that season of *Friday Night Lights*. I felt like if the show ended after the second season, it would have killed me. One reason, it was the middle of the season. We weren't able to put an ending on the season, let alone the show. And also because we had taken such huge criticism for the murder storyline of Season 2, I really wanted the chance to move past that and get the show to a point where it wasn't going to end on 'Oh, they did that stupid murder storyline.'"

For a while, it didn't look like Katims was going to get that shot at redemption. Earlier in the season, a reporter from *Radar* had asked Ben Silverman whether *Friday Night Lights*—which the reporter called "the best show on TV"—would be renewed. Silverman kept trying to tell him to instead watch *30 Rock*, which Silverman considered TV's best show. The reporter stuck to his guns, saying he wanted to keep watching *Friday Night Lights*, and Silverman replied, "I love it. You love it. Unfortunately, no one watches it. That's the thing with shows. People have to watch them. We're NBC, we have a reputation to uphold. And, man, with this writers' strike… Well, we'll see what we can do. But start watching *30 Rock*."

"His negative comments were very useful to us," says David Nevins. "It gave us the heads up that we were on the ax, and we were able to mobilize the forces. Some of those forces included the NBC sales department."

Friday Night Lights had fans in other departments at NBC, and it had fans at other entertainment companies—one of which was looking for a show exactly like it.

"Our needs at DirecTV were very unique," says Eric Shanks, who was president of the satellite company at the time. "For us, it was, 'Can you have different content outside of sports that would make someone switch from cable to DirecTV? At DirecTV we had a bunch of sports, and people are passionate about sports, so we asked, 'What is the equivalent entertainment content out there with hardcore, passionate fans?'"

DirecTV had already bought a struggling show from NBC, the supernatural daytime soap *Passions*, and the experiment had worked well enough that Shanks was looking to try again, this time aiming for something with more overt appeal to the sports fans who formed the core of his subscriber base.

"Everybody knew that *Friday Night Lights* was on the bubble," Shanks says. "Really, the guy that should be given a lot of credit for saving it is Tom Arnold. I was at Sundance with Tom. He and I are roommates every year at a hotel in Sundance. We were having dinner with Ben Silverman, who was running NBC at the time. Tom was the one who put that together, and at that dinner, eating Chinese food in Park City, we decided to save *Friday Night Lights*. It was like a round peg in a round hole. It fit perfectly."

DirecTV agreed to foot what Nevins estimates as $1 million of the $2.2 million per-episode production costs, in return for an exclusive window to show the third season before it aired on NBC. It was, at the start, a one-year experiment, but it was the reprieve Katims needed.

When a great show has a bad season, it usually comes late in the run, and it usually signals an inexorable creative decline. Shows that go bad don't as a rule get better. But *Friday Night Lights* did. After some deliberation about continuing the Season 2 storylines to their logical conclusion, the writers decided that a clean break from that season would be best for all involved. The story resumed the following fall, all the dangling plotlines were ignored (Santiago vanished, as did Lyla's brief career as a Christian radio talk show host), and like a penny in a fountain, wishing that the second season hadn't happened made it so(*). *Friday Night Lights* was *Friday Night Lights* again, once again capable of inducing goosebumps, laughter, and tears whenever it wanted.

(*) Many newcomers to the show have heard the horror stories about Season 2, and ask if they should just skip right from Season 1 to 3. I always tell them to watch it all, not only because there's enough isolated greatness to make it worth suffering through the dumb stuff, but because the ability to tell jokes about Landry Clarke's murderous ways is among the great shared joys of being an FNL fan. And if you don't watch, you don't get to make those jokes.

It was a transitional year for the show, in which Katims and company had to adjust to a shorter 13-episode season(*) while preparing to say goodbye to most of their young characters. Where other teen series often prolonged their kids' time in high school or followed them all to college, Katims knew that this show was about the town, the team, and the coach, and it would feel phony to not let most of the kids graduate, especially after he had already futzed around with their ages(**) in the earlier seasons. Over the course of Season 3, Coach helps Smash get a spot on the team at Texas A&M; Street moves to the northeast to be with the mother of his baby (and, somewhat improbably, get a job as a junior sports agent, despite having only a GED); and Tim, Matt, Tyra, and Lyla all move with varying degrees of enthusiasm towards collegiate life.

(*) Friday Night Lights had always had the depth and fine characterization of a cable drama; making each season the length of one only made the similarities more obvious.

(**) In the pilot, Street, Riggins, and Lyla are presented as lifelong friends going back to early childhood, yet the later chronology of the

series makes Tim and Lyla out to be high school sophomores during Street's senior year. And Landry, who's been shown driving a car on his own since the first episode, is one of two characters (along with Julie) to not graduate until the fourth season, meaning he either somehow got his driver's license as a 15-year-old freshman or else (despite being the smartest kid on the show) was held back a year or two.

Much of the season deals with the quarterback controversy between gutsy but limited Matt Saracen and J.D. McCoy, a rocket-armed freshman whose wealthy, bullying father Joe has been preparing him for the NFL since infancy. Unsure of whether DirecTV would want to continue the series, Katims once again had to write an episode that could work as a series finale, while also setting things up for a new season. He wrote a beaut: "Tomorrow Blues," in which the seniors graduate, and Joe McCoy arranges to have Eric lose his job. As a consolation, the school board offers Eric the position as coach at East Dillon High, the long-dormant school on the poorer, blacker side of town, with minimal facilities and budget, and no players of any portfolio. (An earlier episode had cleverly shown Joe, Buddy Garrity, and the other boosters gerrymandering the school districts so all the good prospects would be Panthers.) Tami reassures Eric, "No matter what happens, no matter where you go, no matter what you do, I'm gonna be right behind you. Always and always and always," and we close on the lovely, bittersweet image of Coach and Mrs. Coach standing on the neglected East Dillon football field, pondering this cruel twist of fate but still together to face the challenges to come.

"The whole impetus for moving the show to East Dillon had to do with the fact that we were graduating basically the entire football team," says Katims. "It was such a challenge as a writer to be losing all of these characters we had spent three years falling in love with. They all had to move on. The writers and I felt that to try to reinvent Coach with a new Panther team would be tough. It would be hard not to compare these new teammates with the characters we had spent three years investing in. So the idea of East Dillon came up in the writers' room. This was a different side of town. The series shifted from a show where Coach Taylor was dealing with huge expectations on him, to a situation where there were no expectations. No expectations, no resources. It was a totally different dynamic. It felt like we could reinvent the show just enough so that the audience could see this team as something new, and not compare it to the Panthers."

And the writers would get to tell the stories of East Dillon, because DirecTV extended the agreement with NBC for two more seasons.

"We had done some research," says Eric Shanks, "and we had found that maybe not a lot of people, but there were enough people, that said *Friday Night Lights* had somehow influenced their decision in coming to DirecTV, that it made sense to continue. And you know what? Between Jason and the cast and Pete, you're in one of those rare situations where you become emotionally attached, and you kind of have the ability to continue on a project that you love, and you can justify it. It would have been a shame. It would have been a disaster if the show had ended before it was ready. It was part business, and part clear eyes, full hearts."

Peter Berg had long ago handed the keys to Katims, but he returned to direct the Season 4 premiere, and to help cast the four new characters faced with the heavy burden of replacing the audience's favorites: Vince Howard (Michael B. Jordan, a.k.a. Wallace from *The Wire*), the son of a drug addict who joins the team as an alternative to juvenile detention, and turns out to be a great quarterback; Luke Cafferty (Matt Lauria), a would-be Panthers star frustrated to find himself on the woeful East Dillon Lions when the Taylors realize what part of town he really lives in; Jess Merriweather (Jurnee Smollett), football-crazed daughter of the quarterback from the last relevant Lions team; and Becky Sproles (Madison Burge), aspiring beauty queen and new neighbor of Tim Riggins, after Riggins quits college and moves into the Airstream trailer in her mother's backyard.

"During the third season, [Berg] called and said, 'I really want to come back and direct an episode of the show,'" says Katims. "I said, 'If you want to come back, this is the one you should direct,' because I knew it was essentially like doing a pilot, and it was when we were losing Jeffrey Reiner. So there was no more perfect of a time for him to do it. That was the one time he came back and was very day-to-day, active on the show. In prepping that episode, we were casting these new roles, and Pete was still there to do that. Clearly, you can tell from the pilot how good he is at it. It was exciting for me, because I had never actually worked with him as a director."

This reinvention of the show shouldn't have worked—but did. Though Julie and Landry wound up at East Dillon High, and Tim and Matt were still hanging around town for different reasons, the final seasons were essentially a spin-off that had retained Coach and Mrs. Coach as the main characters. We were at a new school, with new characters, and not only asked to root for a new team, but root *against* the one that had meant so much to us the past three seasons.

"I had a lot of trepidation about turning the team we'd rooted for for three years into the villains," says Katims. "I didn't know how that would go. But I was watching the second episode of the fourth season in, [and] there's a pep rally scene where the crowd boos Tami Taylor off the stage. I was watching in the editing room and I instantly hated the Panthers. For three years, the Panthers were everything, and in one scene I hated them."

The new setting allowed the show to deal even more with race and class than it had in the early years, and while the new characters all fit in comfortably (especially Vince), the older ones weren't forgotten. In an hour that was emotionally devastating even by the usual tear-jerking *FNL* standards, Matt has to cope with the death of his father in an IED explosion in Iraq—and with the fact that he's being asked to grieve a man who essentially abandoned him to care for Grandma Saracen and raise himself alone. The Riggins brothers and Landry take Matt out for some beers to take his mind off of things; instead, a drunk Matt decides to break into the mortuary to get a look inside his dad's coffin, which the funeral director had previously suggested he not open. Matt sees the state of his father's remains, but the way the scene is shot, the audience doesn't. And we don't need to, because the look of abject horror on Zach Gilford's face(*) tells us everything.

(*) As much as the subject matter, I think the unrelenting emotionality of Friday Night Lights *also prevented it from being a bigger hit. This was a show that worked you like a speed bag, and made you feel the characters' pain—and also, at times, joy—more deeply than any other show on television at the time. And most viewers don't want to be put through the wringer like that every week.*

During those final seasons, Katims had to deal with executives at both NBC and DirecTV, which could have been creatively stifling, but actually gave him unexpected freedom. The DirecTV people had no major issues with content, and for NBC, *Friday Night Lights* had the lowest of profiles, practically treated as if it were one of the foreign imports the network was acquiring as cheap scripted programming for the spring and summer.

In the fourth season, Becky gets pregnant after having un-protected sex with Luke. Her mother had given birth to her as a teenager; Becky, not wanting to repeat the cycle (and after some counseling from Tami that gets Mrs. Coach in trouble), gets an abortion. Bea Arthur's character on *Maude* had famously gotten an abortion in the '70s, but the issue had become so politicized that a broadcast-network character virtually never went through with one in the decades since. If a regular character on a network show got pregnant and considered an abortion, she would either change her mind or conveniently miscarry. But Katims was allowed to go through with the story as planned.

Katims admits, "I went into that storyline naively" and was surprised when his fellow producers suggested they would need a backup plan for when the network said no. "But remarkably, it wasn't something I remember there being a lot of flak about. The Standards [executives] were rightfully concerned that any facts we were stating were accurate, if we talked about statistics. They were very concerned about putting out false information. But as far as I can remember, there was never a big conversation about whether or not we could tell the story. I do think at that point, we were just flying way under the radar, too, with the network. I think it made it a little bit less [problematic], for some reason, because it was going to run first on DirecTV."

Friday Night Lights had always trafficked in certain sports-movie clichés, and therefore it was easy to predict many of the beats of the final two seasons: that the Lions would start out as massive underdogs, then win a moral victory by knocking the hated Pan-thers out of the playoffs, then become genuinely good by the second year. But the execution of the individual story beats—Eric's initial difficulty adjusting to the mindset and culture of his new players; Vince's father getting out of prison and inserting himself between his son and Coach; Luke facing the reality that he's not good enough to get a college scholarship—were at the show's usual elevated level. And by the end of the final season, these characters and this team had been through so much together that we wanted to see them win it all, cliché or not. And Katims still found a way to mix defeat with victory. The Lions win the state championship, but are disbanded right afterwards; the town has decided it only has enough money to support one football team, and that team will of course be the Panthers.

All the conclusions in the finale have that same mix of emotions, where characters get some of what they want, but never everything. Matt and Julie get engaged, but the Taylors aren't pleased they're doing it so young. Luke and Becky pledge their love for each other, but with no promising college opportunities, Luke enlists in the Army. Tim and Tyra get back together for a few days, but they recognize that while they love each other, their ambitions (his to build a ranch house in Dillon, hers to travel the world and go into politics) likely won't reconcile.

And in the most important storyline, Eric rejects a lucrative offer to coach the "super team" of players from both sides of town, finally recognizing that it's time to let Tami's dreams take precedence, and moves with her to Philadelphia when she surprisingly(*) gets a job as dean of admissions at an elite college. This had always been a show about a marriage as much as it was about football, and we close (for real, this time) with the Taylors arm in arm, walking happily off the field of Eric's new team, where the players don't yet know the "clear eyes, full hearts" chant but will learn it in time.

(*) As with Street's sports agent career, it's best not to think too closely about many of the happy endings given to these characters we loved.

The DirecTV deal had given three additional years to a show that would have been canceled after two under the traditional business model. In the past, shows would occasionally leap from one network to another, but not ones as low-rated as *Friday Night Lights* was. The boom in technology and viewing options created an avenue that hadn't existed before, and DirecTV followed the *FNL* deal with one to resurrect *Damages* after FX canceled it. The *Damages* experiment led DirecTV to announce it was getting out of the series-saving business, but other paths have opened since then. *Arrested Development*, the critically adored Fox sitcom (also developed at Imagine under David Nevins), returned with new episodes in 2013 as part of Netflix's streaming video service.

"I think with all this hunger for programming," says Nevins, "there are going to be things that don't fit or aren't quite big enough for a big guy, but could make sense for a small guy if you can make the economics work. There's a handful of shows. With the explosion of other distributors, I think there's life after death in one place if you have loyalty and love."

For a while, it looked like even *Friday Night Lights* had more life in it, thanks to the loyalty and love of the people who made it. The book that became a movie that became a TV show was discussed for a while as the subject of yet another movie—this time a direct sequel to the TV series—until Kyle Chandler finally said he didn't want to do it, given how well the show had already ended.

Berg wanted to do a TV show because he realized a movie ultimately couldn't contain all the stories and themes of the book, and the TV show proved in spades how right the medium was for the subject. The show also got three different outstanding endings. Before Coach took his ball and went home, I asked Katims why he and everyone else felt like they wanted to translate the material back into its previous medium.

"Certainly, part of the joy of doing this," Katims explained, "was we would get to be in this world again, and the fans would get to do the same—to be with Coach and Tami for another couple of hours. But that's not a reason to make a movie. You make a movie if you have a great story to tell. We came up with a direction, and I worked with some of the writers who had been working on the show for all of the seasons, and we did what we would do with an episode, but it was a movie. We only did it because we felt like we had a great story to tell and didn't feel redundant to everything that's already been there. If we do get to make the movie, it will be a great kind of next chapter."

Like the character he played so well for five seasons, Chandler seems the type not easily moved off a decision once he makes it. And he's probably right about this one. But I would never count against him changing his mind, nor against a theoretical movie sequel being great. After seeing *Friday Night Lights* pull off as many improbable real-life comebacks as the Panthers and Lions did fictional ones over the years, anything seems possible so long as we remember the "clear eyes" motto.

CHAPTER 11

It's a time machine...
AMC gets into the game
*with **Mad Men***

The ad man stands before a pair of potential clients, each of them eager to hear how he plans to market the advanced technology at the heart of their new product. He says "new" can create an itch with consumers, but he learned long ago that appealing to their nostalgia is a stronger approach.

"In Greek, nostalgia literally means 'the pain from an old wound,'" Don Draper tells the men from Kodak. "It's a twinge in your heart, far more powerful than memory alone."

By the summer of 2007, it was already easy for TV fans to feel nostalgic about this second golden age. *The Sopranos* had just ended. *Deadwood* and *Six Feet Under* were done. *The Shield* and *The Wire* each had only one season to go, and HBO's initial drama burst had been followed by the short-lived likes of *John from Cincinnati*, *Carnivale*, and *Rome*. We had been lucky enough to witness this unprecedented wave of quality drama, but all great things come to an end, right? If we were lucky, we thought, maybe we'd see another *Sopranos* 5 or 10 years down the line.

Instead, it only took 39 days from the infamous cut to black for a worthy successor to appear—one with a *Sopranos* bloodline, and on a network that, like FX a few years earlier, was just looking to get noticed.

Don Draper, the anti-hero of *Mad Men*, at first glance would seem to have nothing in common with Tony Soprano. He's sleek and classically handsome, where Tony was large and sweaty. He's eloquent; Tony was vulgar. He represents the kind of vintage man's man Tony longed to see (and be) when he asked, "What happened to Gary Cooper?"

But Don Draper isn't what he seems under that polished surface. He's as flawed and complicated and fascinating as any other great character of this period, and he's at the center of a show that masterfully explores the difference between perception and reality.

And perception was at the heart of why AMC wound up extending the revolution with *Mad Men*.

AMC, which used to be short for American Movie Classics, had been playing second fiddle for years to Turner Classic Movies. "AMC was a black and white movie network, but TCM was the 'good' black and white movie network," says Rob Sorcher, an executive who was hired in 2002 to reformat AMC so the movies would feature commercial interruptions.

TV critics complained about the ads, but ratings went up as a result, and AMC CEO Josh Sapan came to Sorcher with a new mission, and with four magic words.

"Josh Sapan wanted to get into original programming," says Sorcher. "His directive to me was, 'We need a *Sopranos*.'"

Sorcher tried to explain that HBO had been in the original series business for years before *The Sopranos* came along, but Sapan was unmoved.

"His point was this: AMC doesn't need to worry about ratings at that moment of time," recalls Sorcher. "What AMC needs is a show, a critically acclaimed and audience-craved show that would make us undroppable to cable operators. Because AMC, as a movie network, was mostly second-tier movies or ones you could get anywhere, unaffiliated with a larger cable empire like Viacom or Turner. They were very worried that the likes of Comcast were creating their own movie channels, and that they would be dropped completely off of systems. Josh knew that he had to have something that the public wanted really badly."

Sorcher wasn't sure how seriously the company was going to take this plan. He knew he needed "somebody who was focused on finding material, was good with material, and could comfortably make their way through L.A." while he was based in New York, but he was reluctant to hire someone away from his or her current job for a gig that could evaporate in six months. Eventually, he turned to screenwriter Christina Wayne.

"When I went in to meet with Rob, I was pretty skeptical and didn't want to do it," says Wayne. "When you're a screenwriter, it's pretty embarrassing to go over to the other side. When I met with Rob, I realized immediately we had a similar love for film, and we hit it off. He started talking about how AMC was looking for someone to put their stamp on the network with original scripted programming. At the time, I had been watching *Sopranos* and *Sex and the City* and *Six Feet Under* on HBO. I had never really watched TV prior to that. I thought, 'Wow, this is a way to do HBO on basic cable.' I agreed to come on as a consultant for six months, because I didn't want to admit to my friends that I had gone over to the dark side."

Sapan wanted to test the waters with a movie or miniseries—

preferably a Western, since those always rated well on the channel—and Wayne asked her agent, Nancy Etz, to find her some scripts. One was *Broken Trail*, which already had Robert Duvall attached to star and Walter Hill to direct. Wayne had never much cared for the genre, but she found herself getting emotional as she read the *Broken Trail* script on the flight back to New York.

"I thought, 'If I respond to it, and I'm not a Western fan, then it's a broader audience,'" says Wayne. "That was March. We went into production in August. Within a week, we got approval from [AMC executive] Ed Carroll and Josh for millions of dollars, with Sony as the studio. It was one of those whirlwind, insane, 'never happens in the business world' things where you get approval to make something that's only half-written at that point."

In Sorcher's early days at AMC, he says, the channel's original series were cheap, unscripted fare that "was costing $100,000 an episode, or $150,000." Even with Sony as the studio, "*Broken Trail* was at least four million bucks to us. This was the greatest single investment in the history of the channel.

"But here's the thing in my mind the whole time," he adds. "I'm at AMC, none of this has been done before. If I make something that's lousy from a quality point of view—if it's critically panned—and then it doesn't do a rating, then everything is shit. Why bother? But if we make something that's critically acclaimed, then having a great rating on it was just an upside. The reason to do it is not ratings. My boss has told me that ratings, in that moment, don't matter."

Ratings may not have mattered, but they didn't hurt, either. *Broken Trail* drew nearly 10 million viewers in July of 2006, a number that Charlie Collier—who was preparing to become the new president of AMC that fall—couldn't believe.

"I saw the number and said, 'That's gotta be a typo,'" says Collier. "But it showed that the movies and originals could live side by side in an interesting way." In the build-up to the miniseries' debut, AMC had been running a string of the best Westerns in the network's library, all of them hyping the original production.

The *Broken Trail* ratings told Sorcher, "If we put on the right show, they were coming." More importantly, to him, the miniseries' quality—it would win four Emmys, including Outstanding Miniseries and acting awards for Duvall and Thomas Haden Church—suggested this small creative team (Sorcher, Wayne, and their colleague Vlad Wolynetz) had what it took to find the next *Sopranos* that Sapan was looking for.

"We gained a certain confidence, going through that," says Sorcher. "We said, 'Hey, we have the taste.'"

Wayne had returned to Los Angeles a month after finding the *Broken Trail* script, and "Word had spread at this point," she says. "It was clear there was a new buyer in town, and people were lining up to have meetings. Not that we had done anything, but people are excited whenever there's a checkbook." She took a meeting at the management company Industry Entertainment, where she was peppered with questions about what AMC wanted. Someone asked if the network was open to period pieces; she noted that with all the period films at the channel, it might be a good fit.

"At the end of the meeting, a junior manager named Ira Liss handed me *Mad Men*," she says. "He said, 'Everybody has passed on this. It's been around for years, but I think it's exactly what you're looking for.'"

Matthew Weiner wrote the *Mad Men* script on spec not because he needed a job, but because he wanted a different one. He had attended film school at USC and wanted to be a serious filmmaker, but his career to that point had largely involved sitcom writing jobs, most recently on the staff of *Becker*, a CBS sitcom starring Ted Danson as a cranky Bronx physician.

"[*Becker*] was a great job to get, and it was a hard job to get," Weiner told me before the final batch of *Mad Men* episodes debuted. "It was a move in success, but my heart wasn't in it."

Inspired by the words of former boss Tom Palmer—"If you can write, you can write your way out of anything. You can change your life"—and stories of other TV writers who had left successful shows because they aspired to something grander, he decided, "I'm just gonna write because I want to feel like a writer again. I don't want to feel like I'm in this kind of machine. It wasn't touching my life, what I was writing."

He had always been fascinated with the transition from the late '50s into the early '60s, and with the world of advertising. (One of his early TV scripts was an unaired episode of the Fox sitcom *Party Girl*, which had a joke where "John Cameron Mitchell came in all battered and bruised because he had been dressed as a giant martini for Halloween and two ad execs had accosted him.") He began researching the period as a hobby—"Like this is my mistress," he says—going so far as to deploy researchers to go to the library and study the tobacco campaigns at the time, or to simply help him navigate the primitive version of the Internet. ("I hired someone to go on Prodigy for me because I couldn't figure it out.")

A few years into the research, and feeling confident that life at the dawn of the '60s "wasn't that different" from the world in which he lived, Weiner began work in earnest.

He wrote a script set in 1960 that detailed an eventful day in the life of Don Draper, an apparent master of the advertising universe and creative director at the Sterling Cooper agency. Over the

course of the story, Don has a dalliance with his beatnik girlfriend
Midge and flirts with a potential new client, Jewish department
store owner Rachel Menken. (When Rachel talks about old-fashioned notions of love, Don tells her, "What you call 'love' was invented by guys like me to sell nylons.") Don's naïve new secretary
Peggy Olson is given a blunt crash course in surviving the job from
office manager Joan Holloway—among other tips, Joan suggests
Peggy go home, stand naked in front of a mirror with a bag over
her head, and "Really evaluate where your strengths and weaknesses
are. And be honest"—gets a prescription for birth control(*), and
goes to bed with weaselly accounts man Pete Campbell.

   *(*) Weiner later told me that he was initially going to start the se-
ries in 1959, but wanted to include the pill, which didn't hit the market until the following year.*

   The hour's centerpiece is a pitch meeting with the agency's biggest client, Lucky Strike cigarettes, which needs a new approach
now that the Surgeon General has made it illegal for any tobacco
company to claim smoking provides health benefits. Don realizes
this is a golden opportunity to start their marketing over from
scratch—the tagline he suggests, "It's toasted," was a real Lucky
Strike slogan Weiner appropriated—and explains to the tobacco
executives the nature of what he does for a living.

   "Advertising is based on one thing: happiness," he tells them. "And
you know what happiness is? Happiness is the smell of a new car. It's
freedom from fear. It's a billboard on the side of the road that screams
with reassurance that whatever you're doing, it's okay. You are okay."

   At the end of the script, Don takes the train home to the sub-
urbs, where his wife Betty and two kids are waiting for him, unaware of what he's been up to in the city all day.

   In 2008, Weiner told the *Washington Post* that he considered

Don Draper "a demon who lives inside me," and that he wrote the script because he was feeling "really unhappy, dissatisfied, and wondered what was wrong with me... I had a wife and three kids, and I had a complete lack of gratitude for what I had."

Whatever dark feelings were driving the script, and whatever desires Weiner had to get out of comedy, they weren't apparent to his new colleagues at *Becker*. Writer/director Ken Levine, an Emmy-winning veteran of *M*A*S*H* and *Cheers*, says, "Matt was very bright. He also was like a really good cheerleader in the show. He brought a real good, positive energy, and was very funny, was very helpful in the room, would pitch an awful lot of ideas. He was a very nice addition."

Levine compares Weiner in those days to working with *Modern Family* creators Steven Levitan and Christopher Lloyd as young writers on *Frasier*; in each case, the drive and desire to both do extra work and soak up knowledge made it clear they had aspirations beyond serving on someone else's staff.

As Weiner worked on *Becker*, he was putting the *Mad Men* script in the hands of every writer he knew, hoping it would lead somewhere—if not to making *Mad Men* itself, then to working on a show like the one in his head. Eventually, he pushed his agent, who worked at the same agency that represented both David Chase and *Six Feet Under* creator Alan Ball, to get it to one of those two men. The agent got it to Chase, who was coincidentally staffing up for the fifth *Sopranos* season.

"We were looking for writers," says Chase. "I read a bunch of material when I was on hiatus, and [*Mad Men*] was one of them. I thought it was remarkable. It held my interest. I didn't feel like I'd seen it 100 times. The characters were good, and it was a great way to look at American culture, through an advertising agency."

Chase hired Weiner, and quickly saw the same qualities that had appealed to Levine on *Becker*.

"He was very energetic," says Chase. "He's extremely intelligent, and tasteful. Showrunning is very difficult from the standpoint of other writers, and listening to input, and who's responsible for coming up with ideas. And because the showrunner is the creator and is the one who had the original voice, it mostly falls to him to do the story work, because other people seem to not be on the same page—at least initially. Matt, he would suggest ideas, and even though those ideas would be rebuffed or modified beyond recognition, he never stopped. He was so enthusiastic—enthusiastic about the show, about his own ideas, about the possibilities, about life."

Weiner wrote or co-wrote 11 *Sopranos* episodes, including memorable outings "The Test Dream," "Kennedy and Heidi," and the series' penultimate episode, "The Blue Comet." Dissatisfaction with one's lot in life would be a frequent theme of his episodes (albeit one present throughout *The Sopranos* as a whole); in Season 6's "Luxury Lounge," Christopher goes to Los Angeles to pitch Ben Kingsley on starring in his slasher film, and is dismayed to learn that a movie star's lifestyle is more gluttonous than anything a wiseguy could dream of.

With *The Sopranos* approaching an ending, Weiner asked Chase about sponsoring *Mad Men* with HBO. The tale of how this HBO-style drama, from a writer on the quintessential HBO drama, somehow didn't wind up at HBO is one of those stories like the end of *Deadwood*, where the only thing all the parties can agree on is the end result.

"I gave it to [HBO] to look at," says Chase. "HBO's big question was whether I would stay with [*Mad Men*]. I said I was not. I was doing a TV show, and this was the last series I would want to be doing. At that point, there was also discussion from Matt's point of view that I would direct the pilot, which would have made it more appealing for them. I was very interested in directing that pilot, but in the end, I just kept thinking to myself, 'Somehow or other, if I'm associated with the show in any way, I'll get pulled into it, he won't be happy with that, and I won't be happy because I don't want to be doing it.' So I said, 'No, I wouldn't have any contact with the show.' I most certainly tried and tried to get them to say yes."

"We never passed on *Mad Men*," insists Chris Albrecht. "It wasn't available to us. I'll give you my recollection of it. Matt Weiner was a writer for David Chase. *The Sopranos* was on the air. We didn't fuck with David Chase. We didn't fuck with his writers. Carolyn [Strauss] and I looked at each other and said, 'We're not going to set Matt Weiner up to leave David Chase. We're not going to enable that.' The first time that I ever remember reading *Mad Men* was after it had been developed at AMC. It was a show set in New York. It was a period piece. This was the time when the bloom was off the rose, and people were coming after us, and the articles people were writing were, 'Everything's set in New York' or 'Everything's a period piece.' This was set in New York *and* it was a period piece. And it wasn't available to us, and it was Matt Weiner. My old friends at HBO like to blame me and Carolyn for not having *Mad Men*, but that is an apocryphal story; that is not the way it happened."

Strauss, who has heard about passing on *Mad Men* so often that she rolls her eyes at the mere mention of it, says she wasn't really worried about offending Chase, who was supportive of Weiner making the show, and that "It was more a matter of timing and stuff that we already had, really. Basically, we had a bunch of stuff, he was working on *Sopranos*, the timing was wrong for us... Matt will forever hate me, but it makes his writing better. So if I can do that for him, it's a service I offer him."

Whatever the reason, *Mad Men* was still available when Ira Liss handed it to Christina Wayne. As a screenwriter, Wayne had tried unsuccessfully to option the movie rights to the Richard Yates novel *Revolutionary Road*, set in the same period as *Mad Men* and also dealing with a dysfunctional marriage and the contrast between tidy suburban living and professional life in Manhattan, "So it personally grabbed me. I knew when I gave it to Rob, he had come from an advertising background, and he would respond to it as well."

"On the surface, it was belligerently uncommercial," says Sorcher. "It's period. People smoke. Everyone's unlikable. It's about advertising, which seems like the most boring thing you could have a show be about. Everything is stacked against it, in terms of what it is on paper."

Broken Trail was a perfect fit for the AMC movie library, but as Sorcher, Wayne, and Wolynetz discussed the first ongoing series of this era(*), they realized that, as Sorcher puts it, if they tried to simply find a series to match a genre in the library, "We would not end up with something of real distinction and quality."

(*) Though Mad Men *is treated by the current AMC regime as the network's first scripted series, it was preceded by* Remember WENN, *a late '90s drama set at a Pittsburgh radio station in the 1940s.*

In Weiner's first meeting with the AMC executives, the enthusiasm and intelligence he had displayed in his previous job was on full display.

"We met with Matt and he pitched this thing beat by beat, all the way through," says Sorcher. "He really impressed me. I was truly blown away by this meeting. It was something special in the way that I felt like, 'Oh, if we do this, and do it right, this is going to be something amazing.' Part of me doubted if we could leap and get there, but it felt like the right mark to shoot for."

Weiner was committed to the final *Sopranos* season, but there was a long production hiatus between the first 12 episodes of that season and the final nine—a hiatus that would allow Weiner to employ much of the well-oiled *Sopranos* production machine to make the *Mad Men* pilot.

Sorcher had liked the script so much that he only gave Weiner one significant note: "Don Draper needs to have a secret."

"I was a little concerned," Sorcher explains. "Everyone seemed so unlikable in this thing. It was a bit of a fearful note. [The script] read as a beautifully encapsulated little movie, but what's bringing you back? And what's going to make him more vulnerable? It really came from Tony Soprano. I watched *The Sopranos* and said, 'Oh, he sees a shrink. That's the vulnerable side of him.'"

Weiner thought about Sorcher's suggestion, and remembered *The Horseshoe*, an unfinished movie script he had worked on before getting his first TV job. "It was the story of the 20th century, and about one of these guys who was one of the giants of the century, starting with his childhood in rural poverty," Weiner recalls. "And the last scene on page 80 is this guy, Dick Whitman, dropping off another man's body, his brother running after the train. And then it dissolved to him getting off the train and it says 'Ossining, 1960.' And I was like, 'This is the same character. This is the same story.'"

So Don Draper and Dick Whitman became one and the same: Dick, the dirt-poor bastard son of an alcoholic farmer and a local prostitute, who would assume the name of his dead commanding officer in Korea.

All that would be explained later, though—the only two changes to the pilot itself are a glimpse of Don's Purple Heart, and the faint sound of an explosion as he naps and dreams on his office couch—but now Weiner had to find an actor capable of playing both faces of this character. Preferably, it would be an unknown.

"This was not a financial concern, finding someone new," he told me in 2009. "I said it was *Sopranos* casting. Lorraine Bracco had been an Oscar nominee, I knew her, but every other person on that show, as far as I was concerned, it was their first job, and they were that person. It's like watching a French film: you don't know the stars, so they *are* the characters. I wanted to do that."

Enter Jon Hamm, an actor with the kind of square-jawed, classically handsome look that, with the right haircut, made him look he had stepped right out of a cab from 1960. It was a look Hollywood had largely lost interest in by the 21st century, and though Hamm worked regularly, it was in a string of unremarkable roles: a hunky fireman on NBC's *Providence*, a hunky cop on Lifetime's *The Division*, a hunky single dad on ABC's *What About Brian?*, etc.

"To put it in a baseball analogy, I was a guy that had made the big leagues but hadn't really distinguished himself," Hamm says of his career to that point. "Sort of a career .250 hitter, and decent defense. Somebody that had a lot of upside, but you weren't sure where he was going. At a certain point, there's a thing where you go, 'Well, we gave it a shot, it didn't really work.' Fortunately, I got a tremendous break and was picked for a part that was suited for me very well."

Hamm read *Mad Men* and knew instantly that it was a great script, and a great role, but "I realized very quickly that I was at the very, very bottom of the list. I figured, there's only one way to get it, and that's to show up."

Hamm showed up, and showed up, and showed up again. He auditioned so many times—for casting directors Kim Miscia and Beth Bowling, for Weiner, on multiple tapes for the AMC executives in New York—that he eventually played nearly every Don scene in the script.

"Jon had been getting parts doing a certain kind of thing," Weiner told me in 2009, "but he came in and read it, and I just saw a bunch of things I hadn't seen before: sincerity, intelligence, obviously he was handsome and had an old-fashioned leading man thing, but he also had a soulfulness that said this man came from somewhere. And I intuited that immediately."

Weiner narrowed his choices to a couple of actors, thought of Hamm, "and I asked myself a question: 'When this man goes home to his wife at the end of the pilot, are you going to hate him?' And I said, 'No, I will not hate him.'"

Weiner had his man, but Christina Wayne wasn't sold on what she saw on the audition tape.

"I watched it, and to be honest, you couldn't see it on the tape," she says. "He seemed really nervous. And when he has his hair floppy, he's not Don Draper. He just didn't do it. It was really hard to tell, and it was a poor quality tape."

She asked for another tape and was no more impressed by it, but wanted to trust Weiner's creative instincts. Finally, she flew Hamm to New York to meet with him and Alan Taylor, a *Sopranos* veteran who was going to direct the *Mad Men* pilot, over drinks.

"And the minute I saw him in person, I got it," she says. "He was this great-looking, super-charming guy that was getting lost on that super-crappy tape."

On the elevator ride down from the hotel bar, Wayne leaned over to Hamm and whispered in his ear, "Of course, you know you have the job." Hamm smiled and said, "Well, no, I didn't know. Thank you for confirming it."

The rest of the ensemble coalesced around Hamm. Wayne wanted actress January Jones to audition for Betty, but the part was so small in the pilot script that Jones's manager insisted that she instead read for Peggy, which seemed like the better role at the time.

"Matt sees her read and says, 'She's terrible for Peggy,'" recalls Wayne, who explained the Betty hang-up. "Matt created a scene for her to read, so all of a sudden, she came back in, and here's Grace Kelly. He saw it immediately."

Sony had been AMC's partner on *Broken Trail*, but no studio wanted to produce the *Mad Men* pilot—executives at each one apparently agreeing with Sorcher's "belligerently uncommercial" assessment of the script. Sorcher eventually got the money to fund the $3 million pilot in-house, and recruited Radical Media as the production company, since AMC wasn't equipped at the time to make a show like this on its own.

Weiner, Taylor, and *The Sopranos* crew filmed the pilot over 10 days in New York. (The series itself would film in Los Angeles because Weiner wanted to move his family back there.) The pilot in general, and Hamm in particular, were everything Weiner had promised: smart, beautiful, and so evocative of the period that one could be forgiven for assuming this *was* a film from the 1960s, and Jon Hamm some long-forgotten movie star.

"No one has a development story like that," Weiner says. "They were so hands off. They were so respectful of the fact that I'd been in TV a long time, that I had a passion for the story, and that they liked what I did. Christina Wayne was very clear that the glory would be standing behind me, not in front of me, in some weird way. There were no layers of notes. There were no layers of anything."

Weiner's *Sopranos* commitment would keep him busy for nearly a year, time AMC used to negotiate a deal with the Lionsgate studio (where Sorcher and Wayne both had friends in the executive ranks) to produce the series.

AMC had a great pilot. They had a studio to help carry the financial load. Now the network needed to let the world know a show like this existed—on a channel people only thought of as the place to watch *The Godfather* five times in a row on a Saturday.

"We had told people for 20 years, 'Come to us for a movie when you feel like it!'" says Charlie Collier, who arrived after the *Mad Men* pilot was produced but before the series debuted. "And now we were saying, 'Come to us on Thursdays at 10.'"(*)

(*) *From the second season on,* Mad Men *aired on Sundays, which HBO had turned into the night where audiences expected to find sophisticated cable dramas, but that first year it aired on Thursdays.*

AMC's vice president of public relations Theano Apostolou decided to enlist the New York media elite to spread the gospel by hosting a lunch at Michael's restaurant, with Arianna Huffington moderating a discussion with Weiner, ad executive Jerry Della Femina, and *New York Observer* owner Jared Kushner.

"We did this panel just talking about the ad game back then, media now and then, and female sexual politics in the workplace," says Apostolou. "I thought the key was we serve them Jack Daniels for lunch. Jack Daniel's was an advertiser for the first season before we'd ever aired. I will tell you, nobody wanted to leave that lunch."

Meanwhile, AMC was using the commercial breaks Sorcher had instituted to promote the July 19, 2007, premiere around the clock.

"Our greatest strength was we could focus on one thing," says Collier. "If you looked at our air in the weeks leading up to *Mad*

Men, it was all *Mad Men*, all the time. And we're a broad-reach net-work. Over a month, you reach the fans who like *Pretty Woman*, and *Cool Hand Luke*, and everyone in between. And you use the time to hyper-promote to them. It was in every break, in every way."

Mad Men wasn't as perfect a match with the network's movie library as *Broken Trail*—as a lead-in for the premiere, AMC ran *Goodfellas*, which took place in the same era but was tonally very different—nor was it an instant hit. The first season averaged about 900,000 viewers per week—an acceptable number, but far from *Broken Trail*.

Still, renewal (which came late in the first season) wasn't that hard a decision.

"You looked at *Mad Men* and critically, you couldn't be more pleased," says Collier. "Ratings-wise, it was usually at [our prime-time] average, if not above it, and you had people time shifting even more than before. We were trying to get a sense of how people were watching. Matt was the first to say that even more people were watching the show than the numbers suggested, and we felt that catch-up [viewing] would be our greatest friend(*). We had a show on a network that people didn't know to come for scripted [dramas]. *Mad Men* was a transformational event for our network, but it didn't happen with the flick of a light switch."

(*) Indeed, the show's viewership has gone up every year, as new viewers have sampled the series in between seasons via DVR, DVD, On Demand, and streaming video services.

And over the course of that first season, Weiner established a recipe for the series that he would vary a bit each year: a mix of historical events (Sterling Cooper tries to insert itself into the pres-idential election—on Nixon's side, of course), workplace intrigue (Pete Campbell aches for Don's approval), personal strife (Don treats Betty like a child, and sends her to a shrink who reports back to him on each session), and *lots* of liquor and cigarettes(*).

(*) Like the swearing on Deadwood, *the sheer amount of alcohol and tobacco consumed was so great that it dominated early coverage of the series—along with similar debates about how historically accurate this was—until critics and viewers came to accept it as a part of Don Draper's world, whether or not it exactly reflected the lifestyle of real ad men of this era.*

Also, there was mystery. The name "Dick Whitman" is first mentioned early in the third episode, when a passenger on the commuter train recognizes Don from their days in the Army, but it's not clear whether our hero has changed his name or if the other man is simply mistaken. Over the course of the season, Weiner begins giving us bigger pieces of the puzzle: the half brother Dick ran away from when he stole the real Don Draper's name; a flashback to young Dick befriending a hobo who teaches him the most formative lesson of his life (when things get bad, run away); a postcoital confession to Rachel Menken about the nature of his birth. But no one figured out where the story was actually going.

"There were so many theories: 'Don's Jewish,' 'Don's this, and Don's that,'" recalls Jon Hamm. "The story that Matt was telling was so specific, and so not obvious in a thematic way that it was almost impossible to guess. And I think that's good. That it's a story about a person we can actually humanize and not treat as this symbol for something else. He's not meant to be a metaphor. He's meant to be a man."

In a secondary mystery of sorts, Peggy puts on weight over the course of the season, with actress Elisabeth Moss wearing a series of gradually expanding prosthetics. Fans began debating whether she was pregnant—she had, after all, slept with Pete (Vincent Kart-

heiser) for the first time on the day she got the birth-control prescription—and whether a woman would be that pregnant and not
realize it. It was a debate that was happening inside AMC, where
the executives knew that Peggy really was carrying Pete's baby(*).

*(*) January Jones was pregnant during filming of the fifth season,
and the prosthetics and fat suit got another workout, but this time for
a story where Betty was just gaining weight, eating her feelings when
her second marriage didn't magically cure her unhappiness.*

"Oh, God, we would talk about that all the time," says Christina Wayne. "I would tell Matt, 'There's no way a woman would
be pregnant and not know it.' And he said, 'Oh, there's all these
cases.' And I've now seen many documentaries on cable. I've been
pregnant, and I can't imagine walking around not knowing. It
seemed highly unbelievable to me, but I guess if you're that psy-
chologically fucked up, it can happen."

Everything comes to a head in the final two episodes of Season
1. In "Nixon vs. Kennedy," Pete confronts Don with evidence of
the identity theft and tries to blackmail him for a promotion to
the firm's head of accounts. We see flashbacks to Dick Whitman in
Korea, and in the present, Don tries to pull the hobo's trick again
and run away with Rachel, who's horrified to see her lover give in
to his true, cowardly nature.

In 2009, Weiner told me about an editing session on that Don/
Rachel scene: "I walk in and the editor says, 'I think you're going to
freak out.' 'Freak out good?' 'No, I think we have a huge problem
here. He's so weak.' I said, 'Let me see the scene,' and I watched
it, and it was exactly what I wanted. The man is in a panic, he's
desperate, and Jon committed to that. He wasn't trying to protect
the character. He knew that this is what the guy would do. And he
did it even more than I imagined. He's so vulnerable in that scene.

What he committed to there was something, and part of it hope-fully has to do with his feeling of safety, that I'm not going to lead him astray, and part of it has to do with that cast, and they are all risk-takers."

Don refuses to yield to Pete, but when Pete spills the beans to founding partner Bert Cooper (played by Robert Morse from the '60s musical *How to Succeed in Business Without Really Trying*), the inscrutable Cooper ponders the idea for a moment, then asks, "Who cares?" Who Don Draper was doesn't matter to him; who Don Draper is now, what people other than Pete Campbell think of him, and the value Don brings to the agency are what's impor-tant to Cooper.

In the finale, "The Wheel," Don is shaken to learn his brother hanged himself after Don paid him to leave town. Peggy (who had stunned her sexist colleagues by displaying an aptitude for creative work) gets promoted to copywriter, but discovers that her recent bouts of indigestion were actually labor pains. And after a season of trying to escape the wife and children who make him feel like a stranger in his own life, Don realizes how much they really mean to him while he's giving the pitch of his life.

Weiner directed the finale, in what would become an annual tradition, and in it he constructed a scene that synthesized every-thing he wanted to do with the period, the world of advertising, and the character of Don Draper. Don is pitching Kodak on their new slide projector, which they want to promote as a great tech-nological achievement. He explains the value of nostalgia to them, then begins using the device to show slides of his own family. In the dark room, we see the Drapers look much happier together than they've been over the course of this season, and we see Don Draper, his face half-lit by the projector, struggling to keep his emotions in check as—pausing every few beats to advance the projector and show another image of the life he only seems to appreciate when he's not fully part of it—he says, "This device isn't a spaceship. It's a time machine. It goes backwards, and forwards. It takes us to a place where we ache to go again. It's not called 'The Wheel.' It's called 'The Carousel.' It lets us travel the way a child travels: around and around, and back home again, to a place where we know we are loved."

It's Thanksgiving, and Don has already told an unhappy Betty to take the kids without him to her father's place in Pennsylvania, but when he takes the train home to Ossining, he's overjoyed to find them still there. He tells Betty he'll be glad to go with them, kisses her, hugs Sally and Bobby, and all is right with the world.

At least, that's how Wayne says Weiner's script originally ended.

"We all read it and said, 'That's a really nice ending. There's the end of the movie, and nobody's coming back,'" says Wayne. "Why would you end the show at the end of Season 1? It's cable. Nobody should be happy."

Wayne called Weiner, and she says their discussion about the final scene turned into a debate, and then into something more— "Matt can go to a place of screaming and yelling," she says, "which I don't particularly mind; having been a screenwriter and having so many screenwriter friends, I know how passionate you have to be to protect your baby"—and eventually they reached an impasse and hung up. Weiner called Wayne back, late at night, and she says she suggested that the scene as written could work, but only if it was a fake-out: Don's dream of what would be waiting for him at the end of the day, rather than the empty house that's actually there.

"He told me that when he realized why he didn't want to change it, 'I cried,'" she says. "And I said, 'Why?' He said, 'I just wanted my characters to be happy. I love them so much.' When you have somebody who cares that much about the show and feels that passionately about something, that's what you live for, to do what we do. He was like, 'I realized I was wrong, and that I do need to change it.' Those are my favorite moments from working on *Mad Men* with Matt, and that's why I love and adore him so much. I think somebody who does battle internally with what the best thing is, and has that kind of passion—that's why it's the best show every year."

Weiner says the decision to potentially end the show with that episode was more of a defensive one: despite the critical acclaim and the improvement over AMC's previous ratings in that time-slot, he had been given no assurances that the show would be renewed, and he didn't want Don's story to feel unfinished in the event of cancellation.

"It wasn't childish," he says. "[Christina and I] had a very respectful relationship, and for me it was a matter of 'I got lucky enough to do a season of the show. I'm not gonna sit and wait around for them to pull the trigger and have my show just be cut off in the middle of a sentence.'"

With that dispute resolved, Weiner had given AMC an incredible first season of television, one that dealt incisively with gender and class, politics and pop culture, and the earliest hints of the generation gap that would flower later in the decade (and become a major theme of each ensuing season).

If the audience wasn't entirely made up of media types at this point, it seemed as if the entirety of the media was watching the show, and writing think pieces on everything from the duality of Don Draper and what it meant for a show about advertising to give its main character a false identity; to the wit and wisdom of John

Slattery as name partner Roger Sterling; to what the curvaceous figure of Christina Hendricks as Joan said about the image of women in 1960 versus 2007. *Mad Men* also had the good timing to come along just as the idea of TV critics reviewing each episode of a series was becoming widespread; every episode offered much to analyze, and suddenly there were many places to find that analysis.

Mad Men had debuted in the summer, right at the start of the next Emmy eligibility period, so its first shot at industry validation came from the Golden Globes, in what became one of the more bizarre awards shows in Hollywood history. Because of the writers' strike, there was no traditional ceremony, and no guests at all: simply a televised press conference announcing the winners. Theano Apostolou rented out the roof deck at the Chateau Marmont and invited everyone who had worked on the show. Nobody got to give a televised speech when Hamm won(*), nor when the series won the best drama award, but more people from the show got to attend this party than would have been there for the "real" Globes, and they all got to celebrate their unlikely achievement together.

(*) Though the show's cast won two Screen Actors Guild ensemble awards, no Mad Men *actor won an Emmy for their work on the show until Jon Hamm got one in his very last shot at the trophy in the fall of 2015. ("There has been a terrible mistake, clearly," Hamm joked, after literally crawling onto the stage to accept the award.) And even with Hamm's last-second win, the actors from the show (both regular cast members and guest stars) went a stunning 1-for-37 in Emmy chances over the years, which isn't at all what you would expect from a show so celebrated in almost every other area.*

"I have one personal theory," says Weiner, "which is that the acting style is different on the show. That it's very naturalistic and not showy.

I don't write Emmy scenes for them either. Maybe that's it. Elisabeth Moss always jokes whenever she works somewhere else, people are always like, 'Cry your eyes out.' And I'm almost like, 'Don't cry. Do everything you can not to cry,' because I feel like that produces more emotion in the audience."

"We were the little show that nobody watched," says Hamm, "and it got a lot of press, but literally most people thought it was on A&E. We thought even though we weren't going to win, it was just nice to be invited—which is an approach I've taken ever since then. When I won and the show won, we kind of lost it. We freaked out, and were so happy, because it was unexpected."

"It was this big insiders' club," says Wayne, "and when we won, it was like this explosion. People were weeping. I don't know that I'll ever top that moment, career-wise, in terms of how everybody felt. I don't think I'll be in that situation again. It was so unique. It just became this thing, and from that moment on, it's never really stopped. That was when it stopped being this obscure little weird, 'Who are these people? Where did they come from?' show. All of us had this thing where we came up in the business never having been recognized for what we'd done before, so this was their moment where it was like, 'We did it.'"

When the 2008 Emmys rolled around, *Mad Men* was one of three series (FX's *Damages* and Showtime's *Dexter* were the other two) to crash the Outstanding Drama Series category, which had previously been the province of the broadcast networks and HBO. The final season of *The Sopranos* had won the award the previous year, and the baton was officially passed when *Mad Men* won it in the first year of the post-*Sopranos* era.

Weiner and company had just proved they could make 13 great episodes. Now they were going to do it again, this time as the champ rather than the unknown challenger. Many fans had expected the story to resume shortly after the events of "The Wheel" so we could see what happened with the baby (and whether the birth affected Peggy's promotion), the Draper marriage, etc. Instead, Season 2 picks up nearly 15 months later, on Valentine's Day 1962. Don and Betty seem happy again (though he's unable to perform sexually during a romantic hotel getaway). Peggy is back at work (and thin again) after a mysterious three-month absence following "The Wheel" (and it appears in an early episode that her sister is raising Peggy's baby as her own). Deeply closeted art director Salvatore Romano (Bryan Batt) has gotten married, and Joan (who ended a long affair with Roger late in Season 1) is getting serious with a handsome doctor. Some of these gaps are filled in later—we learn that Peggy's sister had her own baby around the same time as Peggy, and in the Season 2 finale, Peggy tells a stunned Pete that she gave birth to their son before putting him up for adoption—while others, in what will become a pattern for the series, are left for the viewer to decide what happened and why.

Though the fashions and popular culture still resemble what we think of as the 1950s rather than the '60s, hints of the counter-culture become stronger when Don is pushed to hire a pair of clever young copywriters named Kurt (Eden Gali) and Smitty (Patrick Cavanaugh), who can give Sterling Cooper access to the youth market that's so hard to reach.

"There have been a million ways the folks on this avenue have tried to tell our generation what to do," Smitty tells a prospective client. "Except we don't want to be told what to do. That's over. We want to find things for ourselves. We want to *feel*."

It's already a huge leap from someone like Paul Kinsey (Michael

Gladis), a Draper underling born only a few years before Smitty, but who grew up in a generation where being older was something to be admired, not feared. (Paul takes on various middle-age affectations like a pipe and a beard and is, unsurprisingly, left behind as the decade marches along. When he reappears in a later season, he's a lost soul who has joined Hare Krishna.)

At the start of the third season, Weiner told me that the goal of the series was to look at this incredibly well-analyzed decade not from the familiar Baby Boomer point of view (though there's some of that in the story of young Sally Draper, played by the exceptional child actress Kiernan Shipka), but from people like Don and Joan and even Pete, who were already adults when the clock struck midnight on 1960.

Season 2 also challenges our feelings about Don as he gets involved in an affair with Bobbie Barrett (Melinda McGraw), the manipulative wife and manager of a popular comedian employed in a Sterling Cooper marketing campaign. Bobbie and her husband keep causing trouble for the agency, even after Don sleeps with Bobbie in the front seat of his car, so when they cross paths outside a restaurant bathroom, he slips his hand under her skirt, puts it between her legs, and whispers, "Believe me: I will ruin him. Do what I say."

It was far from the first dark moment for Don (nor would it be the last), but it still unnerved many viewers, and launched a debate over whether the show expected us to celebrate his behavior, condemn it, or simply observe it.

"As uncomfortable as it may be for people," Weiner told me at the end of that season, "they go on to have a relationship, and it's based on their knowledge of their inner selves. To me, you can look at is as a perversion or as violence, but there are sexual re-

lationships based on power, it was specific to them, and I think
Bobbie Barrett was extremely aroused by that experience, by Don
being in charge."

Hamm says he was concerned at first when he read the script
for that scene, but "I feel like I've got a pretty healthy sense of trust
in Matt to make this an interesting character. If you look at Walter
White [from *Breaking Bad*] or Tony Soprano, it's a similar situation. Gone are the days of trying to make our leads some sort of
mythically described 'likable.' I remember Matt telling me stories
about David Chase going, 'Why do people like Tony Soprano?
This guy is a murderer.' And when David made the decision to
have Tony kill Christopher, that was partly in response to that:
'That's what this guy does.' And I think that scene is true to Don's
character. There is no lightening of that."

In 2009, Weiner told me, "I always want Don to be a little meaner
than Jon does," but that his star will commit to whatever material
he's given. "I realized I should not be scared of going all the way.
He'll play stuff different than I imagined it. I am rarely disappointed,
though. And if I am, it's usually because I'm a control freak."

Chase says he never noticed Weiner specifically observing the
way he ran *The Sopranos*, but the stories the *Mad Men* crew tell
about how hard they all worked to re-create the look of the period—and of how very particular Weiner's requests could sometimes be—suggest a similar obsession with detail.

Costume designer Janie Bryant (who previously worked on
Deadwood) once told me about a friendly argument she had with
Weiner regarding a dress that would be removed right before a sex
scene. "I had an amazing dress that had buttons down the front,"
she recalled, "but he said, 'Janie, unzipping is sexier.' So I said,
'Okay, fine. We'll unzip.'" She found a different dress.

"There's a lot of fetishism about the props and the wardrobe," *Mad Men* executive producer Scott Hornbacher (a fellow *Sopranos* alum) told me before the start of Season 2. "There's a lot of stressing and angsting and gnashing of teeth as people try to find and make these things."

"The great part about it is that he knows exactly what he wants," says Hamm. "And he's very specific in his descriptions, and very knowledgeable about the world. For a person who's running a show to have all of the answers, so that you can come up to him and say, 'I don't understand what this, this, and this is,' and for him to then be able to say, 'Well, it's because of something that hasn't happened yet, but trust me, it will happen,' and then it *does* happen, that's how he earns your trust and he repays your trust. That is something that I've learned from Matt over the years. That's the great part of Matt. The downside of Matt is that he can be so detail-oriented that it becomes, 'Enough, enough. Give me my space. Let me do my job now. You don't have to do everyone's job.' But I think every creative person has that energy—they want to help, they want to create, they want to do it all themselves."

The detail work turned *Mad Men* itself into a time machine like the Kodak slide projector. The show sent us backwards in time, and then forwards again, observing the march of social progress (or the lack thereof). It re-created the period so well that very quickly the viewer focused not on the fashions or the alcohol, but on the beautiful stories that Weiner and his team were telling, and the many layers of meaning to be found in each one.

Season 2's "Maidenform," for instance, deals with the way people see themselves versus the way they're viewed by the world around them. It's a gorgeous jewel box of an episode, filled with literal and figurative reflections, including a bra campaign featuring the same model made up to look like Marilyn Monroe and Jackie Kennedy. The next episode, "The Gold Violin," takes its title from a short story written by Sterling Cooper accounts man Ken Cosgrove (Aaron Staton), inspired by an instrument he saw at a museum that he says was "Perfect in every way, except it couldn't make music." Throughout the hour, we see symbols of wealth, status, and power (a museum board position for Don, a Norman Rockwell–esque picnic for the Draper family) that turn out to be just as hollow and fake (Don got the museum gig due to someone else's work, the Drapers leave their lovely picnic spot covered with their litter) as the violin.

One of those symbols is a Mark Rothko painting of red squares that Bert Cooper has recently purchased for $10,000, leading the staff to wonder what it means and what their boss sees in it. (It turns out he just bought it as an investment.)

"I don't think it's supposed to be explained," suggests Ken.

"I'm an artist, okay?" says Sal. "It must mean *something*."

"Maybe it doesn't," says Ken. "Maybe you're just supposed to experience it. Because when you look at it, you do feel something, right? It's like looking into something very deep. You could fall in."

"The Gold Violin" aired a week after I had written a 2,000-word dissertation on the use of mirrors in "Maidenform," and I wondered if perhaps the Rothko scene was Weiner's way of suggesting that the *Mad Men* commentariat was overthinking things. At the end of the season, though, he told me, "Look, the show cries out to be analyzed. I leave so many gaps in communication." He credited David Chase with encouraging him to tell stories this way, saying, "We talked about so many things on that show, and it's just what happens, and I don't know what it means, and I can't put it into words, but hopefully through the magic of film, people will get it."

Fortunately, people got enough of it, and Weiner's storytelling confidence and ambition only grew as the series moved along. The third season, set in 1963, hints at the impending British pop-culture explosion by having a London firm buy Sterling Cooper, which leaves Bert, Roger, and Don eventually feeling adrift in their own company. The season culminates with the *Mad Men* version of a heist film, as the three partners, English liaison Lane Pryce (Jared Harris), Pete, Peggy, Joan, and a few others figure out a way to bolt the agency, steal the most important clients, and start anew as Sterling Cooper Draper Pryce. Though *Mad Men* built its reputation on dense, metaphor-laden storytelling, some of its greatest pleasures could be more visceral and/or comic, like Don coming across a locked room in the office they're ransacking and deciding the simplest solution is to kick the door in, or the run of sick jokes told after a newly arrived British executive gets maimed by a lawn-mower during a drunken office party. (Paul: "He might lose his foot." Roger: "Right when he got it in the door.")

The first season peaked with the Nixon/Kennedy election, the second with the Cuban Missile Crisis, and the third with Kennedy's assassination—but Weiner always viewed the series as a character story that just happened to be set in a rich historical era. He had initially not wanted, for instance, to do a JFK assassination episode, feeling that ground was too well trodden, but began Season 3 when he did because he wanted to see the birth of the child Don and Betty had conceived during a dark period in their marriage in Season 2.

But *Mad Men* deftly managed to tell character stories and social stories at the same time, and was rarely better than when it dealt with the gender politics of the '60s. We're introduced to Betty as a polished Grace Kelly doppelganger who's being cheated on by her husband, but who also seems to be a cold, impatient mother to her kids; to Joan as a knockout who wields her abundant sexuality like a weapon; and to Peggy as a wide-eyed innocent being taken advantage of by both the men and women in that office. But their personalities, and their situations, prove far more complicated.

Betty, we discover, grew up in an emotionally abusive environment that made her ill-suited for traditional suburban wifedom and motherhood(*), and who may be an overgrown child at times but doesn't deserve to be treated like one by Don. Joan seems to have all the power in that office, yet when she turns out to be perfectly suited to run the agency's new television department, the idea of giving her the job never so much as occurs to any of the men there. (Joan also gets raped on the floor of Don's office by the doctor fiancé who's perfect on paper and a creep in reality.) Peggy is mocked and dismissed and manipulated by those around her at first, but in time she becomes the most confident, liberated woman—both professionally and sexually—on the show.

(*) *Every now and then, we see Betty moping around the house in a bathrobe, and it's easy to imagine her turning into Livia Soprano, who gave birth to Tony during this period.*

The opening title sequence for the series depicts a man with Don Draper's silhouette who begins plummeting to earth when his office and the skyscraper that contains it disappear out from under him. In time, Peggy's rise in the series begins to intersect with the suggestion that Don Draper is the falling man. His marriage to Betty ends after she discovers the truth about Dick Whitman and Korea, sending Don into an alcoholic tailspin for much of Season 4, leaving Peggy (and Pete Campbell, who becomes far more capable—and at times sympathetic—as the years pass) to keep the new agency alive.

Don hits rock bottom in the series' finest hour, "The Suit-case," which is essentially a two-character play about Don and Peggy stuck in the office through a tumultuous night. She wants to leave for a birthday dinner with her boyfriend, while he needs company to avoid placing the phone call that will tell him that Anna Draper (Melinda Page Hamilton)—the widow of the real Don, and the one person on Earth with whom this Don feels truly comfortable and safe—has died of cancer. Over the course of the episode, Jon Hamm and Elisabeth Moss are asked to play every emotion possible: rage and despair, joy and humiliation, companionship and absolute contempt. In the most iconic mo-ment, Peggy complains that Don took all the credit for an award-winning campaign she helped conceive.

"It's *your job*," he tells her, his voice dripping with condescen-sion. "I give you money. You give me ideas."

"And you never say, 'Thank you,'" she complains, fighting back tears.

"*That's what the money is for!*" he screams.

"I don't know if there are a lot of other people in the world I could do that with other than Lizzie [Moss]," says Hamm, who tried his best during breaks in filming to be extra silly with his co-star to avoid the angst in the script from dragging them and the crew down. "It is an emotional thing where you have to break down and cry in front of 40 crew members, and you're emotionally raw. It's like taking off all your clothes and saying, 'Well, here we go.' I was happy to get the chance to do it with her, because she's a special talent."

"The Suitcase" came after a run of episodes that ended with doors being closed. As tragic night turns into another day at work, Don and Peggy make their peace(*), get back to work on another campaign, and as Peggy exits Don's office, she asks if he wants the door open or closed. "Open," he tells her, and all is momentarily right with the world.

(*) That peace is signified by Don placing his hand on top of Peggy's as they study an ad mock-up. Even for a show with acute attention to the little things and a great institutional memory, this is an impressive callback, returning all the way to a scene in the very first episode where Peggy, misunderstanding a piece of Joan's advice, makes a clumsy, unwanted pass at Don by putting her hand on top of his. The motif continues in an amazing scene late in Season 5 where Don, struggling to accept that Peggy is leaving for another agency, kisses that hand as a goodbye gesture, then holds on to it for an uncomfortably long period of time, leaving Peggy as the dominant one who gets to pull away and tell him, "Don't be a stranger."

Don sobers up, but this still isn't the happy ending Christina Wayne had feared at the end of Season 1. By now, Weiner knew the show was going to run awhile, and he brought us into Season 5 in strange new territory: Don is remarried to his former secretary Megan Calvet (Jessica Paré), a struggling actress into whom Don invests far too many of his hopes and dreams of happiness. The Don of Season 5 isn't a lush, but he's distracted from work in a different way—in time to be eclipsed by both Peggy and Michael Ginsberg (Ben Feldman), a young copywriter with no respect for Don or his authority, the biggest indicator yet of the widening generation gap—and he's not acting at all like the Don we met in Season 1.

Perhaps as a result, the fifth season is an experimental one. The show had never been tied to a specific formula for episodes, but Season 5 seemed to push even the outer stylistic limits Weiner had already established. One episode, set right after the Richard Speck nursing-school massacre in Chicago, was constructed as a prolonged nightmare for Don, Joan, and several other characters; another, in which Roger and his unhappy trophy wife take LSD, was presented as a dramatic triptych, with time and its three individual stories running forwards, backwards and sideways to suggest Roger's state of mind under the drug's influence.

That fifth season was written after a prolonged, at times publicly ugly contract dispute among Weiner, Lionsgate, and AMC. It's tempting to read the increased level of strife at Sterling Cooper Draper Pryce—Lane and Pete have a bare-knuckle boxing match in the conference room; Pete pressures Joan into whoring herself out to land Jaguar as a client (though Joan gets a partnership stake out of the deal); and Lane hangs himself in his office after Don catches him embezzling money from the firm to cover a tax debt— as Weiner venting his frustration over the rancorous negotiation, but he denied that to me at the end of the season.

"I was really interested in the opposite," he insisted. "I tried to put that out of my mind. I'm an artist, and there's no doubt that going through that experience influences everything. But no. Other than the fact that I felt the growth of Sterling Cooper mirrored the growth of AMC, which is it came upon them suddenly and they may not have been prepared for it, and I thought that was an interesting story. That's not a judgment of AMC, that's just a part of inside baseball about business."

AMC had by this point transformed massively from the seat-of-the-pants operation that found *Mad Men* in the first place. Sorcher, Wayne, and Wolynetz had all moved on to other jobs. The network that once had to beg studios to partner with them on shows was now producing series in-house—including *The Walking Dead*, a zombie drama whose enormous ratings instantly made *Mad Men* look like the boutique hit it had always been.

Mad Men was no longer the most popular show on the network, but it was still the creative standard-bearer for all of dramatic television, having won four Outstanding Drama Series Emmys in a row, tying it with *Hill Street Blues, L.A. Law,* and *The West Wing* for the most ever. Before the fifth season began, Weiner lamented to me that they were now the old show in the category—"I still want my special excuses: *We're new! You don't understand us!* I think we're an underdog. We're always going to be an underdog."—and was proven right when Showtime's *Homeland* prevented *Mad Men* from winning a record fifth in a row.

The industry had come to believe that *Mad Men* had legitimate competition, but Weiner didn't buy it. When I noted near the end of the series that *Mad Men* had inspired many other shows of its type, Weiner said, "I still think it's the only show of its type.

"You've got to just sit back and be what you are," he added, "which is glad to be here, glad to be on peoples' minds and happy that you didn't mess it up. As competitive as we are, I don't feel that way in reference to other shows. I don't like shows that I see that I don't think are that great that get astounding welcomings and huge fanfare and amazing reviews. And then I watch it and I'm like, 'I don't agree.' I've never liked that."

Weiner had long been reluctant to think beyond the current season that he was writing—"I want the end of every season to feel like the end of the series," he told me after the first half of the bifurcated seventh and final season—though he had always hoped to make it to the end of the '60s, and to hit certain signposts along the way. At the start of Season 3, he told me, "I would like to see them get to the end of this [decade], and that was my original intention when I wrote the pilot. My idea was, 'What is it going to be like for someone who is already an adult?' Let's take away all the boomer rosy haze. This guy's an adult. Pete's in his twenties, Peggy is in her twenties. What was it like for them to sit back and watch this happen? And no matter what happens—Summer of Love, the Beatles, Woodstock, Rolling Stones—when you get to 1970, 'My Way' is still in the top ten songs. You know what I mean? That's what I'm interested in. And I would love to see where they are. I would love to see this sense of how things turned out."

When the contract negotiation with Lionsgate ended, Weiner now had an idea of how long the series would run, and how much story he could cover. As he told novelist A. M. Homes in the one interview he did after the series finale, emerging from that negotiation gave him clarity on how he wanted to conclude Don's story, and that of several other major characters. He had an image in his head for the final shot of the series; now he would have to start steering towards it.

"I know the commercial realities of trying to do a television show," Weiner told me before the seventh season began, "and the greatest luxury is that after Seasons 5, 6, and 7 were ordered, all the actors were secured, everything was secured, and I knew I was going to be able to follow through towards the end of the show."

As the show moved deeper into the decade's second half—when the '60s became "the Sixties" of Flower Power, Vietnam, and Nixon—Weiner found himself not only having to travel more well-trod pop culture territory, but tweaking the way he told stories. The show would continue to experiment with form, often reflecting drugs that the characters had taken (a Season 6 episode with half of the agency high on amphetamines played more like a parody of *Mad Men* than the genuine article), and its symbolism and exploration of theme would become more overt than ever.

"That was part of the story of the era of the '60s: the crudeness of the language," Weiner told Homes. "We started making it less and less poetic, less implied—less subtle, quite honestly, deliberately."

Season 6 would be—to the frustration of some *Mad Men* viewers—about the repetition of old patterns. When the simple fantasy of Megan gives way to her more complicated reality, Don has another affair with a brunette (his married neighbor Sylvia, played by Linda Cardellini) and engages in some of the dominating behavior that typified his relationship with Bobbie Barrett. (On a trip to see Bobby's summer camp, he also falls back into bed with Betty, who's more comfortable getting to be Don's other woman, even for one night, than she ever was as his wife.) Pete Campbell again finds himself at odds with a handsome and charismatic impostor in closeted accounts man Bob Benson (James Wolk), and while he briefly seems to have learned his lesson about trying to challenge such a person, he can't control his temper(*) when Bob's friend Manolo marries and then appears to murder Pete's senile mother while out at sea. Don and his rival Ted Chaough (Kevin Rahm) decide to merge their agencies to land a Chevy account, which results in Joan again getting to show Peggy (who had fled to Ted's shop so she could get away from her abusive relationship with Don) to her office, and Roger again getting to fire obnoxious account executive Burt Peterson, who had previously been canned during Season 3's British rule. Before she dies, Pete's mother informs him, "They shot that poor Kennedy boy," and he assumes her ailing mind has taken her back to 1963, because who could imagine that two Kennedy brothers would be gunned down within five years of each other?

(*) Mad Men *had many lines of dialogue that were funnier on paper, but Vincent Kartheiser's incredulous reaction when Bob pleasantly asks how Pete's doing in the midst of this—"NOT GREAT, BOB!"—is easily the show's greatest piece of comic delivery.*

Though *Mad Men* took place in a tumultuous, well-chronicled decade, Weiner had always been reluctant to turn his characters into more sophisticated versions of Forrest Gump, constantly intersecting with all the iconic moments of the Sixties. The results supported that approach: episodes set on the day of the Nixon/ Kennedy election, or during the Cuban Missile Crisis, didn't run from those events, but mainly treated them as metaphors for what the characters were going through (an uncertain power struggle at Sterling Cooper and the fragile state of the Draper marriage, respectively), and were among the series' best, where Season 3's "The Grown-Ups," largely devoted to horrified characters watching news of the JFK assassination, was among its more dramatically inert installments.

With 1968, history could no longer hide in the background, because the bad news was everywhere. An advertising awards dinner is interrupted by news of Martin Luther King's assassination(*), and the agency shuts down for the day so everyone can cope with this national tragedy. (Don, reluctant to put on sackcloth and ashes, instead takes Bobby to see *Planet of the Apes*, and father and son are both struck by the parallels to contemporary race relations.) The Tet Offensive, Bobby Kennedy's murder, the violence at the Democratic National Convention, and all the other dark news of the year didn't just stay on the television, but became part of the characters' everyday lives and angst.

(*) While Mad Men *went deep into many of the period's big social issues, the civil rights movement was never remotely as prominent as, say, the rise of feminism. Early on, Paul Kinsey dates an African American woman and goes on a Freedom Ride with her, and in later seasons, the agency employs a few black secretaries, notably Dawn (Teyonah Parris), who works for Don and eventually succeeds Joan as*

office manager. But Dawn-centric stories, or even scenes, were rare (if sharp, like the way Dawn and fellow secretary Shirley—the only two black people in that office—address each other by their own name, as an illustration of the confusion so many of their white co-workers have about them), and the creative arm of the agency was integrated in different ways, with the likes of Peggy and Ginsberg. It's certainly a subject the show could have done more with, but it also doesn't feel unrealistic that a man like Don Draper would move in social circles where the only people of color he routinely interacted with were secretaries or housekeepers.

"I feel like historical events take a while to filter into our life," Weiner told me after that season. "We take the ones that we think, judging from what we can tell, would really impact people's lives. They were not following the civil rights struggle on a daily basis, but when cities started burning down, they started paying attention. We have tried to make it as gradual a process as it really was. By the time 1968 comes, it is a climax to all of the issues that have been filtering through, that they've been ignoring for as long as possible.

"It was a challenge," he added, "because there was so much of it, and it was so bad, that I basically realized that that *was* the story. The story was there was a worldwide revolution going on, and it is creating this deep, deep anxiety as idealism is going up against violence. And I don't think that idealism wins. That is part of what we tried to show: they turned toward the part that they can control, which is their family. It kind of reminds people that, at least at that point, the social structure and 'civilization' is not in great shape, but what can you deal with? You can deal with your family and your children, and that is all over the show, the entire season. We tried to hit it as much as possible. And Don is not capable of doing that as long as he's living a lie with his family."

Eventually, all the lies and mistakes catch up with Don in the same way that all the social issues are coming to a boil throughout the country. Sally walks in on Don and Sylvia in mid-tryst, and as things deteriorate at both work and home, Don decides to go hobo and take Megan with him to California, where she can pursue higher acting ambitions than her daytime soap opera job, while Don can set up the agency's new satellite office and be a continent away from his other problems. At the last minute, Ted pleads for the opportunity to trade places with him, since he's desperate to save his marriage and get away from the temptation of Peggy Olson.

And Don, who has fought for so long to hide his shameful upbringing from the people who only know him in his stolen identity—who once drove his own brother to suicide because he couldn't stand the world knowing who and what he really was— picks the worst possible moment to open up about his past.

The newly rechristened Sterling Cooper & Partners hosts executives from Hershey, who may be looking to switch agencies, and Don pleases them with an invented story about his father taking him to the store to buy a chocolate bar. But as he looks at the miserable Ted, and watches his own hand shake from alcohol withdrawal (having gone cold turkey after landing in the drunk tank earlier in the episode), he decides he has to give the Hershey executives a more honest pitch.

"I was an orphan," he tells them, as well as Roger, Bert Cooper, and the other SC&P partners in the room. "I grew up in Pennsylvania, in a whorehouse." He goes on to talk about how one of the prostitutes would encourage him to steal money from the johns' pockets, and sometimes buy him a Hershey bar with the proceeds. "I would eat it, alone, in my room, with great ceremony, feeling like a normal kid," he tells them, his voice barely above a whisper, his face buried in his hands at the pain of the memory(*). "It said 'sweet' on the package. It was the only sweet thing in my life."

(*) This is perhaps Jon Hamm's best, most vulnerable, scene of the entire series, but the Emmy that year went to Jeff Daniels for delivering a blistering Aaron Sorkin–penned monologue about the state of America in the first episode of The Newsroom. *Entertainment awards are not worth sweating over sometimes.*

After the season, Weiner pointed to several reasons for the ill-timed confession, including the abrupt attempt at sobriety, guilt about Sally, and seeing Ted about to blow up his own life in the way Don so often had.

"And a lot of it's what we tried to do over the course of the season," he told me, "which is to say, 'At a certain point, you have to stop looking outside yourself and look in the mirror and just recognize who you are.'"

The confession, and the decision to let Ted go to California in his stead, blows up Don's life at work and at home. The other partners put Don on a forced leave of absence, in the hope that he'll quit rather than continue punishing them with his erratic behavior, while a furious Megan (who quit the soap already) leaves for the West Coast without him. But it also emboldens Don to reach out to Sally and the boys and show them the whorehouse, candidly saying, "This is where I grew up." It's the first step on a journey of self-discovery that would occupy the show's seventh and final season.

That journey would take longer than expected. AMC executives, inspired by the huge ratings they got from spreading the final *Breaking Bad* season out over two years—and perhaps reluctant to let go of the series that started the network on this journey—decided to use roughly the same plan again with *Mad Men*, opting to air seven episodes in 2014 and another seven in 2015. This did the show no favors. Not only was *Mad Men* not nearly as plot-driven as its channel-mate—there could be no equivalent of the cliffhanger that drove *Breaking Bad* fans wild over its final hiatus—but it had tended to be a slow starter creatively, with early episodes of each season orienting us to the characters' changed circumstances, while the meatier installments came towards the middle and end of the year. Though Weiner looked at these 14 episodes as one season, he also knew he'd be writing two premieres, and two finales, and that each half-season would have to get up to speed with far less track than he normally had to work with.

"The challenge for splitting the season up is that this is the half of something, but we also wanted it to feel like all of something," Weiner told me at the midpoint of that final season.

The confusion between half and all fit nicely with the disorienting way in which the first half of the final season began, with things at Sterling Cooper & Partners turned upside down. Pete and Ted are in exile in California, Joan is working in accounts, new creative director Lou Avery (Allan Havey) has no respect for Peggy or any kind of modern ideas, and while the season opens with a vintage Don Draper pitch, it is delivered—straight to the camera, and to the audience at home—not by the disgraced, housebound Don, but by freelance copywriter Freddy Rumsen (Joel Murray), the man who first noticed Peggy's way with words in Season 1, now letting a bored and lonely Don use him to play Cyrano.

Don's attempts to prostrate himself before Megan, who has moved into a house in the Hollywood Hills, and the SC&P partners, who agree to let him return to work under a mortifying set of restrictions (no drinking, no being alone with clients, reporting to Lou—and, eventually, Peggy), seem to be getting him nowhere. And Peggy, having gone through a parade of unimpressive love interests—including Pete, Ted, alcoholic accounts man Duck Phillips (Mark Moses), and self-righteous reporter Abe (Charlie Hofheimer)—and still feeling guilt over the child she chose not to parent, even as that choice allowed her to rise so quickly in her career, feels miserable as she turns 30 and has to work on an ad campaign for fast food chain Burger Chef that forces her to think a lot about motherhood. Eventually, in the climax of that season's "The Strategy," Don and Peggy—mentor and protégé, estranged colleagues, and should-be-but-are-never-quite friends—find themselves pulling another all-nighter in what was Don's office at the time of "The Suitcase," but now belongs to Lou.

"I worry about a lot of things, but I don't worry about you," Don reassures her after she confesses her worst fears.

"What do you worry about?" she wonders, baffled.

"That I never did anything, and that I don't have anyone," he admits.

Peggy considers that even the almighty Don Draper could feel this way, and the more pressing question of what would drive a mom of 1969 to take the family to Burger Chef instead of the family dining room, and she has an inspiration about the campaign—right at the instant when, as Weiner had long envisioned, "My Way" comes on the radio. In that moment, Don *is* Frank Sinatra—older, no longer on the cutting edge of style, but still cool and still capable of doing his best work—and he invites Peggy to dance with him. It's a romantic gesture, and yet not—because the two of them having those feelings for each other would have made things too easy for them both, and for the show(*)—and at different times in the song he looks happy and she looks sad, and vice versa, as they think of all they've been through together in this office and the one before it, and all they've lost or given up along the way.

(*) Did Weiner ever consider pairing off Don and Peggy in that way? "In the first or second season," he recalls, "one of the writers came in and had a storyline that was about that. And someone quickly said, 'That's Season 4 if you get there. Don and Peggy can't sleep together until Season 4.' And I always thought that in the back of my mind. There are some entertainment rules about how this thing works, or whatever. . . . I can say that I love their relationship, because it is not chaste, but it is not romantic, but they are in love with each other in so many ways. And it shifts from like brother to father to husband. Sometimes Don's the child, she's the mother. All of that to me is like the richness of the show."

It's a gorgeous moment, and one Weiner could have easily ended the series on. Instead, it wasn't even the mid-season finale. The series would instead go into its final pause a week later with "Waterloo," an episode that played like a *Mad Men* Greatest Hits double album. There would be yet another historical moment made personal, as Neil Armstrong's first step onto the lunar surface inspires Sally to kiss a boy and Bert Cooper to utter his final word— "Bravo"—before dying suddenly(*). There would be yet another last-minute agency restructuring, as Roger—finally accepting the burden and responsibilities of leadership in the aftermath of Cooper's death—arranges to sell SC&P to McCann-Erickson, saving Don's job and making all the partners rich in the process. And there would be another deeply personal and moving pitch, only this time delivered by Peggy (who even gets photographed from the back of her head, a signature Don Draper image), weaving her original Burger Chef idea together with her own buried maternal instincts, everyone's feelings about the moon landing, and the larger turmoil of the period, to promise, "There may be chaos at home, but there's family supper at Burger Chef."

(*) One of Cooper's most memorable moments prior to this episode came when he dictated the obituary for elderly secretary Miss Blankenship, noting, "She was born in 1898 in a barn. She died on the 37th floor of a skyscraper. She's an astronaut." And what's the last thing he sees before he dies? Mad Men: like the elephant that Peggy briefly wanted to put into a Samsonite ad, it never forgets.

Another week, and another episode that could have easily been the series finale. "Waterloo" even featured a musical number of its own, as Don (who has been periodically visited by ghosts throughout the series) has a vision of Bert Cooper (clad, as he so often was in life, in his stocking feet) leading a group of secretaries in a rousing version of "The Best Things in Life Are Free." It was a nod to Robert Morse's musical past (something Weiner had been itching to do since he hired the man) and to the historic moment (Cooper warbles, "The moon belongs to everyone"). But it was also a warning of what was to come. Financially, Don and the other surviving partners were set for life, but what kind of life would that be?

The day after "Waterloo" aired, Weiner told me, "I hope that people listen to the words to the song to some degree, and know that there is some bittersweetness to having all that material success. It is not really life. No one can own it. Do I want people to feel like something bad is going to happen? Yes, we're always playing on that. I was laughing at the fact that the story of Don's success in the company is something where the tension was created, because on *Mad Men*, you can't believe that something horrible isn't going to happen."

This was Memorial Day of 2014, and because Weiner was producing the whole final season at once (unlike his counterparts at *Breaking Bad*, who got to take a production hiatus midway through), he was working on the last *Mad Men* script that day.

"I've given up a lot of holidays to the show," he said. "For me, it's more about slowly settling my relationship with this fiction that has been such a huge, lucky part of my life. If I didn't have so much work to do, I would be crying."

Weiner had come to *Mad Men* from *The Sopranos*, a show whose creator had suggested that personal growth and change, while not impossible, were very difficult and rare. Weiner's own show had taken place in a decade of enormous social change, yet as we watched Don, Betty, Pete, and others continually backslide from promises to change their behavior, we wondered if anyone other than Peggy would exit the '60s(*) a substantially different person from the one who had entered the decade.

(*) For all that fans had obsessed over dates in the series—an obses-sion Weiner had encouraged through his strictness with critics about concealing when each new season was set—Mad Men jumped into a new decade with no fanfare at all. "Waterloo" ends in July 1969, and mid-season premiere "Severance" takes place in April 1970. The final time jump meant the show didn't deal with Woodstock, but it's not like any of the regulars (other than maybe Sally) would have attended, and I guess once you've seen man walk on the moon, you might as well skip ahead to the '70s.

The final half-season would, as usual, start slowly, leaving fans grumbling over the amount of time devoted to Megan, who had already ended things with Don in "Waterloo," and whom the au-dience had never entirely embraced; to Sally's old friend (who also had a very complicated relationship with Betty) Glen Bishop (played by Weiner's son Marten); and to Diana (Elizabeth Reaser), a depressed waitress Don has a brief and unsatisfying affair with.

But the episodes were meticulously stripping away everything of value to Don: his marriage, his furniture, his apartment, his kids (doing just fine with Betty and her second husband, Henry), a large chunk of his fortune (he impulsively writes Megan a $1 million check as an apology for bringing her into the mess of his life), and even the agency, which was supposed to operate as an independent satellite of McCann, but which gets swallowed whole by the advertising behemoth less than a year after the acquisition. And in the process, *Mad Men* gave its audience the stirring finishing kick they had been hoping for.

Much like it had on *The Sopranos*, these final episodes would feel like they were as much about a TV show ending as about the conclusion of the stories on that show. In "Time & Life," Don proposes yet another crazy last-second agency shuffle to escape being absorbed by McCann, this time involving everyone moving to the California office. It's the show's last great heist, only we're so close to the end that it doesn't work out: the executives at McCann, so happy to finally have Don in the fold after a decade of chasing him, don't even let him finish making the California pitch. In "Lost Horizon," while most of the surviving staff has moved over to McCann headquarters(*), Peggy and Roger stick around the gutted SC&P offices, which look like a set that's been struck, drinking and toasting to all the great adventures they had there. (Naval veteran Roger: "This was a hell of a boat, you know?") Old characters like Duck return for curtain calls, and others are seen off, one by one.

(*) *Not only was the* Mad Men *pilot filmed in New York, but Weiner told A. M. Homes that it filmed in what was the real McCann building, and on what was that agency's creative floor in 1970, bringing things neatly full circle.*

Weiner had once told Christina Wayne that he wanted his characters to be happy, and though he put them through hell—right through these final episodes—he found ways to give most of them some kind of happy ending, often demonstrating how much they had grown from the start of the series.

Peggy makes peace with her decision about the baby, matures enough to strut into McCann (with Bert Cooper's octopus porn painting—a gift from Roger—tucked under her arm) ready to conquer the place, and eventually realizes that her close friend, art director Stan Rizzo (Jay R. Ferguson), is the perfect man for her. (That relationship "had to be proved to me," Weiner told Homes, sounding still a bit skeptical about a story that would climax with *Mad Men* resembling a conventional romantic comedy more closely than it ever had before.) Pete, whose bottomless appetite for more love/respect/power/etc. had cost him his marriage and more, finally recognizes what a good life he had and makes a sincere and convincing plea for ex-wife Trudy (Alison Brie) to take him back and follow him to an exciting new job in Wichita. Roger stops chasing younger women and marries Megan's mother, Marie (Julia Ormond), to the amusement of Don and Joan. And Joan, who once upon a time saw a job at Sterling Cooper as merely a stepping-stone to a cushy life with a rich husband, and who sneered at Peggy's attempts to play the man's game, ends up a single mother who would rather devote her energies to starting her own production company than party with the aging sugar daddy who doesn't want her to work. (Also, she leaves McCann over sexual harassment, threatening to call the ACLU and various feminist leaders about the issue in a way that would have disgusted the Joan of 1960.)

Even Betty gets a happy ending of sorts, depending on how

you look at it. She's diagnosed with advanced lung cancer—the inevitable cost of all those years Don spent pushing cigarettes, even after the Surgeon General's warning about its dangers—but she had told Don back in the first season that she would rather die young. And in facing a premature death, she demonstrates a level of wisdom and self-awareness that wasn't always present in life. (In Season 3, when her dying father wants to discuss his funeral arrangements, Betty whines that she's his "little girl" and shouldn't have to hear about this; here, she calmly instructs Sally on what to do after she's gone, even as Sally is the one covering her ears.) Betty had been a hard character to love for many *Mad Men* fans, and her final episodes seemed to give the audience a newfound appreciation for both her and January Jones.

"I knew very early on" that Betty would die at the series' end, Weiner told A. M. Homes. "Her mother had just died in the pilot, and I felt this woman wasn't going to live long. We loved the idea of her realizing her purpose in life right when she ran out of time. To me, despite all the emotions that I feel for these people, that moment when she was in the kitchen and [Henry asks why she's going back to school], and she goes, 'Why was I ever doing it?' If she's not dying of cancer, that's not a good line."

So if everyone else had grown and changed and turned out, for the most part, much better than where they had started, where did that leave Don?

On a cliff in California, dreaming up what Weiner would describe as "the greatest commercial ever made."

Probably.

Don, who has spent much of the final season being dismissive of his entire profession—when Peggy tells him her career goal is to "create something of lasting value," he wounds her by laughing at the idea that she (or anyone) could do that in advertising—realizes that McCann doesn't need him any more than Megan, Betty, or his kids do, and walks out of a meeting for one last hobo odyssey, first in search of Diana, then in search of himself. Along the way, he gives up most of his remaining possessions, including his car, until he's just a man in jeans (the man in the gray flannel suit, now in blue denim) with nothing but a sack filled with clothes, cash, and Anna Draper's engagement ring. Along the way, though, he encounters some fellow veterans who absolve him for his role in the real Don Draper's death, as well as a young Dick Whitman type whom he spares from a similar life spent looking over his shoulder. At the end of the series' penultimate episode, we see Don sitting on a bus bench in the middle of nowhere, Oklahoma, with a wry smile on his face and a world of possibilities open to him.

It was a strange period for Don—Weiner told A. M. Homes that his desire was to do "an episode of *The Fugitive*, where Don comes to town, and he could be anyone, or anything"—and for Jon Hamm, who spent most of his final weeks on the series separate from all the actors with whom he had spent so much of the past decade. In the finale, Don has important conversations with Sally, Betty, and Peggy, but all happen on the phone. (The first two, Hamm was able to film with Shipka and Jones nearby feeding him their dialogue, but he played the series' final Don/Peggy scene with Moss hundreds of miles away, on the other end of a real telephone line.)

"It was weird, honestly," says Hamm. "It was a very specific choice by Matt. I think it worked for the story, obviously. We're telling the story of a guy trying to find himself, through isolation, and through removing himself from patterns of his life.

So it was thematically and, from a story standpoint, was useful, and it was very effective. But from an acting standpoint, it was hard. I would have preferred to have had scenes in person with people. But I understood that that's where the story was taking us, and that's what needed to be done. And I think the proof is in the pudding. It very much reflects that sense of solitude and loneliness and dissatisfaction and confusion that Don is going through."

Don, grief-stricken to learn about Betty—and consumed with guilt over Sally and Betty's suggestion that they not only don't need him to come home to help, but would prefer he remain absent—follows Anna Draper's troubled niece Stephanie (Caity Lotz) to a fictionalized version of the Esalen Institute, a New Age retreat in Big Sur. The group therapy sessions only make Stephanie feel worse, and Don (whom she still knows as Dick Whitman) tries to give her the same bad advice he has applied to so much of his own life: "You can put this behind you. It'll get easier as you move forward."

"Oh, Dick," she tells him sadly, "I don't think you're right about that."

Stephanie does run away, though, stranding Don at the edge of America, forcing him to call the person who most understands him—even if she is somehow one of the few major *Mad Men* characters to never learn about his true identity—for help. Hamm and Moss aren't physically together for their last scene, but their interaction is just as intimate and powerful as the best of "The Suitcase" and "The Strategy."

Peggy scolds him for running out on her and the rest of the SC&P diehards with no explanation, then asks, "What did you ever do that was so bad?"

"I broke all my vows," he tells her, nearly catatonic. "I scandalized my child, took another man's name, and made nothing of it."

"That's not true," she argues, pleading with him to come home, where all will be forgiven, and where he would get the chance to work on the Holy Grail of ad accounts: Coca-Cola.

A sad and lost Don sits in another Esalen group therapy session, where a man named Leonard(*) describes feeling ignored and unloved by the world. Listening to Leonard's description of a dream he had about being an item in the fridge that no one wanted to take out is like a dam bursting inside Don, and he wraps his arms around the stranger, both weeping openly. When next we see Don, he's no longer looking at the other Esalen people with his usual dismissive contempt, but with a sense of camaraderie and openness. He sits on a cliff for a morning chant, and as he delivers his "Om . . . " with perfect sincerity, an idea occurs to him that spreads a huge grin across his face(**).

(*) *Weiner explained to Homes that he told his casting directors, "It's probably the most important role in the series. I need somebody who's not famous, and who can cry, and really do it. Like, ugly, real crying." No pressure whatsoever! But character actor Evan Arnold didn't succumb to the burden of that description, and made Leonard into a person in only a few minutes of screen time.*

(**) *What was Jon Hamm thinking as he played the final glimpse of Don Draper that we would ever see? He had a lot of different emotions running through his head, trying to power that grin, but at the same time, "I just remember hoping that I didn't mess it up, and that I didn't fall off the cliff."*

And suddenly . . . we are on a different hill, with a different group of people who are nonetheless costumed similarly to many of the ones Don has just met—one woman wears her hair in iden-

tical ribbons to those sported by the Esalen receptionist—each one
carrying a familiar soda bottle and singing a song that would be
very familiar to *Mad Men* viewers of a certain age:

> *I'd like to buy the world a home*
> *And furnish it with love*
> *Grow apple trees and honey bees*
> *And snow white turtle doves*
> *I'd like to teach the world to sing*
> *In perfect harmony*
> *I'd like to buy the world a Coke*
> *And keep it company*

Many of the dramas created in the wake of *The Sopranos* had
concluded in ways that angered their fans, but none since that cut
to black had ended on a note that proved so instantly perplexing
to so much of the audience. Was Weiner saying that Don had written the famous Coke ad? Was he trying to contrast the genuine nature of Don's Esalen experience with a manufactured version of it
designed to sell sugar water? And if Weiner *was* assigning fictional
credit for the real ad to his protagonist(*), then was this meant to
be an uplifting ending where Don Draper finally becomes a whole
enough man to create such an iconic ad, or a cynical one where
Don again takes a real piece of life and finds a way to commodify it?

(*) *Season 5 ended with Peggy vying for the chance to write the
campaign that would launch Virginia Slims cigarettes. After that finale, I asked Weiner if he was angling to have Peggy to write "You've
come a long way, baby," since that tagline summed up so much of her
own journey. "That's such a famous campaign written by such a distinctive person that I would never do that," he insisted, having previ-*

ously let his characters use only one real ad slogan ("It's toasted," which dated back to 1917) on the show. Of course, creators are allowed to change their minds, even on "never." Weiner had once said he didn't anticipate doing a JFK assassination episode, given how familiar that subject was in pop culture, and he wound up doing that, too.

Much as it happened in the wake of *The Sopranos* finale, some people weren't content to agree to disagree, whether on the question of whether Don wrote the ad or on what that said about the man and the show itself. Though Weiner's talk with A. M. Homes a few nights after the finale strongly implied that Don had written the ad, it also acknowledged that *Mad Men* was a series that not only didn't need to be definitively solved, but tended to work better when two smart people could look at the same scene and take two completely different ideas from it.

"I have always been able to live with ambiguities," he told Homes. "I don't really understand a lot of things that regular people understand, that's part of it. So holding those things in my head [someone might ask], 'Well, which is it?' Why does it have to be one or the other?"

Back in Season 2, I was convinced Duck Phillips had fallen off the wagon during the events of "Maidenform," but a later episode made clear that *this* was when he was having his first drink in a long time. "There's no reason to know that" he hadn't drunk in "Maidenform," Weiner told me at the end of the season. "It's like when we talked about everyone last year thinking Dick Whitman was Jewish. There are ambiguities of communication, and I don't judge people for misinterpreting. That's the whole show to me: take what you want from it. None of it's wrong."

The Coke ad would be Weiner's ultimate invitation to take what you wanted from *Mad Men*. In the days after the finale, I read arguments for why Don had obviously written the ad, and why he had obviously not, and whether we should admire him for having done it, or once again take pity on such a hollow man who could lose everything he thought that mattered to him, travel thousands of miles, experience a complete emotional breakdown, make peace with his feelings of inadequacy, and somehow come out the other side with . . . a Coke ad. (To borrow the title of the song that closed out the mid-season premiere, some looked at the finale and asked, "Is that all there is?") It was the series finale as Rorschach test, and your take depended as much on your pre-existing feelings about advertising, man's ability to evolve, and even Coke vs. Pepsi as it did on what Weiner actually presented in those closing minutes.

"I think it's a realization by Don of exactly who he is," suggests Jon Hamm. "We spent [years] following this guy who's essentially running away from his reality, and running away from who he is, who he is stated to be, and running away from what he's good at. And it culminates in the ultimate running away, in this long, lonely journey on the road. At the end of that journey, he comes to that moment of peace and clarity about who he is. And it has nothing to do with his name or his past, or anything other than that it is the purest expression of what he does. And what he does is create advertising. And I think that's really the meaning, if there's a larger meaning to it, and an explanation for what happened. Don comes to a realization that this is what he does, and this is who he is, and this is the story of the moment. This is how he solves the cultural malaise, or cultural confusion of the moment: 'Let's get together and hold hands and drink Coke.'"

"I did hear rumblings about people saying the ad being corny," Weiner told Homes. "And it's a little bit disturbing to me. I get back to the cynicism. I'm not saying that advertising's not corny.

But the people who find that ad corny are probably experiencing life that way and are missing out on something. Five years before that, black people and white people couldn't even be in an ad together. The idea [was] that some enlightened state, and not just co-option, might have created something that is very pure. And yeah, there's soda in there with the good feeling. But that ad, to me, it's the best ad ever made. And it comes from a very good place, which is a desire to sell Coca-Cola, but you shouldn't write everything off. The ambiguous relationship we have with advertising is part of why I did the show. . . . I felt like that ad in particular is so much of its time, so beautiful, and I don't think as villainous as the snark of today thinks it is."

"I don't necessarily find it that cynical," says Hamm. "As I say, it's an expression of what this person is. And I don't think it's a backsliding, necessarily. But I don't think there's a world in which Don Draper goes away, finds peace and harmony, and just lives at Esalen. I don't think that's being true to this person we've seen all these years, either. I think Don, in his best moments, is that quintessential ad man. And I think Don in his worst moments is a person who takes advantage of people and mistreats people. Maybe he's accentuated the positive in his life, and hopefully eliminated some of the negative."

Part of the reason those of us who land on the cynical side of things do so is because of the way Weiner constructed the final sequence. Going from Don's grin of realization to the Coke ad, with nothing in between—say, cutting back and forth from the ad to glimpses (scored to the Coke jingle) of Don returning to his life in New York (whether working alongside Peggy at McCann, checking in on the kids, or both)—suggests that the sum total of Don's experience throughout the series, and especially through this final cross-country journey of self-discovery, is him writing a better ad. Or, at least, it suggests that this is by far the most important thing he gets out of it. That doesn't feel untrue to the nature of the series—the opening credits, which show Don falling away from everything in his life, only to end up seated comfortably in his chair, looking as powerful and confident as ever, had more or less promised this *exact* journey—but if you had stuck around for 92 hours, hoping for better from Don even as his actions kept reminding you of how much worse he could get, then seeing that grin immediately translated into the Coke ad and nothing else . . . well, there was a reason some people didn't want to instantly accept that he had written the damn thing.

Even Hamm wonders about what we might have seen had Weiner opted to show us more of Don past his epiphany.

"The thing I would be interested in is what is the reconciliation or the fallout with his children?" he says. "How does he then go back and repair the damage to the people that he cares about in his life? His children and his wife and his long-term protégé, and Roger. I think those are the people that, had the story gone on for another episode or two, we would have seen this new person come back and begin to repair those relationships. I think that's what he actually learned. I think the big two aha moments for Don, other than the literal aha moment of the last frame, is when he confronts Stephanie and she says you can't walk away from your problems— the advice he's been giving himself and other people over the last seven seasons is not a great way to process emotional turmoil— and the moment in the therapy session when he hears this man tell the story of not being appreciated and not being seen and heard and understood. I think both of those things land very heavily on Don, and he hears them, for the first time."

An author may have certain intentions when he writes a story, but he has no control over how his audience chooses to interpret the work. Weiner made his feelings clear, but he also acknowledged that the series had become bigger than its creator by the end.

"I did think, 'Why not end this show with the greatest commercial ever made?'" he told Homes. "But what it means to people and everything? I am not for ambiguity for ambiguity's sake, but it was nice to have your cake and eat it too, in terms of *What is advertising, who is Don, and what is that thing?*"

Months earlier, at the series wrap party, Weiner told the assembled cast and crew, "When I was on *The Sopranos*, someone said to me, 'You better enjoy it. It doesn't get any better than this.' And look what happened? We've had this amazing experience together, but don't ever for a second stop dreaming that this is as good as it gets, because you have no idea what can happen to you. This may really be as good as it gets for me, but none of you should think that way."

By this point, *Mad Men* itself had taught the rest of the TV drama business that this was not as good as things could get. The show's success inspired other channels and content providers to get into the prestige drama game (in the same way that FX's success with *The Shield* and its successors led AMC to this point), unleashing a flood of great content that would have seemed unthinkable even in those 39 days between when Tony Soprano's world went to black and Don Draper's lit up for the first time. Whether or not Weiner approves of all the critical hosannas bestowed upon his descendants, and whether or not many of them approach *Mad Men* at its very best—and even at an advanced age, episodes like "The Strategy," "Waterloo," and "Time & Life" were reminders that when the show was hitting on all cylinders, there was *Mad Men* (and, before that last year, *Breaking Bad*), and then there was everything else on television—there could be no question that there was simply more overall greatness in the medium than there had ever been, often in places that had once been as obscure as AMC.

Before the final season began, I asked Weiner what he would do if he had an actual time machine like the figurative one Don once told Kodak about, and could travel back to tell his younger sitcom-writing self what was coming up for him.

"I'm still having trouble believing it happened," he told me. "I don't think I could have convinced myself that it was going to happen. It's just a fantasy.

"It's an incredible experience," he added. "It has been so creatively satisfying, and I can speak for the other people involved. We all feel so much of our lives were explored and utilized in this process. That's kind of your fantasy as an artist, to try to find meaning in all of that, and it's happened to our characters. They've had success, they've had way more dramatic lives than we have, but the story of the show has always been about—I always joke in the writers room, when I'm pitching a story, the key phrase is 'But he doesn't know it.' Like, 'something happens, but she doesn't know it.' That's been the experience of the show on some level: that you can't realize that it's happened."

CHAPTER 12

I am the one who knocks!...
Breaking Bad gives the recession
the villain it deserves

The pictures come at you, first beautiful, then disorienting.

A cloud pushes over a Southwestern mesa. A pair of khaki pants floats through the breeze, so full of air that it looks like it has an invisible, topless man inside. Then an RV runs over the pants, tearing down a desert highway, a drab green shirt mysteriously dangling off the passenger-side mirror. We see inside the RV, driven by a middle-aged, slightly doughy white man wearing only a ventilator mask, shoes, socks, and tighty-whities. There's a younger man slumped over the passenger seat, and two more sprawled along the floor in the back, sliding to and fro as the camper bumps along the road.

Our driver's mask fogs up, and he veers off the highway and into a ditch. He runs outside, coughs and breathes and flings the mask away, panicking as he hears approaching sirens. He puts on the green shirt, then plunges back into the RV to grab a pistol from one of the men lying on the ground, plus his wallet and a camcorder, runs back outside. He starts recording and gives his name as Walter Hartwell White.

"To all law-enforcement entities, this is not an admission of guilt. I am speaking to my family now," he says, barely keeping it together as he records messages of love to his wife Skyler and son Walter Jr., before concluding, "There are going to be some things that you'll come to learn about me in the next few days. I just want you to know that no matter how it may look, I only had you in my heart. Goodbye."

He turns the camera off and neatly lays it on the ground next to his wallet, hears approaching sirens, waddles into the middle of the road with his shirt tucked into the back of his underpants, and points the gun at whoever is coming around the bend.

As the show cuts to the twangy, menacing musical sting that accompanies the brief *Breaking Bad* title sequence, you are no doubt having the exact two responses the show's creator, Vince Gilligan, wants from you: "What the hell was that?" followed by "More, please. Now."

That opening sequence hooks virtually everyone who sees it, and in script form, it's what lured actor Bryan Cranston to keep reading and then go for the career-altering role of Walter White. As *Breaking Bad* would continue to do, year after Emmy-winning year, the start of the pilot plunges the viewer into a nightmare world—involving a high school chemistry teacher who begins cooking crystal meth to support his family in the wake of a lung-cancer diagnosis—full of dark choices, macabre violence, and gorgeous, surreal imagery.

Over its landmark run, *Breaking Bad* has told us the story of a man we should relate to—a smart man, a husband and father dealing with the pressures so many of us have faced through this recession (though the series was developed and debuted right before the economy crashed), pushed to make bad choices—and consistently challenged our willingness to forgive him his many awful deeds as he becomes more arrogant and unequivocally evil. It told that story at a pace that was at times unusually measured, at others heart-stoppingly quick, as both Walter White and his writers kept finding themselves forced to improvise escapes from impossible circumstances. And it told those stories with a stunning visual style that was equal to, or better than, many crime films produced with a much larger budget, on a much longer schedule.

Mad Men could have been a fluke. If HBO hadn't followed *Oz* with *The Sopranos*, and then *Six Feet Under*, or if FX hadn't followed *The Shield* with *Nip/Tuck* and *Rescue Me*, we'd look at those channels (and perhaps this era) very differently. And AMC happened to follow one all-time-classic drama series with another one that, like *Mad Men*, had struggled to find a home elsewhere.

Vince Gilligan's TV career began on *The X-Files*. His colleague Howard Gordon says there was a clear demarcation on the writing staff between people like himself, Glen Morgan, and James Wong, who could write the show viewers had come to expect each week; and resident geniuses Darin Morgan and Gilligan, who had a more peculiar approach to the series that often inserted humor (and, at times, outright parody) into what was usually a very grim drama. One of the Gilligan-written episodes even cast Darin Morgan in the central role, as a shape-shifter who uses his abilities to score with women who otherwise wouldn't give him the time of day.

"Vince has a voice that blows your mind," says Gordon. "When I say the word 'genius,' I mean that, as a writer, I can look at what Glen and Jim did and admire it, but say, 'I get how they did that. Maybe

I can reverse-engineer that and do a passable imitation.' Darin and Vince assembled the most improbable elements into a story."

"I don't think of myself as a particularly funny person," says Gilligan, "and yet when I started writing movie scripts, I gravitated towards writing comedies... one of my concerns when I got *The X-Files* job was, 'Am I gonna be able to write darkness and drama and tension?' People who only know me from *Breaking Bad* would be amused to hear that, but I was the light, quirky romantic-comedy guy, wondering if he was going to fit in with the darkness of *The X-Files*."

A few years after *X-Files* ended, Gilligan was talking with Thomas Schnauz, a film-school classmate who had worked with him on both *X-Files* and its short-lived spin-off, *The Lone Gunmen*. Both men were bemoaning the lack of writing jobs like the ones they had shared. As a joke, Schnauz (who would become a *Breaking Bad* writer himself) mentioned an article he had read about a man who put a meth lab in the back of an RV, and suggested they could try that if their careers went further south.

"And as we were laughing about it, it was one of those eureka moments that are few and far between for a writer," recalls Gilligan. "There was a click in my head. What that click was, was a moment of intense curiosity, and coming up with a character who was very much like myself: law-abiding, and who would nonetheless do such a thing, and put a meth lab in an RV, and willfully transform himself into a criminal. The character popped into my head in a proverbial flash of lightning, and it took hold of my imagination from there.

"In hindsight, I'm glad I didn't talk myself out of pursuing it," he adds. "It would have been relatively easy, because on paper, this show doesn't make a lot of sense that it would work as it does. We're talking about a 50-year-old man, and right there, TV executives aren't going to want to build a show around a 50-year-old man, and you find out by the first-act break that he's dying of cancer, that's another strike against you. And if you realize that his means of amassing money for his family is to cook crystal meth, maybe you say to yourself, 'Man, that's three strikes right there.'"

Gilligan took the idea—which he always breaks down as, "We're going to take Mr. Chips and turn him into Scarface"—to Sony executives Zack Van Amburg and Jamie Erlicht, with whom he had recently worked on a pilot script for CBS(*).

(*) That script, for the lighthearted cop drama Battle Creek, *would eventually be revived in the wake of* Breaking Bad, *though it only lasted one season, and Gilligan's involvement was minimal.*

"I pitched it to them," he says, "and five to ten minutes into the pitch, I had this out-of-body experience where I'm watching myself pitch and I'm thinking, 'This is the goddamn stupidest idea I've ever heard.' There were these blank, affectless expressions on their faces that indicated how nuts they thought this idea was. But I got through this pitch, and they both stared at me. It didn't look good, their expressions. But they kept their poker faces and said, 'All right, good to see you.'"

A week later, though, Van Amburg and Erlicht told Gilligan they wanted to make the show, though they had encountered some of the same skepticism Gilligan felt during the pitch.

"What I found out years later," Gilligan says, "is in between the pitch and when they called me, they went to their boss, Michael Lynton at Sony. He has told me personally that he said, famously, 'That is the single worst idea for a television series I've ever heard in my life.' But he hired them to make calls like this, so if they were excited by it, it was their reputations."

Everyone knew that the crystal-meth business would be a non-starter at the broadcast networks, so Gilligan pitched it to HBO and TNT, without success. Showtime declined to take the meeting, since they were already working on *Weeds*, a dramedy about a suburban widow who starts dealing marijuana to pay the bills, and a show whose existence Gilligan didn't learn of until he went to pitch *Breaking Bad* to FX.

"Five minutes into the pitch with John Landgraf," Gilligan says, "he said, 'This sounds a little like *Weeds*.' And I'm like, 'I'm sorry, what? What's *Weeds*?' As he explained it to me, I could feel all the blood leave my face."

Fortunately, Gilligan's pitch sounded different enough that Landgraf ordered a script. Gilligan spent 10 happy months developing the show at FX before Landgraf chose to green-light another series, *The Riches*, about a family of gypsy con artists (who also, co-incidentally, used an RV as their base of operations).

"It was a really good script," says Landgraf. "But there's so much about what a series ultimately becomes that's still unknown before the pilot is cast and shot, and also before the second and third episode have been written. At that time, we had *The Shield*, *Nip/Tuck*, and *Rescue Me*: three shows with four male protagonists you might describe as anti-heroes. And we were saying to ourselves, 'Well, are we just the anti-hero network? Is that our brand?' I certainly regret not having *Breaking Bad*. But what I don't regret is the decision to make FX more than just the anti-hero network. And I don't regret the experimentation that led to *Damages* and the other shows we have on the air now, or being in the comedy business or all the other things we did. We said, 'If we have a fourth dark anti-hero show, then that's it. That's what we are and that's all that we are.'

And then, obviously, Vince went and cast it the way he cast it, and made it the way he made it, and the rest is history."

"They had to make a tough call at FX," says Gilligan, "and I would've made the same call. *Breaking Bad*, thank God it is a success critically, but it's not a show that's an easy sell."

Had this happened even a few years earlier, *Breaking Bad* would have ceased to exist. But there was a new player in town in AMC, where executives Rob Sorcher and Christina Wayne were pondering what kind of series they could use to follow *Mad Men*, and began looking at their movie library for inspiration.

"We had been talking a lot about movies at the channel that had rated well, like the *Death Wish* movies, or *Falling Down*," says Wayne, "so we had talked about looking for something like that: man against the world, but anti-hero."

AMC had recently hired Jeremy Elice from FX to help develop shows, and Gilligan's agent Mark Gordon made sure to get the *Breaking Bad* script in the hands of someone who had liked it at his old job.

"Jeremy brought the script in to me," says Sorcher, "and he said, 'It's a high school teacher, diagnosed with terminal cancer and becomes a crystal meth dealer.' I'm thinking, just on the logline alone, how contemporary it sounded compared to everything else we were looking at(*)."

(*) "After Mad Men, *we saw every period piece known to man," says AMC president Charlie Collier, who arrived at the channel after* Breaking Bad *was already in development. "I would come in to work, and there would be messages pitching flappers, and Motown. 'We've got a period piece for you!' We had a lot of conversations about not wanting to be a period-piece network, even though we had the word 'classic' in our name at the time."*

The world hadn't seen *Mad Men* yet, Gilligan says, "So when Mark Gordon asked me if I knew what AMC was, I said, 'Yeah, I watch *Short Circuit 2* on it. I watch old Stallone movies on it. That's all they do, right? Why not just send it to the food channel? It's a show about cooking, after all.' Little did I know what was in the offing as far as AMC was concerned, and they were as good as their word from day one. They said they wanted to make this into a television series, and I secretly thought, 'Yeah, right.' They said all the nice things you say in meetings, and I smiled and nodded and drank the free scotch and figured, 'Hey, this is a pleasant enough way to spend a half hour and nothing will ever come of it.' I was so glad to have been proven wrong."

The AMC executives were impressed with Gilligan, so much so that Sorcher took another big gamble after they decided to order a *Breaking Bad* pilot.

Sorcher asked Gilligan whom he might like to direct it, and while Gilligan paused to assemble a mental wish list, "Rob spoke up and said, 'Hey, how about you direct it?'" says Gilligan, who to that point had only two *X-Files* episodes on his directorial résumé. "I thought I was on *Candid Camera*, but I said, 'Yeah, that's good,' because I had indeed harbored aspirations of being a director. I never thought in a million years that a major network would let someone who had directed two hours of television direct a pilot. It was just an amazing, one-of-a-kind, win-the-lottery sort of situation. You had this deader than a doornail property of mine picked up by an upstart network and then you had the head of the network suggest I direct the pilot myself."

"You could take one read of the pilot script and know that every frame of this had been thought out visually," says Sorcher. "The directorial approach was there on the pages, to the point where I felt like the script was a transcription of a shot film… In talking to Vince about directors, I hadn't ever encountered anyone in Hollywood who sounded so reasonable, nice, and full of common sense answers and folksy practicality. I guess it was just his damn accent. But that sure worked out well."

Gilligan was relatively new to directing, but he had an ace up his sleeve: John Toll. The Oscar-winning cinematographer of *Legends of the Fall* and *Braveheart* was friendly with Gilligan (they were supposed to work on a movie together, but it ultimately didn't get made), and he had a hole in his schedule in between two movie assignments. Shooting the *Breaking Bad* pilot with Gilligan would give Toll a reason to keep his crew together during that gap.

Gilligan picked up a bunch of photography books at the local Barnes & Noble, put Post-it notes on pages that evoked the look he wanted for the series, and began discussing the visual style of what would become the most cinematographically daring show on television.

"I knew that once we knew our characters, we didn't have to have them perfectly lit," says Gilligan. "I wanted light that was sculptured and textured. We didn't need to see the faces of everyone we were watching and listening to."

Matt Weiner had wanted an unknown for Don Draper. The actor Vince Gilligan chose for Walter White was a known quantity—just one known for a very different kind of performance.

Bryan Cranston had been a working actor for nearly 25 years, starting small (he was a car thief on an episode of *CHiPs*), then working steadily but mostly anonymously (save a recurring *Seinfeld* role as kinky dentist Tim Whatley) before hitting it big in his mid-40s as Hal, the panicky father on Fox's *Malcolm in the Middle*.

The sitcom was designed around the kids, but everyone quickly realized that the biggest laughs came from Cranston and Jane Kaczmarek as the parents, and more and more of the stories were geared around them. Cranston, who was nominated for three Emmys for the role, proved to be an actor without vanity, frequently appearing in his underwear and other unflattering outfits (in one episode, Hal becomes a competitive speed-walker and dons a bright red and yellow body stocking).

"I hate to say it, but if I'd only known him from *Malcolm*, I never would have thought of him," Gilligan told me in 2009. Instead, the interest came from an *X-Files* episode Gilligan wrote called "Drive," in which Cranston played a man who carjacks Mulder because his head will explode if he's not in a moving vehicle going west. As Gilligan explained it, "The guy starts out being a real racist jackass, and you don't like him. But as the episode progresses, his humanity shines through. He doesn't suddenly become a good guy, he doesn't have some deathbed transformation, and yet he has to have a basic humanity so that you respond to him by the end of the hour."

Cranston pulled it off in "Drive," and Gilligan needed a similar quality from Walter White. Walt might start off as a sympathetic character, but Gilligan knew that there was darkness in his past— we learn that he quit a lucrative business over wounded pride, and later stubbornly chooses to keep cooking meth rather than take money from his ex-partners(*)—and would be far more in the future. The premise was a tough enough sell as it was; if his star didn't have that core of humanity, viewers might flee long before the full Scarface transformation. And Cranston's comic gifts would also be useful for the black humor Gilligan wanted to incorporate throughout the show.

(*) One of the few pieces of backstory the show never fully explained was exactly why Walt walked away from Gray Matter Technologies, the company he founded with girlfriend Gretchen and their friend Elliott. The gist of it, according to longtime Breaking Bad *writer Peter Gould, is that Gretchen takes Walt to meet her parents in their grand Rhode Island estate, and Walt, self-conscious about his working-class roots, "feels less than" and abandons her in the middle of the trip with no explanation, causing her to end the relationship and begin dating Elliott. Suddenly miserable on the wrong side of this love triangle, Walt cashes out at a low point for Gray Matter, then resents Gretchen and Elliott's success without him so much that he refuses several offers, even before the events of the series, to reward his early work at the company.*

First Gilligan had to get the attention of Cranston, who was looking through a stack of pilot scripts for his first post-*Malcolm* job, and who didn't particularly remember Gilligan when his agent mentioned they had worked together before.

"Most pilot scripts are very difficult to get through," Cranston told me in 2009. "You want them to be great, and they're not… But with Vince's script, I picked it up and read, 'A guy in tighty-whitey underwear, he's got a respirator on, he's driving a Winnebago. Two dead bodies are sliding back and forth,' and I'm like, 'What the fuck? What? What?' And I had to catch up! I had to catch up! And that was his lure. He was just fishing. And before you know it, you're engrossed, and I read it cover to cover without stopping."

Gilligan had hooked his big fish, and now Cranston began doing what he could to flesh out Walter White beyond what was already on the page.

"Once I signed the contract and was doing the show," Cranston said, "I had visions of how this guy [should look]. I thought he should be a little chunky. This guy went to seed a bit emotionally, and it should manifest itself physically. He should be pale. And I thought that his invisibility to himself, because of his lost opportunities and depression, should kind of form a mask."

Costume designer Kathleen Detoro ran with Cranston's suggestions that Walt's life should be colorless, coming up with a wardrobe full of muted greens and browns. Cranston wanted an "impotent" mustache for the character—"I wanted the mustache to have people subconsciously go, 'What's the point of that mustache? It doesn't make any sense. Why would you bother if that's all you can grow?'"—and makeup artist Frieda Valenzuela took all the red highlights out of his hair and thinned out the mustache until you could see skin underneath. Cranston also packed 10 additional pounds onto his usually slim frame so he would look particularly nonthreatening when Walt is cooking meth in his undies.

"Bryan, God bless him, is one of the most courageous actors I've ever even heard of, let alone worked with," Gilligan told me in 2009. When he was directing the pilot, "I had a moment where I wimped out, and I could have really done damage to our show. In the very early stage, we were set to film the scene where he's in his underpants. I said, 'Gee, are you comfortable in underpants, wouldn't you rather be in sweatpants?' And he said, 'Why?' I said, 'I don't know, are you comfortable?' And he said, 'No, I'm not comfortable, but that's the whole point. What's important for the story here?' I said, 'Well, underpants, I guess,' and I asked him what kind of underpants he was comfortable with. He said, 'What kind of underpants are more pathetic?' And I said, 'Well, saggy jockey shorts,' and he said, 'That's right. That's what I should wear.'"

The pilot was filmed on location in Albuquerque, and deals with Walt being diagnosed with inoperable lung cancer, then going into business with his former student Jesse Pinkman (Aaron Paul), who's been using what he remembers from Mr. White's chemistry class to become part of the local meth trade, under the pseudonym Cap'n Cook. (Jesse's secret ingredient: chili powder.) After Jesse buys an RV with Walt's savings to use as a mobile meth lab, Walt takes charge of the cooking, telling Jesse, "You and I will not make garbage. We will produce a chemically pure and stable product that performs as advertised." He's as good as his word, but the product is ultimately *too* good: Krazy-8 and Emilio, the local dealers Jesse takes a sample to, decide to steal the formula and kill these two losers. Walt is able to save himself and Jesse through some clever mixing of chemicals—the first of many times in the series his brain will prove to be more dangerous than an opponent's gun—and the incoming sirens he hears in the opening teaser prove to be fire trucks racing to put out a brushfire Walt and Jesse had inadvertently started earlier. He returns home to his wife Skyler (Anna Gunn), with whom we've seen he shares a loving but passionless marriage, climbs into bed, and shocks her with spontaneous, vigorous sex that prompts her to ask a question that will echo through the rest of the series:

"Walt, is that you?"

Is it? At this stage of our viewership, it doesn't seem like it. It seems like the two death sentences our man receives in this hour—first from the oncologist, then from Krazy-8—have woken him up from years of slumber, and made him act in ways his wife couldn't imagine. But as *Breaking Bad* moves along, we begin to see that this is who Walter White was all along, and it's only his changed circumstances that have revealed him as a man capable of these things.

The executives at AMC loved the finished product. AMC is a sibling of the Independent Film Channel, and Charlie Collier screened the pilot for his bosses Josh Sapan and Ed Carroll at the IFC Center in New York. Collier asked them what they thought, "and Ed said—and I knew this was high praise for them—'If you added 20 minutes to this, it's the best independent film of the year.'"

Mad Men had been a tough call as a period piece, but it also had the benefit of a *Sopranos* pedigree, easy opportunities for product integration (many of Sterling Cooper's clients are brands that still exist), a kind of Hollywood glamour, and an overall classiness. *Breaking Bad* was set in flyover country and had a drab, middle-aged protagonist who was A) dying of cancer, and B) dealing with it by going into the drug business. And he wasn't even making pot, coke, or heroin—all of which have been the subject of sexy, iconic movies—but crystal meth, a downmarket product which had no slick showbiz antecedent.

"*Breaking Bad* was about the biggest risk we could have taken at the time," says Collier. "If you're an ad-supported cable network, looking to move from a beautiful period piece and match it with something modern-day, you would quickly say there is no context for saying yes to this show. My background was ad sales, so I knew my advertisers would need a year to see it. *This crystal meth show brought to you by...* It was one of those shows where you had to believe so much in the content that you thought it would cure all ills."

Ultimately, Collier, Sorcher, and Wayne believed enough in the content, and their bosses believed enough in them, to give *Breaking Bad* a green light in June of 2007, a few weeks before the world got to see *Mad Men*.

"Vince is so nice," says Collier, one of many testimonials to the good Southern manners of the Virginia-born Gilligan. "One of the first things he said was, 'I can't believe you guys are making this show!'"

Breaking Bad debuted at 10 p.m. on Sunday, January 20, 2008, the night of the NFC Championship Game between the New York Giants and Green Bay Packers. The AMC executives knew that they needed male viewers to tune in, and the football game was set to end in time for men to be channel surfing just as Walter White's pants went flying through the air. Instead, Giants kicker Lawrence Tynes missed two field goal attempts that would have won the game in regulation, and the contest went into overtime, when Tynes finally kicked a winner at 10:15.

"For the first 15 minutes, we were up against a 50 [ratings] share," says Collier, who already knew he would have to be patient with *Breaking Bad*, and now would have to be even more so thanks to Tynes's faulty aim.

Patience would be required for viewers as well, once they got past the *Breaking Bad* pilot. The first episode covers a lot of story ground (as most pilots do), moving Walter White from school-teacher to meth cook to killer (albeit in self-defense) in the course of a single hour. The second and third episodes slowed things down significantly, and laid out how *Breaking Bad* would pace itself going forward.

We pick up immediately after the end of the pilot, with Walt and Skyler in mid-coitus, then go back out to the desert, where Walt and Jesse are surveying the damage to the RV, and discover that while Emilio remains very much dead, Krazy-8 is still breathing, barely. Now they have one corpse to dispose of, and one human being's fate to decide. Walt is new to a life of crime, and Jesse to crime at this level, so they split their responsibilities in the only way that makes sense to them: a coin flip. Jesse will dissolve

Emilio's body in acid, per Walt's detailed instructions, while Walt will shoot Krazy-8, whose neck is bicycle-locked to a support beam in Jesse's basement.

Simple, right? Except nothing on *Breaking Bad* is ever in the same zip code as simple.

Jesse skips over several of the steps Walt told him to follow and dissolves not only Emilio's corpse, but the bathtub itself *and* the floor and first-floor ceiling beneath it, creating a much bigger, more disgusting mess for the both of them to clean up. And though Walt was willing to kill two men when they had him under threat of imminent death, he finds it much harder to pull the trigger under saner circumstances. Krazy-8, calm and helpless, convinces Walt of his humanity enough that Walt is ready to let him go for nothing more than a promise to live and let live, until he realizes that Krazy-8 has hoarded a shard of a ceramic plate that Walt broke earlier, and is just waiting for the chance to use it as a weapon. Shedding a tear as he does it, Walt chokes the life out of Krazy-8 with the bike lock, then falls to his knees weeping and muttering, "I'm sorry. I'm so sorry."

This was not at all how Walter White expected his career in the meth business to begin. Nor, frankly, was it how I was expecting it to begin. Given the presence of Cranston (in *Malcolm*-style undies, no less), I had gone into the pilot expecting...well, *Weeds 2: The Methening*. And the pilot had left me expecting something darker, but not quite *this* dark, and graphic, and extremely restrained in its pace(*). Not a third episode that opens with Walter White cleaning Emilio's liquefied remains off of Jesse's living room floor, spends the mid-section on him coughing up a lung, and closes with Krazy-8's agonizing death.

(*) When the show returned for its second season, I felt as if Gil-

ligan and company had made a huge leap forward in what they were
doing and how. In hindsight (and particularly in revisiting those early
episodes for this book), I think it's less the show that changed (though
there were improvements) than my perception of it. Like The Wire,
the pace and tone are so unusual that you have to re-learn how to
watch a TV show.

But this is exactly what Gilligan wanted *Breaking Bad* to be: an
epic crime drama driven by process.

"To me, that is the story," Gilligan told me before the second
season. "To me, this is the story about the in-between moments. I
think we've all seen the big moments in any crime story. You can't
top a movie like *The Godfather*. So what can I do as a filmmaker?
At least I can show the stuff that nobody else bothers to show.
The in-between moments really are the story in *Breaking Bad*—the
moments of metamorphosis, of a guy transforming from a good,
law-abiding citizen to a drug kingpin. It is the story of metamorphosis, and metamorphosis in real life is slow. It's the way stalac-
tites grow, you stare at it and there's nothing, but you come back
100 years later and there's growth."

So when Walt and Jesse need to get rid of a body, we have to
learn exactly how they'll do it—which pays off beautifully in later
seasons, when their corpse-disposal technique becomes an understood, almost casual detail in the middle of far more complex
scenes. When, early in the second season, Walt and Jesse decide
they have to kill violent local kingpin Tuco Salamanca before he
kills them, we get a scene where Walt picks apart each of Jesse's
murder plans, pointing out all the flaws in his logic as if they were
back in the classroom and Jesse had just handed in a shoddy term
paper. Under Gilligan, *Breaking Bad* would not take shortcuts. He
was going to turn Mr. Chips into Scarface, and show us each and

every painful step along that journey, not skipping over all the logistical questions the way a typical gangster story would.

But just as Walt had a lot to learn about this business, so did Gilligan. His original plan, for instance, was to kill off Jesse by the end of the first season, feeling the character would have served his purpose by introducing Walt to the world of meth, and that Walt's journey through it would be more terrifying if he didn't have his guide anymore.

"Fairly early on in the process of shooting the season," Gilligan says, "I did jettison that idea, because Aaron Paul was such a star."

"Vince was having lunch with the other writers," Paul recalled before the fifth season began, "and they brought me over and said, 'You know, we were going to kill Jesse off in the first season.' And I still haven't read the next episode yet! And I go, 'Yeah, what does that mean?' Vince says, 'Well, that's not going to happen anymore.' ... I guess once he shot the pilot, that changed his mind. He wanted to keep Jesse around. Thank God."

But even after he decided to spare Jesse to preserve the crackling rapport between Cranston and Paul, Gilligan says, "My fear was that we didn't have an interesting or exciting enough show—that not enough was happening. . . .We were going to put everything, including the kitchen sink, into that final episode [of Season 1]. We would have had to practically start over, character-wise, family-wise, and it would have been very tricky indeed."

Instead, production had to shut down two episodes early, thanks to the writers' strike, which Gilligan says, "saved me from my inadvertent self-destructive impulses."

As Gilligan and writer Peter Gould now recall, the creative team came up with two different ways to end the first season with a bang. In one, the White house would be invaded by criminals who knew Walt and took Walter Jr. (RJ Mitte) and a pregnant Skyler hostage to demand Walt's drug money; a terrified Skyler would insist that they had the wrong house, right as Walt produced a bag full of cash he had hidden in a vent, the season ending on her horrified look of understanding.

"It would have been a great scene and I don't know where the hell we would have gone after that," says Gould.

The other also involved a character discovering Walt's secret identity in the worst possible way: Walt witnesses Tuco shooting Steve Gomez (Steven Michael Quezada), partner of Walt's DEA agent brother-in-law Hank (Dean Norris), and as Gomez bleeds to death, he recognizes Walter White standing there. Terrified of both Tuco and the chance of prison if he saves Gomez's life, Walt instead runs off into the night, covered in the lawman's blood.

Both ideas had to be scrapped due to the strike—a frustrating turn of events at the time for which Gilligan is forever grateful in hindsight.

"It would have been arguably a more exciting Season 1," Gilligan says, "but it would have left us with so many fewer avenues and ultimately we might have had one or two fewer seasons, or we would've had one or two seasons where we had gone past the apex and were starting to slide into familiarity."

In another way, the timing of the strike couldn't have been better, because it happened late enough for *Breaking Bad* to produce enough episodes to qualify for Emmy submission. The show was nominated for four Emmys, including Gilligan for directing the pilot and John Toll for shooting it. Cranston was up for the drama lead actor category, against, among others, man of the moment Jon Hamm and *Boston Legal* star James Spader, who had won the category three of the previous four years. On hype, Cranston seemingly had no shot, but Emmy voters have to actually watch a submitted episode by each nominee, and it was hard to ignore the mesmerizing, emotionally naked work of Cranston—just as it would be three more times over the run of the series, when he was again the deserving winner.

Charlier Collier, who was in the Emmy audience that night with the casts of both his nominated shows, watched Cranston walk up to the stage, "and I leaned over to those guys and said, 'Wow, we're not just one show. We're a network.'"

By then, Collier had already renewed *Breaking Bad* for a second season. The ratings had been unimpressive, and the reviews less universally adoring than the ones for *Mad Men*, but the executives at AMC liked the show, thought it paired well with a lot of movies in the library, and wanted to see what Gilligan could do with a full, uninterrupted season.

And the polite man from Virginia was about to repay their kindness with one of the greatest sustained runs in the history of the medium.

The first season had abruptly ended on Walt and Jesse watching Tuco beat an underling to death for the mildest of offenses. The second season returns to that moment, but only after a bizarre sequence of black-and-white images from Walt's backyard, all set to the sound of ever-louder sirens in the distance: water dripping from a hose, a snail creeping along a wall, a wind chime idly turning, a plastic eyeball bobbing along the surface of the pool, and a charred pink teddy bear (the only color in the sequence) floating near the bottom. As the season shows Walt and Jesse getting more serious about establishing their own business, we occasionally return to those black-and-white images, getting slightly more information each time, until it's clear some kind of major tragedy happened at Walt's house that left multiple bodies on the ground. In the finale, the event is revealed as a midair collision between two planes(*) that's the last domino to fall from all of Walt and Jesse's recent actions.

(*) *Gilligan had left a trail of clues for viewers with the titles of the four episodes to feature the black-and-white openings. Put together, they read "737 Down Over ABQ."*

"In simple terms," Gilligan told me after the finale, "we just wanted a giant moment of showmanship to end the season. And what better way than to have a rain of fire coming down around our protagonist's ears, sort of like the judgment of God? It seemed like a big showmanship moment, and to visualize, in one fell swoop, all the terrible grief that Walt has wrought upon his loved ones, and the community at large."

Gilligan's showmanship had already been on display throughout the season, as both the creative team and Walter White gained enormous confidence in what they were doing.

Tuco was meant to be the big bad of season 2, but actor Raymond Cruz had to return to his day job on TNT's *The Closer* sooner than expected. Tuco dies(*), leaving a power vacuum for Walt—who has taken to wearing a black porkpie hat and sunglasses and using the alias Heisenberg (after the Nobel-winning physicist) when he's out in public—and Jesse to fill.

(*) *Tuco takes Walt and Jesse prisoner for an episode, where they meet his uncle Hector (Mark Margolis), a once-feared drug lord now wheelchair-bound thanks to a stroke, able to communicate only with a brass service bell. They barely escape with their lives, and Tuco is ultimately killed by Hank, who's been out looking for the missing Walt.*

"It worked out better for us," says Peter Gould, "because the absence of Tuco meant that Walt and Jesse had to try to make the business work on their own. A lot of the fun we had was imagining the things that would go wrong if two people who were not educated in the world of drug dealing tried to create an empire."

They hire cheerfully sleazy defense lawyer Saul Goodman (Bob Odenkirk, tweaking his usual comic persona just enough to fit in) to get them out of a jam, and Saul offers to be Tom Hagen to Walt's Don Corleone. Saul helps dramatically expand the scope and efficiency of their business, and introduces them to two men who will figure prominently in later seasons: Gus Fring (Giancarlo Esposito), a calculating businessman who uses his fried chicken restaurants as cover for a meth distribution network; and ex-cop Mike Ehrmantraut (Jonathan Banks), Gus's ultra-competent fixer(*).

(*) Though the second season was mapped out in many ways, the introduction of the unflappable yet weary Mike was a fluke. He first appears in the season finale to help Jesse with a problem that, in the script, Saul was going to deal with. But as Jonathan Banks told me after he left the show midway through the fifth season, Bob Odenkirk had a preexisting commitment to his recurring role on How I Met Your Mother, *and the writers came up with Mike as a one-shot character. "I'd never seen the show," Banks said, "and I thought, 'I'll go in here, I'll guest star and I'll be gone.' It didn't turn out that way."*

The show became bolder and more macabre in its depiction of violence, and the way it advanced the story arcs. *Breaking Bad* wasn't by this point just the kind of show that would put the severed head of guest star Danny Trejo on top of a tortoise during a story where Hank goes south of the border on a DEA mission; it was the kind of show that would put Danny Trejo's severed head on top of an *exploding* tortoise that would kill several of Hank's colleagues.

The exploding tortoise episode opens with a *narcocorrido*—a traditional Mexican folk ballad about drug dealers—that efficiently details the rise of Heisenberg, and how he's coming to be viewed by the cartel, in a catchy 3-minute Spanish tune.

At the same time, it's amazing how quickly the series is able to shift our sympathies away from Walt and towards Jesse. Walt is introduced as the identifiable suburban dad under enormous pressure. Walter Jr. has cerebral palsy. The family is struggling financially, and Walt has to work a humiliating second job at a car wash, often waiting on his own students. His health insurance doesn't cover the experimental cancer treatments he needs to stay alive. He is, on the surface, the recession era's everyman. Walt's chosen method for solving his problems is horrifying, but the impulse behind it is understandable, and Cranston's performance is so great that you feel for him despite these appalling acts.

Yet the second season seems determined to undermine our affection for Walt. Where once it was thrilling to see Walt order Jesse around, or briefly take the upper hand with Tuco by blowing up his office, Walt's criminal career begins to reveal an ugly side of his personality that was, again, likely always there, but constrained by circumstance. In the second-season premiere, Walt returns from a terrifying encounter with Tuco and tries to force himself on Skyler in the family kitchen before she pushes him away. He goes from ordering Jesse around to flat-out bullying him, and a remarkable role reversal occurs thanks to the writing and the naked emotions of Aaron Paul's performance: Jesse Pinkman, the clownish meth cook who was designed as a disposable plot device, turns into the conscience of the series, and each unpleasant turn in the Walt/Jesse relationship makes us empathize with Jesse more and Walt less. Gilligan had cast Cranston because he wanted someone who could find the humanity inside a monster, but it turned out that Cranston was even better at showing the monster struggling to escape its frail human cage, while Paul shone brightest when displaying the vulnerability of a low-rent crook the average viewer would cross the street to avoid.

The second season features the first of several great, secret betrayals in the relationship between the two partners. Jesse moves into a new apartment and begins dating his landlady Jane (Krysten Ritter), a recovering heroin addict who falls off the wagon while Jesse is struggling with the murder of his friend Combo by a rival drug crew. The drugs bring out the worst in Jane (*), who threatens to expose Walt's life of crime if he doesn't give Jesse his cut from a batch they cooked for Gus Fring. Walt finds Jesse and Jane sleeping off a high, and his attempt to wake Jesse to reason with him pushes Jane into a position where she begins choking on her own vomit—and Walt, after an initial impulse to help her, decides to let nature take its course, crying as he watches her die but doing nothing to stop it. (It's Jane's father, an air-traffic controller, who causes the plane crash while distracted by grief.)

(*) Early on in that season, the writing staff started calling Jane "Yoko Ono," as the woman who would be blamed for breaking up the band.

"I've gotta say, AMC and Sony are ballsy," Gilligan told me after that season. "AMC particularly, they don't ever second-guess us. They don't ever say, 'Gee, is this too out there? Is this too rawboned or rough-edged?' Having said that, the one time this season they were a little freaked out was when we sent them the outline, they went, 'Wait, Walt lets her choke to death on her own vomit?' They were right to worry about the audience losing their desire to want to watch the guy: 'Are they going to lose their empathy for him forever?' I said, 'I don't know.' We danced around it, talked about shooting multiple endings where he leaves and she chokes to death out of his sight. But then we said, 'Go big or go home.' … We've come this far, let's be honest about it. I give 'em great credit."

Walt's cancer goes into remission late in that season, giving Walt yet another excuse to quit the meth business, but the impulse to cook—to be a respected, dangerous man rather than the schnook he was pre-diagnosis—is too strong to resist. He eventually loses his teaching job due to his erratic behavior, and Skyler kicks him out of the house when she begins to suspect he's dealing drugs, removing most of his tethers to the civilized world. (As a way to seize some control of a situation she never asked for, Skyler will eventually insist on using her accounting skills to launder Walt's drug money.)

Yet no matter what heinous things Walt would do in this season or later ones, for some viewers he remained the unquestionable hero of the piece, the guy they liked and rooted for no matter what(*).

(*) Because the revolutionary dramas were mostly about men, and male anti-heroes at that, and because viewers tend to bond most with the main character of a show, there was a side effect to the era, where characters who on paper should be the sympathetic ones become hated by viewers for opposing the protagonist. And the greatest vitriol has been unfortunately saved for wives like Skyler White, Corrine Mackey, Carmela Soprano, and Betty Draper, who are viewed by some viewers as irredeemable bitches, no matter how poorly they're treated by their husbands. (Male antagonists get more of a pass from these viewers, because "they're just doing their job.") None of the wives are entirely uncompromised (of these four, Corrine comes the closest), but it can be disheartening to see these great shows encourage some of their fans' sexist impulses.

"I have to say it does surprise me," Gilligan says of the viewers who kept cheering on Walt after he'd clearly become a monster. "I'll take whatever reaction we can get, just so long as people are having an emotional reaction to the show. I want there to be a vigorous debate about these characters, first and foremost Walter White. To my way of thinking, *Breaking Bad* is an experiment in television. Historically, television is about stasis. It's about maintaining a character at a certain place in time, sometimes for years or decades on end. None of us are standing still, we're getting older by the second, and there's something comforting about being able to revisit these favorite characters still being how we remembered them. But time does not stand still, and I thought it'd be interesting as an experiment to create a television show where a major point of the show was change—to see a good man transform into a bad man.

"I figured what would happen is that we would lose sympathy for Walt with every subsequent episode we produced—that people would start to sympathize less and less with Walt," he adds. "But there are some people who, come hell or high water, will never lose sympathy for Walt. Some lost sympathy way back in Season 1, and bell-curve-wise, the average person lost sympathy around when he watched Jane die and didn't intervene. Everyone has their moment. That's the experiment, and that's the thing that keeps the show fresh and interesting for me."

The series became not just more morally adventurous in Season 2, but visually, thanks to the arrival of Michael Slovis (an Emmy-winner for his work on *CSI*) as the new director of photography.

"I worship the ground Michael Slovis walks on," says Michelle MacLaren, an *X-Files* alum who began directing for *Breaking Bad* in that second season. "First of all, his lighting is spectacular. Michael has an incredible eye. We don't have a lot of time on the show, so Michael is really brave in how he does things. He doesn't use a ton of lights. He's not afraid to shoot silhouette or shadows or not do two eyes."

MacLaren's first episode was Season 2's "4 Days Out," which Gilligan had conceived of as a "bottle show"—industry jargon for an episode filmed largely on pre-existing sets, with minimal use of guest stars, to keep the budget tight. The plot involves Jesse and Walt getting stranded in the desert when the RV battery dies during a cook, and was merely an excuse to sit back and watch Bryan Cranston and Aaron Paul bounce off each other for the entire hour. The plan was to film almost all of it inside the cramped RV set in the studio, but MacLaren began pushing more and more of the action outdoors, letting Slovis work his magic with the Southwestern landscape and gorgeous natural light—and turning what was supposed to be a cheap episode into what Gilligan called the most expensive one they had made(*) to that point.

(*) "It is so not the most expensive one!" MacLaren says with a laugh. "He says that just to get my goat." Later in the interview, when we discuss a later episode where Walt, Jesse, and Mike steal methylamine from a cargo train, she pauses to note that that was the most expensive episode ever.

But the money is all on the screen, as we can appreciate the beauty of the scenery, and even of the process Walt and Jesse use to produce their terrible drug. As the show does from time to time, the camera breaks the fourth wall that's supposed to separate the characters from the viewers, as it looks like Walt and Jesse are pouring a batch of chemicals directly onto the TV screen. It's one of many shots employed by MacLaren and the other *Breaking Bad* directors that call attention to themselves; others include a shot from the perspective of a shovel Jesse is toting on his shoulder, or a tracking shot at a nihilistic party at Jesse's house as seen from the Roomba that's futilely trying to clean up messes as they're made.

"I'm a firm believer that you shouldn't do a shot for the sake of a cool shot, unless the shot serves the story," says MacLaren. "Yes, Roomba-cam is something that isn't a conventional way of telling the story, but it does still tell the story, in that you're moving through the living room, and you're seeing that everybody's passed out, they've been partying all night, there's drugs and beer everywhere, and then one of the meth heads picks it up and starts taking it apart. That one shot tells what you may have used three or four different shots to tell the same story, and it's a fun way of telling it."

Much of Season 2 had been carefully plotted in advance, and it was great. But *Breaking Bad* wouldn't get into the pantheon-level-drama conversation until its third season, which Gilligan and company wrote by the seat of their pants.

"Season 2, we were very proud of, and I liked that," Gilligan told me after the third season. "It appealed to me intellectually, the idea of a circular season where the beginning images are also the end images. But that was miserably hard to figure out. We spent four or five weeks just sitting around with our heads in our hands."

The third season introduces the Cousins, a pair of silent, unstoppable killers in matching sharkskin suits who come north of the border looking for the man responsible for their cousin Tuco's death—specifically, Walter White, who put Tuco in position to be shot by Hank. The Cousins, played by brothers Luis and Daniel Moncada(*), made an instant impression on the audience, and the plan was for them to lurk in the background all season before attempting to kill Walt in the finale. But as Gilligan watched footage of the Moncadas at work, he realized that the Cousins were not the type of men who would wait and wait and wait; they would move swiftly towards their target, and it was hard to imagine Walt being able to stop them.

(*) Luis Moncada was an ex-con turned actor who impressed the Breaking Bad *casting director so much that he was asked to come back with his brother, even though Daniel had never had a paid acting role before. Michelle MacLaren recalls that Daniel was so nervous his first few days that he barely spoke. When she went to compliment him on his poise during a scene where the Cousins walk away from an exploding truck, "Daniel looked at me and said the first full sentence I had heard out of his mouth in three days: 'A shoe flew over my head.'"*

So, much as Walt and Jesse so often have to do when their brilliant plan blows up in the first 30 seconds, Gilligan had to improvise. The Cousins had to be taken off the board, surprising losers in a parking lot shootout with Hank—the scene, at the end of Season 3's "One Minute" (also directed by MacLaren), is among the most suspenseful ever put on television—and the mild-mannered Chicken Man himself, Gus Fring, replaced them as the next big bad. For the first time, Walt would be doing battle with a kindred spirit, as the precise, logic-driven Gus was very much the kind of criminal Walt had always fancied himself as (even if, as Gus pointed out in an early encounter, Walt is actually incredibly reckless).

"We actively try to paint ourselves into corners at the end of episodes—at the end of seasons, at the end of scenes sometimes—and then we try to extricate ourselves from those corners," Gilligan told me after the third season. "The Cousins were one of those corners, in a sense. We created these guys, wound them up and set them loose, and then we spent a lot of hours and days in the writers room asking questions of ourselves: *What happens next? How do these guys who are so desperate to kill Walt, what keeps them at bay?*

Well, I guess the only thing that keeps them at bay would be Gus. Then suddenly we're realizing Gus is playing this whole game on a much higher level than we writers even thought in the first place."

Gus sets Walt up in an elaborate, top-of-the-line underground meth lab. Walt is handsomely compensated for his work, but life as a glorified clock-puncher doesn't befit the great Heisenberg, who begins to chafe at having a boss. Jesse becomes fixated on a pair of Gus's dealers who ordered the murders of both Combo and the 10-year-old boy(*) who shot Combo, and when Gus refuses to intervene—and, worse, Walt seems to side with Gus and the men who turn little boys into dealers and killers—Jesse decides to get rid of them himself. He approaches them, gun out, trembling, almost surely about to die in the attempt, when Walt's familiar green Pontiac Aztek roars in between them and runs over both dealers. One dies instantly, and Walt shoots the other in the head with his own gun, before staring at Jesse and telling him—with as much meaning as any three-letter word can contain—"Run."

(*) In one of those cosmic twists of fate that sometimes drive the series' plot, the underage killer is the kid brother of Jesse's new girlfriend Andrea (Emily Rios).

It's one of many classic gangster moments for Walter White. It's also a big step on his journey from everyman to supervillain, and one Vince Gilligan was more prepared to take than the normally fearless actor playing him.

"When I read that [scene], I thought different things than when I saw it," Cranston told me before the fifth season. "The way I played it was he gets out of the car, it was all impulsive what he did, to save Jesse, and now it's 'Oh my God, oh my God,' and this one's crawling around underneath looking for his gun, so I have to take the gun. I take the gun, I look at him, I look at Jesse, am thinking, 'What to do? What to do?' I look around for witnesses, there are no witnesses, I look back at him, he's writhing in pain, and I think, 'Oh, shit. There's only one thing I can do.' And I look at Jesse, and he's in shock, and now I have to get the courage to do it. I look, and think, 'Jesus, just do it!' And BAM! And 'Run.' So there was a culmination of thought: witnesses, threat, this guy, ugh, ugh. It was a thought process. And they cut it together, and it was BAM! BAM! 'Run.' I saw that, and I went, 'Holy shit.' That's an example of Vince's trajectory not being on the same track as mine. I thought he was still in 'Oh my God, oh my God, what did I just do,' and Vince is thinking, 'I'm taking control, he's the threat, bang, kill him, tell my partner to get out of here.' It was one of those moments where it pushes you back in the seat of your chair."

Gus has been plotting all along to have his chemist, the eccentric but harmless Gale Boetticher (David Costabile), figure out how to produce Walt's trademark blue meth on his own so the operation wouldn't have to rely on such an erratic personality. Walt's homicidal disobedience with the two dealers appears to seal his fate, and Jesse's, but Walt sends Jesse—who, to this point in their on-again, off-again partnership, has somehow managed to avoid killing anyone—to murder Gale, while a seething Mike is left to figure out how he just got hustled by Walter freaking White.

Season 3 ends on Jesse pulling the trigger, and we return for Season 4 with Gilligan and company again demonstrating the value of patient, disciplined storytelling with "Box Cutter," an episode where Walt and Jesse spend most of the hour in the lab as prisoners to Mike and his lackey Victor, waiting for Gus to arrive and mete out his punishment. Though we see Gus in a season-opening flashback to Gale setting up the lab, his first appearance in the present comes two-thirds of the way through the episode. He enters the lab, and as Walt tries to talk his way out of a death sentence, Gus silently changes out of his suit and into protective lab gear, studies his two treasonous employees, gets the eponymous box cutter out of a cabinet, and calmly slits the throat of Victor (who made the fatal mistake of being seen by witnesses at Gale's apartment). Gus holds Victor while he bleeds out, never flinching as he stares down both Walt and Jesse. He gets changed *again* and walks to the exit, almost exactly 10 minutes after he entered, and utters his only line of the entire scene:

"Well? Get back to work."

It's an almost absurdly tense scene—after he left the show, Esposito told me he considered it "the crowning moment of my career"—and one that turns Season 4 into a riveting cat-and-mouse game between Heisenberg and the Chicken Man. Gus has his organization—Mike in particular—and limitless resources, and after a while he has Jesse, too, who finds in Mike the father figure Walt always refused to be. All Walt has is his brain, and while we've seen its power in the past, Gus is just as smart—and, after we begin to get pieces of his backstory, including an understandable vendetta against Hector Salamanca(*), perhaps more sympathetic—and doesn't suffer from Walt's crippling hubris.

(*) In a flashback, we see a still healthy Hector murder Gus's partner Max on orders of Mexican cartel boss Don Eladio (played by Steven Bauer from Scarface*), who explains that he won't also kill Gus because he knows of Gus's past in Chile. That history, like the exact nature of the Walt/Gretchen split, would become a source of fertile speculation among* Breaking Bad *fandom, especially since the show never really elaborated on it. Sam Catlin, who wrote that episode with George Mastras, says, "Eladio spares Gus out of consideration for his*

reputation as a powerfully connected secret policeman in Pinochet's Chile. Maybe Eladio had dealings with other Chileans he didn't wish to alienate, but he wasn't specifically forbidden to kill him. He spared him out of respect for his reputation." Mastras adds that Eladio also wanted to get into business with Gus, whose reputation, precision, and audacity impressed him, even though the way Gus and Max manipulated his organization into getting this meeting was too much of a public offense to go unpunished. "Given (his) respect for Gus" he says, "Don Eladio is inclined to let Gus live, so long as someone dies (Max) so he can save face in front of his men." Gus is forced to become the cartel's employee, rather than its partner, which motivates the revenge he orchestrates throughout Seasons 3 and 4.

When the local cops find Gale's lab notes and assume that he's Heisenberg, Walt can't stand the idea of an inferior chemist getting credit for his work, and inadvertently talks Hank into reopening the case. When Skyler, fearing for their lives, suggests they need to run because they're in danger, an incredulous, boastful Walt replies, "Who are you talking to right now? Who is it you think you see? Do you know how much I make a year? I mean, even if I told you, you wouldn't believe it. Do you know what would happen if I suddenly decided to stop going into work? A business so big it could be listed on the NASDAQ goes belly-up. It disappears. Ceases to exist without me. No, you clearly don't know who you're talking to. I am not in danger, Skyler. I *am* the danger. A guy opens his door and gets shot, and you think that of me? No. I *am* the one who knocks."

The One Who Knocks is still The One Who Thinks, and in the end, that proves to be enough. Walt tricks Jesse back over to his side by poisoning Andrea's son Brock (not fatally, but just barely) and making it look like Gus did it, then recruits Hector as his weapon against Gus. The old man rings his bell one last time, detonating a bomb Walt has placed under his wheelchair and sending Gus—half his face destroyed in the blast—staggering out of the room, straightening his tie as one final tic of a dying but still precise man.

A few episodes earlier, Walt had planned to purchase new identities for himself, Skyler, and the kids and escape, only to discover that the money he kept stored in the crawl space under the house was gone, and that Skyler had given it to her ex-lover, for reasons we were privy to but Walt wasn't. That hour concludes with an overhead shot of Walt lying in the crawl space—framed through the access hatch like he's a body in a casket—laughing maniacally over this cruel karmic joke. The imagery suggests, as Cranston put it to me, "Walter White is dead, and Heisenberg rises from the ashes. And that's basically what happens."

After Gus dies and a terrified Skyler asks what happened, Walt tells her, "I won," and the first half of the fifth and final season(*) shows a Walter White resplendent and insufferable in victory. Mike's still around for a while to question Walt's decision making, until he underestimates Walt once too often and takes a fatal shot to the gut. (In typical no-nonsense fashion, Mike's final words are to interrupt Walt's hollow apology by telling him, "Shut the fuck up, and let me die in peace.") Jesse retires from the business, unable to deal with either the danger or the guilt, and with the help of one of Gus and Mike's former corporate contacts, Lydia (Laura Fraser), Walt is able to take his business international, generating so much money in only a few months that Skyler gives up on trying to launder any of it.

(*) When Gilligan and AMC decided the story was reaching an endpoint, the network ordered 16 episodes and decided to split them up

into two blocs of 8, airing nearly a year apart. Contractually, though, they're all considered part of one season, the same way that HBO accounting dealt with the last 21 episodes of The Sopranos, *which aired over a period of 15 months. AMC would similarly split the final* Mad Men *season over two calendar years.*

For most of the series, Walt had been an underdog facing the constant threat of death, and that, coupled with the appeal of Bryan Cranston, lent the character some level of relatability no matter how monstrous his actions (letting Jane die, poisoning Brock) may have been. With no real threat to his power base, the Walt at the start of this final season is a particularly arrogant, unpleasant individual. During his 51st birthday party, Skyler (whom Walt has forced to take him back) wanders into the pool, more at peace with the idea of drowning than she's been with living next to this monster, and later confesses to her husband that "All I can do is wait."

When he asks for what, she replies simply, "For the cancer to come back."

Though Walt is at the peak of his powers for much of these eight episodes, we know it won't last. The season begins with yet another flash-forward, this time to more than a year in the future, set in and around a local Denny's. A bearded Walt has apparently returned to Albuquerque after some time away, is using an assumed identity, is taking pills again (have Skyler's wishes about the cancer come true?), seems twitchy and desperate, and for some reason needs to buy a large machine gun from his favorite local gun dealer (played by Jim Beaver from *Deadwood*). Sometime in the future, it's clear, Walt's empire is going to go very, very awry, and the first half of the final season concludes with a big hint as to why, as Hank—who has had many, many clues to Heisenberg's true identity over the years, but could never make the leap of thinking of his dweeby brother-in-law as a master criminal—has what Gilligan calls "quite literally an 'oh, shit' moment" when he finds a poetry book inscribed from Gale to Walt while using Walt's bathroom. It's a book that the careful, brilliant drug lord who Walt believes himself to be would have thrown out long ago, but he's just cocky enough to keep it around, because the inscription—from a man whose murder Walt arranged—is a testimony to his own genius.

Through those first 54 episodes, *Breaking Bad* had been a devastating character portrait of a brilliant but deeply flawed man placed in chaotic circumstances. The writing, direction, and performance of Bryan Cranston let us see every facet of the man they call Heisenberg, and supporting characters like Jesse, Skyler, Hank, Gus, and Mike were drawn almost as vividly. But the series was also more plot-driven than a *Mad Men* or even a *Sopranos*, and that put an enormous amount of pressure on Gilligan as he and his writers convened to figure out the final eight episodes and the proper conclusion to their crime epic.

"It literally kept me awake at night for months," Gilligan says, "worrying that our ending wouldn't be satisfying enough."

A scene in the first half of the final season finds Walt coming face-to-face with his cinematic inspiration, as he and Walter Jr. watch Al Pacino in *Scarface*. "Everyone dies in this movie, don't they?" Walt asks. The line was an improvisation by Bryan Cranston, and as the writers entered the home stretch, they weren't necessarily committed to killing off their protagonist.

"In the early days, it seemed to me fitting that Walt should die at the end of the show," says Gilligan. "But then as the series progressed, we tried to keep all avenues open. We thought for a while there would be a wild shootout and he would be wounded and he would be lying on a gurney in a hospital hallway, waiting to be treated. Maybe he would expire on the gurney, alone and unknown in the hallway, or lie there blankly staring at the ceiling, waiting for something to happen. And we talked about the possibility of him getting away, so everything was fair game."

More troublesome was finding a target for that machine gun in Walt's trunk from the season-opening flash-forward, which was introduced simply because Gilligan liked the image, and not because he had a concrete plan for how to get Walt from his present situation to that future one.

"We wanted to have a feeling that this was all going somewhere," recalls Peter Gould. "The machine gun was us putting down a marker saying, 'No matter what happens, there's going to be some kind of apocalyptic last stand here.' I will tell you, there were so many times when we broke Season 5, Vince said, 'God, what would we do, the world would be open to us if we hadn't put the machine gun in the trunk? Why oh why did we have to do that?'"

The writers had enjoyed painting Walt and Jesse into corners to see how they would make it out; now it was their turn to do the same. And just as the results of Walt's improvised solutions were often more spectacular than his initial plans, so too was the *Breaking Bad* stretch run, a relentless machine that gave the audience every great and terrible thing they could have possibly wanted.

The final 8 episodes masterfully knock over every domino that had been carefully positioned over the previous 54. Hank confronts Walt with his discovery, but finds himself boxed in by his quarry's bottomless capacity for deception, as Walt records a bogus confession painting Hank as Heisenberg and Walt as the innocent chemist forced to work for him. As Skyler had hoped for (and the flash-forward hinted at), Walt's cancer returns. An attempt to send a guilt-ridden Jesse out of town backfires when he finally realizes it was Walt who poisoned Brock, turning Jesse and Hank into unlikely allies scheming to take down Walt once and for all.

With Mike dead and Jesse and then Walt retiring, the organization is gradually taken over by a more remorseless brand of criminal: dead-eyed thief and killer Todd (Jesse Plemons from *Friday Night Lights*, finally on a show where homicide wasn't out of place) as the new cook, Todd's Uncle Jack (Michael Bowen) and his white supremacist gang as the muscle, and the paranoid, cold Lydia handling distribution. Walt and Jesse's crew had never exactly been warm and fuzzy, but there was a sense of amateurism to them for so long that it felt startling to see the empire in the hands of these nasty professionals.

Everything comes to a head right where it all began: at To'hajiilee, the Navajo reservation where Walt and Jesse had their first cook, and where a paranoid Walt has hidden his entire fortune. Jesse and Hank trick Walt into thinking they've found his buried treasure and will burn it if he doesn't show up, and for a few brief minutes, Hank gets to bask in his victory, taking as much pleasure in slapping the cuffs on the great Heisenberg as the writers did in giving him that moment.

Gilligan recalls the writers approaching the final season with a wish list of things they wanted to see happen before all was said and done, "And one thing on our wish list was, 'I wanna see Hank catch this sonuvabitch.'"

It's a seemingly grand victory, shot in epic spaghetti Western fashion by Michelle MacLaren (who cites Sergio Leone's *Once Upon a Time in the West* as one of her stylistic touchstones for the episode), but it's ultimately a hollow one, because Walt has already called Uncle Jack and his fellow Nazis to the same location, assuming only Jesse will be there to suffer their wrath. "To'hajiilee" ends just as the bullets begin flying between Jack's crew and the badly outgunned Hank and Gomez, with the audience forced to spend the next week with a pit in their collective stomach, certain that bad news would be waiting for them when *Breaking Bad* returned the following Sunday.

But no one had any idea just how awful things would get—nor what dramatic heights *Breaking Bad* would scale in an installment that Gilligan calls the show's best episode ever, and what may be the best hour of dramatic television, period.

The greatness of that episode, "Ozymandias," was, like so much of the series, a collection of happy accidents that left even its Emmy-winning author, longtime *Breaking Bad* writer Moira Walley-Beckett, insisting, "I just got lucky."

The initial plan had been for Gilligan to direct the series' final two episodes, writing the last one himself while Walley-Beckett scripted the penultimate chapter. Peter Gould was set to write and direct the episode that became "Ozymandias." But the writing staff started falling so far behind schedule that Gilligan abandoned plans to direct them both, which resulted in Gould and Walley-Beckett switching spots in the order.

Gilligan knew he wanted the penultimate episode to largely involve Walt in exile in a snowy mountain cabin, which Walley-Beckett was prepared to do as the self-described "poetic, emotional writer" of the group. Instead, she found herself having to bridge the gap between the start of the Jack/Hank shootout and Walt being alone in that cabin, and discovered that she would be responsible for bringing many of the show's most important story arcs to a climax.

"It was just very exciting to break it," she says. "For all these years, we had major things that happened, but we spaced them out. But all of a sudden, all these major things happened in one episode."

Hank is murdered by Uncle Jack, but only after he gets to stand up to both Walt (as Walt pleads for his brother-in-law's life, Hank sneers and tells him, "You're the smartest guy I ever met, and you're too stupid to see he made up his mind ten minutes ago") and his killer (deploying the one muted f-bomb AMC allowed the show to use per season, he tells Jack, "My name is ASAC Schrader, and you can go fuck yourself").

"We wanted Hank to go out like a man, as Vince likes to say," Walley-Beckett explains.

As Jack and the Nazis prepare to drive off with all but one barrelful of Walt's fortune and Jesse as their prisoner, Walt chooses this of all moments to tell Jesse about his failure to save Jane's life, because he needs somewhere to direct his impotent rage and once again can't accept fault for anything.

"Basically, Walt is killing him," Walley-Beckett says of how she approached the moment of truth, for which the writing staff had spent years brainstorming scenarios. "He may as well have stabbed him with a weapon in the heart, in pure, vile retribution. Because, as ever, Walt cannot take the blame."

While Walt is rolling the last bit of his cash through the desert—in a sly visual gag that provides the present-day part of the episode with its only light moment, he pushes the barrel right past the pair of khaki pants that floated through the air in the series' opening seconds—Hank's wife Marie (Betsy Brandt), unaware of all that's transpired since he called her to celebrate Walt's arrest, insists that Skyler finally tell Walter Jr. the truth about his father. The stunned teenager directs all his anger at the only parent in front of him, telling Skyler, "If all this is true, and you knew about it, then you're as bad as him."

Instead of coming home to more news of Walt's arrest, Skyler finds the man himself in the house, covered in dirt from his desert ordeal and refusing to explain why they should pack up their lives and follow him. Knowing that Hank would never simply let Walt go, Skyler prods Walt until he acknowledges the murder (while, as always, trying to duck any blame), at which point things go nuclear: she grabs a carving knife and orders Walt out of the house before he speaks again(*), then slashes his hand when he refuses to listen and begins rolling around the living room with him, fighting for control of the knife while Junior is frozen with horror at all that's happening.

(*) Skyler's "Don't say one more word" was a last-minute addition made after Walley-Beckett and Anna Gunn conferred on set. "It's very rare that we make changes on the fly," says Walley-Beckett, "but we were talking, and we thought that all Walt fuckin' does is talk and talk and talk and lie and lie and tell stories and bamboozle and coerce what it is that he needs, and it's words words words that add up to disaster and mayhem, and so 'Don't say one more word.' It was so exciting and powerful that we wrote that in."

Given the apocalyptic nature of the episode, it seems not only possible, but almost inevitable, that Walt will once again win a physical struggle and Skyler will end up dead on the living room floor. Instead, Junior finally wills himself to move, tackling his father and then crouching in front of his mother like a human shield.

As Walt stares at his terrified wife and son, he bellows, "WHAT THE HELL IS WRONG WITH YOU?!?! WE'RE A FAMILY!!!"

Then he pauses for seven seconds that feel like an eternity, before repeating, in a defeated whisper, "We're a family."

Those seven seconds, and the realization that comes with them, are everything the show has been building itself to for the previous 59 hours. They are every illusion Walter White has ever had about himself being shattered. They are the terrified faces of his wife and son as they huddle together on the floor, trying to wish him into the cornfield. They are all the bogus self-rationalizations he has told himself and others being dipped in acid until they are no longer identifiable by forensic science. They are Walter White finally, after so much time and so much sin, coming to terms with everything he has lost—everything he has caused himself to lose, through one terrible choice after another.

But even that realization doesn't take complete hold of him. As Junior dials 911 and tells the cops that his father, as Walt once boasted, *is* the danger, Walt goes on autopilot to scoop up baby Holly and her diaper bag—"It's irrational, and it's not a punishment," says Walley-Beckett. "It's the last piece of the family that he can take"—and climbs into the truck he bought in the desert, driving off as Skyler sprints after him, wailing to the heavens about her husband's latest unforgivable act.

Once the adrenaline wears off, Walt realizes that Holly will need her decent and healthy mother far more than her dying fugitive father, and drops the baby off at a fire station while placing a threatening call to the house.

"What the hell is wrong with you?" he repeats. "Why can't you do one thing I say? This is your fault. This is what comes of your disrespect! I told you, Skyler, I warned you for a solid year. You cross me, there will be consequences."

The invective he hurls at her is vile by design: Walt knows the police are probably listening, and he's trying to insulate Skyler from prosecution. But the harsh words—"You stupid bitch!" he yells at one point. "How dare you?"—don't come from nowhere(*). Like the fake confession he uses to blackmail Hank, or the many other lies he tells throughout the series, the rant is convincing because it's built on a foundation of truth—of all the resentment Walt has felt about Skyler's refusal to just go along with his criminal activities and bow down before his genius.

(*) The rant is also evocative of some of the uglier comments hurled by the show's less evolved fans at Skyler and/or Anna Gunn, who wrote in a New York Times *op-ed about her uneasiness with the whole phenomenon, which included her finding a message board post asking, "Could somebody tell me where I can find Anna Gunn so I can kill her?" "It was definitely present in my thinking," says Walley-Beckett, even though she didn't deliberately try to quote specific online comments about Skyler, "which I find completely distressing. Personally, it just seems like such a two-dimensional way to look at the fact that she was actually a pretty normal person reacting to Walt's behavior over the years. It's just that people were so voracious in their appetites for this strange heroism, this Mr. Chips into Scarface dream, that she was the enemy and the obstacle to his hero's journey. So I understand why the Skyler backlash happened, but I also find it disappointingly two-dimensional, in terms of investigation."*

The episode ends with Walt sitting on an Albuqerque hillside, surrounded by the Bear Canyon Arroyo Spillway Dam, whose design resembles a cemetery, with only the barrel of cash beside him, rather than the family he hoped would follow him into hiding. A faded red minivan pulls up, driven by Saul's disappearance expert Ed (who will be played in the following episode by character actor Robert Forster), and Walt rides off to an uncertain future, having

destroyed everyone around him in a manner evoking the Percy
Bysshe Shelley poem that gives the episode its name:

> *"My name is Ozymandias, king of kings:*
> *Look on my works, ye Mighty, and despair!"*
> *Nothing beside remains. Round the decay*
> *Of that colossal wreck, boundless and bare*
> *The lone and level sands stretch far away.*

In script form alone, "Ozymandias" was so powerful that Walley-Beckett says she started getting phone calls from the cast, "And
the actors were weeping and going 'Holy shit,' or Dean just saying, 'Thanks for my death, motherfucker. It's great.'" Even earlier
in the process, when it was essentially a multi-page plot synopsis,
its effect was so potent that its eventual director, Rian Johnson,
says he had to put it down several times to walk away and get his
head together. When he finally finished it, "My initial reaction
was, 'Really? We get to do this one? Vince doesn't want it? No? I'm
not complaining.'"

Johnson had first worked on the show with season 3's "Fly," a
divisive but memorable episode where Walt and Jesse spend the
entire hour chasing a single insect that's found its way into Gus's
super lab. (Unlike "4 Days Out," it was a bottle show that remained corked.) Gilligan had recruited Johnson because he enjoyed his neo-noir movie *Brick* and detected a similar sensibility,
and Johnson and Walley-Beckett (who co-wrote "Fly" with Sam
Catlin) got along so well that they dubbed each other "the Wonder
Twins," after the alien shape-shifter sidekicks from the *Superfriends*
cartoon. When Gilligan told her to pick her director for the epi-
sode(*), Johnson was her first and only choice.

(*)Peter Gould could be a sympathetic figure in all this as the guy bumped from doing "Ozymandias." But he's okay with it, both because the episode he ultimately wrote and directed, "Granite State," is terrific in its own right, and because, as he says humbly, "Lucky for us, Rian Johnson was available to direct that one. ('Ozymandias') would not have been the right episode for me to direct, I can tell you that."

Johnson was ready for it all: the scope of the desert sequence, which consumed nearly half the episode's running time (and required waivers from the various Hollywood guilds so the episode's credits could be delayed until after it was done, lest they distract from the intensity of the moment), the horror of the fight over the carving knife, Skyler's agony over the abduction of Holly, and the half-playacting, half-not nature of Walt's phone call.

Johnson, a fan of the show in addition to a part-time director on it, recalled the previous times that Skyler had pondered calling the police on her husband, not to mention the utter failure the one time she tried it in Season 3. So as she went for the knife, he made sure to frame it right next to that phone—as he puts it, "the lady or the tiger?"—and even to have a mirrored version of that shot in an earlier flashback set on the day of Walt and Jesse's first meth cook.

That entire sequence in and around the White house would be the most emotionally intense part of the entire series, but the writer and director responsible for it didn't find their actors agonizing over what they would have to go through.

"Everybody there was armed and dangerous and ready for that scene," says Walley-Beckett. "They'd waited five years for it. They just nailed it, take after take. There was no torture, like, 'I can't get there!' Everybody was right there."

"It's funny: the hard part was the argument before" the knife fight, says Johnson. "The actual fight itself, in this episode especially, was almost a nice little break. It was a nice little release of tension. Now we're doing this shot, and that shot, and we're doing a fight, and it's physical work with the stunt guys. It was almost play time a little bit. I actually remember that being one of the more straight-up fun parts of the shoot."

When it came time for that crucial pause between Walt's two utterances of "we're a family," Johnson realized Cranston needed no help from him: "The only direction I gave him there was his eyeline. Obviously, he knew what was happening with Walt at that moment, and the significance of that moment. He took the time he needed to take there. That was all Bryan."

Skyler chasing after Walt's truck on foot, then dropping to her knees in the middle of the street, was more difficult for Anna Gunn, but as much for the physical nature of the act—which she had to repeat for take after take—as for having to channel those raw emotions again and again. As if a sign from a deity who didn't want to see Skyler White suffer quite this much, filming of that sequence was delayed by a freak hailstorm, then by the crew's efforts to blow-dry the street so it would match the earlier footage.

If the fates disapproved of Skyler's circumstances, they smiled on the manner in which her daughter would be returned to her. As scripted, the scene where Walt decides he has to give Holly back to her mother just involved him changing her diaper and realizing his mistake from the innocent expression on her face. Bryan Cranston's a world-class actor who could have conveyed that without much help from his infant co-star, but many takes into the scene, the baby exponentially increased the moment's gravity by saying "Mama."

"I remember so distinctly being at the monitor with Moira," says Johnson, "and both of our mouths dropped open, and we looked at each other and said, 'God bless this baby.' It's not like we brought the baby on for the first time and that happened. We had shot enough with the baby that we were starting to get worried we were going to get something that worked. We were at the point where we were ready to start calling for our own mamas. The baby felt the general vibe of the room. And the fact that Bryan just played right into it, and just knew exactly how to play off this magical thing that was happening—that was pretty incredible for me to see."

"It's just a perfect episode," says Vince Gilligan. "Rian Johnson is a brilliant director, Moira Walley-Beckett wrote a brilliant episode, and we had those two factors working for us. But it was also just a culmination of a great many emotions and actions that had come before it. It was a culmination of a great many other good episodes and high emotion. It really wrapped things up very tragically."

If you look at the series' final four episodes, they each in their way could function as the end of the series: "To'hajiilee," if you edit out Uncle Jack's arrival, is the (relatively) happy ending where law and order triumphs over criminality; "Ozymandias" is Walt losing everything and everyone he ever cared about, and finally being made to confront the destruction he caused; "Granite State," where Jack and the Nazis terrorize everyone (including Jesse, whom they keep as a slave to cook Walt-quality meth) while Walt sits alone in his New Hampshire cabin, barely able to do anything without coughing, is a deconstruction of the myth of Heisenberg and Walt's initial belief that he could make a fortune in the drug business without hurting anyone; while the actual finale, "Felina," brings Walt back to Albuquerque to settle all family business.

This *Choose Your Own Adventure*-style approach to the ending was no accident. As Gilligan admits, "We were very greedy. The expression 'have our cake and eat it too,' was said so often, it could have been a drinking game."

Had the series ended with "Ozymandias," it would have been one of the boldest conclusions to any great drama, and likely the darkest. (Though *The Shield* finale would be close.) A *Breaking Bad* that concludes with Walt riding off into anonymity, having ruined the lives of his family and friends, might have aroused anger on the level of *The Sopranos* or *Lost* finales, but it could potentially have turned the entire series into something talked about only in hushed tones among the faithful, and introduced to newcomers with equal parts envy and empathy.

"Emotionally, there is a real argument to be made that the show is over two episodes from the end," Gilligan acknowledges. "The final two episodes are Walt picking up the pieces, as much as he can, and putting things as right as he possibly can. Having said that, his family is irreparably torn apart, and always will be. The last two episodes are really about him putting things as right as he can, which is to say, he can't do much."

Of the seeming finality of "Ozymandias," Peter Gould remembers worrying, "At the time, I didn't see it as a feature, but as a bug: Are we bringing the whole to a complete climax too early?"

"I don't think ["Ozymandias"] would have been enough of an ending," argues Moira Walley-Beckett. "It would have been poetic and sparse, but I don't think it would have felt as full as it ended up feeling. We didn't get closure on Walt and Jesse, on Walt and Skyler and [Walter Jr.]. Some of the heart of the series, we torched it, we shot it up, we stabbed it up, we chewed it and burnt it with acid, but we didn't see the aftermath. We didn't get closure. I think it was really important to finish out the Walt and Jesse story."

The finale offers closure in abundance—perhaps too much for a show that had by design always been so messy, but never in a way that felt like a betrayal of how the *Breaking Bad* universe operated.

Having failed at getting the remaining cash to his family—in "Granite State," he figures out a way to clandestinely call Walter Jr. (now going by the nickname Flynn to avoid any association with his father), only to have his bitter son snarl at him, "Why don't you just die already?"—Walt is on the verge of turning himself into the authorities when he sees Charlie Rose interviewing Gretchen and Elliott, who are trying to distance themselves from their infamous ex-partner. Inspired by the sight of them, he steals a car and drives home to blackmail them into laundering his remaining cash to look like a charitable donation to Flynn and Holly, using the threat of "hit men" (in actuality, Jesse's old pals Badger and Skinny Pete standing in the woods with laser pointers) to make sure they'll comply. Upon learning that his trademark blue meth is still on the market, he assumes Jesse has teamed up with the Nazis and buys the machine gun to take them all out(*).

(*) It wasn't until those final eight episodes were being outlined that the writers decided the Nazis should be the gun's intended victims. As Thomas Schnauz recalls, they had previously considered having Walt use it to break Jesse out of prison, or to eliminate the drug crew run by Declan, who briefly handled Walt's distribution before the Nazis wiped them out. Also finally deployed, after years of hanging over the proceedings like Chekhov's gun: the ricin capsule that Walt had originally made for Jesse to use on Gus, and which was later part of the scheme to make Jesse think Gus had poisoned Brock. "That damn ricin kept appearing and disappearing!" Gilligan says with a laugh. Many scenarios were broached—Schnauz says at one point, Jesse was going to use it to kill Hank—including Walt taking it himself at the very end.

Instead, Walt slips it into a packet of the sweetener he knows Lydia always puts in her tea, sentencing her to a slow and agonizing death for her many sins. "Lydia, as awful as she was, would be out there still, and go on to thrive and survive," says Gilligan." I couldn't stomach the thought of that, and I didn't want to see her shot or killed in some violent manner. That's the closet chauvinist in me. Dying in a Shakespearean manner from poison seemed fitting."

First, though, he has to stop by the shabby apartment where Skyler and the kids have been living since Walt's identity was exposed to the world, to say a proper goodbye, to give Skyler a piece of evidence (the GPS coordinates to where the Nazis buried the bodies of Hank and Gomez) that could help her cut a deal with the prosecutor, and to utter the words that no one ever expected him to say out loud.

As Skyler assumes he's going to once again tell the lie that he did all of this for the family, a quiet, peaceful, and self-aware Walt interrupts her to say, plainly, "I did it for me. I liked it. I was good at it. And I was . . . really . . . I was alive." (It's less showy than many of Bryan Cranston's other moments in the series, but the way he closes his eyes immediately after the confession, clearly thinking of all the things that happened because he kept chasing that feeling, is remarkable.)

Walt finally admitting his true motivation to himself and Skyler is "the one argument for having those final two episodes," says Gilligan. "It could be argued that he sees in 'Ozymandias' the damage he's done to his family. But I wanted it a little more explicit. In the writers room over the years, I had said a few times, 'This guy is astoundingly untrue to himself. This guy lies to himself like no character I've ever heard of. This guy can rationalize any kind of bad behavior. Isn't it time for him to just cop to the fact that he's a villain? That he is doing it for himself?' Sam Catlin, one of my writers, said a wise thing two or three years before those final episodes: 'I think that the show is over the moment Walt realizes that he's been rationalizing. Once he admits to himself who he truly is, in that very moment, the show is over.'"

The show actually runs for another 20 minutes after that admission, but as Gilligan bluntly puts it, the rest of the episode— in which all the Nazis die (most with the machine gun; Jack and Todd at the hands of, respectively, Walt and Jesse), a physically and emotionally scarred Jesse chooses to drive off to his freedom rather than shooting Mr. White at Walt's own request, and Walt dies from a stray round from the Nazi massacre, surrounded by the meth-cooking equipment he designed—as "housekeeping. It's hopefully very cinematic housekeeping, but the final act of *Breaking Bad* is just housekeeping. Walt has already emotionally ended the series by telling his wife, 'I did it for me. I liked it.'"

Unlike the conclusions to *The Sopranos, Lost, Battlestar Galactica,* or some of this era's other greats, there would be no ambiguity over exactly what happened(*), nor controversy over how Gilligan chose to end it. Some fans might have preferred more of Jesse's story in the final season, while others (including me on some days) might have preferred that the series ended with "Ozymandias" or "Granite State," rather than letting Walt have one last victory, even a pyrrhic one. But on the whole, the conclusion of *Breaking Bad* felt of a piece with all that had come before it.

(*) Technically, there are still the questions of whether Jesse eludes capture and what happens to the money Walt wanted Gretchen and Elliott to give to his kids. "I'm very simplistic, in that sense," says Gil-

ligan. *"I think Jesse got away, and the brilliance and completeness of Walt's plan [with the money] bore fruit. And maybe on some level, Skyler, I can see with my mind's eye, that she would kind of figure it out that Walt somehow made it happen. But I think she would turn a blind eye to it at that late date, when a lot of the immediate anger had worn off. I'm talking years later. I think she might think, 'Hmm, this sounds a little fishy.' But on the other hand, she might not question it too forcefully."*

Also, there were some fans (including TV critic Emily Nussbaum, novelist Joyce Carol Oates, and comedian Norm Macdonald) who suggested that Walt's ability to gain a final victory and redeem himself even slightly made it feel, intentionally or not, as if the entire finale was a fantasy taking place in the mind of a powerless, dying Walt as he sits in the frozen car he's trying to steal in New Hampshire. Gilligan has denied that this was ever his plan, and that would go against the series' operating logic to that point, as well as what we knew from the text. (A Walt who never returns to Albuquerque, for instance, has no idea that Jesse has become Todd's slave.)

The God's POV shot of Walt's body lying amid the meth equipment wasn't the final thing filmed for the series. Nor was anything else in "Felina." Instead, "Ozymandias" would be the end of *Breaking Bad* in a practical way, if not a narrative one. The last scene filmed was that episode's flashback teaser, which had to be held for the end so Cranston and Paul could shave off all the facial hair their characters had grown in the interim. Rian Johnson returned to direct it, eager to finally shoot a scene inside the RV, and to film something relatively light after all the tragedy of the rest of the episode.

"It was such a relief for us to be back in the days of tightiewhities and stupid Jesse in the RV," says Moira Walley-Beckett. "The actors were so relieved. It had been such a run and was so fraught, those last few episodes. And suddenly, here at the end, the stakes were pretty low again."

Everyone was looking for ways to prolong the experience. Because so much of the time was spent filming the RV's interior, Michelle MacLaren says, "It almost looked like a stage play, and I said to Vince, 'We should take the show to Broadway.'" Walley-Beckett recalls that Aaron Paul spent much of the day "moping around in the most adorable, delightful way, going, 'This is terrible! I hate this! What is happening?!?!'"

As they neared the very last shot of the series—a close-up on Paul's face as Jesse calls Mr. White a dick—Johnson says, "I think [Paul] kept flubbing his lines intentionally when he got the sense we were close to the end, because he didn't want the final take to happen.

"But it did. Vince called 'Cut' on the final shot, and then that was it. That was *Breaking Bad.*"

Before that final "Cut," Gilligan had been noticeably separate from the crew and cast throughout the day. As Walley-Beckett recalls, "To curb all the emotions that were swelling up in him, he brought his big camera, and would disappear up into the red rocks and take photos from a long way away."

Breaking Bad had exceeded Gilligan's wildest dreams. It won 16 Emmys, including four for Cranston, three for Paul, two for Anna Gunn, and Outstanding Drama Series trophies for both halves of the final season. It evolved from a private joke between Gilligan and Tom Schnauz into what Walley-Beckett called "this tiny little show that we weren't sure anybody was ever going to care about except for us," then—with the influx of viewers who had caught up

via DVD and Netflix so they could watch the final episodes live—
became a bona fide hit whose finale was watched by more than 10
million people.

Gilligan admits, "I worry about not pleasing people in general.
I'm very needy in that sense as a writer and a director." With the
end of *Breaking Bad*, he pleased people enough that he shouldn't
lose sleep over it anymore.

A *Breaking Bad* follow-up project, however, would inspire more
late night angst for Gilligan, Peter Gould, and others.

That show, *Better Call Saul*, is set six years before Walter White's
cancer diagnosis, following the ways that both Saul Goodman (or,
as he was known then, Jimmy McGill) and Mike Ehrmantraut
broke bad on the path to meeting the great Heisenberg. The setting, characters, and crew are familiar, and so is much of the frustration of trying to make these stories work.

While Gould was in the midst of plotting out *Saul* Season 2, we
spoke about what a headache it had been to find a target for Walt's
machine gun, and he said, "We're banging our heads against the
wall right now, and it's not so terribly dissimilar. The inspiration
came before, and maybe it will this time, too."

Gilligan loves sharing the credit for his work—it's a running
gag on the *Breaking Bad* and *Better Call Saul* podcasts, moderated
by editor Kelley Dixon, that Gilligan is always effusive to the point
of long-windedness in his praise of his cast and crew—but during
one of our conversations, he admitted he often had trouble re-
membering exactly who solved certain storytelling problems, and
when exactly those solutions came.

"That seems like a bad thing," he says, "but it's actually a good
thing. I always liken it to the pain I hear that's involved in childbirth.
Women forget the pain of childbirth, otherwise they wouldn't have

a second child. I feel like it's that way coming up with these stories. It's so goddamn hard coming up with these episodes that you kind of have to forget; otherwise you wouldn't go into Season 2."

Gilligan would force himself to forget, again and again, but the result was a long-form televised character study that no one who watched could ever hope, or want, to forget.

EPILOGUE

Don't stop believing...
The lasting legacy of the revolution

It's inarguable that the shows in this book (and other dramas from the period, including *Six Feet Under* and *Rescue Me*) expanded the boundaries of what's possible on television. The kinds of dramas made today, and the number of outlets for them, don't exist without *The Sopranos* and company.

"I think things definitely changed," says Shawn Ryan. "I don't see how you can look at where TV was 15 years ago and see where it is now and not see the difference."

But not everyone I interviewed for the book agreed on the depth, or permanence, of these changes.

"There's a lot that's still promised by television that's not delivered," says David Simon. "I think some good work's been done, some good work continues to be done, but I'm not sure television's punching at its weight to any degree where we should be patting ourselves on the back."

And when David Milch talked about the period when *Deadwood* and *The Sopranos* were made, it was with a wistful tone suggesting that, even though he still had a contract to produce series for HBO, something had shifted in the nature of the business.

HBO had once advertised itself with the slogan, "It's not TV. It's HBO." By the time *The Sopranos* ended, the rest of TV had started to catch up. AMC and Showtime began winning Emmys in categories that HBO had dominated, and the new HBO dramas from the middle of the '00s failed to catch on in the public imagination the way *Sopranos* and *Sex and the City* had. HBO found a new big hit in *True Blood*, a vampire drama from *Six Feet Under* creator Alan Ball filled with gore and nudity that no one has ever mistaken for great art. But the network has also rebounded creatively with the period gangster drama *Boardwalk Empire*, the fantasy epic *Game of Thrones*, and the dramedy *Girls*, among others.

AMC also had creative difficulties after that initial burst. *Mad Men* and *Breaking Bad* proved impossible acts to follow. The spy thriller *Rubicon* lasted only a season, more successful at creating atmosphere than telling a coherent story. *The Killing* tried to marry the structure of a network police procedural with the scope and complexity of a cable drama, but viewers didn't find the characters very deep, and grew frustrated with an over-reliance on red herrings; AMC canceled it after the mystery was finally solved, then revived it later to fill an unexpected hole in the schedule. And the Western drama *Hell on Wheels* has been competent so far, but not much more. Like HBO, AMC has found enormous commercial success, but mixed reviews, with a horror series: *The Walking Dead*, based on the comic book about life after a zombie apocalypse.

"I went to the Olympics and we were watching the Dream Team," says AMC's Charlie Collier. "I was with some ad executives who said, '*Mad Men, Breaking Bad, Walking Dead*—you have the starting front line of the Dream Team!' The inevitable question becomes, 'What do you do to replace them?' You don't replace Michael Jordan and Scottie Pippen. What you do is you say, 'Thank goodness we had this moment in time. Let's keep building.'"

Over at FX, *The Shield* passed the baton to *Sons of Anarchy*, a drama about an outlaw biker club from *Shield* writer Kurt Sutter. It's the biggest hit in FX history, and at times achieves the power of its predecessor, but Sutter has written on his blog that critics are sometimes "applying a level of analysis that is best reserved for a David Simon show. *The Wire* we ain't, nor do we aspire to be. For the record, *SOA* is an adrenalized soap opera, it's bloody pulp fiction with highly complex characters."

FX couldn't get people to watch the charming but subtle *Terriers*, but scored a big hit with *American Horror Story*, the latest histrionic show from *Glee* and *Nip/Tuck* producer Ryan Murphy. But the network has developed other artistic successes in recent years that have rated well enough to continue, like *Justified*, a modern-day Western based on a series of Elmore Leonard stories and produced by Graham Yost (who was writing and directing acclaimed HBO miniseries like *From the Earth to the Moon* and *Band of Brothers* around the time *The Sopranos* was taking off); or *Louie*, an uncategorizable but brilliant, deeply personal half-hour series written, directed by, and starring comedian Louis C.K.

Yost, who quit a job on the *Full House* writing staff to work on his script for the movie *Speed*, recalls going back to the ABC sitcom's writers' room a few years later, "and the look on their faces was a little bit like, 'Tell us what it's like out in the world! You made it to features!' Now, in talking to friends, agents and producers I know from the feature world, they will ask me, 'What's it like in television, where you have the freedom to do interesting things?'"

"You can argue about the cause and effect" of the revolution, says Shawn Ryan. "Was the fact that *The Sopranos* and *Six Feet Under* and *The Shield* and *The Wire* all premiered in this 4–5 year period the cause of it? Or was it the beneficiary of a changing dynamic? I think both things benefited from each other, and also from the movies deciding to get out of the $40–50 million good drama business. They don't really make those anymore, and TV has really grabbed that mantle. But I think there has been an effect. I think the fact that we made something that was good and very profitable for FX and increased the value of that network by many factors inspired a lot of other networks like AMC and Syfy and TNT to ramp up their production, and to set their bar higher for things."

"Is TV better because of these shows? Not specifically, but collectively, absolutely," says Kurt Sutter. "*The Sopranos* or *The Shield* or *The Wire* alone did not change TV. What did was the collective effort of what began to happen: creatives taking bigger, smarter, deeper ideas to cable because broadcast said no and features took forever. I know *The Sopranos*, at the very least, made the *Sons of Anarchy* pitch a much easier sell. Not that it couldn't have gotten made, but with the proven success of an outlaw anti-hero, there was a tangible mile marker."

The broadcast networks will still occasionally dabble in less formulaic dramas like *Lone Star* and *Awake* (both created by writer Kyle Killen), NBC's family drama *Parenthood*, or CBS's morally complex legal drama *The Good Wife*, but for the most part they've doubled down on easy-to-market procedural mysteries and reality shows.

"Increasingly the distinction between network and cable is disappearing," says Kyle Killen, "but for now networks still provide a huge platform to try to reach a wide audience from. The downside is it's a long fall from that platform if you miss. I still believe a new network drama is going to pop for both critics and audiences in the next couple seasons and scramble some of the arguments, and I'll keep trying to be there when it does. But over the long haul I believe the network-versus-cable debate is going to go away as they all just become channels."

"I think that there is an appetite for quality that has been stoked, and shows that continue to come along to fill it," says Jane Espenson. She also notes that the rise of non-traditional distribution outlets creates even more opportunity to experiment, which she has with her web comedy series *Husbands*, about a gay couple who wed while drunk and try to make the marriage work. "When [*Husbands* co-creator and star] Brad Bell and I felt that traditional TV wasn't going to give us the freedom to make *Husbands* in the way we wanted to, we made it ourselves. So, if you include online TV, then yes, absolutely, the change has been accomplished."

Chris Albrecht now runs Starz (which has made its own forays into this style of ambitious drama, like Kelsey Grammer as the corrupt mayor of Chicago in *Boss*), while Carolyn Strauss now works as a producer, rather than executive, on HBO shows like *Game of Thrones* and *Tremé*. But whatever the changes in the executive ranks, *Boardwalk Empire* creator (and *Sopranos* alum) Terence Winter says, "You've got this incredible toy box full of resources, including a real powerhouse network behind you. Their whole business model is to do things that are off-kilter. Look at a show like *Girls*. It's different from anything else on TV. That's really the job. I'm totally optimistic. As long as there are the HBOs of the world that are out there trying to achieve this stuff, you can really do some really interesting things."

But others who were there at the start of the revolution have seen boundaries being erected again, even if they're much further out than they were before *The Sopranos*.

"It's like anything else," says Carolyn Strauss. "Anytime you have a little bit of money, you invest it, you try things, you get a lot more money, suddenly you become, 'Ohhhh!' The spotlights on you, everyone's looking at you, and you have something to lose. When you're a frontrunner, you're always a little bit more self-conscious than when you're working in the shadows. Before, we were doing it because it was the only way you could get people to come work with you."

"I think television by nature is cyclical; each time the cycle comes around, you gain a little and you lose a little," says Tom Fontana. "Everybody at this point is having the screws tightened around their thumbs to make more money and figure out what the big hit is. We've come back to the idea of the big hit, even for the cable networks… As much as I would like to say we've had a permanent effect on the medium, I would say the change of the economic environment has had a more substantial effect."

Several producers (though, oddly, not David Milch) compared the period in the early '00s to the Wild West.

"When there's a new frontier and you're breaking things in, a lot of crazy, wild and criminal things are allowed to happen," says David Eick, who doesn't believe his version of *Battlestar Galactica* could be green-lit today. "When the culture becomes established and the rules become set, and people become comfortable, a lot of the experimentation goes away. We're constantly in a state of flux in television. It's a very rickety, unstable business right now. This is not to suggest that the golden days are over. But that particular kind of show, *Battlestar Galactica*—I continue to work in the genre, in both network and in cable, and I'm out there writing and developing and producing, and I'm telling you right now, you couldn't do it today."

"It was a fluke," acknowledges Ron Moore, "but there's always flukes. If you look back through the whole history of television, you experience moments like that—these golden moments, over and over again—and then they go away. 'Oh, that was a golden time, and we're never going back.' From the '50s, when you had *Playhouse 90* and all those shows. That was 'the golden age of television.' Then you had *Hill Street Blues*, *Miami Vice*, *The Cosby Show* in the '80s, or *Seinfeld* in the '90s. There are a lot of flukes and anomalies that then define the television landscape. TV, like film, is scared of change, scared of doing anything different, and fights and fights and fights it. And then one of these shows hits, they're hailed as classics, and people go 'Ohmigod, it's a bright shining moment, and it'll never happen again.' And then it happens again.

"Right now," he adds, "*Mad Men* is one of the best shows on TV, one of the best shows in the history of TV, probably. You could certainly call that a fluke. You can call *Sopranos* an enormous fluke—probably, in my estimation, the best one-hour show ever made in terms of the whole package. And people will go, 'God, that's so long ago, that'll never happen again.' Yes it will... It's certainly not easy to replicate the success of *Galactica*. Lord knows that I've tried. But I do have faith that it'll cycle around again, and we will see great shows once more. It keeps happening, even if you don't know where it's going to come from. You can almost guarantee that the success story of the next great show will be one of 'Nobody believes in us, the network hated it, it tested like shit, they all wanted to cancel it, and sure enough, it became an enormous hit.'"

As Moore was fond of writing on his classic series, all of this has happened before—and if we're lucky, all of it will keep happening again, and again, and again.

EPILOGUE, TAKE TWO

Listen to the thunder...
How TV drama's Wild Wild West has only gotten wilder

The other day for HitFix, I reviewed a superhero cop show that's viewable only on the streaming video network available to owners of PlayStation game consoles. If I could travel back in time to read that sentence to a younger version of myself, his head would have exploded. And I'm not talking about the eight-year-old me whose most prized possessions were his new ColecoVision and his well-read copy of *Justice League of America* #100. I'm talking about the 38-year-old me who was writing the original edition of this book.

The television business has transformed almost as much in the three years since *The Revolution Was Televised* was first published as it did over the 15-odd years of TV history the book covered. I would say that these changes should be the subject of another book entirely, but things keep changing so rapidly, and substantially, that it's possible even this new epilogue will become woefully out of date over the few months between when I finish writing it and when you're reading it.

The fracturing of the viewing audience that made the likes of

The Wire and *Mad Men* possible has accelerated, on all levels of television. Broadcast network shows now get renewed with ratings so small that a few years ago, they would have gotten every executive associated with them fired for cause. And in this topsy-turvy new world, the highest-rated show in all of television, outside of football, is AMC's *The Walking Dead*. The channel whose stars once had to explain to people that they weren't on A&E now sets the mark against which all other TV success is measured.

The grenade that's really blown everything to bits has been Netflix, which has made a vast library of some of the best television ever made available to its audience, all at the click of a button, and all for a much lower price than a traditional cable package. The popularity of Netflix, and to a lesser extent Hulu and Amazon Prime, has radically altered both the manner in which people watch individual shows and the way they pay to access them.

With the Netflix phenomenon has come the culture of the binge, where instead of watching several different shows at once on a week-to-week basis, streaming customers marathon through entire seasons, or even series, before moving on to something else. Some shows like *The Wire* (with its novelistic structure) or *Breaking Bad* (with its propulsive narrative, particularly in later seasons) wind up playing even better as a binge than they did when watched in the traditional, linear fashion. Others like *The Sopranos* and *Mad Men*, which have serialized elements but structure their episodes to function as standalone works of art, can suffer when watched all in a row. When *Mad Men* ended, Matthew Weiner said that if he ever made a show for Netflix, he would fight to keep them from releasing all the episodes at once. And when Netflix revived *Arrested Development* in 2013, its creator, Mitchell Hurwitz, tried, to no avail, to convince his rabid fans to portion the episodes out a few out a time, because comedy can grow tiring when you consume too much in one go.

Netflix et al. have also led to the rise of cord-cutters: people who abandon the cable bundle altogether and simply use a broadband connection to watch the best the streaming world has to offer. On occasion, this proves beneficial to the traditional business model— see the skyrocketed ratings for the stretch run of *Breaking Bad*, fueled largely by people who caught up via Netflix but wanted to see the conclusion in real time—but more often than not, it's taking eyeballs away from the networks who actually pay the freight for these shows, and who may struggle to keep doing that if too many people cut the cord.

(And the current hegemony of Netflix has made a lot of people's media diets very specific. Try convincing viewers to catch up on FX's *The Americans* or NBC's *Hannibal*—two of the best, most ambitious dramas in the recent marketplace, both of which have previous seasons streaming only on Amazon—and you'll get a lot of apologetic shrugs. The HBO catalog is also available in several places, but not Netflix; as cultural critic and media studies professor Anne Helen Petersen wrote for Slate a few years ago, her students had little interest in the likes of *The Wire* and *Deadwood* because, "as far as I can tell, the general sentiment goes something like this: *If it's not on Netflix, why bother?*")

To deal with the rise of cord-cutting, different channels have started to unbundle themselves from cable, as well. This spring, HBO started offering a standalone streaming service to encourage people to stop borrowing HBO Go passwords from friends and relatives when *Game of Thrones* season came around again. CBS and Showtime have their own streaming service, and lots of other channels are expected to follow, which in turn has inspired different distribution outlets to offer pared-down channel offerings. In the end, the consumer will likely wind up paying as much, if not more, for a far smaller selection of channels—these same companies provide the broadband necessary to stream the whole run of *Friends*, after all, and they are not in the business of saving you money.

This new a la carte world could also make it much harder for a latter-day AMC to survive long enough to find its own *Mad Men*, let alone *Walking Dead*. But that's only encouraged every cable channel, streaming service, and gaming platform to rush into the drama marketplace in the hope of becoming indispensible in an unbundled landscape. In a medium where viewing habits are changing almost as fast as the technology to support them, the Quality Drama has become the business's killer app.

Beyond its library of other people's shows, Netflix has started producing its own, with prestigious stars like Kevin Spacey and Robin Wright in the deceptively trashy Washington potboiler *House of Cards*, or the incredibly diverse ensemble of the women's prison dramedy *Orange Is the New Black*. Amazon won awards by casting Jeffrey Tambor as a transgender woman in *Transparent*, and cable channels like Sundance (with its ethereal drama *Rectify*), Cinemax (which has done fun pulp thrillers *Strike Back* and *Banshee*, as well as the period hospital drama *The Knick*, with all episodes directed by Steven Soderbergh), Lifetime (with *UnREAL*, its scripted evisceration of *The Bachelor*), and many more have gotten serious about being part of the conversation.

The producers from the start of the drama revolution compared it to the Wild West, where as new frontiers opened up, old laws didn't apply for a while until each territory was fully settled and absorbed into the larger American experiment. (AMC, for instance, largely let Matt Weiner and Vince Gilligan make the shows they wanted to, where *Walking Dead* has had three different showrunners across five-plus seasons.) The current demand for essential programming means that it's always the Wild West somewhere, whether that's Sundance, or Netflix, or even PlayStation.

"It's a strange thing," says *Breaking Bad* and *Better Call Saul*'s Peter Gould. "It's like a gold rush, or even a bubble. It's a great thing for us who do drama, especially. But I can't help waiting for the other shoe to drop."

That moment could well come, but right now, the demand for shows even the smallest demographic slice will care about has grown so large that it seems no show is ever truly dead. The immediate aftermath of *The Sopranos* in cable television has been compared to the early '70s in movies, when Coppola, Scorsese, Polanski, and other directors brought a new level of intimacy and thematic ambition to the medium, just as the recent success of *Walking Dead* and *Game of Thrones*, which each offer more frequent visceral thrills than their predecessors at AMC and HBO, has been compared to the release of *Jaws* and *Star Wars*, and how the blockbuster mentality pushed those more personal films out of the mainstream. (*Game of Thrones*, which films each episode on multiple continents, and features dragons, epic battles, and armies of the undead, operates on a scale that makes its HBO predecessors look like art films in comparison. But at its best, it also achieves a level of emotional intimacy and nuance that makes it feel worthy of being in the conversation with the others, where *Walking Dead* only occasionally gets anywhere near its AMC forerunners.) The difference here is that there's barely any mainstream left in television at this point. Almost everything outside of football, *Walking Dead*, *Game of Thrones*, and a small handful of network shows

(*NCIS, Big Bang Theory, Empire*) is a niche success, and any show that can satisfy a niche audience has value.

The cancellation threshold has dropped low enough at many networks that the only shows in real danger of ending without warning are the ones nobody cares about. And where canceled shows being revived at other networks used to be a rarity, there are, again, so many networks and subscription services in need of content, and preferably content that people have already heard of, that it's become almost more shocking when a canceled show with a small but vocal fan base *doesn't* resurface somewhere else, whether *The Killing* and *Longmire* following *Arrested Development* to Netflix, or Yahoo reviving NBC's *Community* to make people aware that Yahoo Screen is a thing that exists. The resurrection of long-dead series has become almost commonplace, with sequels for everything from *X-Files* and *Twin Peaks* to the family sitcom *Full House* in the works for 2016 or 2017.

FX's research department, led by Julie Piepenkotter, says that in 2002, the year *The Shield* debuted, there were 36 original scripted dramas and comedies on cable; by 2014, that number had sky-rocketed to 167, along with another two dozen from streaming outlets like Netflix and Hulu. By the end of this year, FX estimates, there will be over 400 original scripted series in primetime across broadcast, cable, and streaming networks. The sheer tonnage of good new stuff available, all the time and from so many places, has led many to refer to this post-revolution period as "TV's new Golden Age," but it's also made it harder than ever for both viewers and critics (whose whole job is to watch and write about television) to keep up with it all. It makes it much more challenging for any one show or even handful of shows to achieve consensus as the current best of the best, and it's made patience with promising but uneven shows a luxury even many critics can't afford. Given the number of recent shows I quickly dropped, but which other critics or fans swear got much better later, I sometimes wonder whether I'd have stuck with a *Buffy* if its first season were to debut today, or even made it to the all-"fuck" scene from *The Wire*'s fourth episode.

(FX CEO John Landgraf recently described the staggering number of new comedies and dramas as "peak TV in America," and suggested that the bubble will have to start deflating a bit in the coming years, simply because the economics don't make sense. For now, though, series order totals keep rising.)

In the land of the blind, the one-eyed man is king. In this new TV land of niches, the one-man show has done pretty well. In 2010, FX debuted *Louie*, created by comedian Louis C.K., who served as the show's only writer, director, and regular actor, along with handling many of the other jobs. C.K. and FX had a simple arrangement: they give him a budget substantially less than the cost of your average cable half-hour series, and he gets minimal involvement from the channel's executives unless he asks for it. *Louie* can be whatever C.K. wants it to be in a given week: a collection of whimsical short stories, a dramatic encounter between Louie and a suicidal friend from his early stand-up days, a travelogue to Miami's Little Havana, or even a more serialized show where Louie auditions to succeed David Letterman, or falls in love with a woman who speaks no English.

Though C.K. has collaborators, the sheer number of jobs he does himself every week makes *Louie* (currently on indefinite hiatus while C.K. lets his batteries recharge) even more of an auteur's show than something like *Sopranos* or *Mad Men*. It's encouraged other storytellers from indie cinema to make the move to television, including *Transparent* from TV-writer-turned-movie-director

Jill Soloway, HBO's *Girls* from Lena Dunham, and HBO's *Togetherness* from filmmaking brothers Jay and Mark Duplass. The 2015 Sundance Film Festival had both significant TV presences—acknowledgment that so much of the best storytelling, and talent, has migrated from the big screen to the small.

"You get to tell unique and very sensitive stories in television, and make a living," Mark Duplass told me at the end of *Togetherness* Season 1, while discussing the appeal of TV to former indie film diehards. "And there's really very few places you can do that today."

This influx of new shows and new voices also meant new kinds of faces on television. The dramas of the revolution had been dominated by middle-aged white male anti-heroes, but there were only so many the medium could support, until eventually the bastard sons of Tony Soprano (on series like AMC's short-lived *Low Winter Sun* and Showtime's more successful *Ray Donovan*) feel just as formulaic as the shows David Chase was rebelling against. There are more shows with complex female leads (*Homeland* heroine Carrie Mathison started out every bit as prickly and complex as her male predecessors), with prominent characters of color (you get both with Shonda Rhimes shows, while last spring, hip-hop soap opera *Empire* became the biggest broadcast network drama success in a decade), and with other types of characters the medium previously had no interest in putting at the center of a show. Once upon a time, a character like Tambor's on *Transparent* would be a one-shot sitcom guest star, and either the butt of the joke or a source of anxiety for one of the series regulars. And *Orange Is the New Black* alone features characters spanning so many different ethnicities, sexualities, and gender identities that (like *Oz* and *The Wire* so many years before) it almost had no choice but to fill its cast largely with unknowns, because how many good opportunities were there for most of these actresses prior to its existence?

What shows like *Louie, Girls,* and *Orange Is the New Black* also have in common is a blurring of the lines between comedy and drama that's left traditional TV awards like the Emmys completely flummoxed as to where to slot anything. *Louie* can be explosively funny, but its best episodes tend to be on the dramatic side, while *Transparent* has many comic elements but an entirely serious lead performance from Tambor. Awards show rules keep being tweaked to make sense of a genre-transcending world, and to deal with the rise of this era's other big new scripted format: the anthology miniseries.

That one was the brainchild of Ryan Murphy for his FX drama *American Horror Story.* Previous Murphy series like *Glee* and *Nip/Tuck* had burned hot, burned bright, and then burned out, sticking around for years as shadows of themselves simply because of the way the business works. With *American Horror Story*, Murphy figured out a happy medium between the anthological likes of *Playhouse 90* and *Twilight Zone* that dominated TV's first Golden Age, and the serialized shows that were emblematic of the current one: one long narrative per season, before returning the following year with new characters (and, at times, actors) in a different setting, but under the same umbrella title.

It was potentially the best of both worlds: the long-term continuity of a creative team and a brand would inspire viewer loyalty (and make new stories easier to market), but the series would never have to creatively suffer for stretching out one concept past its usefulness. Other anthology miniseries soon followed: HBO's *True Detective*, which can lure movie stars (Matthew McConaughey and Woody Harrelson in the brilliant first season; Colin Farrell,

Vince Vaughn, Rachel McAdams, and Taylor Kitsch in the more problematic second) to TV for a short commitment; FX's *Fargo*, which did the impossible in not feeling like a poor imitation of the Coen brothers' film; and ABC's *American Crime*, from Oscar-winning screenwriter John Ridley.

The shows in this book suggested TV's greatest strength over movies was time. You could tell the story of Walter White or Tony Soprano in a film, but we would have never understood them as well, nor reacted quite so strongly to the terrible things they did, if we had only spent two hours with them rather than dozens and dozens. But time is also starting to become the enemy in some parts of the business. The anthology miniseries are an explicit rebuke to the idea that more is always more when it comes to serialized drama. (As a 13-episode miniseries that climaxes with Nicholas Brody blowing himself up, *Homeland* would have been legendary; as an ongoing show that kept Brody alive two more years and kept repeating various plot and character beats until they grew tired, it's a classier *24*.)

And while doing 13 episodes for cable/streaming remains preferable for many creators to doing 22 for network—despite the protestations from the producers of CBS' *The Good Wife* (one of the few broadcast dramas left that aspires to the complexity of cable) that they should get extra credit for making that many—even that number has become high in some places. HBO's typical season length has shrunk to 10 episodes, which started out as a way for *Game of Thrones* to deal with the show's filming logistics, but has now become the benchmark for almost every show they do. Amazon has also stuck to 10, while Sundance, AMC, and others have experimented with doing 6- or 8-episode seasons at times. It's far from the standard (Showtime, FX, and Netflix still do 12 to

13 episodes per season), but it may be the business's way of correcting for the over-saturation of the marketplace; fewer episodes cost fewer dollars, which can be the difference between life and death for something brilliant but marginal like *Tremé*, or *Rectify*.

I first published this book at a time when many of the creators interviewed wondered if the business would ever see their series' likes again. This new version comes at a time when there's such a flood of great TV—even in a year that's said goodbye to *Mad Men*, *Justified*, *Parenthood*, and more—that it seems impossible that this new Golden Age could ever end. The truth likely lies somewhere in the middle of those two extremes, but the business has changed so much in the last few years, in ways both predictable and not, that I wouldn't want to hazard a guess about when or if this ride will stop. I'm just going to pop some onion rings and enjoy it for as long as it goes on and on and on and on. . . .

WHERE ARE THEY NOW?

The men and women who changed TV drama mostly still work in TV, though it hasn't always been easy for them to replicate the magic of these shows.

The Sopranos experience made **David Chase** glad he hadn't left television quite yet, but it didn't make him want to do another ongoing series.

"It made me more aware of the possibilities of what you could do on television," he says, "but I had six or seven years of it, which was enough. But when I say I want to do a movie, people say, 'Why? You get to spend so much time with these characters, you know them so well. They're indelible.' I say, 'Okay. So Rick and Ilsa [from *Casablanca*], they're not indelible?' 'Well, yeah, of course.' 'Charles Foster Kane, he's not indelible?' 'Well, yeah, but…' So I don't know what it really means. [On TV], there's more of it, and you can get into more detail. I guess maybe this is what it comes down to: in a television show, you can spend a lot of money on very little small things about people."

Chase finally got to break into the film business with 2012's

Not Fade Away, a period piece about a '60s Jersey garage band, which featured James Gandolfini in a supporting role. Gandolfini himself died of a heart attack on a 2013 vacation in Rome; his funeral was attended by most of *The Sopranos* cast and crew, and Chase delivered the closing eulogy, written as a letter to his late friend, at several points comparing the volatile but beloved actor with the character he played so wonderfully.

"So Tony Soprano never changed, people say," Chase said. "He got darker. I don't know how they can misunderstand that. He tried and he tried and he tried. And you tried and you tried, more than most of us, and harder than most of us, and sometimes you tried too hard."

At present, Chase is developing *A Ribbon of Dreams*, a miniseries project for HBO about the early days of Hollywood.

Former *Lost* partners **Carlton Cuse** and **Damon Lindelof** have gone off in different directions, with Cuse producing a cluster of cable dramas (including vampire thriller *The Strain* for FX, and *Psycho* prequel *Bates Motel* and resurrection mystery *The Returned* for A&E), while Lindelof has toggled between film (whether collaborating with *Lost* co-creator J.J. Abrams on the recent *Star Trek* films or writing the likes of *Prometheus* and *Tomorrowland*) and television (including vampire thriller *The Strain* for FX, *Psycho* prequel *Bates Motel* for A&E, and sci-fi series *Colony* for USA).

David Eick, Ronald D. Moore, and **Jane Espenson** all worked on the short-lived *Battlestar Galactica* prequel *Caprica*, which struggled to find an audience while telling more planet-bound stories. (Another prequel, *Battlestar Galactica: Blood & Chrome*, recently escaped from development hell, at least long enough for viewers to watch the pilot episode.) Eick also tried to reinvent another mediocre '70s property with NBC's *Bionic Woman*, a troubled production that went through a cavalcade of showrunners (including Jason Katims), without the results he and Moore had with *Battlestar*.

"We were left alone to do something interesting [with *BSG*]," Eick says. "They didn't have any interest in leaving us alone on *Bionic Woman*."

Moore had another adaptation success with *Outlander*, a Starz fantasy series about an English nurse who travels back in time to the Scottish Highlands. Espenson is a producer on ABC's *Once Upon a Time*, and co-created the critically acclaimed web comedy *Husbands*. **David Weddle** and **Bradley Thompson** currently work on *The Strain* with Carlton Cuse.

After *Oz*, **Tom Fontana** tried going back to the broadcast networks, without much success or fulfillment. In the summer of 2012, he once again produced the first original drama for a cable network, as co-creator of BBC America's *Copper*, a nineteenth-century police procedural that Christina Wayne (who had moved on to *Copper* studio Cineflix) originally developed at AMC as a possible follow-up to *Breaking Bad*. *Copper* ran two seasons; Fontana continues developing projects.

"I'd certainly want to be somebody who's known for trying something that nobody's tried," Fontana says. "I will also say I'm more interested in working at a place that will let me tell the stories I want to tell than being forced to tell stories that I don't want to tell just so I can get on the air."

Vince Gilligan stayed within the Albuquerque city limits for his next major project, the *Breaking Bad* prequel *Better Call Saul*, starring Bob Odenkirk and Jonathan Banks and co-created by Gilligan and **Peter Gould**. The first season generated good ratings and even better reviews—it was a stronger debut season, frankly, than

Breaking Bad had, though we'll see if *Saul* can make similar leaps in its later years—but even before it debuted, no one involved was worried about it potentially tarnishing the parent show's legacy.

"*Breaking Bad* exists," Odenkirk says. "There's a lot of good DVDs of it, so that's not going to go away. Your DVDs will not be erased by the existence of *Better Call Saul*."

A few days before the new show's debut, Gilligan told me, "I am worried right now as we speak about how *Better Call Saul* will be received. I'm very anxious about it. But I don't worry about it messing up the legacy of *Breaking Bad*. I think Bob is exactly right. *Breaking Bad* is what it is. It exists, and it will not cease to exist, and I don't think it can be stained by anything that comes after it."

24 veteran **Howard Gordon** has been busy enough for three or four producers in recent years. His output (sometimes as hands-on showrunner, sometime as one cook among many) has included the Showtime thriller *Homeland*, which broke *Mad Men*'s consecutive win streak for the drama series Emmy; the brilliant-but-canceled NBC drama *Awake*, about a cop living in two different realities; the miniseries revival *24: Live Another Day*; *Tyrant*, an FX drama set in a fictional Middle Eastern dictator-ship; TNT's *Legends*, about an FBI undercover operative; and a new Fox drama called *Lookinglass*.

After *Friday Night Lights*, **Jason Katims** unexpectedly found himself as a go-to adapter of movies for TV, with a critically ac-claimed five-season run on *Parenthood* (which would eventually feature half the *FNL* cast in guest-starring roles, along with a brief web series where Landry and Billy Riggins come to the Bay Area and hang out with some of the Bravermans) and two seasons of the comedy *About a Boy*, both for NBC.

David Milch's post-*Deadwood* series both ended abruptly. He continues to develop projects for HBO, including a long-gestating adaptation of the novels of William Faulkner. Viewers didn't know what to make of *John from Cincinnati*, and HBO canceled *Luck* a few weeks into filming the second season after several horses died during production.

When I interviewed Milch a few days after *Luck* ended, I asked whether he was still satisfied with his relationship with HBO, given three consecutive cancellations.

"Absolutely," he insisted. "Each set of circumstances was unique. You'll have to ask them whether they are [*laughs*], but to this point, they have been as supportive a partner as one could want or imagine. It's my experience that it isn't a useful exercise to try and figure out the other fellow's state of mind. I'm going to keep carrying the water, and we'll hope that the exercise is well-received."

Shawn Ryan has worked steadily since the end of *The Shield*, comfortably shifting back and forth between cable and network. In one season, he did both—*Terriers* for FX, and the cop drama *The Chicago Code* for Fox (both with **Tim Minear**, who now produces FX's *American Horror Story*)—though each show was canceled after 13 episodes. He's also joined the flood of talent going into the streaming video world, with 2016 series set up at both Amazon (*Mad Dogs*, about a group of middle-aged friends on a nightmarish vacation in Belize) and Netflix (*The Get Down*, a period piece about the early days of hip-hop). "The creative community is really intrigued with Amazon and Netflix," he says, "and want to be in business with them."

David Simon has continued his iconoclastic journey through a medium he's never entirely been comfortable in. He followed *The Wire* with *Generation Kill*, a miniseries about recon Marines at the start of the invasion of Iraq, then headed to New Orleans with

Homicide and *The Wire* producer Eric Overmyer to create *Tremé*, a drama about musicians and chefs in post-Katrina New Orleans. It's a series with a rich atmosphere and great performances (the cast includes *Wire* alums Wendell Pierce and Clarke Peters), but without the cops-vs.-drug dealers narrative hook, it proved even less commercial than *The Wire*. Simon once again had to petition HBO for the opportunity to finish his story as planned, and this time got a more drastic compromise: he and Overmyer were given a small lump sum to produce a fourth and final season, which they were able to stretch to make five episodes, half the length of a regular *Tremé* season.

"I'm not made for television," says Simon. "I'm really not. I don't say that with any haughty, 'I'm a literary artist' attitude. I'm not trying to pull rank on television. I'm just not made for what the medium is. It's far more powerful than prose. I don't know how you can be a writer pretending to be a writer, or a grown-up pretending to be a writer, and start a story and not finish the story. I don't know how you waste your life doing that."

The Wire itself has only continued to grow in esteem, helped in part by President Obama being a very public fan of the show; recently, POTUS even invited Simon to the White House for a public discussion of the series and the many flaws of the War on Drugs.

Simon's latest HBO show, the political miniseries *Show Me a Hero*, debuted in August; he's developing another series for the channel, starring James Franco, set in the porn industry of the 1970s.

At this writing, **Matthew Weiner** has not announced any post–*Mad Men* plans.

Joss Whedon spent several years as master of the Marvel cinematic universe, co-creating the *Agents of S.H.I.E.L.D.* TV spin-off, helping to oversee other films, and writing and directing *Avengers: Age of Ultron*. That last experience—though resulting in a film that felt very much like the concluding arc of a season of *Buffy*—left him feeling burnt out on the Marvel experience, and he expressed a desire to return to more personal projects (like his literally homemade 2012 film version of *Much Ado About Nothing*). His former *Buffy* and *Angel* partner **David Greenwalt** has gone back to the supernatural well with the NBC drama *Grimm*, now in its fifth season.

ACKNOWLEDGMENTS

Though this book was initially self-published, it was never a one-man effort.

First and foremost, I have to thank my incredible wife, Marian, and our amazing kids, Julia and Ben, for putting up with my lengthy disappearances during the writing of the book, and for providing me with the best possible motivation to finish each chapter so I could go home to them.

Literary agent Anthony Mattero convinced me I didn't want *Stop Being a Hater and Learn to Love The O.C.* to be the only line in my bibliography, and Ted Griffin not only urged me to listen to that advice, but helped give this book a much better title than he gave his own show, *Terriers*.

Sarah D. Bunting has been the best editor I could ask for, understanding exactly what I was going for (sometimes better than I did) while being unafraid to tell me when certain sections needed Walter White to come along and blow them up. Ken Levine was my guru in the world of self-publishing, encouraging at every step of the process. Lauren Spiegel at Touchstone helped make this an easy, happy transition from self-publishing to mainstream, now that the book (and this updated edition) comes to you from Touchstone. Thanks also to my new agent Amy Williams for her help with this edition.

I had the great fortune to have Matt Zoller Seitz as my partner on *the Star-Ledger*'s TV page, not only because he handed *The Sopranos* beat to me after three seasons but because his talent and passion pushed me to become a much better writer in the process. This book doesn't exist without him, nor without my former *Ledger* bosses Susan Olds and Mark Di Ionno, who trusted me with the TV beat at a very young age and put me in a position to cover this great period. I also couldn't have written this without the generosity of my bosses at HitFix.com, Dan Fienberg, Gregory Ellwood, Richard Rushfield, and Jennifer Sargent, who gave me the extra time I needed to get it done. And, in Dan's case, he allowed some of his own productivity to slide by as he served as an invaluable sounding board for me the same way he has every day of the last decade.

I'm grateful to everyone who submitted to fresh interviews for the book, many of them people I've interviewed so often in the past that I'm impressed they had new things left to say. I'm also indebted to the many network (and sports) PR people who helped arrange many of those interviews and/or were ready, willing, and able to answer whatever obscure history questions I had, including Diego Aldana, Theano Apostolou, Karen Barragan, Tobe Becker, Dan Bell, Marnie Black, Bill Brennan, Lou D'Ermillio, Olivia Dupuis, Akiva Griffith, Pat Hanlon, Karen Jones, Jessica Nevarez, Dominic Pagone, Shannon Ryan, and John Solberg.

Finally, I'd like to thank my other TV critic friends, including Mo Ryan, Linda Holmes, Tara Ariano, Todd VanDerWerff, Phil Rosenthal, Rich Heldenfels, Ryan McGee, and Myles McNutt for letting me bounce ideas off of them at all hours of the day and night.